PUBLISHER'S INTRODUCTION

Welcome to the world of digital publishing ~ the book you now hold in your hand, was printed using the latest state of the art digital technology. The advent of print-on-demand has forever changed the publishing process and never has information been so accessible. It is our hope that this book serves your informational needs for years to come. If this is your first exposure to digital publishing, we hope that you are pleased with the results. Many more titles of interest to the classic automobile and motorcycle enthusiast, collector and restorer are available via our website at www.VelocePress.com. We hope that you find this title as interesting as we do.

NOTE FROM THE PUBLISHER

The information presented is true and complete to the best of our knowledge, as it was extracted from the original official Japanese publication. However, please note that the translation from Japanese to English is presented exactly as it appears in the original publication, and may seem a little 'quirky' some 50 plus years later.

TRADEMARKS

We recognize that some words, model names and designations, for example, mentioned herein are the property of the trademark holder. We use them for identification purposes only. This is not an official publication.

INFORMATION ABOUT THIS PUBLICATION

This publication is a 'must have' resource for any Japanese motor vehicle enthusiast and an invaluable reference for the automotive historian. It chronicles the emergence of Japanese motor vehicles on the worldwide market and many of the vehicles featured within are highly collectible today. It also contains information on manufacturers (and their products) that are no longer in business or have been absorbed by the current Japanese automotive giants.

While every care has been taken to ensure correctness of the information, it is obviously not possible to guarantee complete freedom from errors or omissions or to accept liability arising from such errors or omissions. Therefore, any individual that uses the information contained within acknowledges that there is a risk factor involved and that the publisher or its associates cannot be held responsible for any liability resulting from the use of that information.

COMPLETE CATALOG

of

JAPANESE MOTOR VEHICLES

Automobiles
Scooters
Motorcycles
Trucks
Buses
Components

Copyrighted and published 1961

by

FLOYD CLYMER

World's Largest Publisher of Books Relating to Automobiles, Motorcycles, Motor Racing, and Americana

1268 SOUTH ALVARADO STREET, LOS ANGELES 6, CALIFORNIA

Mt. Fuji. Hundreds of thousands of people climb this mountain during the season every year, and are struck with wonder to see from the summit the magnificent sunrise. The summit is 3,776 meter above the sea level and the highest in Japan. In summer time buses ply between the foot of the mountain and a point of 2,400 m. high carrying even aged women and small children. On the way there is an aid station with oxygen inhalers.

ANNOUNCEMENT

During my recent visit to Japan I attended the Tokyo Motor Show, which was not only unique but considerably different from the many shows I have visited in various cities of the United States, or in Paris, London, Brussels, Frankfurt or Turin.

Tremendous enthusiasm is evidenced everywhere in Japan over any vehicle that runs on wheels — from bicycles to the largest trucks and busses. During my stay in Japan I visited many of the automobile and motorcycle factories, where I test drove the cars and rode the motorcycles. Much to my surprise, I found manufacturing methods and mass production as modern as one would find in many factories in this or any other country. Japan actually is not a pioneer in automobile manufacturing and, for this reason, it is all the more astounding to find such progress.

Many will be surprised to know that in Japan more makes (not in numbers) of automobiles and trucks are now manufactured than in any other country. In the production of three-wheeled vehicles Japan probably builds more makes and has a larger total production than all other countries in the world combined. Japan now leads every other country in the production of motorcycles — again a surprise.

Recently, when in fabulous Tokyo, now nearing 10,000,000 population and the largest city in the world, I gave a talk on cars and motorcycles of the world. Some 300 Japanese automotive executives, engineers, journalists, and enthusiasts attended the show in Yahama Hall in the Ginza district of Tokyo. With me I had films of the Indianapolis "500" Mile Race, Mobilgas Economy Run, Catalina Motorcycle Race, and other U. S. films that seemed to fascinate those who attended.

The tremendous number of three-wheeled vehicles in use was impressive. The number of motorcycles, mopeds, scooters and pedal bicycles on the streets of Tokyo, and even in the small towns and rural districts, was evidence of how the Japanese people become enthusiastic — in not almost fanatic — about almost any product that runs on wheels.

During my stay there I made arrangements with the Japan Motor Industrial Federation, through their president, G. Asahara, to secure the U. S. publishing rights for what I consider the most complete, interesting, educational and unique catalog of all vehicles manufactured in any one country.

This book is reproduced exactly as it was printed in Japan. It is reproduced by offset process and, therefore, no change has been made in the text — which is in what we might call Japanese-English. The wording in some instances is somewhat different from the way we would have written it, but it gives a good idea of Japanese methods of presentation and their editorial translation from Japanese to the English language. They did a better job than we could had we tried to translate any text from English to Japanese.

We, as the world's largest publishers of automotive books, make no recommendation as to choice of any make of automobile, bus, scooter, moped, motorcycle, truck or any other vehicle manufactured in any country. This book, like many of our other publications, is published for the benefit of enthusiasts and collectors who are interested in learning more about automotive products manufactured in all countries of the world. We have never published a more comprehensive book.

I hope you find this book interesting, and I feel sure that you will.

Floyd Clymer

WITH FLOYD CLYMER IN JAPAN

Clymer looks at, but can't read Japanese sign while testing Datsun Bluebird near Tokyo.

Busy assembly line at Honda Motorcycle factory where employees dress in white uniforms.

When 14 years old Clymer learned to ride a motorcycle backwards, and never forgot how. Here, much to the amusement (and amazement) of a Honda test rider, he turns a lap on the Honda test track as rider follows.

At Toyopet factory test course, near Nagoya, Clymer drives Toyopet Crown over obstacle course consisting of rocks and stones of all shapes and sizes imbedded in concrete. This was indeed a tough test section that Toyopet took in stride.

The castle and cherry blossoms are both the syombols of Japanese building and flower. The picture shows the Hirosaki Castle and the cherry trees in full bloom. It will be interesting for motor fans to find that all Japanese castles are of the monocoque structure, made of dark timber and snow white walls.
Photo : Japan Tourist Association

CONTENTS

Overseas Activities of Japanese Motor Vehicles
- Japanese Car won Special Prize in the World's 10,000-mile Rally 13
- Japanese Motorcycles won Prizes in the T. T. Race 16
- Japanese Vehicles Running in Foreign Lands 17
  - In Southeast Asia 18
  - In Near and Middle East 20
  - In Central and South America 22
  - In North America 25
- Japanese Cars at Foreign Motor Shows 26

Japan's Motor Industry
- Its Development 29
- What It Is To-day 33
- Statistics 38

Oldtimers of Japanese Car 47

Some Aspects of Japan's Basic Industries and Motor-Factory Installations 50

Topical Technics
- Passenger Cars 57
- Buses 66
- Trucks 74
- Motorcycles and Scooters 82
- Jeep Types 89

Tokyo Motor Show 92

Principal Automobile Makers in Japan 101

Vehicle Illustrations with Features and Specifications
- Passenger Car 131
- Bus 141
- Light Commercial Vehicle 151
- Light Truck 158
- Heavy-Duty Truck 168
- Tank Lorry 174
- Fire Engine 177
- Jeep Type 180
- Dump Truck & Construction Equipment 184
- Three-Wheeler 199
- Motor Scooter 213
- Motorcycle 218

Manufacturer's List
- I. Cars, Buses, Trucks & Three-Wheelers 241
- II. Motorcycles & Motor Scooters 242
- III. Auto Parts & Accessories 242

Index 253

Special New Car Supplement 257

BIG FOUR OF MODERN CITIES IN JAPAN

The picture (top left) shows the special express train and tourists bus speeding on the Tokaido line which links Tokyo, Yokohama and Osaka. With Mt. Fuji in the back-ground, the coast is washed by the waves of the Pacific Ocean.

In the picture (bottom left), you will see a modern street in Tokyo. It makes a striking contrast with the sight of the Imperial Palace only 500 meters away from this street. The Castle of the Palace was built in 1457 and has been the seat of Mikado's court since 1868.

The picture (top right) shows the port of Yokohama about 30 km (19 mi.) to the west from Tokyo. Yokohama was the main entrance to Japan for the visitors from the overseas in the days before the air line was opened. Adjacent to the port, there is an industrial area with many manufacturing plants, such as automobile factory, ship-building yard and steel mills. Thirty years ago, Ford built an assembly plant in this area.

Nagoya (center right) is situated at the midway of Tokyo and Osaka and is the fourth largest city in Japan. In recent years, Nagoya made a rapid growth as an industrial city and is called "Detroit of Japan".

Osaka (bottom right) is the second largest city in Japan having as its satellite several industrial towns. Osaka Castle was built in 1582 and since the city has long flourished as the largest commercial city of the Western Japan. Kobe is a beautiful port city extending from the east to west over the narrow strip of land between the hills and the sea and loved by foreign residents as the Hongkong of Japan. Formerly, General Motors had in the city an assembly plant for cars similar to the Ford plant in Yokohama. A project is under way to construct the express way to link Tokyo and Osaka in about three hours.

DRIVING HIGHWAYS

While Japan is widely known for its beauty of landscape, Japanese roads are notorious for their poorest in all the world. Under the pressure caused by the dramatic expansion of motor car holding in recent years, new construction and improvement works are under way in all parts of this country as the most urgent public work of the nation.

The picture (top) shows the Higashiyama motor way running from the ancient city of Kyoto to the Biwa lake side.

The picture (left) shows the traffic scene near Ochanomizu, Tokyo. Look the fleet of cars on the bridge and the subway car (painted in red) running into the underground of another road.

The Manazuru Highway (bottom left) extends 71 miles along the pacific coast from Takyo to Atami Hot Spa City.

The picture (top) shows Yurakucho of Tokyo where an elevated motor way runs in parallel with the famous Ginza street. Under this motor way, there is a long narrow shopping arcade which has numerous provision stores, restaurants and buffets. The subway runs under this arcade.

The picture (right) shows the Seikai Bridge in Sasebo, Kyushu island, the former naval base. The span of this bridge extends 316 meters and is claimed to be the third longest bridge of the kind in the world. Between the Kyushu island and the main land three car traffic was made possible by the opening of the under seas tunnel, 3,461 meters long, in the spring of 1958.

Yokohama Bypass, (bottom) was opened recently and offers the shortest motor road to Tokyo.

These are the pictures showing Japanese girls of today visiting the temples and shrines in her every day wear (top), visiting dress (below), and the best Kimono (right).

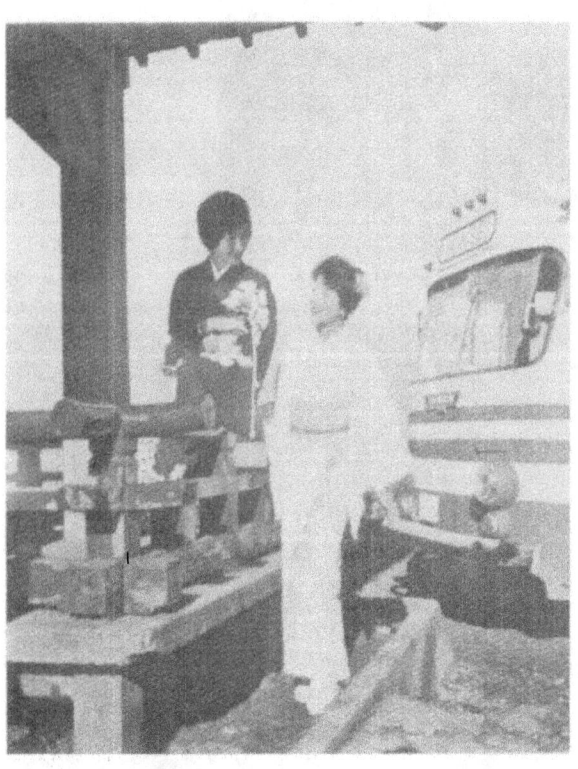

The splendid Work of the ancient Fine Arts. One of the sinewy couple statues of Deva kings in Toshogu Shrine at Nikko; one with an open mouth and the other with a mouth shut. They guard the gates of big Buddhist temples. Japan's typical temples such as Daibutsu of Nara and Kamakura have these Deva gates.

Noh play is a traditional drama of old Japan and is still played at several stages in Tokyo. The players wear the masks and costumes, most of which are the refined works of the ancient great craftsmen.

Japanese Car won Special Prize in the World's 10,000-mile Rally

Australian Mobilgas Rally, 1958

The Round-Australia Auto Rally is the World's toughest and most gruelling events held every year with entries from all car producing nations. Japan's first entry in this Aussie Rally was made in 1957 by Toyopet which won third place. In 1958 Rally, Japanese Datsun also took part and won the first place in a group outrivalling the Morris Minor, Renault Dauphine cars.

The followings are the copies of newspaper cuttings reporting about the Rally.

Round-Australia Auto Rally Opens

Sydney (Kyodo-Reuter)—Drivers and cars of many nations start competition Wednesday in one of the world's toughest and most gruelling events—the 10,000 miles Round-Australia car reliability rally.

Between competitors and the prize money, totaling 13,500 sterling, lies a 19-day nightmare of natural and mechanical hazards, and, greatest enemy of all—time.

The course aims at providing a searching test of the skill of drivers and navigators, and the reliability of the cars.

The trial will start from Sydney and finish in Melbourne on Sept. 7. It will take competitors through bush, desert and lush countryside and over broad highways and along barely distinguishable tracks plunging down into dry rocky creek beds. The course includes sections seldom before traversed by cars.

Each car, all 1951 models or later, will carry a gallon of water for each member of its crew, sufficient food to last each of the crew one week, a first aid kit and special safety aids.

Overseas interest in Round-Australia trails has increased each year, and this year's event has brought entries from Japan, the United States, Czechoslovakia, Canada, New Zealand and West Germany.

The Japanese contingent is the biggest ever, with 10 drivers and 5 cars entered. The cars are Toyopets and Datsuns.

From Czechoslovakia will come a team of three Skodas, and the other overseas factory entry so far is a Porche from West Germany.

More than 50 Australian firms have joined with the sponsors to swell the prize money.

The winner will receive an additional 1,200 sterling if he decides to compete in the 1959 Monte Carlo rally. Included in the prize list is 600 sterling for women competitors.

Japanese in High Hopes as Aussie Rally Starts

Special to The Japan Times

Sydney—Sixty-seven cars—including three Toyopets and two Datsuns—left Sydney's Bondi Beach Wednesday morning to begin the 10,000-mile Round Australia Rally.

The cars faced tough going in the southern part of Australia because of widespread floods.

The Japanese crews, the center of attraction at the start, were beseiged by autograph hunters.

Mrs. Misako Togo, dressed in white over-alls and polished black flying boots, received loud applause as she and her husband, Yukiyasu, and their Australian navigator, Evan Thomas, roared off in their Toyopet.

Japanese Consul General Kazuyoshi Inagaki shook hands with every Japanese crewmember before the start. Tuesday night, the Japanese were Inagaki's guests at a reception.

Rally officials invited Inagaki to act as starter for a number of cars and he sent them off with a swing of a big Australian flag.

The Japanese cars were gaily painted with advertisements and insignia. Their crews had high hopes of winning the foreign section of the rally.

In contrast to last year, the Japanese entries this year have a fully-organized serving organization to maintain them along the route. Serving agents have been appointed around Australia and spare part have been flown to Perth and Darwin where the cars will stop for maintenance.

The 800-mile road between Sydney and Melbourne is reasonably good. However, when cars cross the Victoria border they will have to detour because of raging floodwaters in many parts of the state.

On arrival in Melbourne Thursday, the cars will stay 10 hours before continuing on.

The foreign representation is bigger than usual with six Czechoslovakian, one German, one New Zealand and the five Japanese entered.

Japan Car Leading in One Class

The Brisbane Telegraph, September 4, 1958—A Japanese car today is leading in one section of the Mobilgas trial but the other may win the "booby prize."

The crews of the cars, both Datsuns, entered by the Nissan Motor Co., Ltd., Yokohama, appear to have little stamina.

This is because they have not been able to obtain meals of rice or other foods in their ordinary diet.

They are drinking gallons of pineapple and grapefruit juice.

In the run into Brisbane one crew member could drive only 60 miles before he had to rest.

The cars are the smallest to reach Brisbane with a three-man crew in any round-Australia trial.

Crocodile Latest Rally Obstacle

Perth (Kyodo-Reuter)—A large crocodile held up a car during the 10,000 mile round-Australian Mobilgas trial Friday.

It squatted across the road into Derby, hot dusty trial checkpoint in the north of Western Australia.

Driver Lou Kent said he had to hit the crocodile several times with his shovel before it made off into the scrub.

The leader of the three Japanese cars still in the trial arrived in Derby with a badly dented bonnet after colliding with a wallaby.

Datsun Declared 1,000 cc Winner

Melbourne (Kyodo-Reuter)—The Japanese Nissan motor company's Datsun car won the class for vehicles up to 1,000 c.c. in the 10,100-mile round-Australia reliability trial, which ended here on Saturday.

The Datsun took the award, scoring 1,129 points, after the Confederation of Motor Sports national court of appeal had revised the provisional placings.

The courts decision makes Eddie Perkins of Victoria the winner of the trial and puts the provisional winner Greg Cusack of Canberra in second place. Both drove Volkswagens.

Datsun Car Driver Gets Special Prize

Melbourne (UPI)—Japanese Datsun driver Yasuhara Nanba won a special prize for cars not exceeding 1,000 cubic centimeters, with a total of 416 points in the Mobiloil race here Sunday.

A factory-entered Czechoslovakian Skoda, driven by Kent Ubman, of New South Wales, won a special prize for being the leading overseas entrant, with a loss of 146 points. Thirty-four of the original 72 cars reached the final checkpoint at Albert Park in Melbourne Sunday. Another entrant, limping toward Melbourne, finally withdrew Sunday at Central Victoria.

Nanba's Datsun finished 24th and another Datsun, driven by Yoshitane Oya, was 35th with a loss of 1,296 points.

Datsun car entering the finish line after making the whole course in 1958 Australian Mobilgas Rally.

Datsun car, the winner in the Australian Rally, on display at the fifth Tokyo Motor Show

Japanese Motorcycles Won Prizes in the T.T. Race

Toward the end of May, 1959, many veteran motorcycle riders rushed to the Isle of Man from various countries to participate in the speed competitions for the world's most honorable prizes, and among them were a group of Japanese riders.

The event was the world-famous International Tourist Trophy Race what we call the T. T. Race. On June 1, the eagerly-awaited 40th T. T. Race was opened, in which a Japanese team participated for the first time. It was the "Honda" team.

The Honda team was the only participant from the Far East, and their appearance produced so great a sensation that, even during their training, they were greeted with applause wherever they went.

In the T. T. Race, there were several classes of competitions: 500 c.c. Senior, 350 c.c. Junior, Light Weight 250 c.c., Ultra Light Weight 125 c.c. and 500 c.c. Sidecar. It was in the Ultra Light Weight Class that the Honda team entered the first competition at the race.

Among the spectators, a great deal of interest was given as to what results the new participant from Japan would show. Needless to say, the Honda riders were heavily handi-capped compared with other veterans having past experience in the T. T. Race.

In the 125 c.c. class competition, 34 racers including 4 Hondas started out in full readiness. However, 16 failed halfway and only 7 racers succeeded to finish the whole course length of 107.9 miles.

The Honda riders made considerable efforts in competing with powerful veterans, and at the finish of their hard run was crowned with success. Although it was their first attempt at the Isle of Man, the Honda team won 4 prizes including the manufacturer's team prize.

The press immediately reported the results of the Japanese riders, and the news quickly travelled all over the world. Mr. John Griffith of the British Publication "Motorcycle," and a well-known commentator on motorcycle races, said to the effect that the Honda racers were basically original models, and their engine, mechanism, design and small detailed parts showed the result of advanced research work; riders were also of the first rank.

The Honda racers were the RC 142 models with 124.7 c.c. engines developing 18.5 HP at 14,000 rpm. and conclusively demonstrated the superiority of Japanese motorcycles in the world racing arena. Incidentally, Honda is making preparations for participation in the 250 c.c. (left) competition of the 1960 T. T. Race.

Starting London in the Spring, 1956, two Asahi newspaper-men set out for a long distance tour in Toyopet car visiting over twenty different lands.
After eight months trying drive through vast deserts and steep hills, they reached Tokyo in December, the same year.
Throughout the whole course of 50,000 kilometers (31,000 mi.), the car gave not a single trouble in spite of all adverse climatic and road condition. Their manuscript was published under the title of " 50,000 kilometers Drive from London to Tokyo " and has been received as the best seller.

The motor caravan of three-wheelers, motorcycles and scooters made a goodwill visit to South-east Asian countries leaving Tokyo in November, 1958. The city first visted was Saigon, thence the caravan proceeded to Cambodia, Viet-Num and Laos, and went as far as Thailand. Then it visited Singapore, after passing through Malay Peninsula.
From there the caravan arrived in Djakarta, Indonesia, where it completed its 4,500 kilometer course and came back in January, 1959.
The similar visit is scheduled to be made to other parts of the world.

Japanese Vehicles Running in Foreign Lands

The Toyopet Land Cruiser " Sankei Milagro ", with two Sankei special correspondents at the wheel made a round-the-continent drive in South America.
They left the port of Laguaira, Venezuela on January 1, 1958, and traversed the rocky hills of the Andes. They visited Colombia, Equador, Peru, Bolivia, Chile, Argentina, Uruguay and Paraguay.
After visiting those ten different countries in South America, they finally arrived in Brazil and attended the Jubilee held on June 18, 1958, commemorating the arrival of the first Japanese emigrant in Brazil.

In 1958, the Waseda University student team including two young ladies made an exploration tour to the Tropical Africa covering the total route 10,000 kilometers (6,200 mi.) driving a couple of Datsun Carrier models, with a successful result.
On January 1, 1958, they landed at Monbasa, Kenya, and proceeded to the capital, Nairobi. From there they attempted to climb Mt. Kilimanjaro and succeeded in conquering the snowy peak.
On Feb. 14, they started and drove through Belgian Congo and French Equadol Africa as far as to Stanleyville. During the course, they hardly put up any hotel, but passed nights in and on their cars which were prepared with camping equipments.

Nissan Bus in Thailand

Hino Blue Ribbon in Thailand

Toyo-Ace Canvas Bus in Thailand

Japanese Vehicles Running in Foreign Lands

Nissan Bus & Truck in Thailand

Isuzu Bus in Burma

Isuzu Dump Truck in Burma

Datsun Sedan in Thailand   Toyota Land Cruiser in Thailand

It is only after the war that the Japanese motor industry commenced its export business, and the annual exports were on a low level of 1,000 units until several years ago. Since 1956, however, vehicle exports have shown a marked increase in pace with the rapid rise in domestic production.

In 1955, total exports exclusive of three-wheelers, motorcycles and motor scooters were 1,241 units, followed by 2,446 units in 1956, 6,554 units in 1957 and 10,234 units in 1958. This means that since 1956, Japan's motor vehicle exports have almost doubled every year. Today, Japanese-made vehicles are used in more than 70 countries.

Japanese motor vehicles have been enjoying enormous popularity in Southeast Asia as adequate means of transport. Our statistics show that up to the present Okinawa purchased 4,000 units, Taiwan (Formosa) 4,700 units, Philippines 530 units, Indonesia 720 units, Burma 3,100 units, Malaya 220 units, Ceylon 100 units, Singapore 280 units and Thailand 5,000 units.

India, Pakistan, North Borneo, Korea, Laos, Cambodia, Viet Nam, Hong Kong and Portuguese Goa also are important customers of the Japanese motor industry.

In Southeast Asia, nearly 20,000 military vehicles produced by our motor industry are playing an important role as modern mobile units to secure national defense.

To Burma, Indonesia and Philippines, a considerable number of motor vehicles have been shipped from Japan as war reparations. These vehicles are used mainly for construction and development in these countries.

In Bangkok, capital of Thailand, a branch office of Toyota Motor is very active in assembling, selling, after-sale servicing, etc. Modern selling systems including installment plans have been widely adopted and travelling service units are dispatched to local districts away from the capital to assure the customers of satisfactory after-sale service.

In Bangkok, many Japanese-made modern buses are running on the main streets for transporting the people, while Japanese small trucks and passenger cars are receiving popularity among motorists in Thailand.

Burma is another important customer for Japanese vehicles. Apart from normal exports, about 3,000 vehicles of various kinds have been shipped as war reparations from Japan.

On Sundays and holidays, a great number of people go to the Pagoda, symbol of Rangoon,

Hino Bus in Rangoon   Hino Bus in Ceylon

Datsun Sedan in Egypt   Isuzu Fighter in Egypt

and to the Royal Lake, riding on the rear platform of small Japanese trucks which have conveniently installed chairs and canvas.

You will see on the streets of Rangoon quite a number of modern-styled Isuzu and Hino buses running at high speed. It is still fresh in our memory that the Burmese Government decided to ban horse carriages in Rangoon to be replaced by Japanese trucks.

A leading newspaper published in Rangoon reported about the decision like this: "Japanese small trucks are becoming a notorious feature of the capital.... a traffic revolution is breaking out."

To Ceylon, about 100 Japanese vehicles have been shipped up to the present. Last year, 30 units of Hino buses and Isuzu large trucks were exported. Through full activities of agents set up in Colombo, the export of our passenger cars is expected to increase greatly in the future.

In Malaya, the number of Japanese cars and trucks, such as Datsun, Toyopet and Prince Skyline, has been on the increase. In the near future, several hundreds of Datsun will be exported. In view of promising prospects, it will not be long before a plant is established in Malaya to assemble Japanese vehicles.

Taiwan has been using almost all Japanese makes—Isuzu, Toyota, Nissan, Hino, Fuji Precision, Minsei, Tokyu Kurogane, etc. Isuzu has exported the larger number of diesel-engined buses.

Under a contract between Nissan and an enterprise in Taiwan to assemble and eventually manufacture Nissan products, the first large truck was introduced on March 28, 1959. The Taiwanese plant now assembles Nissan trucks and Datsun trucks, using a number of items of locally manufactured products.

To sum up, most of Japanese motor vehicle exports to Southeast Asia have been accounted for by trucks and buses. In particular, the demand for Japanese diesel-powered vehicles has been increasing. Incidentally, Japanese diesel-engined vehicles now hold the first rank in the world production.

Japan has exported a number of motor vehicles to the Middle East and Africa. Up to the present, about 570 units have been shipped to Syria, 800 units to Iran, 320 units to Egypt, 750 units to Kuwait, 120 units to Aden and 190 units to Saudi Arabia. In addition, a number of vehicles have been delivered to Iran, Jordan, Oman, Bahrein, Lebanon and Qatar.

In Teheran, capital of Iran, Japanese-made passenger cars are being used as very convenient

Toyota Truck in Aden   Toyopet Crown in Kuwait

Minsei Bus in Addis Ababa, Ethiopia

Nissan Patrol in Danaseus City, Syria

taxi which are very popular among the public.

The export of Japanese vehicles to Africa began a couple of years ago. So far, the Union of South Africa imported 250 motor vehicles from Japan.

In Addis Ababa, capital of Ethiopia, Japanese small trucks and 4-wheel drive vehicles are received very well. An Ethiopian soldier commented on Japanese vehicles, "We hear Japan ranks the top in shipbuilding. Japanese cameras and transistor radios are excellent. Japan is so highly industrialized a country, I have had firm dependence on Japanese vehicles, too."

In Paraguay, a parade is to be held on August 15, the country's Independence Day. One year recently, at the head of the parade came high-ranking military officers riding on Japanese-made 4-wheel drive vehicles, followed in succession by many soldiers standing on Japanese trucks.

4-wheel drive vehicles—Toyota's Land Cruiser, Nissan's Patrol and Mitsubishi's Jeep—are chief export items of the Japanese motor industry. In Latin American countries, Venezuela and Cuba are big customers for Japanese 4-wheel drive vehicles.

La Paz, capital of Bolivia, 3,500 meters above the sea and surrounded by the Andes mountains, is in need of many vehicles with high performance especially in climbing. After a series of tests and studies of various foreign vehicles, the Metropolitan Special Police Board decided to use Japanese makes. Now in the uplands capital, Japanese vehicles are seen running to the satisfaction of the authorities concerned.

Costa Rica is using a large number of Japanese 4-wheel drive vehicles for police patrol. In addition, many such vehicles are used for agricultural activities.

It is a scene often seen in Costa Rica that customers bring their horses and carriages into dealer shops as a downpayment for Japanese vehicles. Of course, other foreign 4-wheel drive vehicles are also used, however a Japanese Land Cruiser is serving as a private car of the President of Costa Rica.

So popular are Japanese vehicles in Costa Rica that a race horse appeared, named after Toyota. One day the "Toyota" took the lead and won. But the "Toyota" continued running for a while. Fans at the bench shouted, "Push the brake pedal of that Toyota!"

Reputation of Mitsubishi buses in Santiago is well-known in not only Chile but also other countries. The Mitsubishi buses, purchased after keen competitions among many foreign manufacturers, are displaying their excellent

Hino Bus in Greece   Hino Buses in Greece

Isuzu Bus in Asuncion, Paraguay   President of Paraguay on a Toyota Land Cruiser

performance, coming up to the expectations of the transport authorities. So far 600 Mitsubishi buses have been supplied to Chile.

In Arica, free port in Chile, an assembly plant is operated under the agreement signed between Nissan Motor and a local firm. Some component parts produced in Chile are used, but many knocked-down shipments are sent from Japan. The demand for the car is increasing so much that market prospects are very encouraging.

Brazil is steadily growing as a motor vehicle manufacturing country. A number of foreign firms have invested to assemble and eventually manufacture their vehicles in the country.

Toyota Motor established a plant near Sao Paulo, where Land Cruisers are assembled by use of locally manufactured parts together with Japanese products. This is the first Japanese plant ever to be set up in the overseas markets.

In Mexico, Mexico Nissan Motor Sales Company was organized in 1959 by the cooperation of Mexican interests. Nissan Motor is now sending knocked-down shipments to the plant where Datsun sedans and trucks are assembled. The first car built there was purchased by the First Lady.

Toyota Motor is setting up an assembly plant in Bogota, Colombia to meet increasing demands for their vehicles. Last year, Isuzu buses were shipped to Paraguay and Minsei trucks to Guatemala. These vehicles are highly evaluated and are made a subject of talk.

Japanese motor vehicles are exported sometimes on barter basis. Recently, a leading businessman of Guatemala visited Japan to conclude a contract for barter trade. With the contract signed, Japan will ship some 300 cars and trucks, and buy raw cotton, lumber and sugar.

The already high reputation of Japanese motor vehicles abroad has been increased by the start of export to the U.S.

In January, 1958, Toyopet and Datsun cars made their successful appearance at the Los Angels Automobile Show and created a sensation among the visitors. They were the only participants from Asia and the first post-war cars to be shown before the public in the U.S. and yet they stood comparison with many other foreign cars.

Toyopet and Toyota vehicles are handled through U.S. Toyota Motor Sales Co., Inc. in Los Angels. The company has distributors and dealers in the East and West Coasts.

Nissan Motor is increasing Datsun sales through distributors and many dealers in the

Datsun Sedan in Venezuela   Mitsubishi-Jeep in Argentina

Mitsubishi-Jeep Fighter in Chile   Mitsubishi Fuso Bus in Chile

East and West Coasts. Fuji Precision, manufacturer of Prince Skyline and other products, is concentrating in the West Coast at present.

Hawaii is having a small-car boom. Japan began export of passenger cars only a couple of years ago, and already more than 500 units were shipped from Japan.

One of the contributing factors for the popularity of Japanese cars in Hawaii is that Japan holds a favorable geographical position. Usually, European cars for Hawaii are sent to a North American port, where they are unloaded once and loaded again on another ship for Hawaii. This troublesome shipping makes their cost inevitably higher.

Moreover, Japanese-made cars today are favorably comparable with European cars in performance, fuel consumption, etc. At an Economy Trial held under the sponsorship of a Hawaiian dealer of Japanese cars, the Japanese cars completed the whole course (6,300 miles) with remarkable results. Since the event, his car sales has rapidly increased.

The biggest purchaser of Japanese vehicles in Europe is Spain. So far, some 700 large trucks have been shipped from Isuzu, Hino and Minsei plants. Exports to Australia also have been on an upward trend.

Japanese motorcycle industry is also in a prosperous condition. Annual exports have increased to the level of 20,000 units inclusive of motor scooters. Major customers are Australia, Mexico, Malaya, Burma, and the U.S.

As economical means of transportation, these types of vehicles have a strong appeal. With the increase of national income prevailing in various countries, there will be much greater demands for motorcycles and motor scooters. Japanese products will meet such demands to a large extent, since they are highly evaluated in many a country.

To popularize the modern high-performance Japanese products, a caravan consisting of motorcycles and motor scooters visited Viet Nam, Cambodia, Laos, Thailand, Malaya, Singapore, Indonesia and Philippines from the end of 1958 to the spring of 1959.

From February, 1960, another caravan visited Mexico, Guatemala, Honduras, El Salvador, Nicaragua, Costa Rica and Panama. These caravans achieved substantial results and at the same time contributed toward a better understanding of the peoples.

❖ ❖ ❖

Minsei Truck in Spain   Hino Truck in Spain

Toyota Truck & Land Cruiser in Thailand

Toyota Land Cruiser in Caracas City, Venezuela

Some of 600 "Prince Skyline" cars landed at the port of Oakland in the San Francisco Bay.

Hino Dump Truck in Hawaii, U.S.A.

Toyota Land Cruiser in Florida, U.S.A.

Toyopet Crown at Golden Gate Bridge in San Francisco, U.S.A.

JAPANESE CARS AT FOREIGN MOTOR SHOWS

The 44th Salon de Paris was held from the 3rd through the 13th of October, 1957, in Paris at Grand Palais situated at the centre of the city.
The Prince Skyline model of Japanese made participated in the exhibition there and gained fame for its excellent efficiency.

Toyopet Crown exhibited together with other models by Toyota Motor at the 1959 San Francisco Automobile Show.

Datsun Sports Car exhibited with Datsun Bluebird at the Los Angels Imported Car Show in March, 1959.

NOTES

JAPAN'S MOTOR INDUSTRY

Its Development and What It Is Today

DEVELOPMENT

Early Period

The first motor car made its appearance on the streets of Yokohama in 1899, when a foreign merchant, a resident of Yokohama, imported an electric tricycle "Progress" for his private use. But, it disappeared shortly thereafter because it fell into the sea in an accident.

The second car, an American four-wheeled electric car was presented by Japanese residents in San Francisco to the Imperial Household in 1900, as a wedding gift to Crown Prince Yoshihito (father of the present Emperor). This car also met with similar misfortune because it ran into the palace moat on its trial run. Whereupon, the elderly councilors of the Mikado's Court decreed that the motor car was too dangerous a carriage to be used by a member of the Imperial family.

Thereafter, motor cars were imported into Japan by foreign residents in Yokohama and Kobe and made their appearance on the streets before the curious eyes of the Japanese people.

In November, 1901, an enterprising Tokyo merchant by name of Tamijiro Matsui started a motor car business in Ginza, Tokyo, under the name of "Motor Shokai." His aim was to sell a few motor cars imported by a foreign merchant but there remains no record that any business was done at this shop.

Forerunners

In the summer of 1902, the "Motor Shokai" was taken over together with cars in stock by Shintaro Yoshida, a proprietor of "Sorinsha," a bicycle dealer, who had just returned from the U.S. where he visited to buy bicycles. He was deeply impressed by the progress of the motor industry in the United States and brought home two horizontal two-cylinder engines of 12 and 18 HP each. He started a motor car business under the new name of "Automobile Shokai."

An electrical engineer, Komanosuke Uchiyama, who learned something about motor cars in Vladivostok, assisted Yoshida to build a four-passenger car in 1902, with the aforesaid 12 HP engine. Although it was not good enough to be sold, this car was the first motor car built in Japan. Using the other 18 HP engine, Yoshida and Uchiyama built another car, a twelve-passenger motor cab, in the fall of the same year at the request of a cab company in Hiroshima. Uchiyama delivered this car to the customer by driving it about 620 miles from Tokyo. However, this car was not in service long because of the lack of good tires.

In 1904, Torao Yamaba of Okayama built a steam-engine car for a cab company in Okayama. In May of the same year, a trial was made at Okayama in the presence of admiring spectators.

In 1907, Yoshida and Uchiyama made their third car, a car equipped with a under-the-floor horizontal gas engine, one of the most advanced cars in its days. A total of 17 cars of this type was built by the same makers and the cars were commonly called by the name of "Takuri." In the trial run, Prince Arisugawa, a member of the Imperial family, had a ride in this car. He was an owner of a "Darracq" car bought in France and was a great motor fan in those days. Ten motor cars, foreign and domestic, joined in this trial run which was about 30 miles into the suburb of Tokyo. This was the first motor car rally held in Japan.

This was in the year 1907, about twenty years after Gottlieb Daimler of Germany invented the first gas engine car in 1885, about ten years after Henry Ford succeeded in building a two-cylinder 4 HP car and one year after the Austin Motor Company was formed in Britain.

In the following year, 1908, Rinosuke Yoneyama of Tokyo made a single-cylinder car and the next year, Miyata Works, Ltd. built another car as an experiment.

In 1911, four military trucks were built for experiments in the Tokyo and Osaka Arsenals in accordance with the plans designed by the Army Technological Laboratory.

A few years later (1912), a new car was built by Masujiro Hashimoto of Tokyo and was named "DAT" taking the initials of the names of the three sponsors. This car is the predecessor of the popular small cars "DATSUN" now being produced by the present Nissan Motor Co., Ltd.

Notwithstanding these relatively early efforts, Japan's motor industry made little progress until recent years mostly owing to the backward economic and social conditions.

In Japan, motor cars had been used only by a small number of people who were always very interested in picking the newest type of foreign car of the time and paying little attention to the unshapely domestic cars. Because of lack of domestic demand, the industry found it very difficult to get support from the government and financial quarters to improve its production facilities.

In 1922, Masaya Toyokawa, a great motor fan, organized Hakuyosha, Ltd. in Tokyo, and started the commercial production of a small car powered by an air-cooled engine, the first of its kind in those days, under the name of "Otomo." The total production for two years was 250 and some were shipped to Shanghai, but this firm had to close down its plant in 1927, under the pressure of competition from foreign cars.

Growth under the Assistance of Government Subsidy

Finding the strategic value of motor vehicles, the Japanese Army commenced investigation of military vehicles of foreign origin as early as in 1907. As previously mentioned, the army succeeded to make four military trucks in 1911, at the Tokyo and Osaka Arsenals. After a series of tests, the military authorities fully understood the strategic importance of the motor vehicles and influenced the government to pass a law in 1918, to pay subsidies to motor vehicle manufacturers for the purpose of improving production facilities. Owners of specified cars and trucks were also paid subsidies which increased the number of owners in this group.

This government subsidy served as the incentive to induce competent engineering firms such as Ishikawajima Dockyard & Engineering Co., Ltd., Tokyo Gas & Electric Co., Ltd. and DAT Motors Co., Ltd. to make cars and trucks in comformity with the military specifications. The above subsidy policy of the government is said to be responsible for the later trend in the Japanese motor industry laying special emphasis on the manufacture of trucks and buses rather than cars.

The Great Quake of 1923, The Turning Point

On September 1, 1923, the Great Earthquake shook the Tokyo and Yokohama area and killed hundreds of thousands of people and destroyed the larger parts of both cities by fire, disrupting all urban and suburban railway traffic. At the time of the Quake, passengers were transported mostly by imported taxi cabs, buses and trucks, and it was learned by this experience that motor vehicles could be operated on a paying basis for transporting passengers. While all railway traffic was suspended by the Quake for many weeks, motor vehicles played an important part in transporting passengers and goods, and fully demonstrated their true value before the public. The recovery work of the tramways was delayed and consequently, the Tokyo Electric Tram Bureau placed an order with Ford Motor Company, U.S.A., for inmediate shipment of 1,000 bus chassis. On their arrival, the said Bureau built and mounted on the bus chassis clumsy bodies and put them into service in the Tokyo area. For some time, these unshapely vehicles were the most popular buses among the people of Tokyo and was called by the pet name of "Entaro."

The Great Earthquake gave the stimulus to the Japanese public to use motor cars and trucks more extensively, and American cars began being imported by private motorcar dealers because of their earlier delivery than European makes.

In September, 1924, Ford's survey team landed in Yokohama to see how the Ford buses were being used and to make general market study. Deeply impressed by the energetic efforts being made to reconstruct the destroyed cities, they reported to their head office about the high potentiality of the Japanese market. Thereupon, Ford decided to get started in Japan and in December of the same year, they organized the Japan Ford Motors. In March of the following year, the company went into assembling cars by modern conveyor system.

At the end of 1926, General Motors in Japan was formed in Osaka and started assembly operations of Chevrolet cars. The spectacular sales activities of the above U.S. manufacturers brought about the demands of the Japanese people for motor cars, contributing a great deal to cultivating the market for the motor industry.

It was inevitable, on the other hand, that the increasing competition from the above U.S. car manufacturers began to overshadow the future development of the domestic motor industry. This condition continued until shipment of motor parts from the U.S. stopped, and Ford and G.M. closed down their assembly plants in Japan as the result of the Foreign Exchange Control Law passed in 1939.

Supported by the military motor vehicle subsidy, some of the manufacturers survived the strong competition from the U.S. manufacturers. These were Ishikawajima, Tokyo Gas & Electric,

DAT, Mitsubishi Kobe Dockyard (the predecessor of the present Mitsubishi Nippon Heavy-Industries, Ltd.) and Ohta Motors, some of whom had started the manufacture of trucks and cars as early as in 1917.

Toyota and Nissan Got Started in 1933

In 1933, both the Dat Division of the Motor Industry, Ltd. and Toyoda Automatic Loom Works announced to start the production of cars and trucks. The former changed its name as Nissan Motor Co., Ltd. in 1934, and the latter formed Toyota Motor Co., Ltd. in 1937. In a few years, both companies went into mass production of motor trucks and cars. About the same time, the military car divisions of Ishikawajima, Tokyo Gas & Electric, and DAT Motors were amalgamated into the Motor Industry, Ltd., the predecessor of the present Isuzu Motor Co., Ltd. and Hino Motors, Ltd.

In 1935, the present Minsei Diesel Engineering Co., Ltd. went into production of diesel trucks and buses under the name of Japan Diesel Industries, Ltd.

It was at this time when Japan's motor industry had laid a concrete foundation for its future prosperity. The production of motor vehicles including trucks, buses and cars reached a total of 46,498 units in 1941, and this was the record figure for Japan's motor industry in pre-war days.

In December, 1941, at the start of the Pacific War, the motor industry gradually began to suffer from the growing shortage of materials, and production continued to dwindle down to less than 10,000 trucks and buses by 1945, the year of Japan's surrender.

A Spectacular Post-War Development

In 1945, the year of the return of Peace, found Japan's inland transportation in an extremely confused state. Of about 110,000 total motor vehicle registrations, inclusive of cars, trucks and buses, less than 80,000 were found to be fit for service. The condition of operation was on a very low level owing to the lack of fuel. Everyday life of the people was on the brink of crisis due to shortage of foods and other daily necessities from the lack of transportation facilities.

Recovery of inland transportation was taken up by the government as one of the major problems of the time. Fortunately, the production facilities of the motor industry had suffered relatively minor damage from the war and the resumption of truck production was ordered by the occupation authorities during 1945, using the materials then available. The ban of the manufacture of cars was lifted in 1949, and cars were again put in production the same year. Thus, production was resumed by almost all the former motor vehicle manufacturers and also two big firms, Mitsubishi Heavy Industries, Reorganized, Ltd. and Fuji Precision Machinery Co., Ltd., joined in as newcomers. As a result, motor vehicle production facilities showed a dramatic expansion in the following years.

In vehicle registration, 1948 figures surpassed the prewar peak of the 1938 output, and the 1953 figures broke the record production figure of 1941, since then production has been showing a steady increase year after year.

This dramatic development of our motor industry was due largely to the liberation of national trade and industry from the long wartime controls. Under the intense competition, wholesalers and retailers had to speed up delivery of their merchandise by using private trucks and wagons. And as the nation's living standard improved, the private tourist bus business opened extensive sight-seeing services and also long distance bus services of passengers.

The rapid increase of private car registrations is a marvelous reflection of the surging upward trend of business activities in recent years. In addition, the rapid expansion of motorcycle registration, is due to the enthusiastic backing of the motor boom among the younger generation.

This dramatic growth in the motor industry is the outcome of innumerable factors and came like a windfall to the motor manufacturers of this country. Supported by the strong upward trend of demand from the domestic market, the manufacturers have been able to expand their capacities with the modernized production facilities to its present level.

Three-Wheelers

As stated previously, the first car imported into Japan in 1899, happened to be an American three-wheeler electric motor car.

About 10 years later a two front and one rear wheeled motor car was reportedly made in Tokyo in 1911, and another car of the same type called "YAMATA" was built in Osaka in 1916, though no further details are now available about them. In 1917, William R. Gorham, an American citizen later naturalized a Japanese, built a one front and two rear wheeled motor car for his crippled friend. In 1919, the building of Gorham's three-wheeler was started in Osaka on a commercial basis and a small number of vehicles were sent to the market. The above are the forerunners of the Japanese three-wheeled cars which are now well known all over the world as a champion of the Japanese motor cars.

The motorized three-wheelers came into popular use for the first time during the period immediately following the year of the Great Quake in the Tokyo and Yokohama area.

In a few years following the Great Quake of 1923, motor vehicles such as cars, trucks, buses, etc. became a more important means of transporting goods and passengers in this country.

In those days, motor vehicles were mostly of foreign origin too big and too expensive to be used by medium and small traders. The three-wheeler was introduced to meet the demand from the majority of the people for a smaller and speedy vehicle.

The start was made by importing a "Smith" motor from the U.S. having ½-1 HP, and was attached to bicycles and pedal tricycle without too much difficulty. Bicycles and tricycles attached with this motor were permitted by the Home Office to be driven on the roads without any driver's license. Since these vehicles could carry only small load of 165 lbs at best, 3 HP engines were imported to be used in order to carry 330–413 lbs. The government specifications for these motor vehicles in those days were as follows:

Engine, piston displacement	350 c.c.
Width of vehicle	0.9 meters
Length of vehicle	2.4 meters
Transmission of speeds	2
Speed per hr.	up to 25.6 km.
Load	150–187.5 kg.
Price of vehicle	about ¥600

The Home Office gave approval on each three-wheeler produced by the makers and ordered that every car approved, a blueprint showing its structure be issued as proof to license the vehicle. No driver's license was required for this vehicle.

In February, 1930, official notice was given indicating the undermentioned specifications under which any person was permitted to make motorized three-wheelers:

Piston displacement	
4 cycles	500 c.c.
2 cycles	350 c.c.
Width of the vehicle	1.2 meters
Length of the vehicle	2.8 meters
Number of persons	1 person

By this change, three-wheeler car manufacturing was opened to general machine makers and interest in the three-wheeler manufacturing was started among big machinery makers. In a rapid succession, many three-wheelers were introduced into the market. They were "Daihatsu" of Hatsudoki Seizo Kaisha, Ltd. (the predecessor of the present Daihatsu Kogyo K.K.), Osaka, "Mazda" of Toyo Kogyo Co., Ltd., Hiroshima, "Kurogane" of Nippon Motor, Ltd., (predecessor of the present Tokyu Kurogane Motor Co., Ltd.), Tokyo, and "Giant" of Teikoku Seiki, Ltd. (presently the Aichi Machine Industry Co., Ltd.) of Nagoya, etc. All these three-wheelers are built entirely in Japan.

To cope with the increasing use of motorized three-wheelers throughout the country and also to meet the need of revisions of the Motor Car Control Law of the time, the government revised the Control Law, including the control of light cars or motorbicycles and the three-wheelers, in August, 1933. By this revision, the piston displacement of the three-wheeler engine was increased from 500 c.c. to 750 c.c., and the demand for three-wheelers were further increased. Production of passenger cars was permitted by this law and the era for light four-wheelers began its development in those days.

In 1937, trouble occurred between China and Japan, and Japan gradually went into wartime controls and consequently the motor industry, especially in the light cars, had to suffer under the increasing short supply of fuel. After 1937, the pre-war peak, the output of motor vehicles continued to drop year by year.

However, the post-war development of motorized three-wheelers is indeed beyond all expectation. The production of three-wheelers in 1948, outstripped the prewar record of 15,230 units in 1937, and made a zooming rise year after year reaching to the 10 months total ending October 31, 1959, of 122,505 units, about an 800 percent increase compared with pre-war peak figure.

Motorcycles & Scooters

The first motorbicycle, a "Thomas" brand, was imported into this country in 1902, by a foreign merchant, residing in Yokohama. Around 1907, a "Smith" motor was brought home from the U.S. and attached to a bicycle. In 1908, Torao Yamaba of Okayama, the inventor of a steam engine car, developed a gasoline engine motorbicycle inspired by an American who did stunts riding on his motorcycle. This is the oldest motorbicycle made in Japan. In 1913, the present big bicycle maker, Miyata Works, made two motorbicycles, "Asahi" and "X," and in 1924, Murata Iron Works, Tokyo, made the "Giant" motorcycle with the assistance of Komanosuke Uchiyama, and Rikuo Nainenki (the predecessor of the present Rikuo Motorcycle Co., Ltd.) succeeded in making a domestic "Harley" motorcycles. These earlier activities of the forerunners of Japan's motorcycle makers were entirely overshadowed by the fleet of foreign-made motorcycles, such as "Sunbeam," "Douglas," "Harley-Davidson," "Henderson," "Indian," etc., and admired by Japanese motor fans of those days. These foreign motorcycles began to disappear from the street as the foreign exchange control was strengthened by the government. However, the pre-war activity in this segment of the motor industry had remained at very low level. The total motorcycle production in 1940, the pre-war peak year, stood at a little more than 3,000 units, mostly for the police requisition, rather than popular use.

A tremendous expansion in motorcycle manufacturing came after the war when all Japanese scientific and technical capacities were liberated from war production and concentrated for peaceful purposes. This gigantic expansion of the motorcycle industry can be seen in the zooming rise of its output in the last two years:

1958	503,087 motorcycles and scooters
January—October, 1959	695,722 motorcycles and scooters

WHAT IT IS TODAY

Thanks to the booming domestic and overseas demand for all motor vehicles in the past years, the industry is now making ceaseless expansion at a rate unknown in the industry's history. Motor vehicle output for 1958, recorded 790,267 units which is broken down into:

Cars	50,643
Trucks	130,066
Buses	7,594
Three-wheelers	98,877
Motorcycles	389,869
Motor scooters	113,218

Total output for the ten months ending October 31, 1959, reached 1,029,436 units which includes:

Cars	63,179
Trucks	142,499
Buses	5,531
Three-wheelers	122,505
Motorcycles	592,752
Motor scooters	102,970

The total production of 1959 is estimated to exceed the figures for the preceding year by approximately 450,000 units.

Cars

The cars made in Japan are mostly of the compact type with engines under 1,500 c.c. These small cars are very popular because of the narrow and congested roads of this country and of its low fuel consumption. Of the total 63,179 cars produced during the ten months ending October 31, 1959, 62,424 units are small cars of this type or 99% of the total.

The small cars include 4,341 light cars with engine cylinder capacity under 360 c.c. The cars with over 1,500 c.c. engines, long left out of production after the war, was brought back in production program since the beginning of 1959, although still in relatively small number.

In Japan, motor vehicles are classified by the motor vehicle regulations, according to cylinder displacement, such as under 360 c.c., 500 c.c., 1,000 c.c., 1,500 c.c., and over 1,500 c.c. And each division is subject to the discriminating rules for duty assessment and operator's licensing standard. Therefore, motor vehicle manufacturers have placed their efforts to design their products so that they give the highest performance within the respective division limits.

People's Car Idea

In 1955, a white paper was published on an idea for a people's car containing suggestions from government quarters for development of a low priced high-efficiency small car with engine capacity of 350—500 c.c. for use by people in the medium and low income brackets.

This paper caused an active argument in and out of the industry as to its feasibility and the news was even reported in the overseas presses. For some years, this seemed to have been forgotten by the people, however, at the Tokyo Motor Show of 1959, a new small car of an original design was displayed by a manufacturer who had presumably adopted the people's car idea.

The "people's car" has been in the mind of some of motor vehicle manufacturers, and it will be interesting to see how their people's car idea will develop in their future models.

The cars made in Japan have long been known for their durability and low fuel consumption. But today Japanese car manufacturers have to improve their products by upgrading structural efficiency, appearance and comfort in order to meet the satisfaction of aspirant and progressive demands of domestic motor fans and also to compete with foreign manufacturers in the overseas market.

Trucks

Of the total 142,499 trucks manufactured in the 10 months ending October 31, 1959, the light trucks with engines ranging of 360 c.c. to 1,500 c.c. amounted to 104,108 units or 73% of the total and the remaining 37,510 units (26%) are heavy trucks with engines of over 1,500 c.c.

Before 1955, the production of the heavy trucks was more than that of the light ones. But, since 1955, the output of heavy trucks has reduced year by year, being replaced by the light trucks with engines under 1,500 c.c.

This trend indicates the rapid expansion of private truck ownership among medium income firms in this country in recent years. Heavy trucks are in constant demand mostly from higher income industrial customers and transportation and trucking concerns.

During the 10 months ending October 31, 1959, Japan produced a total of 142,499 trucks, of which gasoline trucks consisted of 85% and diesel trucks only 15%. However, in heavy-duty trucks, diesels predominate, sharing almost 70% of the total.

The heavy duty trucks are mostly of cargo, stake or semi-stake models, all fit for long haulage and used by trucking concerns and large industrial firms.

In the light commercial group, the so-called "Pick-up" trucks are most popular and enjoy a rapid increasing demand in this country. Those made in semi-cab-over model are now in extensive use together with full cab-over model light vans. The stylish delivery vans have made their appearance on the road. These are built on car chassis having comfortable driver and passenger cabs with the smooth performance of a car.

In addition to the above-mentioned models, the industry supplies for military defense or civil services a number of special trucks, such as tractor trucks, four and six-wheel drive vehicles including the diesel Jeep, a new development of the motor industry of this country.

Buses

Total output of buses during the 10 months ending October 31, 1959, amounted to 5,531 units against that of 7,594 units for 1958. For the past two years, bus production has remained at lower level than that of 1957, when some overseas bus companies were in the market.

Japanese buses are available in almost any type including "Bonnet," "Cab-over," "Rear or Under-floor engined" and also in the expensive aircushioned model.

Japanese vehicle manufacturers and their highly trained engineers and scientists are prepared, at the request of the customers, to design and manufacture any special types of bus, tailor-made to suit local climatic and other conditions at a most competitive price.

Special Purpose Vehicles

Under this group, dump-trucks, tank lorries, fire-engines, crane trucks, tractor shovels, concrete mixers, etc. are produced in this country. In addition to the above, there are many special function vehicles such as the so-called "PR cars" with speaker and movie-projector; radio and TV relay car, show-case car, medical clinic car, and cooking and other demonstration cars.

Having close cooperation from experts of other industrial fields, Japan's motor manufacturers are prepared to accept orders for any of these special cars and execute it to the complete satisfaction of the customer.

Three-Wheelers

The output of three wheelers in Japan during the 10 months ending October 31, 1959, totaled 122,505 units of which 60,209 units are light three-wheeled trucks of under 360 c.c., and the balance, 62,296 units, are heavy three-wheelers of over 360 c.c. Before 1958, most of the three-wheelers had engines ranging from 360 c.c. to 1,500 c.c., but since 1958, the light tricycles made rapid increase in its production and popularity.

The three-wheeled trucks with engines ranging 360—1,500 c.c. had their peak year in 1957, with their total output of 111,257 units. Since 1957, the production shows a gradual decrease and in 1959, the output is estimated at about 75,000 units.

With the introduction of the low-priced and handy light tricycles, they have rapidly displaced the heavier units. Some of these light tricycles were shipped to the U.S.

Motorcycles

Motorcycles manufactured in this country fall into several groups, depending on the cylinder capacity, heavy type with engine over 250 c.c., the medium type with 126—250 c.c. engines, the light type with 51—125 c.c. engines and the extra light "moped" with less than 50 c.c. engine.

The output during the 10 months ending October 31, 1959, totaled 592,752 units, about 200,000 units more than the 1958 total of 389,869 units. The total production in 1959, is estimated to exceed 700,000 units showing 90% increase compared with the 1958 total.

Special interest is in the "moped," with engine under 50 c.c., which was formerly designed to be attached to the conventional bicycle frame.

This "moped" is being well received by young motor fans nation-wide, owing to its low-price, low fuel consumption and also its simplicity to get a operator's license.

Its output during the 10 months ending October 31, 1959, reached 236,197 units showing a 460% increase compared with the 1958 figure.

Motor Scooters

Like the motorcycles, the heavy scooters with engine of over 250 c.c. lost popularity from about 1954, and the lighter types have taken their places.

Of the total output of 102,970 units for the 10 months ending October 31, 1959, the medium type with engines ranging 126–250 c.c. represents 48,117 units or 48% and the light scooters with engines ranging 51–125 c.c. shared 54,853 units or 52% of the total. The total production of motor scooters for 1959, is estimated surpass that of 1958.

Manufacturing Methods

Notwithstanding the relatively early start of manufacturing vehicles in 1907, Japan's motor industry lagged behind showing very slow progress during the next 30 years. However, the advent of industrialization was seen in 1936, when some of the manufacturers imported mass production systems for the first time.

After a series of improvement made in the manufacturing methods an automation system has now been adopted by the industry under which all production processes such as forging, casting, press work, coating, etc. are going in a well-planned uninterrupted stream. The cars completed in the assembly line moves to the test ground to undergo strict examination.

Every component part which goes into the Japanese motor vehicles is domestically made and all accessories such as tires and tubes, batteries, wires, ignition plugs, etc. are the products of the industries which share the prosperity with the motor industry.

All Japanese products are marketed only after

passing the strictest examination and the customers are certain to find them the most dependable being free from any fault.

Rapidly Growing Vehicle Registrations

The domestic demand for motor vehicles is on a steadily increasing trend year by year with the resultant rise in the number of vehicle ownerships. The statistics show that the number of motor vehicle registrations in August, 1959, totaled 2,588,882 including 290,556 cars, 523,569 trucks, 50,130 buses, 66,467 special purpose vehicles, 679,804 three-wheelers and 978,356 motorcycles and motor scooters.

This total registration is nearly an increase of twelve times as compared with that of 1938, the peak year of the prewar time.

The group including cars, trucks and buses increased more than six times while the motorcycles and three-wheelers increased nearly nineteen times—the most spectacular expansion unknown in the record of any country of the world.

This phenomenal expansion of the total number of vehicles, it is believed, is the result of the liberation of all national activity controls influenced by the occupation after the war.

Since the termination of the war, Japanese industry and trade, released from wartime controls, have resumed their full activities to enrich the daily lives of the people. The growing competition made industrial and commercial circles speed up delivery of goods by using their own vehicles instead of relying on the railway and road transport. And as a result of increasing business activities in recent years, the taxi business continued to enjoy booming years and to own a private car has become a must for an active businessman.

Sightseeing bus business also has been enjoying profitable years supported by the mounting popularity among the people.

The total private car registrations showed a marvellous increase up to the index of 859 compared with the figure of 1950 as 100. During the same period, small car with engine under 1,500 c.c. made gigantic strides in registrations to the index number of 1,265 by the end of 1958, or about 12.7 times compared with the registrations in 1950. During the same period, truck registration index reached 397 or about an increase of four times as compared with the 1950 registrations. The total registrations of light trucks with engine under 1,500 c.c. in private possession shows an index of 855, that is about 8.6 times as that of 1950.

The total tonnage of the cargo hauled by trucks in 1957, reached 750 million tons, that is about 3.4 times as much as the total tonnage transported by railways. Buses carried, during the same year, about 4,700 million passengers compared with the total 4,300 million transported by the National Railways. The total number of users of taxis during 1957 is reported to reach 1,160 million. All these figures show a steady increase.

Of the total motor vehicle registration in March, 1959, domestic cars represents 72%, trucks 98%, buses 99%, and special purpose vehicles 87%, or an average of 89%. In motorcycles and three-wheelers, no foreign makes are seen on the road because domestic vehicles of these types are almost exclusively being used.

Exports

Overseas shipments of motor vehicles in 1958, included 2,357 cars, 7,297 trucks, 346 buses, 243 special purpose vehicles, and 38 trailers making a total of 10,281 units. During the 10 months ending October 31, 1959, Japan exported 4,258 cars, 6,867 trucks, 360 buses, and 631 special purpose vehicles, or totaling 12,116 units.

Total export of motorcycles and three-wheelers in 1958, totaled 8,106 which consisted of: motorcycles 2,427, scooters 5,120 and three-wheelers 559. The export statistics of motor vehicles shipments for the seven months from April 1 to October 31, 1959, show three-wheelers 1,632, motorcycles 8,284, and scooters 3,900 or 13,816 in total. This figure represents more than a 70% increase compared with the total exports in 1958.

Of motor vehicle shipments for the said seven months, 1,632 three-wheelers with engine under 360 c.c. and 296 heavier motor tricycles. The former or light types are becoming popular among U.S. buyers.

Of the total 8,284 motorcycles shipped overseas during the said period, "Moped" with under 50 c.c. engines represents 3,217 units and those with engine exceeding 51 c.c. totaled 5,067. It was a windfall for the industry to see the mopeds originally designed for the domestic market find a good market in the overseas countries.

The above export figures are not large enough to describe the actual scale of Japan's present day motor industry. It was only a few years ago that Japan actually commenced her effort to export her motor vehicles. Up till that time, the Japanese makers had solely been utilizing its production to supply the ever increasing domestic demand. After some ten post-war years, they have finally succeeded to fulfill this demand. They now have enough production capacity, both in production facilities and engineering skill, to ship their products to overseas markets.

The post-war exports of motor vehicles up to October, 1959, totaled 37,848 units including cars, trucks, buses, special purpose vehicles and trailers. The destinations extended to the Asiatic and American Continents, Oceania, European and African Continents or to more than 70 nations.

The major customers were Thailand (4,777 units), U.S.A. (4,717), Formosa (4,263), Okinawa (3,858), Burma (3,149), Venezuela (2,643) Brazil

(1,439), Cuba (1,062), Kuwait (812), Iran (802), Spain (710), and Indonesia (708).

Japan's motor export is now at its very beginning and the future looks very promising. Japanese vehicles have been well received in the overseas markets, and sales networks have been expanding gradually.

A study is now under way, at the request of some overseas customers, on the new concept in which Japanese manufacturers ship motor parts to the customer's country and assembly work is done at the customer's plant under a special agreement. For a stable growth of Japan's motor industry, it is highly desirable to increase its passenger car exports in the future.

Body Industry

Aside from three-wheeled vehicles, motorcycles and motor scooters, Japanese motor vehicles currently manufactured can be roughly classified into passenger cars, buses, trucks and special purpose vehicles. Bodies for these motor vehicles except for passenger cars, are manufactured by body manufacturers.

In Japan, there are about 100 plants engaged in body manufacturing. These firms, which the Japan Auto Body Industry Association comprises, manufacture every variety of superior vehicle bodies to meet customers' requirements. Their products consist of a wide variety: bodies for large and small-size buses, trucks, pick-ups, light vans and special purpose vehicles, such as dump trucks, fire engines, medical service vehicles, publicity vehicles and so on.

Bus Bodies

There are eight leading manufacturers whose total capacity is approximately 12,000 units annually. In addition, ten firms operate bus-body production on local scale with a total bus-body production during the past year was approximately 8,000 units.

Japanese bus-body industry not only supply domestic requirements but also ship their products to oversea countries. The workmanship of bus bodies produced in Japan has been appreciated both at home and abroad. Worthy of special mention is the recent development of all-light metal bodies for buses of special construction which are gaining a general popularity.

Truck Bodies

Usually, standard-size truck bodies are manufactured and mounted on chassis at local body plants. Trucks completed are then delivered through dealers to customers. As to rear bodies, there are a number of standard types and various sizes for the users to choose from.

Total production of standard-size trucks with wheel-bases of four meters and over during the past year was approximately 8,000 units. In addition, special purpose vehicles on truck chassis amounted to 1,500 a month. This category includes dump trucks, tank lorries, concrete mixers, refrigerators, publicity cars and the like.

Small-vehicle Bodies

As in the foreign motor industries, bodies for passenger cars are mass-produced at the car manufacutring plants. However, bodies for small trucks including pick-ups and light vans are mostly manufactured at different body specialist plants.

Due to the conditions prevailing in Japan, production of small vehicles has been showing a continual increase. A brisk demand for small buses has sprung up and the body manufacturers are busily engaged in producing these bus bodies as well.

Auto Parts Industry

In the automobile industry of Japan, auto parts and accessories are manufactured partly by the vehicle makers themselves and partly by other factories specializing in leaf springs, coil springs, bearings, babbit metal, electrical equipments, lamps, horns, tires, brakes, linings, spark plugs, pistons, piston rings, piston pins, cylinder valves, carburetors, pumps, screws, etc. These parts include a large variety of types for new and old, foreign and domestic models. Thus, the auto parts industry holds an essential position in the automobile industry.

The Japanese government has established the quality parts guarantee system under which the products of every maker are subject to inspection every few years. All those parts which passed the inspection can be used with safety.

As mentioned above, some automobile makers themselves produce parts for their own automobiles, and some subcontract them to other factories of special lines. In either case, these parts are sold by retail dealers as genuine parts for spare parts. In prewar times, even the parts of foreign cars had been produced and exported, and it is now expected the production of parts for foreign models will again become very active in near future.

Like that of the auto body industry, the auto parts industry shares an important role in the automobile industry, and consequently, the parts makers are earnestly striving to make quality products to give satisfaction to their customers.

For example, the leaf springs or coil springs of automobiles are extremely important parts which affects the center of gravity, oscillation and life of the vehicle. These are being produced by several well-known factories specializing in springs. After careful examinations, the materials are heated in a mass production conveyor furnace. Of course, the temperature is accurately measured by means of a pyrometer, and after careful heat-treatment consisting of quenching and tempering, they are assembled.

After coiling and heat-treating, valve springs are put under a special process called shot peening. With this process, the life span is lengthened and cracks are prevented.

Pistons are mostly made of light alloy with high temperature resistance and low expansion coefficient, such as Y alloy, and are cast in metallic mould of special design. In order to lengthen their life span, a special thin tin plating is applied.

Also in regard to piston rings, many special factories are operating and manufacturing with scientific methods. Each product is cast in an individual casting and is finished after grind lapping. In the course of inspecting the products, pressure distribution of all areas is measured by means of piezo-electricity. This is done to turn out quality products, and usually such efforts cannot commonly be seen in foreign countries.

Special porcelain and electrode are used in making spark plugs. The most effective designs of which are being mass-produced.

As in Europe and in the United States, large factories in Japan are turning out tires. Regarding batteries, if we consider the fact that the Japanese designs are noted for their special processed lead oxide, we can determine the degree to which they have been developed.

In regard to the bearing industry, there are several factories producing this item on a large scale. It is a fact worth noting that ball, roller and needle bearings which are comparable to those made in Europe, are being mass-produced.

Annual Production of Machinery Industry 1955-1956 (Unit: 1 billion yen)

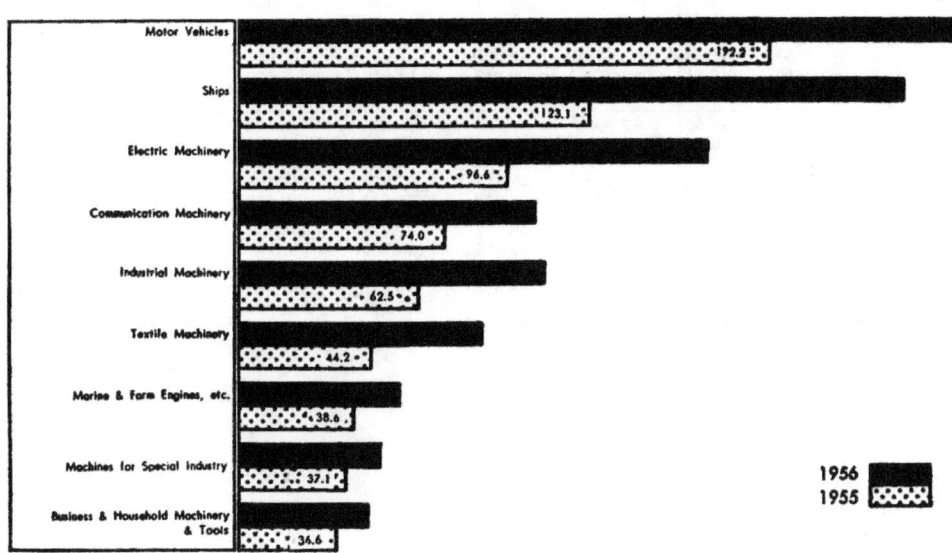

Annual Export of Machinery Products 1958 (Unit: 1 million dollars)

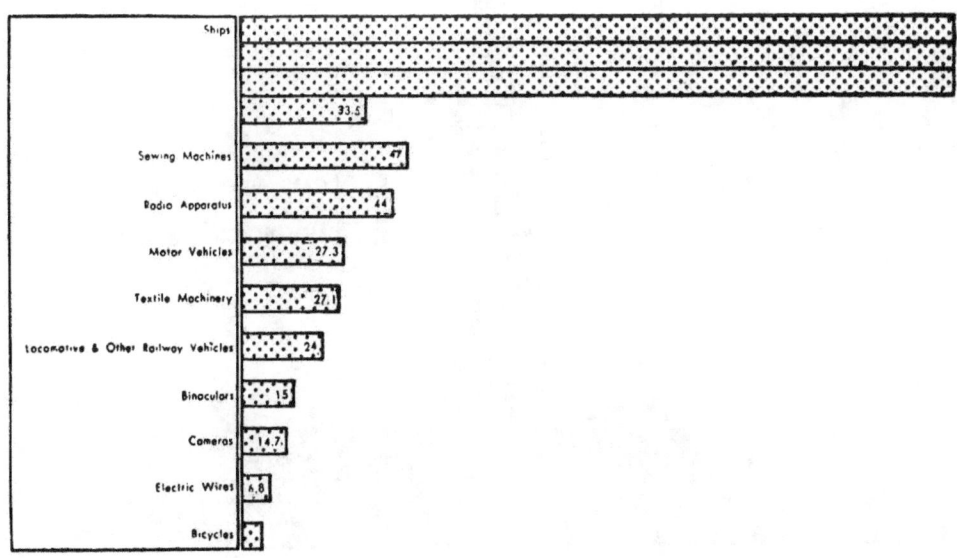

STATISTICS

PRODUCTION

MOTOR VEHICLE PRODUCTION

Table 1 1930 —— 1959

YEAR	CARS	TRUCKS	BUSES	TOTAL	3-WHEELERS	MOTOR-CYCLES	MOTOR SCOOTERS	TOTAL 2-& 3-WHEELERS	GRAND TOTAL
Japanese Fiscal Year (Apr. to Mar.)									
1930	—	458		458	300	1,350	—	1,650	2,108
1931	—	436		436	552	1,200	—	1,752	2,188
1932	—	880		880	1,511	1,365	—	1,876	3,756
1933	—	1,681		1,681	2,372	1,400	—	3,772	5,453
1934	—	2,787		2,787	3,438	1,500	—	4,938	7,725
1935	—	5,089	Included with Trucks	5,089	10,358	1,672	—	12,030	17,119
1936	847	11,339		12,186	12,840	1,446	—	14,286	26,472
1937	1,819	16,236		18,055	15,236	2,492	—	17,728	35,783
1938	1,774	22,614		24,388	10,685	2,483	—	13,168	37,556
1939	856	33,658		34,514	8,194	2,429	—	10,623	45,137
1940	1,633	44,408		46,041	8,252	3,037	—	11,289	57,330
1941	1,065	45,433		46,498	4,666	2,596	—	7,262	53,760
1942	705	36,483		37,188	3,821	2,189	—	6,010	43,198
1943	207	25,672		25,879	2,259	1,965	—	4,224	30,103
1944	19	21,743		21,762	1,338	1,029	—	2,367	24,129
1945 (Apr. to Aug.)	—	6,726		6,726	380	127	—	507	7,233
Year ended Dec.									
1945 (Sept. to Dec.)	—	1,461	—	1,461	—	—	—	—	1,461
1946	—	14,914	7	14,921	2,692	211	8	2,911	17,832
1947	110	11,106	104	11,320	7,432	387	1,623	9,442	20,762
1948	381	19,211	775	20,367	16,852	1,000	6,757	24,609	44,976
1949	1,070	25,560	2,070	28,700	26,727	1,766	7,423	35,916	64,616
1950	1,594	26,501	3,502	31,597	35,498	2,633	4,958	43,089	74,686
1951	3,611	30,817	4,062	38,490	43,802	11,510	12,799	68,111	106,601
1952	4,837	29,960	4,169	38,966	62,224	48,800	30,445	141,469	180,435
1953	8,789	36,147	4,842	49,778	97,484	111,716	54,713	263,913	313,691
1954	14,472	49,852	5,749	70,073	98,081	119,632	44,841	262,554	332,627
1955	20,268	43,857	4,807	68,932	87,904	204,304	55,000	347,208	416,140
1956	32,056	72,958	6,052	111,066	105,409	258,298	74,462	438,169	549,235
1957	47,121	126,820	8,036	181,977	114,937	308,926	101,143	525,006	706,983
1958	50,643	130,066	7,594	188,303	98,877	389,869	113,218	601,964	790,267
1959 (Jan. to Oct.)	63,179	142,499	5,531	211,209	122,505	592,752	102,970	818,227	1,029,436

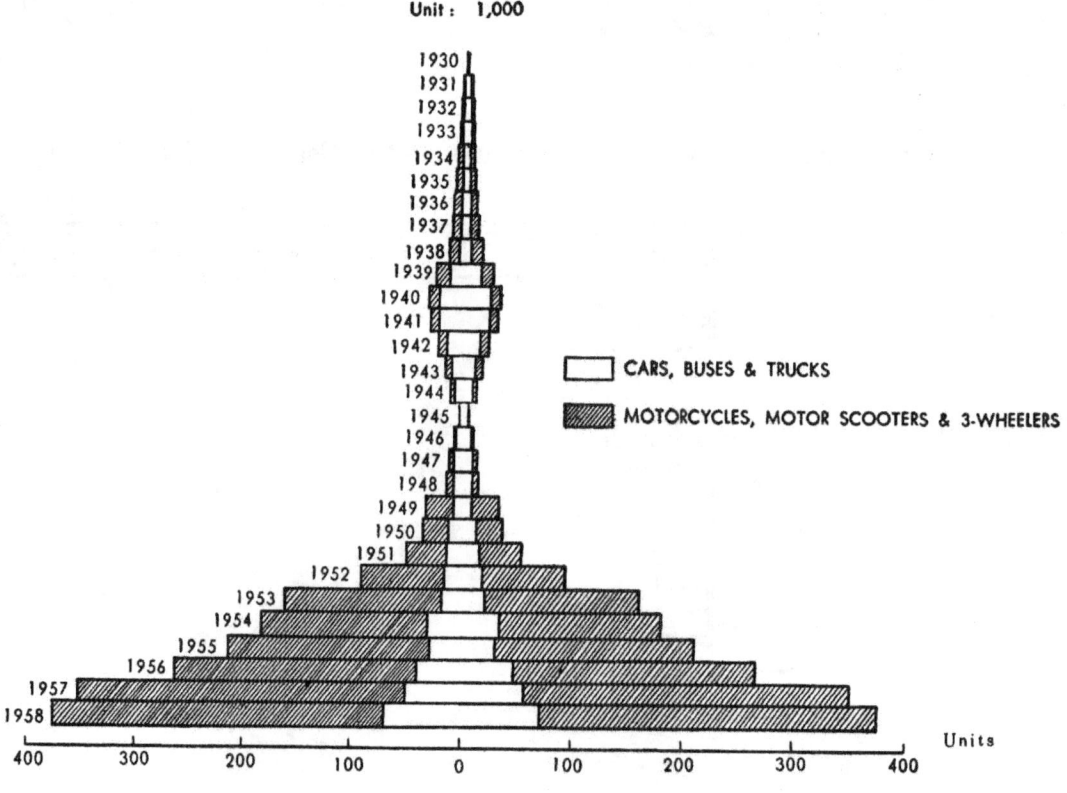

PRODUCTION FIGURE

Unit: 1,000

CARS, BUSES & TRUCKS

MOTORCYCLES, MOTOR SCOOTERS & 3-WHEELERS

STATISTICS
PRODUCTION

CAR, BUS PRODUCTION FIGURE

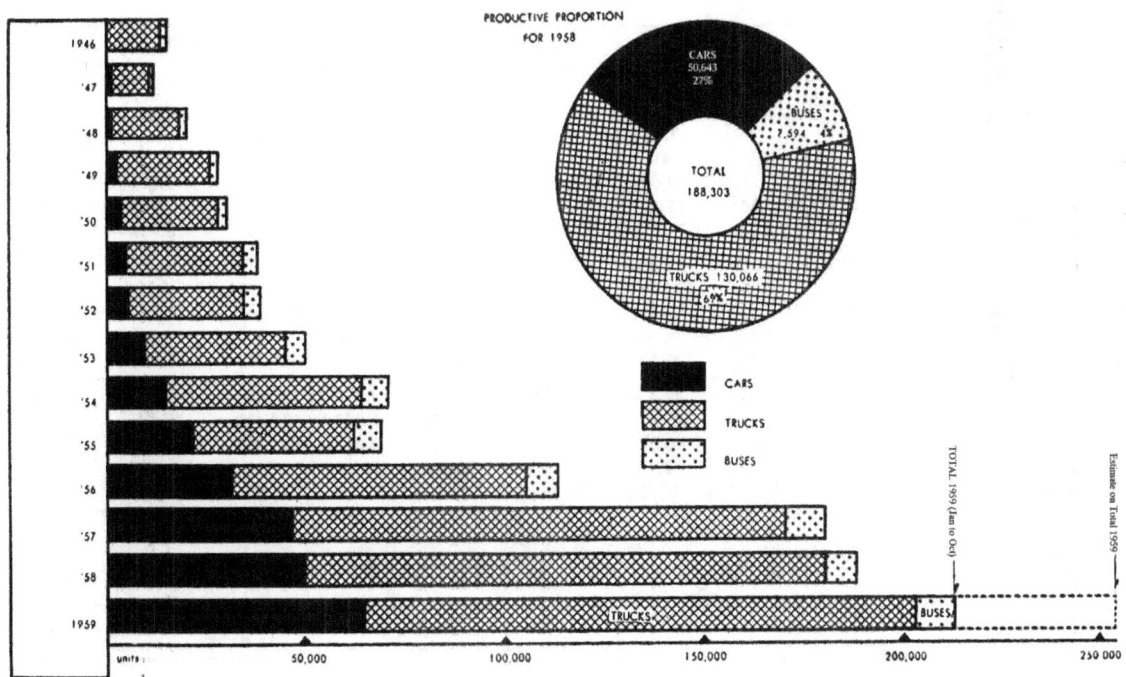

3-WHEELER MOTORCYCLE, MOTOR SCOOTER PRODUCTION FIGURE

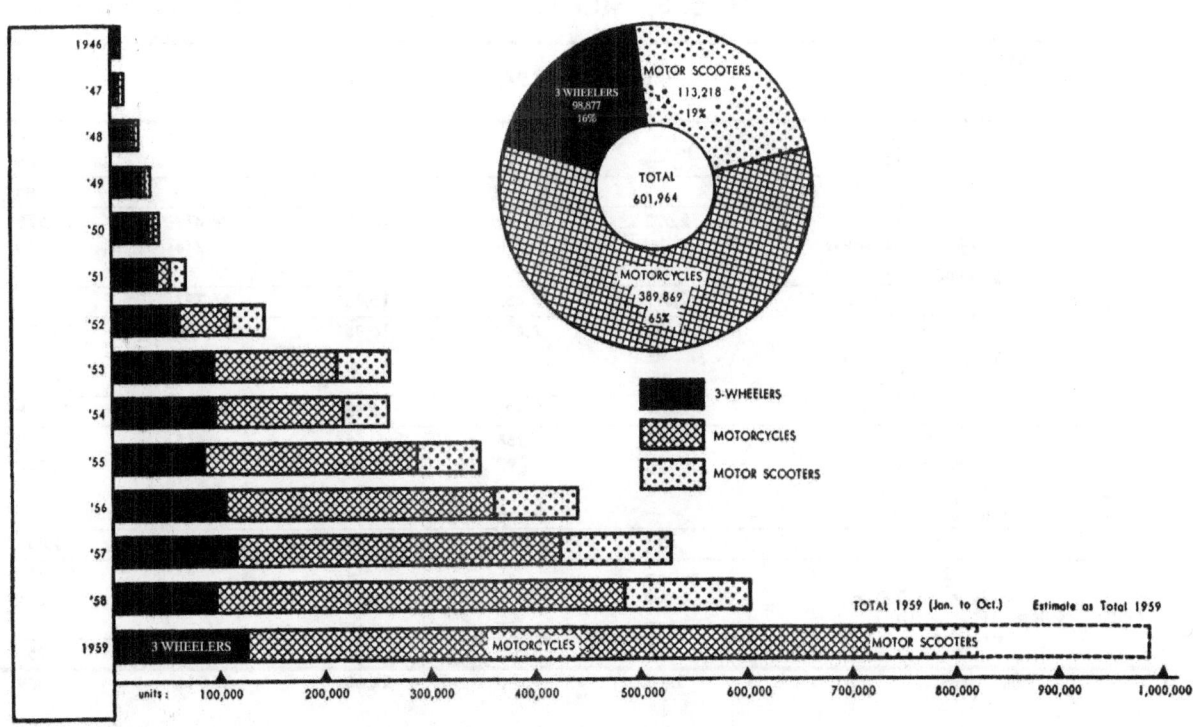

STATISTICS

PRODUCTION

CARS, TRUCKS, BUSES, by Cylinder Capacity Groups 1945 — 1959

Table 2

Year ended Dec.	CARS			TRUCKS			BUSES	GRAND TOTAL		
	Exc. 1,500 cc.	Not Exc. 1,500 cc.	Total	Exc. 1,500 cc.	Not Exc. 1,500 cc.	Total	Exc. 1,500 cc.	Exc. 1,500 cc.	Not Exc. 1,500 cc.	Total
1945 (Sept. to Dec.)	—	—	—	1,461	—	1,461	—	1,461	—	1,461
1946	—	—	—	14,178	736	14,914	7	14,185	736	14,921
1947	50	60	110	9,522	1,584	11,106	104	9,676	1,644	11,320
1948	3	378	381	15,649	3,562	19,211	775	16,427	3,940	20,367
1949	—	1,070	1,070	17,712	7,843	25,560	2,070	19,782	8,918	28,700
1950	—	1,594	1,594	17,576	8,925	26,501	3,502	21,078	10,519	31,597
1951	—	3,611	3,611	22,633	8,184	30,817	4,062	26,695	11,795	38,490
1952	—	4,837	4,837	19,595	10,365	29,960	4,169	23,764	15,202	38,966
1953	—	8,789	8,789	24,490	11,657	36,147	4,842	29,332	20,446	49,778
1954	—	14,472	14,472	31,767	18,085	49,852	5,749	37,516	32,557	70,073
1955	—	20,268	20,268	22,352	21,505	43,857	4,807	27,159	41,773	68,932
1956	—	32,056	32,056	29,433	43,525	72,958	6,052	35,485	75,581	111,066
1957	—	47,121	47,121	46,352	80,468	126,820	8,036	54,388	127,589	181,977
1958	—	50,643	50,643	39,416	90,650	130,066	7,594	47,010	141,293	188,303
1959 (Jan. to Oct.)	755	62,424	63,179	37,510	104,989	142,499	5,531	43,796	167,413	211,209

Table 3

Detail Figures, Jan. to Oct., 1959

Classification	CARS	TRUCKS	BUSES	TOTAL
Up to 360 cc.	4,341	781	—	5,122
361 to 1,000 cc.	24,167	104,208	—	162,291
1,001 to 1,500 cc.	33,916			
Over 1,500 cc.	755	37,510	5,531	43,796
Total	63,179	142,499	5,531	211,209

Table 6

3-WHEELERS, MOTORCYCLES, MOTOR SCOOTERS—by

Vehicles Classified by Cylinder Capacity Groups			1946	1947	1948	1949	1950
3-wheelers	Up to 360 cc.	Trucks	—	—	—	—	—
		Cars	—	—	—	—	85
		Total	—	—	—	—	85
	361 cc. to 1,500 cc.	Trucks	2,692	7,432	16,852	26,479	34,278
		Fire Trucks	—	—	—	248	150
		Cars	—	—	—	—	985
		Total	2,692	7,432	16,852	26,727	35,413
	Grand Total	Trucks	2,692	7,432	16,852	26,479	34,278
		Fire Trucks	—	—	—	248	150
		Cars	—	—	—	—	1,070
		Total	2,692	7,432	16,852	26,727	35,498
Motorcycles	Over 250 cc.		193	288	564	815	623
	126 cc. to 250 cc.		18	99	436	951	2,010
	51 cc. to 125 cc.		—	—	—	—	—
	Up to 50 cc.		—	—	—	—	—
	Total		211	387	1,000	1,766	2,633
Motor Scooters	Over 250 cc.		—	—	—	—	457
	126 cc. to 250 cc.		8	1,623	6,757	7,423	4,501
	51 cc. to 125 cc.		—	—	—	—	—
	Total		8	1,623	6,757	7,423	4,958
Grand Total			2,911	9,442	24,609	35,916	43,089

MOTOR VEHICLE PRODUCTION—by Fuel 1945—1959

Table 4

STATISTICS — PRODUCTION

Year ended Dec.	CARS	TRUCKS			BUSES			TOTAL		
	Gasoline	Gasoline	Diesel	Total	Gasoline	Diesel	Total	Gasoline	Diesel	Total
1945 (Sept. to Dec.)	—	1,452	9	1,461	—	—	—	1,452	9	1,461
1946	—	14,791	123	14,914	7	—	7	14,798	123	14,921
1947	110	10,614	492	11,106	103	1	104	10,827	493	11,320
1948	381	18,429	782	19,211	261	514	775	19,071	1,296	20,367
1949	1,070	24,110	1,450	25,560	720	1,350	2,070	25,900	2,800	28,700
1950	1,594	23,980	2,521	26,501	622	2,880	3,502	26,196	5,401	31,597
1951	3,611	26,687	4,130	30,817	848	3,214	4,062	31,146	7,344	38,490
1952	4,837	26,029	3,931	29,960	1,003	3,166	4,169	31,869	7,097	38,966
1953	8,789	31,101	5,046	36,147	859	3,983	4,842	40,749	9,029	49,778
1954	14,472	42,436	7,416	49,852	692	5,057	5,749	57,600	12,473	70,073
1955	20,268	35,263	8,594	43,857	506	4,301	4,807	56,037	12,895	68,932
1956	32,056	61,338	11,620	72,958	480	5,572	6,052	93,874	17,192	111,066
1957	47,121	108,762	18,058	126,820	463	7,573	8,036	156,346	25,631	181,977
1958	50,643	111,196	18,870	130,066	234	7,360	7,594	162,073	26,230	188,303
1959 (Jan. to Oct.)	63,179	120,471	22,028	142,499	157	5,374	5,531	183,807	27,402	211,209

Table 5 TRUCKS—by Fuel & Loading Capacity Groups, 1959 (Jan. to Oct.)

Classification	GASOLINE	DIESEL	TOTAL
Up to 500 kg.	1,020	—	1,020
501 kg. to 1,000 kg.	68,172	—	68,172
1,001 kg. to 2,000 kg.	35,797	—	35,797
2,001 kg. to 5,000 kg.	7,447	4,957	12,404
5,001 kg. to 7,000 kg	760	9,191	13,614
Over 7,000 kg.		3,663	
Other All Wheel-drive Trucks	7,275	4,217	11,492
Total	120,471	22,028	142,499

Cylinder Capacity Groups, 1946—1959

1951	1952	1953	1954	1955	1956	1957	1958	1959 (Jan. to Oct.)
—	—	1,400	1,205	656	1,483	3,501	14,001	60,209
20	—	—	—	—	—	84	1	—
20	—	1,400	1,205	656	1,483	3,585	14,002	60,209
42,498	61,710	95,954	96,782	87,206	103,907	111,257	84,875	62,296
227	101	71	86	42	19	95	—	—
1,057	413	59	8	—	—	—	—	—
43,782	62,224	96,084	96,876	87,248	103,926	111,352	84,875	62,296
42,498	61,710	97,354	97,987	87,862	105,390	114,758	98,876	122,505
227	101	71	86	42	19	95	—	—
1,077	413	59	8	—	—	84	1	—
43,802	62,224	97,484	98,081	87,904	105,409	114,937	98,877	122,505
1,868	4,378	11,858	14,769	6,416	5,570	5,791	5,059	4,185
9,642	44,422	99,858	104,863	91,151	99,565	113,229	122,355	121,511
—	—	—	—	106,737	153,163	189,906	211,694	230,859
—	—	—	—	—	—	—	50,761	236,197
11,510	48,800	111,716	119,632	204,304	258,298	308,926	389,869	592,752
3,545	8,718	3,620	—	—	—	—	—	—
9,254	21,727	51,093	44,841	42,702	48,176	55,966	53,523	48,117
—	—	—	—	12,298	26,286	45,177	59,695	54,853
12,799	30,445	54,713	44,841	55,000	74,462	101,143	113,218	102,970
68,111	141,469	263,913	262,554	347,208	438,169	525,006	601,964	818,227

STATISTICS

EXPORT

MOTOR VEHICLE EXPORT

Table 7 — Classified by Destinations —— 1959 (Jan. to Oct.)

DESTINATIONS	CARS	TRUCKS	BUSES	UTILITY VEHICLES	TOTAL	TOTAL 1947-1959 (Jan. to Oct.)
ASIA						
Aden	7	36	—	4	47	117
Afghanistan	—	1	—	—	1	6
Bahrein	—	4	—	—	4	7
Bonin I.	—	—	—	—	—	1
Burma	29	551	17	—	597	3,149
Cambodia	—	1	—	—	1	10
Ceylon	32	13	10	—	55	93
China	—	—	—	—	—	33
Goa	12	—	—	—	12	40
Hong Kong	14	19	—	—	33	80
India	1	5	—	—	6	19
Indonesia	7	153	1	421	582	708
Iran	191	260	2	—	453	802
Iraq	1	6	—	—	7	37
Jordan	2	8	—	—	10	42
Korea	—	—	—	—	—	464
Kuwait	79	333	—	62	474	812
Laos	2	5	—	—	7	229
Lebanon	3	6	8	—	17	71
Malaya	57	108	—	2	167	234
North Borneo	—	16	—	—	16	81
Okinawa	274	278	48	47	647	3,858
Pakistan	—	10	—	5	15	59
Philippines	20	62	2	20	104	524
Qatar	—	16	—	2	18	18
Sarawak	—	—	—	—	—	2
Saudi Arabia	3	39	—	—	42	176
Singapore	10	48	—	2	60	229
Syria	2	89	4	1	96	550
Taiwan	149	795	240	5	1,189	4,263
Thailand	23	767	1	19	810	4,777
Trucial Oman	—	12	—	—	12	62
Vietnam	5	2	—	—	7	37
Total	923	3,643	333	590	5,489	21,660
AFRICA						
Angola	—	34	—	—	34	88
Cape Verde	—	2	—	—	2	2
Egypt	11	30	—	1	42	297
Etiopia	2	—	—	—	2	71
Fernando Po I.	—	8	—	—	8	12
Ghana	1	20	—	—	21	21
Kenya	1	—	—	—	1	1
Mozambique	—	62	1	2	65	73
Nigeria	—	25	—	—	25	25
Sudan	—	—	—	—	—	11
Union S. A.	32	135	—	—	167	218
Total	47	316	1	3	367	819

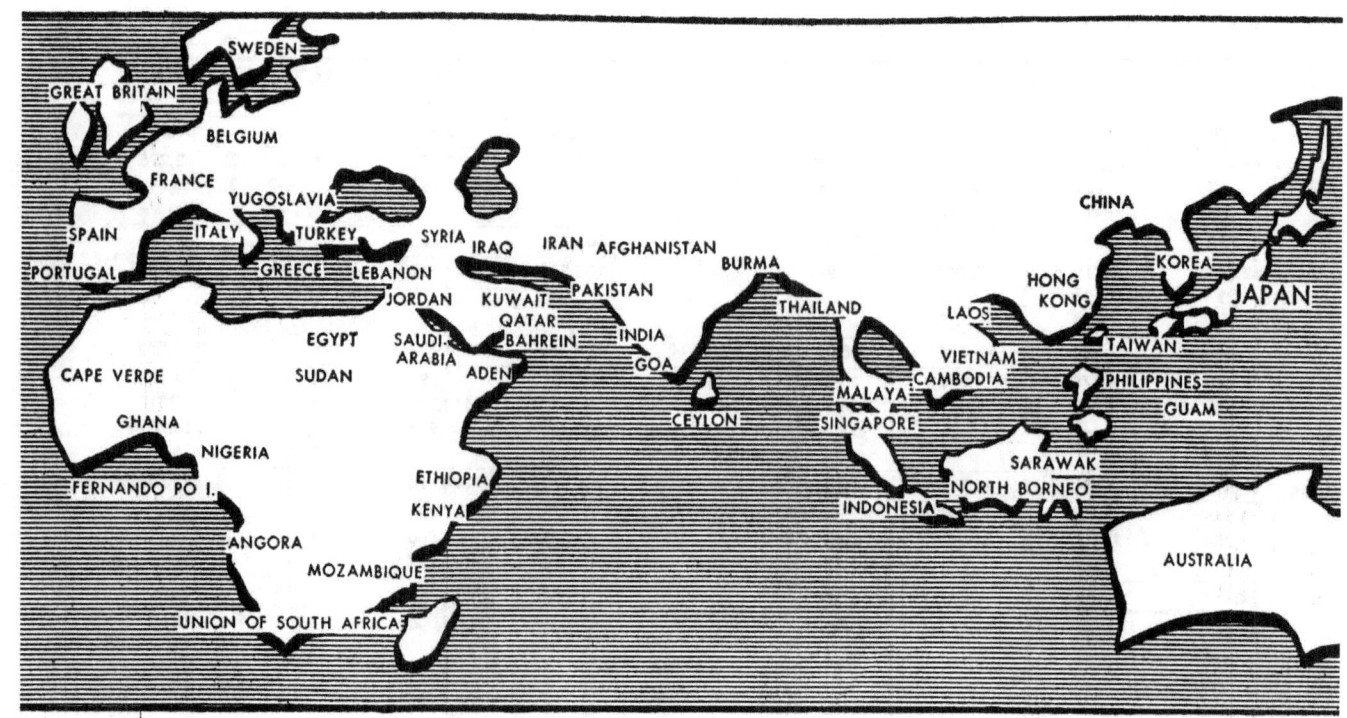

STATISTICS
EXPORT

DESTINATIONS	CARS	TRUCKS	BUSES	UTILITY VEHICLES	TOTAL	TOTAL 1947-1959 (Jan. to Oct.)
AMERICA						
North:						
Alaska	—	—	—	—	—	1
Canada	—	—	—	—	—	2
U. S. A.	2,602	567	—	—	3,169	4,717
Central:						
Costa Rica	—	99	—	1	100	386
Cuba	3	537	—	—	540	1,062
Dominican Rep.	2	20	—	—	22	93
Guatemala	50	122	—	2	174	313
Haiti	—	3	—	—	3	3
Honduras (Br.)	—	10	—	—	10	14
Honduras Rep.	—	26	—	—	26	110
Mexico	201	51	—	—	252	253
Nicaragua	—	21	—	—	21	137
Panama	9	17	—	3	29	33
Port Rico	1	22	—	—	23	175
Salvador	—	19	5	—	24	174
Trinidad I. (Br.)	12	86	—	—	98	104
South:						
Argentina	—	—	—	3	3	235
Bolivia	2	151	—	10	163	285
Brazil	—	—	—	—	—	1,439
Chile	30	—	4	2	36	645
Colombia	—	100	—	—	100	106
Equador	—	2	—	—	2	32
Paraguay	2	74	—	1	77	253
Peru	14	56	1	14	85	229
Surinam	—	—	—	—	—	2
Uruguay	—	—	—	—	—	168
Venezuela	113	550	—	—	663	2,643
Total	3,041	2,533	10	36	5,620	13,614
EUROPE						
Belgium	—	—	—	—	—	4
France	—	—	—	—	—	1
Great Britain	—	—	—	—	—	1
Greece	—	—	12	—	12	18
Italy	—	—	—	—	—	1
Portugal	—	—	—	—	—	4
Spain	1	120	1	1	123	710
Sweden	1	—	—	—	1	1
Turkey	—	1	2	—	3	46
Yugoslavia	—	—	—	—	—	5
Total	2	121	15	1	139	791
OCEANIA						
Australia	2	52	—	—	54	138
Guam	—	36	—	—	36	147
Hawaii	243	166	1	1	411	675
Majuro I.	—	—	—	—	—	1
Marshal Is	—	—	—	—	—	1
Nauru I.	—	—	—	—	—	1
New Hebrides Is.	—	—	—	—	—	1
Total	245	254	1	1	501	964
EXPORT TOTAL	4,258	6,867	360	631	12,116	37,848
Domestic Export & US Army Procurement	4	3,930	—	—	3,934	14,457
GRAND TOTAL	4,262	10,797	360	631	16,050	52,305

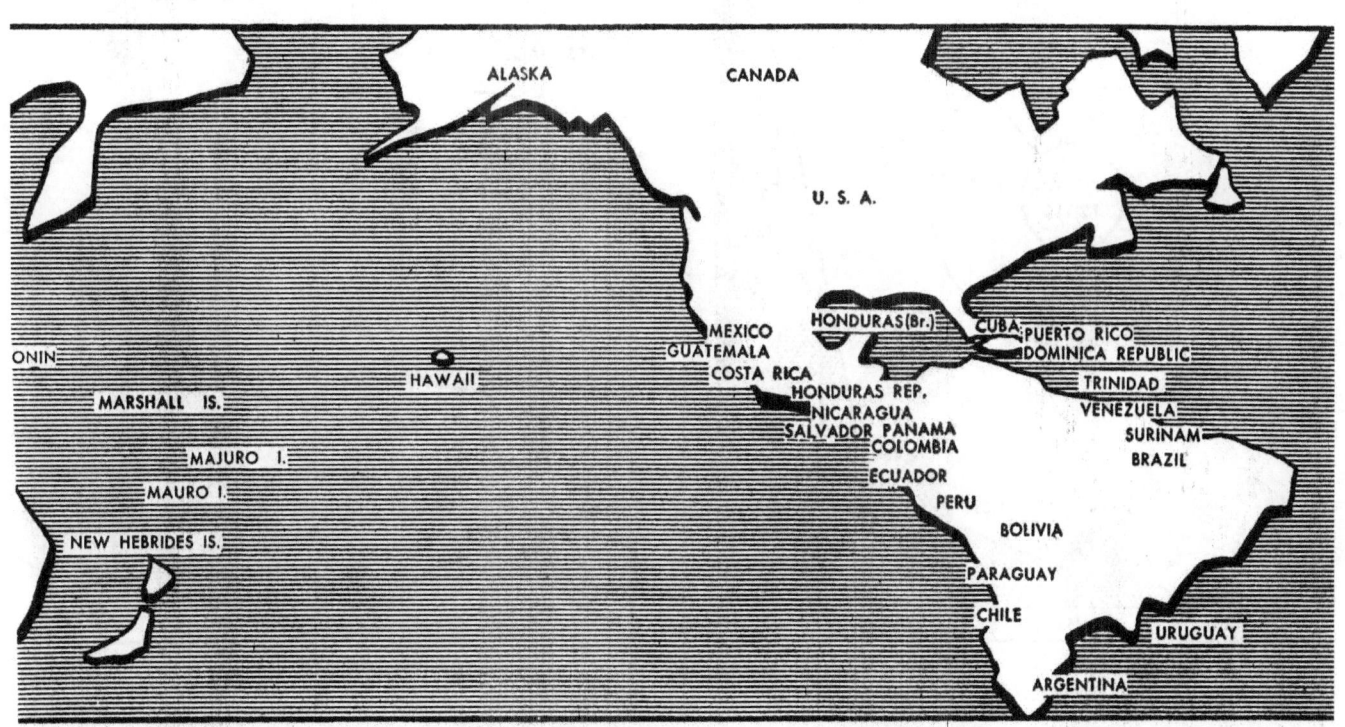

STATISTICS

EXPORT

Table 8

MOTOR VEHICLE EXPORT
1946 —— 1959

	Year ended Dec.	CARS	TRUCKS	BUSES	UTILITY VEHICLES	TRAILERS	TOTAL	3-WHEELERS	MOTOR-CYCLES	MOTOR SCOOTERS	TOTAL 2-& 3-WHEELERS
Overseas Export	1946	—	—	—	—	—	—	—	—	—	—
	1947	1	1	—	—	—	2	—	10	200	210
	1948	—	1	—	—	—	1	63	233	880	1,176
	1949	1	211	4	258	14	488	168	58	489	715
	1950	6	865	93	154	—	1,118	403	64	777	1,244
	1951	—	486	103	37	—	626	299	17	301	617
	1952	—	529	184	142	—	855	19	3	13	35
	1953	-	569	409	119	—	1,097	324	14	187	525
	1954	1	458	308	221	—	988	74	54	87	215
	1955	2	696	322	211	—	1,231	151	143	309	603
	1956	46	1,701	517	183	9	2,456	1,872	168	503	2,543
	1957	407	4,644	632	868	38	6,589	412	494	2,144	3,050
	1958	2,357	7,297	346	243	38	10,281	559	2,427	5,120	8,106
	1959 (Jan. to Oct.)	4,258	6,867	360	631	—	12,116	1,771	9,334	5,487	16,592
	Total	7,079	24,325	3,278	3,067	99	37,848	6,115	13,019	16,497	35,631
Domestic Export	1948	1	5	—	—	—	6				
	1949	9	9	2	—	—	20				
	1950	1	3,626	—	749	—	4,376				
	1951	—	4,792	50	1,265	—	6,107				
	1952	—	—	—	10	—	10				
	1953	—	1	—	—	—	1				
	1957	3	—	—	—	—	3				
	1959 (Jan. to Oct.)	4	3,930	—	—	—	3,934				
	Total	18	12,363	52	2,024	—	14,457				
GRAND TOTAL		7,097	36,688	3,330	5,091	99	52,305				

NOTES: 1. A greater part of the Domestic Exports is vehicles purchased by US Army in Japan.
2. 3-wheelers, Motorcycles, Motor Scooters —— Japan Fiscal Year (Apr. to Mar.) (1959—Apr. to Oct.)

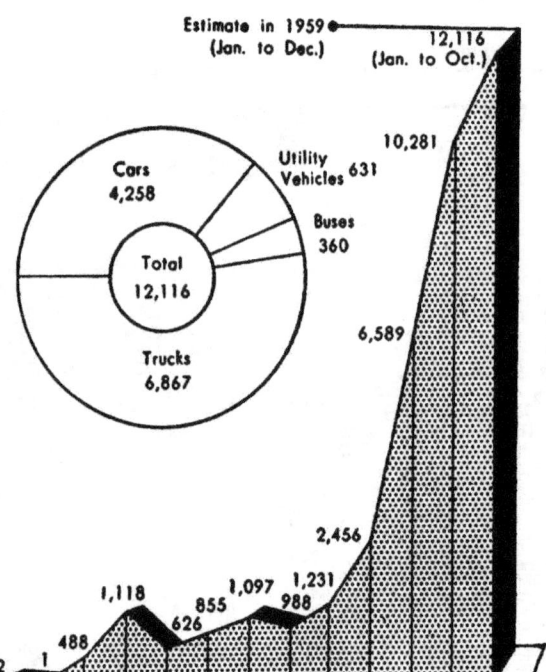

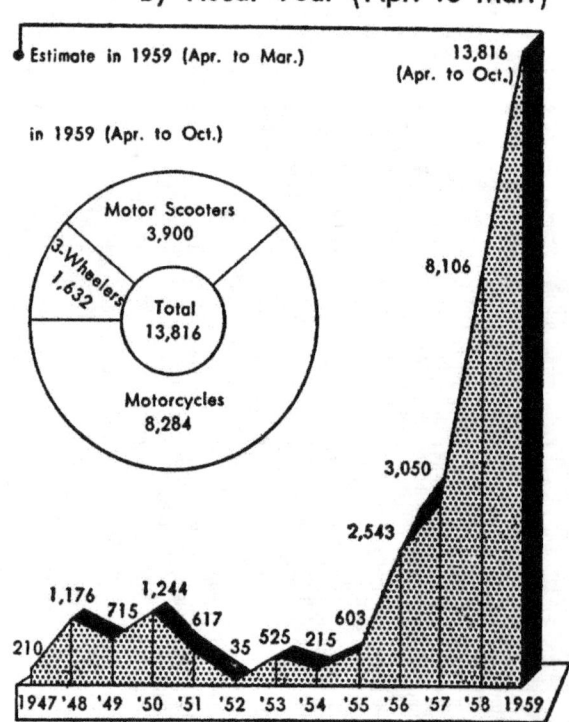

3-Wheelers, Motorcycles & Motor Scooters Exports
—by Fiscal Year (Apr. to Mar.)

MOTOR VEHICLE REGISTRATIONS 1908 — 1944

STATISTICS — REGISTRATIONS

Table 9

Year	CARS	TRUCKS	BUSES	TOTAL	3-WHEELERS	MOTOR-CYCLES	Side Cars	TOTAL 2- & 3-WHEELERS	Special Motor-cycles & others	GRAND TOTAL
1908				9						
1909				19						
1910				121						
1911				235						
1912		(1908 — 1915, Not available)		512						
1913				892						
1914				1,066						
1915				1,244						
1916	1,624	24		1,648						
1917	2,647	25		2,672		(1908 — 1925, Not available)				
1918	4,491	42		4,533						
1919	6,847	204	Included in Cars	7,051						
1920	9,335	644		9,999						
1921	11,228	888		12,116						
1922	13,483	1,383		14,866						
1923	10,666	2,099		12,765						
1924	17,939	6,394		24,333						
1925	21,002	8,162		29,164						
1926	28,256	12,097		40,353	521	7,627	2,323	10,471	141	50,965
1927	18,701	15,987	7,414	52,102	561	10,137	2,880	13,578	426	66,106
1928	33,358	21,719	11,700	66,777	718	10,901	3,097	14,716	225	81,718
1929	37,300	27,541	15,985	80,826	1,135	10,747	3,841	15,723	522	97,071
1930	40,819	30,881	17,522	89,222	2,513	9,625	4,657	16,795	587	106,604
1931	41,765	34,837	21,226	97,828	5,260	10,560	4,078	19,898	515	118,241
1932	42,087	35,939	22,825	100,851	9,074	10,431	4,617	24,122	163	125,136
1933	42,501	33,501	24,822	100,824	11,753	10,011	1,218	22,982	6,006	129,812
1934	45,376	42,667	26,328	114,371	24,388	12,358	972	37,718	4,493	156,582
1935	49,548	47,939	28,428	125,915	30,842	14,094	713	45,649	4,688	176,252
1936	52,359	55,610	28,745	136,714	39,891	13,398	822	54,111	4,388	195,213
1937	60,054	61,132	24,344	145,530	47,869	15,038	1,093	64,000	4,616	214,146
1938	59,317	67,840	24,024	151,181	50,402	15,155	1,084	66,641	4,424	222,246
1939	54,986	71,262	23,181	149,429	50,507	12,360	1,075	63,942	4,232	217,603
1940	52,110	77,561	22,394	152,065	50,420	9,568	1,064	61,052	4,102	217,219
1941	47,924	71,721	21,965	141,610	48,212	5,062	811	54,085	3,306	199,001
1942	60,054	75,365	21,744	134,636	45,883	4,370	702	50,955	2,704	188,295
1943	33,893	76,721	21,502	132,116	41,992	3,450	593	46,039	2,102	180,257
1944	30,401	75,595	16,769	122,765	37,185	1,603	484	39,272	1,498	163,535

Note: 1925—1929 Include Small-sized Trucks

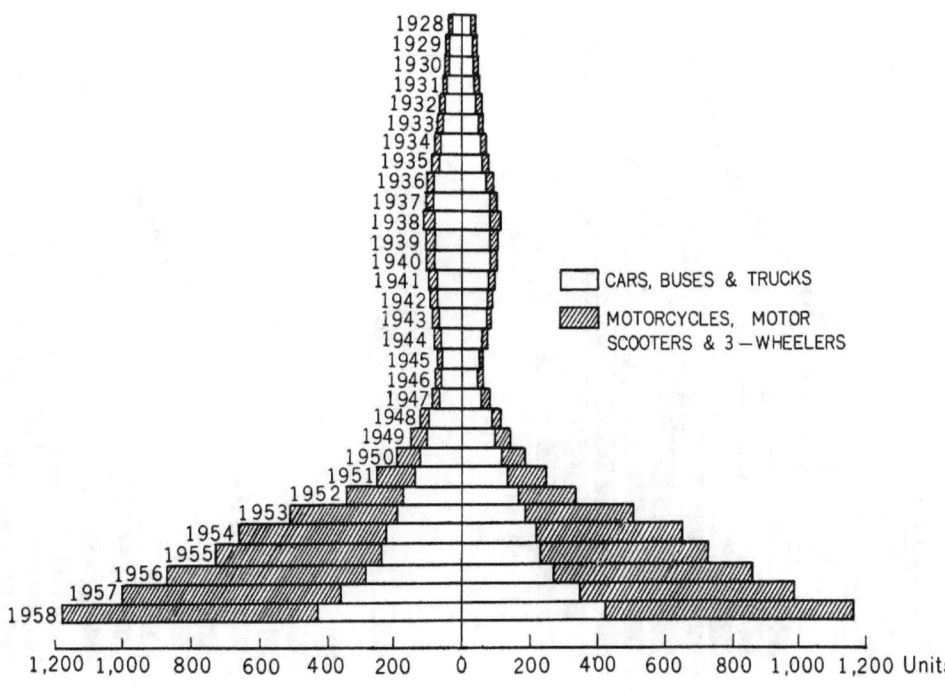

REGISTRATION FIGURE
1928 — 1958 (Unit : 1,000)

☐ CARS, BUSES & TRUCKS
▨ MOTORCYCLES, MOTOR SCOOTERS & 3—WHEELERS

STATISTICS

REGISTRATIONS

MOTOR VEHICLES REGISTRATIONS
1945 —— 1959

Table 10

Year	CARS	TRUCKS	BUSES	UTILITY VEHICLES	TOTAL	3-WHEELERS	MOTORCYCLES MOTOR SCOOTERS	GRAND TOTAL
1945	25,533	72,908	12,792	2,314	113,547	28,500	2,304	144,351
1946	26,863	84,579	12,060	6,678	130,180	33,598	2,869	166,647
1947	26,340	100,618	12,772	10,779	150,509		37,702*	188,211
1948	30,221	122,676	14,704	14,022	181,623		56,624*	238,247
1949	36,265	137,876	16,467	15,541	206,149		106,247*	312,396
1950	42,588	150,612	18,306	17,279	228,785	111,888	46,870	387,543
1951	57,533	169,143	21,220	19,165	267,061	152,734	83,008	502,803
1952	88,354	191,317	24,307	21,704	325,682	213,027	176,506	715,215
1953	114,696	213,455	27,982	26,779	382,912	293,674	349,308	1,025,894
1954	138,518	234,598	31,530	34,924	439,570	367,441	504,770	1,311,781
1955	153,325	250,005	34,187	36,215	473,732	429,491	560,526	1,463,749
1956	181,074	294,213	38,050	44,034	557,371	493,839	667,654	1,718,864
1957	218,524	372,442	42,724	52,825	686,515	553,958	776,865	2,017,338
1958	259,631	454,617	46,957	61,030	822,235	612,342	897,306	2,331,883
1959(August)	290,556	523,569	50,130	66,467	930,722	679,804	978,356	2,588,882

SOURCE: Ministry of Transportation.
NOTES: 1. As of annual year end.
2. *Inclusive of 3-Wheelers, Motorcycles and Motor Scooters.
3. Motorcycles and Motor Scooters are exclusive those of 125c.c. and under.

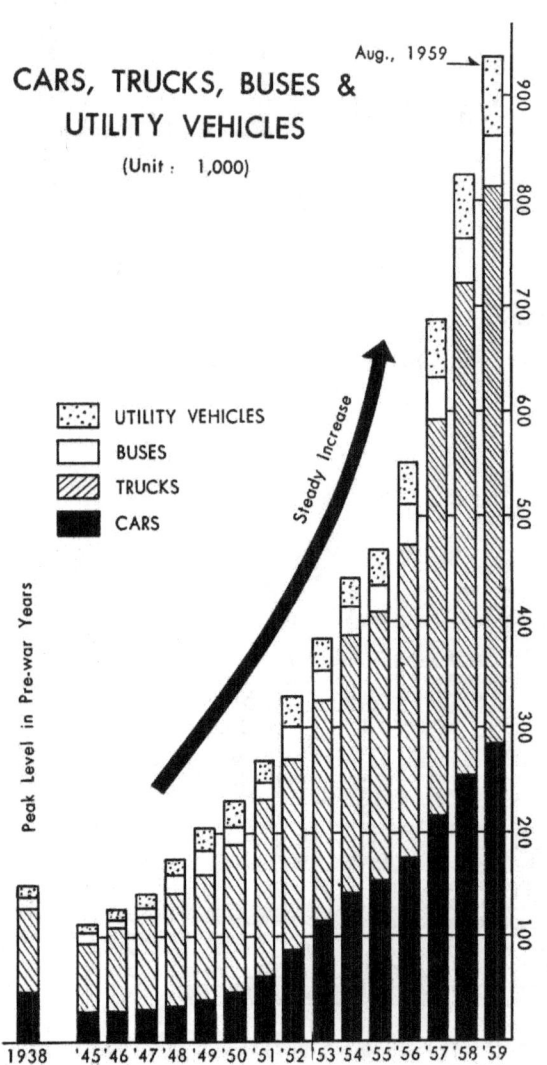

CARS, TRUCKS, BUSES & UTILITY VEHICLES (Unit: 1,000)

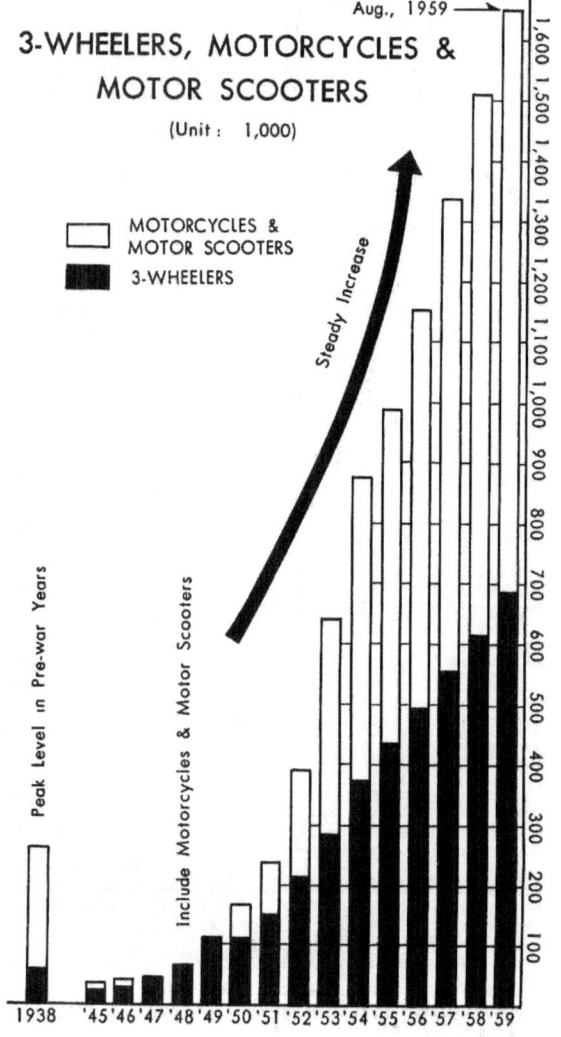

3-WHEELERS, MOTORCYCLES & MOTOR SCOOTERS (Unit: 1,000)

Old Timers of Japan
1907〜1947

Printed here are noteworthy cars manufactured during the forty years from the first appearance of a motor car in Japan. Vehicles built in the early years were mostly modelled on foreign makes, but in 1921 a car original in its design was completed by an enthusiast. It was "Ohtomo." The Ohtomo, equipped with an air-cooled engine, had a technical significance since there was in those days no air-cooled car in all the world. The Ohtomo, exported to Shanghai, had another historical significance as the first Japanese-made car ever to run on foreign roads.

From the year 1933, production capacity was concentrated on military vehicles including large-size passenger cars with the result that production of passenger cars for civilian uses was almost prohibited. Only after the end of World War II (to be exact, in 1949), free production of passenger cars was resumed. Since then the Japanese passenger car industry has made a remarkable development.

1907
Takuri
Tokyo Automobile Works

1914
Dat
The Kwaishinsha Motor Car Works

1917
Experimental Car
Ishikawajima Dockyard Works

1918
Mitsubishi A
Mitsubishi Kobe Dockyard Works

1921
Ohta OS
Ohta Motor Co

1922
Lila
Jitsuyo Jidosha K.K.

1922
Wolseley A9
Ishikawajima Dockyard Works

1924
Ales M
Hakuyosha Co.

1924
Ales S
Hakuyosha Co.

1925
Ohtomo
Hakuyosha Co.

1931
Datsun Road Star
Dat Automobile Manufacturing Co.
(Present Nissan Motor Co., Ltd.)

1932
Datsun 500 cc Coupé
Dat Automobile Manufacturing Co.
(Present Nissan Motor Co., Ltd.)

1932
Mitsubishi Fuso BX33
Mitsubishi Kobe Dockyard Works

1933
Sumida K93
Jidosha Kogyo Co.

1933
Sumida H
Jidosha Kogyo Co.

1935
Ford 8V
Ford Motar Co. of Japan, Ltd.

1935
Chiyoda HF
Jidosha Kogyo Co.

1935
Chevrolet Master de Luxe
General Motors of Japan, Ltd.

1935
Chiyoda H
Jidosha Kogyo Co.

1936
Toyota AB
Toyota Motor Co.

1936
Toyota AA
Toyota Motor Co.

1937
Nissan 70
Nissan Motor Co.

1937
Ohta Cabriolet
Ohta Motor Co.

1940
Toyota BB
Toyota Motor Co.

1943
Toyota AC
Toyota Motor Co.

1944
Toyota B
Toyota Motor Co.

1944
Toyota BC
Toyota Motor Co.

1947
Datsun Standard Sedan
Nissan Motor Co.

Some Aspects of Japan's Basic Industries and Motor-Factory Installations

Electric Power Industry

The rapid development of the electric industry in Japan is amazing. It is now surging along with the achievements in construction machinery. Presently 32 ton bulldozers, 15 ton dump trucks and 2.3 cubic meter powershovels are being manufactured domestically and at much lower prices than imported machines.

These machines are employed in various fields of the construction industries in Japan. To speak of construction works, the construction of dams deserves foremost attention. It is representative of the technical standards of a country in this field, and Japan can proudly show its highly-mechanized dam construction works to foreign visitors.

Almost all dams that Japan can be proud of have been or are constructed by the Electric Power Development Company, Ltd. which was formed in 1952. The company has built the Sakuma Dam and 12 others totalizing 675,300kw in generating capacity. When 14 dams under construction, totalizing 1,396,800kw in generating capacity, are completed, the total capacity of hydroelectric power plants and dams owned and operated by the company will amount for 16 per cent of the nation's total hydroelectric generating capacity.

Japan's electric power industry comprises in nine electric companies and 12 smaller-scale power enterprises which are engaged directly in general power supplies to consumers, the Electric Power Development Company, Ltd. and 27 public and 6 private power enterprises serving as exclusive wholesale suppliers. Power generating equipments of these concerns as of the end of March, 1959, aggregated to about 15,800,000kw, of which 9,900,000kw and 5,900,000 kw are hydro and thermal generation, respectively.

On the other hand, Japan plans for atomic power generation which will be able to generate about 8,000,000 kw of atomic power by fiscal 1975. Under the program, the Atomic Power Generation Company was inaugurated in November, 1957, and a Calder Hall improved-type atomic power plant (capacity 160,000 kw) is scheduled to start generation in fiscal 1963.

Iron and Steel Industry

It was in 1887, when the first blast furnace in Japan was successfully blown in at Kamaishi. Three years later, the first open hearth was installed at the Yokosuka Naval Arsenal and the first integral iron and steel plant went into operation at Yawata under government management. This Yawata plant supplied domestic industries with steel which accounted for more than half of the national production.

At present, Japan has more than sixty major concerns; 8 companies possess blast furnaces, 14 companies own open hearth furnaces, and 44 companies manufacture steel in electric furnaces. Besides, there are 424 smaller-scale enterprises engaged in the rolling, casting, forging and other processing of steel.

World War II had thoroughly paralyzed the iron and steel industry of Japan, but along with the recovery of general economy, the industry was brought to a rehabilitation. The outbreak of the Korean war in 1950, gave an impetus to the development of the industry. Since then the production of steel and iron increased rapidly, and in 1958, figures showed the production of pig iron 7,394,000 tons, crude steel 12,113,000 tons and rolled steel 9,479,000 tons.

The rapid increase of the production of iron and steel in Japan is attributed to the increase

Kurobe Dam (upper): One of the largest dams now being constructed in Japan. Every available mechanical power, including helicopters, has been used for the construction of this gigantic arch dam in the midst of the Japan Alps.

Sakuma Dam (lower): The largest dam ever built in Japan. The construction was completed in 1956. It is a strait concrete dam, 150 meters in height and 294 meters in crest length.

in the following demands:

1. The mechanization of facilities in various industries has made rapid progress.
2. The automobile industry enjoys prosperity and ferro-concrete buildings have increased conspicuously year after year.
3. Since motorcycles and various kinds of electrical appliances have become very popular among the public, the people's daily life is requiring much iron and steel.
4. The increase in export to the U.S.A., India, Thailand, the Philippines, China and other countries of the world.

In 1958, the export of iron and steel totaled 1,830,000 tons in volume and $277 million in value. Among main items of exports were rails, steel plates, steel bars, wire rods and steel pipes. Steel bars were mainly exported to the United States and rails to India, Burma, Thailand, the Philippines and Latin American countries. Further, Japan almost monopolizes the export of rails to India.

Rubber Industry

Japan is the fifth biggest consumer of rubber in the world in the absence of complete statistics from the Soviet Union; only the United States, the United Kingdom, West Germany and France consume more.

In 1958, consumption of new rubber in Japan totaled 146,700 tons and $53,350,000 worth of products were exported. These figures include such items as auto tires, belts, hoses, footwear, bicycle tires, rubberized cloth, toys and sporting goods.

As to the field of auto-tire manufacturing, Japan first began the production over half a century ago. Presently there are six concerns in Japan manufacturing automobile tires and tubes. Most of them have had some connections

1500 ton blast furnace in Tobata Works of Yawata Iron & Steel Co., Ltd.

with overseas manufacturers, and have continued to get technical assistance from abroad along with their independent research. This means that Japan has been constantly modernizing her facilities, enabling her to put out a consistently superior product. Japan's auto-tire factories use more than 50,000 tons of rubber a year, and exports more than $20,000,000 worth.

Nowadays tires have to bear more strenuous use than ever before. Cars travel at higher speeds, mammoth machines used for heavy construction works now use rubber tires, and cross-country buses travel tremendous distances nonstop. To meet these demands, tire manufacturers first developed the tubeless tire. And this in turn created a need for a new tire-cord, something finer, stronger and more resistant to wear. After many tests, nylon was chosen. In Japan,

12 in. four-high reversing plate mill in Tsurumi Works of Nippon Kokan Kabushiki Kaisha

Hot strip mill in Muroran Works of Fuji Iron & Steel Co., Ltd.

nylon cords had first been used in airplane tires. Now, the rayon manufacturers in Japan are trying to strengthen their product to the point that it can be used.

Japanese tires are subject to a whole series of rigid tests. Japanese tires now holds good mileage even with constant use on poor roads and with heavy loads. They come in a multitude of sizes, enabling them to be used in almost any type or size of vehicle produced anywhere in the world.

Motor-Factory Installations

Drop forging or impact-die forging account for the greater part of the tonnage of forgings used for automobiles. On the other hand, in the field of heavier forgings, presses have gained rapidly in popularity. In the past few years, both mechanical and hydraulic presses in wide range of sizes have been installed in mass-production plants.

Horizontal forging machines, or upsetters are often preferred when production quantity justifies the tooling.

Sand casting is still, by far, the most extensively used production casting process and the foundry equipment have highly been mechanized and automatized, however, synthetic sand is fast replacing the natural sand for the better cast surface; the shell-molding process, accordingly, is becoming more and more popular.

For metals of lower melting temperatures, permanent mold or diecasting process is widely adapted with the advantages of better controls for time, temperature and pressure.

Presses of common use are open-back inclinable press, straight-sided, single and double action presses and double-action multiple point presses. In recent years, however, use of presses in lines or automation of presses are being introduced. Quick-action material handling devices electrically or hydraulically operated are gaining preference. Multi-punch progressive presses are another trend of press developments.

To meet vast demands for the important component parts of the cylinder heads, cylinder blocks, transmission boxes, differential casings, considerable use is made of automatic in-line transfer machines built by outstanding machine tool makers in Japan.

Other heavily loaded parts, such as crankshafts, camshafts, axle shafts, are machined and processed through powerful and high-precision machines and they are statically and dynamically balanced to super-critical tolerances.

Wider adaptation of magazines and chutes for automatic loading and unloading is an obvious feature of the modern machine-shop lay-out.

Engines, transmission gear boxes, differential gear casings and other functional units are commonly assembled on wide ranges of conveyors of various types. The assembly lines are equipped with high-speed assembly tools and jigs and high-efficiency mechanical devices and the high standard of manual skill of Japanese workmen are perfectly combined to achieve most praiseworthy workmanship.

Testing equipment comprising engine dynamometers, chassis dynamometers and other devices enabling the operator to take a rapid and accurate check have developed to improve accuracy of the machined dimensions as well as stability of production processes.

Forging shop   Nissan Motor Plant

Press shop   Nissan Motor Plant

Testing course for assembled cars for individual automotive manufacturer is equipped with completely modern testing set-ups, however, the Japanese Government is now making a positive and realistic approach to the construction of a gigantic proving ground available for the public use.

Body assembly work is another field where Japanese world-famous manual dexterity is fully demonstrated, however, the mechanical facilities are none the less in a highly advanced stage. The main framing line and final assembly line are equipped with ingenious fixtures and clamps

Transfer machine for engine drilling - Nissan Motor Plant

Engine testing line — Toyota Motor Plant

Assembly line—Toyota Motor Plant

Testing course—Toyota Motor Plant

and wide range of welding machines are arranged on both sides of assembly conveyors.

As to painting of bodies, both pneumatical spraying and electro-static spraying systems are gaining popularity. Drying is performed almost all by the infra-red drying ovens.

Final assembly of cars is unanimously conducted on a conveyor of considerable length, using high-frequency electric tools and high-speed pneumatic tools. In-process inspections are performed at every important station of the assembly line.

Topical Technics

On Cars, Buses, Trucks, Three-Wheelers, Motorcycles and Motor Scooters

KOHJI KONDO*

The Japan Motor Industrial Federation has requested him to point out some of the technical highlights of the existing automotive engineering in Japan in respect to the new models of vehicles. Because of an immense number of new vehicles and models and limited pages of this book, only an extremely brief resume became available. On the next issue, selection will be made in respect to vehicles and models so as to make the description more detailed.

Japanese Cars for 1960

Until 1959, all passenger cars in Japan were powered by engines with piston displacements less than 1,500 c.c.—an administrative regulation set by the Government.

Completely new car by the name of Prince was launched in 1959 having an engine with a displacement of 1,862 c.c. This epoch-making revelation indicates the advent of a new era for the automotive industrialists in Japan in their undaunted efforts to bring the Japanese-made cars up to an internationally competitive level.

Achievement of this ultimate goal is being reached by modernization of the cars themselves and by overcoming the high price handicap of the cars.

Efforts with respect to the former are being exercised by giving the bodies popular lines and low silhouettes improving the interior trimmings and upholsteries. Other improvements concerning such mechanical items as power plant, suspension system, ventilating system are becoming the objects of concentrated study.

Cutting-down of manufacturing costs are being approached through modernization of manufacturing facilities; transfer machines are being installed in increasing numbers and assembly lines are being reinforced with high-efficiency machinery.

This industrial progress is giving smaller firms opportunities to develope new makes and models of cars—miniature cars with displacements ranging from 360 c.c. to 500 c.c. are being introduced to bring about a so-called "People's Car."

The acceleration of passenger cars is showing an upward trend reaching 1.1–1.85 m/s^2, a figure comparable with the average European cars. This achievement is from the results of modification of gear ratios, reduction of dry weights, and improvements of speed change mechanism.

With respect to the braking ability, efforts have been concentrated in solving this problem by means of incorporating new devices, such as two leading shoes and floating shoes to obtain a more sure and reliable stop.

Maximum car speeds are also rising fast by virtue of rational selection of gear ratio and innovation of the performance of the engine. There are a few cars that can exceed 120 km/h, and buses are also reaching this figure.

Special attention has been paid to lowering fuel consumption with the average fuel consumption rate successfully being reduced by approximately 10% compared to cars of five years ago, especially at low speed where Japanese cars are particularly economical. Overdrive unit is making its début to give substantial fuel economy on the open road.

Employment of independent suspension on all axles for superior riding comfort is one of the most conspicuous design tendencies. Coil springs are used widely for the front axle. Lowering of center of gravity, reduction of unsprung weights, improvements of shock absorbers are outstanding developments of approaching higher standard in riding comfort.

---

* *The author is a mechanical engineer and a Director of Society of Automotive Engineers of Japan, Inc. He is a closest follower of the recent developments of the automotive industry in Japan.*

SUBARU 360
356 c.c.

A distinguishing feature of the suspension system is the marked simplicity of its construction. It is anchored to the body frame by means of special rubber bushings.

The Subaru Standard 360 is mounted with 356 c.c. vertical twin, two-stroke, air-cooled engine developing 16 HP, an excellent specific output contributed by an engine-driven cooling fan. The engine is installed in the rear of the vehicle and drives the rear axle, eliminating the long and heavy propeller shaft. The exhaust silencer is divided into two parts for easier disassembly and cleaning.

The transmission system consists of a three-speed transmission gear box and gear changes are easily performed by a long gear shift lever.

The body is of frameless construction, affording the vehicle an unusual lightness of weight as well as strength. One of the unique features of the Subaru is the independent suspension systems.

The front wheel is mounted at one end of the trailing arm and the opposite end is fixed to a transverse rod which is anchored to the chassis by means of a spring-loaded upright rod.

The rear wheel is fixed to a longswing arm which is anchored to a transverse torsion bar. Any shocks caused by the road bumps are absorbed by the torsion bar and the shock absorbing system consisting of a center spring and a spring rod.

The interior space is large enough to accommodate four full-grown persons and the doors are of the wide opening type ensuring easy entrance and exit.

The rear seats can be folded down, giving ample loading area for luggage and goods. The front seats can be adjusted at three positions in conjunction with the length of the driver's legs, giving him the most comfortable driving postures.

Aiming at better ventilation, the Subaru is provided with door window glass of regulatable type, as well as with a cowl ventilator which introduces cool air into the vehicle to cool the interior.

Both front and rear suspension systems are featured by combined use of a center spiral spring and torsion bars. The trailing arms are used for suspension of wheels. The body is of the unitary construction.

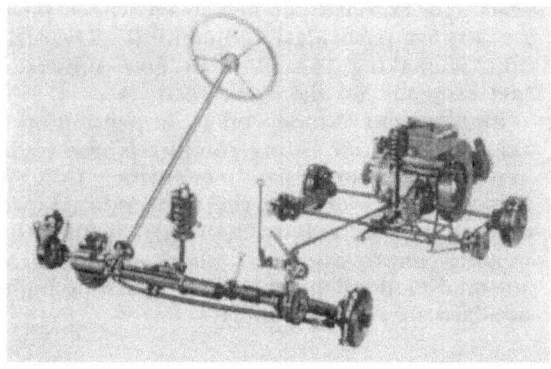

MITSUBISHI 500
493 c.c.

Mitsubishi 500 is powered by 493 c.c. vertical twin air-cooled four-stroke ohv engine developing 20 HP at 4,600 rpm.

The high specific output exceeding 40 HP/l has been the results of many years of accumulation of engineering experiences and study by the manufacturer. Aluminium is used quite exensively for the engine with the object of decreasing the weight of the engine and the vehicle as well. The horse-power-weight ratio, 24.5 kg/HP ranks high as compared to cars of equivalent capacity.

The transmission unit has three speeds and synchromesh on the second and third gears. Gear shifting can easily be done by a lever with I-section.

Engine and other power units are located in the rear of the vehicle which drives the rear axle.

The trailing arms combined with coil-spring-type telescopic shock-absorbers comprise the ining reasonable riding comfort for travel over rough roads and for elimination of rolling and pitching at high speeds. From the same standpoint, the tire size of 55.20-12 has been selected and the tire pressure is of the lowest type.

An interesting technical achievement is the extreme lightness of the car weight, 490 kg. This was made possible by the large use of pres-

Roentgen view showing the rear engine of the MITSUBISHI 500

dependent suspension system on both front and rear wheels.

The body of all-steel frameless construction equipped with two doors offers remarkably comfortable travel for four persons.

Much attention has been given for maintainsings of ample section modulus, distribution of concentrated load over large area and unlimited use of light alloys.

As far as the body styling is concerned, they have produced a body having a most compact and conventional apperance.

MIKASA TOURING
585 c.c.

The Mikasa is a four-seater convertible car, a type of a car rarely found in Japan, featuring exceptional easiness of drive and admirable road holding ability.

These two advantageous features are derived from the employment of the torque converter.

The Mikasa is the only small car in the world which is equipped with this ingenious mechanism of transmission.

This particular touring car is powered by a flat-twin, air-cooled, 585 c.c. four-stroke engine developing 17 HP at 3,800 rpm, mounted in the front of the vehicle. Power of the engine is transmitted to the two-speed gear box through the torque converter, and then to the front axle through the final drive unit.

By virtue of this front wheel drive principle, markedly high standard of road holding is obtained.

The movement of the steering wheel (only two turns from lock to lock) is transferred to the front wheel with the most exact accuracy and at the speed of 60 km/h the right wheel follows the road mark with mathematical exactness. Even when making an abrupt turn, no tendency of drifting is felt and it is possible for the Mikasa to make an acute turn at accelerated speed.

Easiness of driving of the Mikasa is another feature worthy of note.

Having only two pedals on the floor and equipped with shock-absorbing torque converter, the driver is able to operate the car without any rough starting or sudden stoppage with a jerking motion. Acceleration and deceleration are very smooth.

In the congested part of the city, this car is just the thing for threading through traffic without the necessity of endless shifting of gears. When the driver gets accustomed the torque converter, he can start his car with vivid acceleration at the change of the traffic signal.

Basis of this new open four-seater is a pressed steel body structure mounted on the frame of two longitudinal rails of the box section.

The front suspension is comprised by the lower wishbone link and the lower quarter-elliptic leaf spring, and the leaf spring runs parallel to the center line of the car.

The rear suspension is made of a transverse leaf spring and radius arms extending in the longitudinal direction.

The engine bonnet at the front is arranged to swing up in an alligator fashion to give access to the engine and power train.

At the rear the entire tail and rear fender form a rigid shell strengthened by the inner wheel arches and by inner pressings welded between the wheel arches.

As to the body work, the Mikasa Touring is a four-seater pure and simple, but is notable for generous width and leg room. The seats themselves are of the bucket type with foam rubber cushion. The simple instrument panel is of pleasing appearance with a speedometer prominently visible through the steering wheel.

As expected on a car of this type, vision is excellent. To facilitate folding the top, the rear window is of flexible plastic. The side windows are rigid-framed and can be used whether or not the top is in use giving adequate wind protection.

DATSUN BLUEBIRD

1,189 c.c.

The Datsun Bluebird four-door sedan has been designed for the highest standard of quality as well as for economical operation and maintenance costs.

Reduction of the curb weight by 65 kg compared with the last model, Datsun 211, is an indication of the successful realization of the above fundamental principle.

An entirely new four-cylinder over-head valve engine is equipped with a new three-speed transmission box, another change from the traditional four-speed transmission box, affording easier gear-shifting and reducing the weight.

Cam-and-lever steering system was employed with limited reversibility and the steering box was moved from the former position on the frame to a more convenient location on the suspension member with the aim of reducing elastic deformation of the frame.

Some drastic changes have been accomplished on the brake system of the new model, equipping the front wheel with Japan's first uniservo brake system and the rear wheel with the leading and trailing brake system, assuring light dependable control.

The dimension of the brake drum was also changed in connection with the tire size.

Considerable thought has been given for the determination of the tire size. The result was an extra low pressure tire with the size of 5.60-13. Tires of this size are available in any part of the world.

An realized weight reduction was effected by giving the rear axle housing smaller dimensions.

In order to meet overall demands for the independent suspension of the front wheel, an unique wish-bone type independent system was incorporated. It is unique with respect to easiness and exactness of adjustment of the front wheel alignment.

The rear axle is provided with three-leaf spring suspension system of an ample width.

For a quick change of wheel, a special body jack is attached.

Considerable attention has been paid to the construction of the frame, eliminating downward projections from the bottom and giving sturdy mounting to the functional units of the vehicle, as well as the body.

Roentgen view showing the construction of the BLUEBIRD.

The front brake system is provided with a single wheel cylinder, embodying Japan's first uniservo-brake sytem. Brake pedal pressure is intensified by 5½ times by means of an adjuster located at the bottom and the said multiplied pressure is applied to a rear brake shoe.

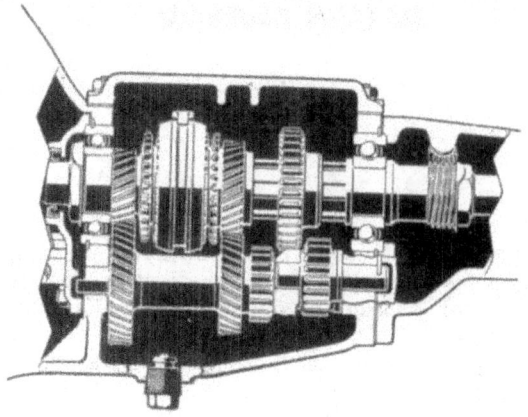

Three-speed Transmission Gear Box with synchromesh engagement for second and third gears. Remote-control type gear-change lever.

With respect to the body, horizontal features are accentuated at the front and rear, giving a much lower side view. The wheelbase was elongated by 60 mm, making driver and passenger sit cradled more comfortably between the axles. The overall height was lowered by 55 mm and the over-all length was shortened by 20 mm compared with the previous model Datsun. The interior width was increased by 30 mm, giving more seating comfort to the passengers.

The vehicle does not have a wrap-round windshield, but it is noteworthy for its extremely thin windshield pillars.

To comply with the demand for more space in the trunk compartment, ample capacity has been provided to place four golf-bags with a spare tire placed horizontally in a recess in the floor board.

The seats are so arranged that five persons can be seated comfortably. The seats are dually cushioned with both seat springs and 40 mm thick foam rubber mattings. The front seat can be adjusted within a distance of 80 mm.

The rear seat is provided with arm rests giving comfortable relaxation.

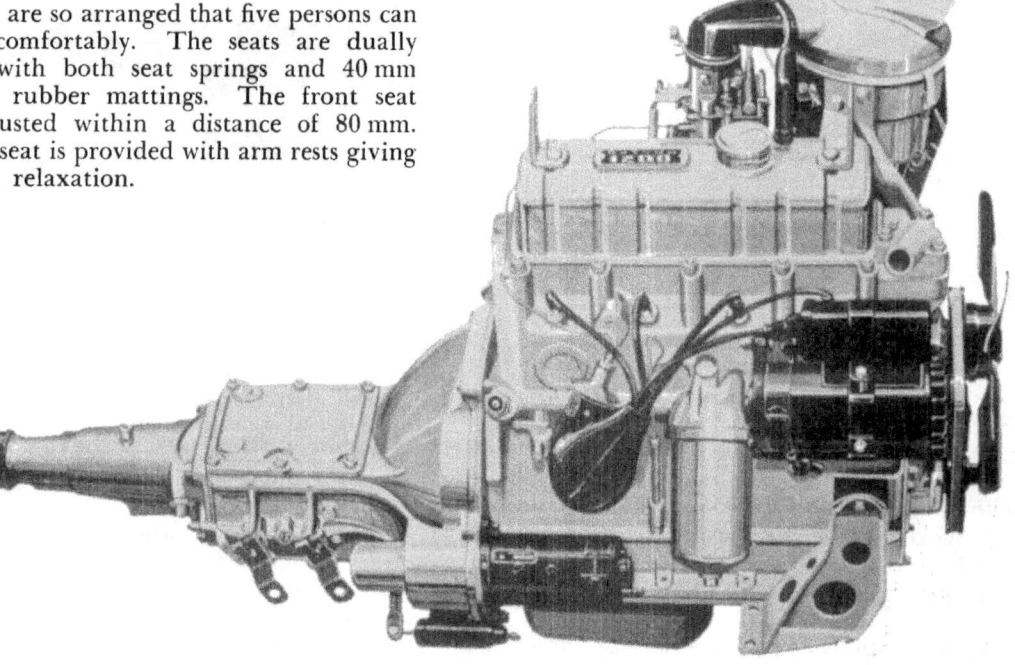

A short-stroke engine with a bore of 73 mm and a stroke of 71 mm having a piston displacement of 1,189 c.c., developing 43 HP.

TOYOPET CROWN DE LUXE
1,453 c.c.

Many advantages of both standard passenger cars and sport cars are incorporated in the Toyopet Crown De Luxe. As a normal passenger car, various improvements have been done to the important functional units, the most outstanding of these is the front end ball joint suspension, the first of its kind to be used in Japan.

By virtue of employing of the ball joint type front-wheel suspension, the customary nose dive when braking has been eliminated to an appreciable extent.

Further, a feeling of stiffness caused by frictional resistance of the conventional type of front suspension was also eliminated. Again this particular type of ball joint suspension aided greatly to reduce the unfavorable steering

The engine is equipped with Japan's first overdrive. It is an electrically operated automatic type, which at a car speed of approximately 40 km/h, the overdrive gear is made to be thrown in automatically.

The Toyopet overdrive does not deviate from the Borg Warner type of overdrive having the same gear ratio, 0.7:1.

The advantages of using this overdrive is as follows:—

(1) If there is no difference of engine revolution between the overdrive engine and the non-overdrive engine, the car speed will be higher by 30%, and if the car speed is assumed equal, then the engine revolution will be lower by 30%.

(2) By virtue of lower engine revolution, engine with an overdrive will last longer than the engine with a conventional type of transmission.

(3) When running on level roads, under normal running speed, the fuel consumption will be reduced by 15–20%.

(4) Engine operation will be much smoother

Two-speed transmission gear box equipped with overdrive; by virtue of the overdrive, the three-speed transmission gear box can be used effectively as a four-speed or five-speed transmission gear box.

condition effected by inaccuracy of the fabrication and assembly of the frame.

A special kind of machining process was given to the contact surfaces of the ball joint components, producing almost frictionless contact of the mating parts.

The steering gear ratio was changed from 23:1 to 20:1, affording improved exactness of steering and quick response of the wheel to the turn of steering wheel.

As to the power plant, the compression ratio was increased from 7.1 to 8.0 producing improved standard of high-speed performance, when fuels of high-octane rating are used.

and riding comfort will be improved appreciably.

Another mechanical feature contributing to give the Toyopet a sport car impression is the usage of smaller wheels. The chassis parts are so designed and constructed that the 13″ diameter wheels can be used 13″ wheels are the easiest size of wheels obtainable in the United States and Europe.

By adoptation of this small wheel, a drastic reduction of unsprung weight totaling approximately 18 kg was effected, another helpful contribution to improved standard of high-speed performance.

The two-barrel carburettor is so constructed that, at lower loads, a single barrel is made to operate for improved fuel economy and, at higher loads, both two barrels are made to operate simultaneously for increased engine power. A new automatic choke system brings the engine to life easily in the coldest season.

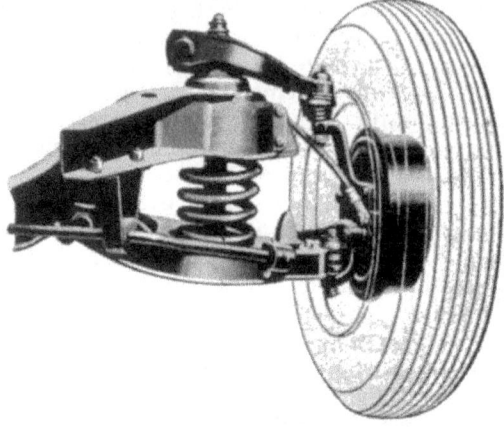

Independent front suspension is incorporated with a coil spring. The king pin is superseded by an universal joint comprising a ball and hemispherical seat.

Much attention has been given to various interior equipment for the convenience of the driver and the passengers.

The control and instruments are laid out in simple business-like fashion consisting of low rectangular shape meters. The indicating needle of the speedometer moves horizontally and when it reaches above the car speed of 40 km/h, it is lighted red. The lighting switch is actuated in four steps and the long parking switch and foglamp lighting switch are consolidated in this single switch.

A new method of locking the engine bonnet was employed allowing the driver to open the bonnet only from the driver's seat without leaving the car, eliminating possibility of unauthorized tampering while the car is left unattended for a period of time.

A unique pop-out type cigar-lighter using a bi-metal device is attached on the instrument panel. By a soft depression of the finger on the button, a redhot lighter is made to pop out.

Engine mounted with a two-barrel carburettor, developing 62 HP.

PRINCE GLORIA

1,862 c.c.

A completely new passenger car powered by a four-stroke engine with a piston displacement of 1,900 c.c. has recently been launched by the Fuji Precision Machinery Co., Ltd.

The engine is the most powerful of all the passenger cars in Japan. It is a modification of the well-known 60 HP engine and it is now developing 80 HP, a type of square engine with both cylinder bore and piston stoke of 84 mm.

By virtue of special design with respect to combustion chamber, piston and piston rings, the engine affords high standard of performance and long life.

In comparison with other passenger cars powered by the same power output, the engine weights remarkably less, measures unusually smaller and the fuel consumption is pronouncedly lower.

The first employment of the De Dion rear axle, consisting of the differential gear casing firmly attached to the frame, resulted in marked reduction of unsprung weight and in lowering the position of center of gravity—a happy combination of advantages of the rigid axle and

Back-bone tray type frame.

De Dion rear axle.

swing axle. This unique arrangement contributes to excellent riding comfort and high-speed road holding ability.

The entire vehicle is supported by the back-bone tray type frame, which is a composite construction of the conventional ladder-type frame and the frameless construction, ensuring lightness of weight and robustness of the structure.

Considerable attention has been devoted to the lowering of the overall height of the vehicle as well as the center of gravity. A high standard of running stability is thus successfully afforded when the car is running at a high velocity or making a formidable climb.

The trunk compartment is provided with a generous accommodating capacity following general tendency of the car design, capable of containing many golf-bags, suit cases and other personal effects. A spare tire can be installed horinzontally in a special recess in the floor board with the top of surface flush with the bottom of the compartment.

As far as the car interior is concerned, it is luxuriously trimmed and equipped. A large steering wheel, instrument panel of combined utility and striking beauty, smooth-operating gear shift lever are all located in appropriate positions.

All upholstery material is of Nylon. The seat cushions are full size and the front edges are raised to give adequate support to the legs.

The rear seats are provided with coat hangers and center armrests. Foam-rubber seat cushions are utilized and they are covered by gorgeous trims giving the interior a modern atmosphere as well as classical; noise and heat insulation materials are also extensively used.

In the rear of the rear seat, a radio speaker is installed additionally to improve the accoustical effects. Receiving of short-wave communications has also become available.

As to he outward appearances, a newly designed golden belt line and eye-catching wheel caps give the car a most luxurious and exciting styling.

Technical Progresses in the Field of Buses

Technical progress in the omnibus field includes strenuous efforts for improving the comfort of the passengers and driver as well as for increasing the seating capacity.

The effort has successfully been realized in a deluxe semi-decker bus accomodating 83 passengers; this particular bus features air-cushion springs, power-assisted steering system and brake system, heating and air conditioning unit and tilting seats.

It is powered by a Diesel engine developing 125 HP with a turbo-supercharger. Maximum speed is in the neighborhood of 112 km/h when accommodating 60 passengers. A special speedometer is conveniently installed above the front windshield so as to keep passengers informed of the actual bus speed.

Recently, the four-head lamp lighting system has been introduced on buses. A labor-saving device incorporating an automatic lubrication system for 40 important oiling points under the floor are being installed which can be operated from a button on the dash board.

Side by side with large-sized buses, buses of reduced dimensions, micro-buses are gaining popularity. The seating capacity of these small buses is approximately 14 passengers.

These buses are designed and constructed to offer the most practical means of transportation to the public. Outstanding features are space-saving under seat engine, air-conditioning system, wide-opening doors, easy-to-mount step board.

MITSUBISHI FUSO SEMI-DECKER BUS AR470

Japan's first one and half decker body has been developed and mounted on a standard bus chassis with modified wheelbase and elongated overhang to suit this bus of luxurious superstructure styling. The bus is powered by a turbo-supercharged Diesel engine developing 185 HP and equipped with a five-speed transmission gear system featuring an overdrive and synchromesh gear system. Engine position permits use of entire floor surface for passenger accommodation and special baggage room. Superb riding comfort is guaranteed by air suspension system, spacious reclinable seats arranged on both sides of sunken gangway, heating and cooling systems.

MITSUBISHI FUSO BUS "AR 470"

with Air Suspension

Air suspension system consists of compressed-air-filled rubber bellows used instead of conventional leaf springs of steel. Hard cushioning thus produced is softened by connecting the bellows with air reservoirs. A radius rod and a Panhard rod controlling the longitudinal and transverse motion of the bellows and a levelling valve keeping the height of the bellows constant constitute the air suspension system.

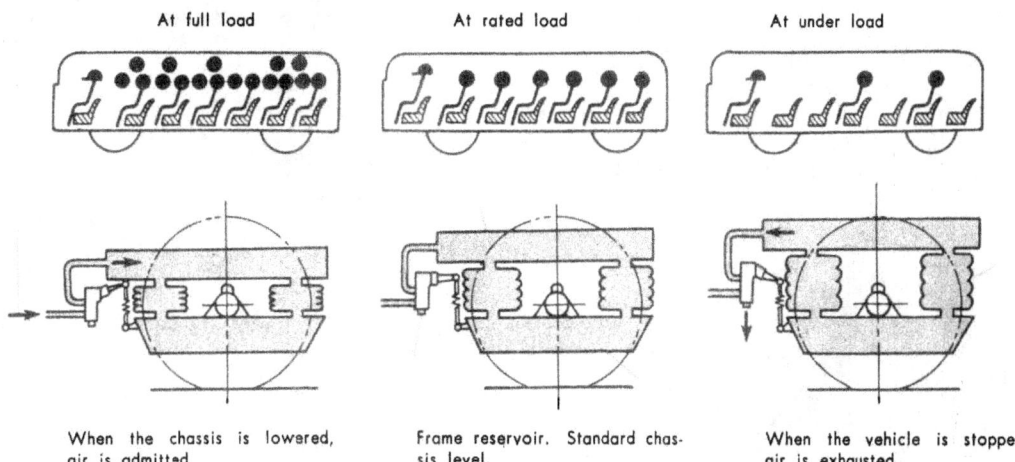

At full load	At rated load	At under load
When the chassis is lowered, air is admitted.	Frame reservoir. Standard chassis level.	When the vehicle is stopped, air is exhausted.

The Mitsubishi AR 470 embodies the results of intensive development work on consolidating wide range of modern equipment into one single bus. By virtue of these efforts, a maximum speed of 112 km/h has successfully been achieved.

Much alterations were made to the principal construction of the chassis—the wheelbase and front overhang were extended. Power-assisted steering system, pneumatic suspension system and automatic centralized greasing device are outstanding features of the bus.

By employment of the five-speed transmission gear box equipped with an overdrive afforded lower fuel consumption even at high-speed conditions. The bus is powered by a turbo-supercharged engine with an ingenious arrangement called boost control in order to prevent black smoke from the exhaust pipe when the vehicle is vividly accelerated.

The body has been built as a semi-decker for improved outside appearance and at the same time, for providing ample space for the luggage storage.

Seats are all reclinable through an angle of 45° in two steps.

A separate engine is mounted for operating the cooling system.

Tires of special design, 11.00-20, 14P have been developed for effecting increased braking efficiency and prevention of side skid on the slippery road.

MINSEI UD BUS

2-cycle Uniflow Diesel Engine with Air Suspension

The RF range of the Minsei Diesel engine buses enjoys the reputation of the first bus in Japan equipped with the air suspension system.

These buses feature the 7,413 c.c. Diesel engine, a two-stroke, six-cylinder unit having a

The UD Engine is an abbreviation of the Uniflow Scavenging System Diesel Engine embodying a special scavenging process of the combustion chamber, an uniflow or one direction flow of the scavenging air. Upon entering the combustion chamber of the cylinder, the flow of air is directed always in a single direction inside the cylinder liner, passing through the inlet port to the outlet port. Speaking in a more exact manner, the UD Engine is a special kind of Diesel engine featured by the port scavenging, overhead valve exhaust and single-direction scavenging systems.

bore of 110 mm and a stroke of 130 mm.

Its power output is 230 HP at 2,000 rpm and the peak torque is 90 kgm at 1,300 rpm. To suit the high performance, the engine is fed by the Root's blower type supercharger and the fuel is supplied by a direct injection unit. A special combustion chamber and multi-orifice injection nozzle of enclosed type ensures quick starting even in the coldest season.

The body accommodating seventy-seven passengers is mounted on two axles and for each axle, a new air suspension system is installed, affording excellent riding comfort and increase in service life.

By virtue of the levelling valve embodied in the air suspension system, the loading platform is maintained at a constant controlled height.

When the bus is being either loaded or unloaded, and the chassis falls or rises relative to the suspension, the consequent movement of the lever causes air to be admitted or exhausted, according to whether the chassis has to be raised or lowered to re-adjust the static height.

The power plant is located at the rear end of the chassis for ease of inspection and servicing.

The driver's seat is located in line with the universal trend of forward-control layout.

Wide-opening folding doors assure easy entering and leaving for the passengers.

An intensive development work has been made by the Minsei Diesel Industry Company, Ltd., in cooperation with the Japanese Government Railroad Engineering Research Institute in respect to the air suspension system, after finalizing the work successfully, they are mounting this particular type of suspension system on all the buses operated by the Government Railroad Ministry.

HINO UNDER-FLOOR ENGINED BUS
with Air Suspension

The Hino Diesel engine bus is well-known for its under-floor arrangement of the power plant, however, more interesting features have been added to this particular vehicle.

The chassis is powered by the 7,698 c.c. Diesel engine, a four stroke, horizontally arranged six-cylinder unit having a bore of 110 mm and a stroke of 135 mm.

Its power output is 200 HP at 2,400 rpm and the peak torque is 62 kgm at 1,800 rpm.

The engine is equipped with a turbo-charger and with a five-speed transmission gear box provided with an overdrive unit. The engine and

Entire floor area is devoted to installation of passenger seats, permitting an increased accommodation capacity of passengers. The position of the engine at the center of the chassis eliminated longitudinal vibration, affording perfect road holding of the vehicle. Inspection and maintenance of the engine can easily be performed by removing the body skirt.

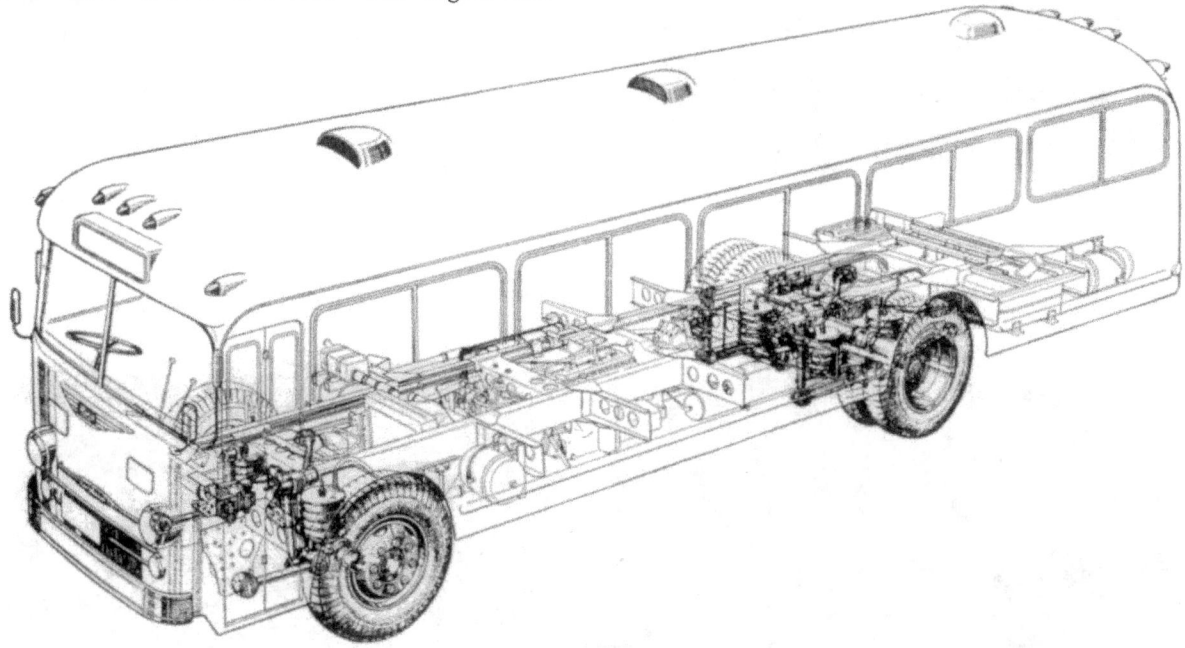

power train are neatly installed underneath the chassis floor.

A special air-suspension system is mounted on each axle for improved riding comfort, elimination of road shocks and increase of vibration damping characteristics. The levelling valves function perfectly for keeping the floor of the bus body at a constant height, regardless of the loading conditions.

The driver's seat is provided with a large and deep windscreen having a wide range of vision. The steering mechanism is reinforced by a power-assisted steering unit.

Passenger seats are reclinable and equipped with electric fans for better ventilation.

The spacious and luxuriously constructed body permits accommodation of 63 passengers.

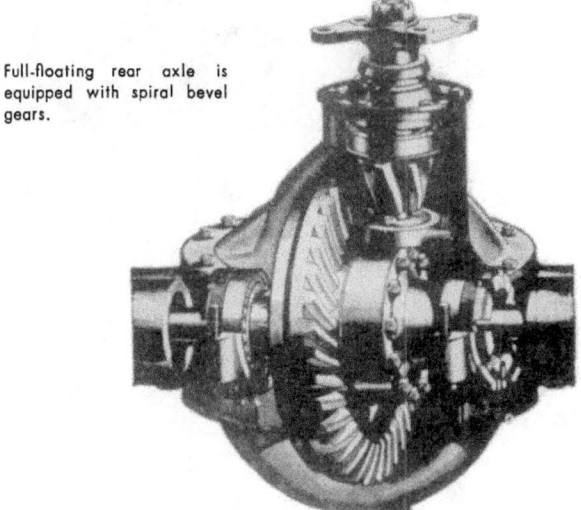

Full-floating rear axle is equipped with spiral bevel gears.

ISUZU BUS "BC 151"

with Air Suspension

Turbocharger-supercharged DH100 Diesel engine developes 230 HP.

The Isuzu bus BC 151 has been modified in many respects aiming at increasing engine power and improving passengers' comfort. The vehicle is powered by a non-supercharged engine developing 180 HP or by a turbo-supercharged engine developing 225 HP. The engine is located at the rear of the chassis.

The engine is equipped with a five-speed transmission gear box and if required, an overdrive is available as optional equipment.

Clutch control system was changed to hydraulic actuation arrangement under the remote control principle, affording increased efficiency and ease of operation.

For brake system, hydraulic brake system is employed reinforced by pneumatic master cylinder.

Power-assisted steering system is employed with a steering wheel of larger diameter.

The body is of the unitary construction with the results of reduced weight and increased stiffness. The dropped central gangway and all forward-faced seats feature the interior. Large areas of heat-insurating and noise silencing glass windows are employed.

The cooling system and air suspension system are another noticeable features.

Seats are inclinable and at the foot of each seat is located a heater box.

The main body of the air suspension system comprises the rubber bellows filled with compressed air. This unique spring system, utilizing compressivity of air, is provided with air reservoirs for increasing spring constant, levelling valves for maintaining the constant chassis height and torque rods and radius rods for controlling longitudinal and traversal swinging motions of the bellows.

PRINCE MICROBUS

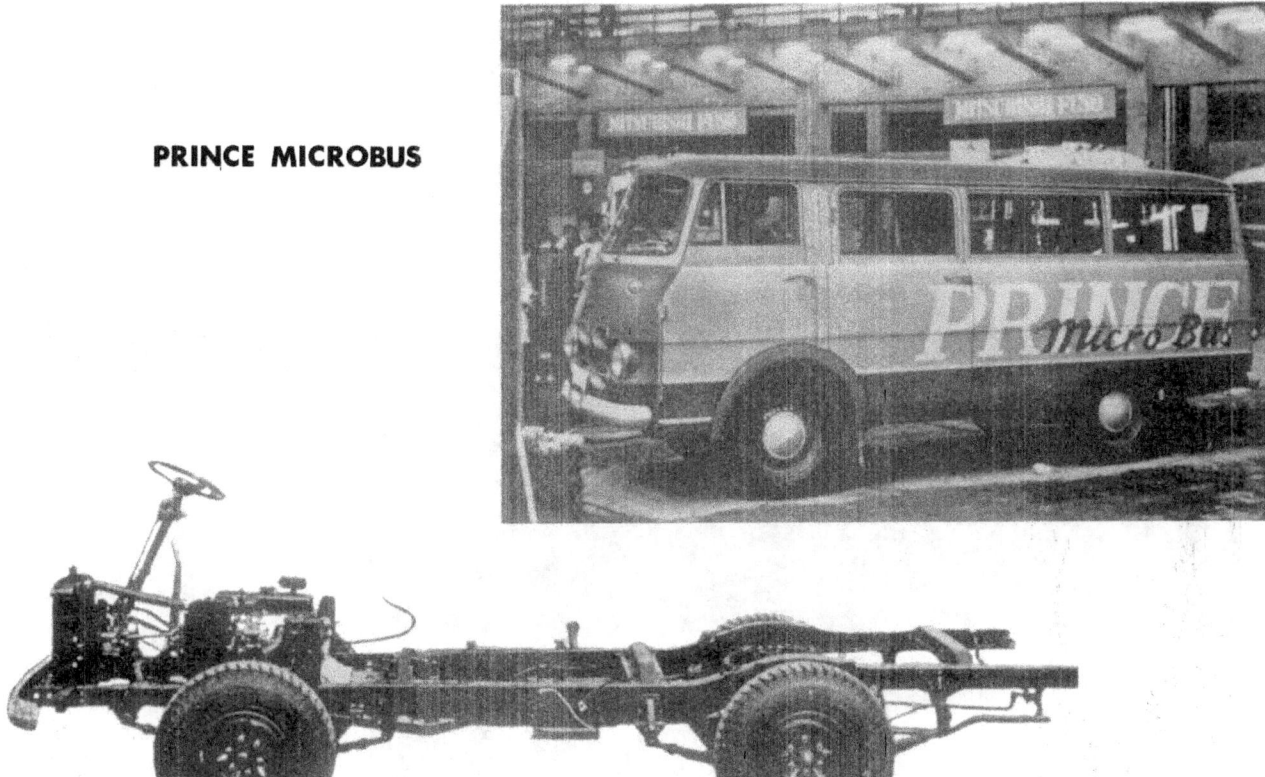

In recent years, marked swing has been created toward small and medium-sized buses for sight-seeing and commuting trips and for other lightload transportation.

The Prince Microbus is a new development for meeting these requirements.

The particular vehicle has the greatest loading area among the competitive vehicles with a loading capacity of 1,250 kg.

It is powered by a four-cylinder, o.h.v. 1,484 c.c. engine developing 70HP at 4,800 rpm. The power plant and other functional parts are snugly located under the driver's seat contributing to shift the driver's seat to the extreme front, yielding increased space for loading and passenger seating.

When the bus body is mounted on the chassis, it can accommodate 14 passengers. Special attention has been given for easier entrance and leaving of the passengers, one of the practical examples is indicated by extremely low boarding step of only 430 mm high.

The driver's seat is located at the foremost part of the chassis ensuring ease and safety of operation. Like the passenger car, the driver's seat gives accommodation to 3 persons.

Large and deep windscreen and side window glasses provide exceptionally wide range of vision for the passengers and the driver as well.

NISSAN CABALL Micro Bus

The engine has a piston displacement of 1,489 c.c. and developes 57 HP. The transmission gear box is equipped with synchronous engagement. Bodies are made for both fourteen and seventeen passengers. Overall dimensions for the bus accommodating fourteen passengers are 4,590 mm long × 1,990 mm high × 1,675 mm wide: the same for the seventeen passenger bus are 4,975 mm long × 2,140 mm high × 1,900 mm wide.

ISUZU ELF Micro Bus

Two different wheelbases, 2,180 mm and 2,460 mm, are available. The bus with 2,180 mm wheelbase gives accommodation to twelve passengers and the other is good for fifteen passengers. These two buses are powered by a common engine, having a piston displacement of 1,491 c.c. and developing 60 HP. The transmission gear box is equipped with synchromesh engagement for the second, third and fourth speeds.

HINO LIGHT AMBULANCE

A conversion of HINO Mini Bus body into an ambulance for transporting patients. A standard HINO chassis is used and bed seats and litters are mounted. The bed seats can be folded up into sofas each accommodating five persons. The bus is driven by an engine mounted in the front. The body floor is mounted in the level of knee-height permitting easy entry and exit.

TOYOPET Micro Bus

The bus is powered by a four cylinder, 1,453 c.c., o.h.v. engine, developing 58 HP. The body offers roomy accommodation for twelve passengers with overall dimensions of overall length: 4,665 mm, overall width: 1,680 mm, overall height: 1,980 mm. An optional model with reclining seats gives generous accommodation for fifteen passengers.

HINO Mini Bus

The bus is powered by a four cylinder, 836 c.c., water-cooled engine of line cylinder arrangement with o.h.v. The engine is mounted in the front end of the chassis leaving spacious room for accommodating eleven passengers. Unitary construction has been adopted for the body. The standard model has the overall dimensions of overall length: 3,930 mm, overall width: 1,690 mm, overall height: 1,880 mm. The transmission gear box is of synchromesh-type equipped with synchromesh engagement for the second, third and fourth gears.

DAIHATSU Micro Bus

The bus is fitted with a 1,478 c.c., tour cylinder, four-stroke, o.h.v., water-cooled engine, developing 53 HP. The bodies are constructed in two different models, the model with standard seats accommodates twelve passengers and the enlarged model with reclining seats accommodates fifteen passengers. The overall dimensions are, overall length: 4,690 mm, overall width: 1,690 mm, overall height: 1,980 mm.

Technical Highlights of Trucks in Japan

There are six outstanding manufacturers of heavy trucks in Japan and the scale of production and standard of production facilities can be compared favorably with those of the United States and other foreign countries.

Considerable progress for improved performance is obviously being made in several directions with the prospect of high-speed motor highways to be constructed in the near future. Quest for increased power is continuing and accelerated speed is the goal at the present time in the field of truck engineering.

The Diesel engines are rapidly encroaching on territory of the gasoline engines and the turbocharged engines are fast gaining universal popularity with the power output extending to 230 HP.

Transmission gear boxes are being improved to cope with requirements for robust construction and dependable operation, as well as requiring a minimum of service attention. Synchromesh gear boxes are in production and being standardized.

The air suspension is attracting much attention and power-assisted steering is obtaining preference.

Multiple axle system is increasing and a manufacturer has employed a double front and single rear axle system. The three axle and the all wheel drive systems are being offered with universal acclaim.

Emphasis is being placed to give more comfort and convenience to the man at the wheel, by providing excellent visibility, better weather protection and climatization. Four head lamp system is also being introduced.

Three-Wheelers

The three-wheeled trucks are Japan's special vehicles of transportation with amazing practicability, having no equal in the world with respect to the quantity of production.

The universally accepted advantages of these particular trucks are their excellent manoeuvability by virtue of single front-wheel, high torsional resistance of the frame because of their triangular construction, and low cost of operation and maintenance.

These trucks are powered by engines developing 20 HP to 60 HP and having a loading capacities ranging from 500 kg to 2,000 kg. Recently, four cylinder engines are gaining more popularity than the traditional two cylinder engines and also the two-stroke and four-stroke engines are equally popular.

The driver's cab is receiving more attention for improving the comfort and convenience of the man at the wheel. The cab with three person seating capacity and circular steering wheel is becoming standard. High rear body capacity is another advantage of this type of truck, ranging from 1.25 m^2 to 1.6 m^2 for the light-type and from 3.04 m^2 to 6.89 m^2 for the heavy-type. Materials of unusual lengths can be carried by using the extra long rear bodies ranging from 2.1 m to 2.5 m for 1-tonners and from 2.5 m to 4.8 m.

TOYOTA HEAVY TRUCK "FA71"

with 2-Speed Rear Axle

The Toyota Truck FA71 embodies the results of intensive development work accumulated since the early days of Japan's automotive industry.

It is now enjoying the well-established reputation as a truck of unsurpassed power output, unmatched strength and perfect ease of handling, featuring the Japan's first two-speed rear axle.

This particular truck is powered by a gasoline engine, a six-cylinder unit, having a bore of

Two-speed rear axle permits wider range of speed reduction and provides freedom of selection of the most appropriate gear-ratio for negotiating severe running conditions over rough terrains or for high speed operations on speedways.

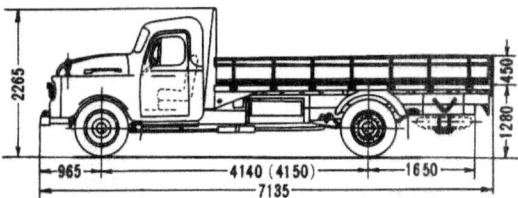

90 mm and a stroke of 101.6 mm. Its power output is 110 HP at 3,400 rpm and the peak torque is 27.5 kgm at 2,000 rpm. A Diesel engine of a similar specification is available on application. Four-point suspension of engine for better balance and accurately horizontal arrangement of inlet manifold for improved fuel distribution are notable features. The transmission gear box is equipped with synchromesh engagement for the 2nd, 3rd and top gears.

The rear axle is of the two-speed full-floating Hypoid type and selection of the high and low gear ratio can be performed by means of a push-button located on the shift lever in the driver's cabin. By virtue of this special arrangement, exceptionally high standard of performance can be gained when running on the highway or off-highway.

The cargo rear body is provided with generous overall dimensions with a load carrying capacity of 5,000 kg.

In tune with the recent developments in frame design, it is aimed at reducing vehicle weights and the floor heights, and at affording greater stiffness.

A roomy and comfortable driver's cabin is another feature, provided with accommodation for three passengers.

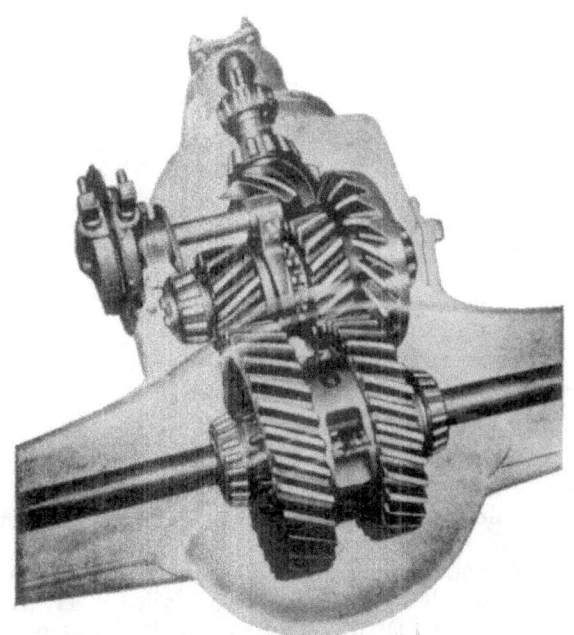

Transmission system is of a selective sliding gear type provided with a four-speed transmission gear box with synchromesh engagement for second, third and top gears.

MITSUBISHI "JUPITER"

with Light Diesel Engine

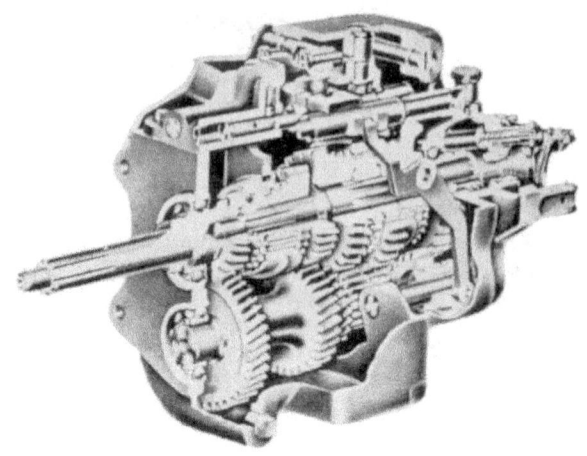

Full-synchromesh transmission gear box.

The Mitsubishi Jupiter has been launched quite recently to meet ever increasing demand for a truck of medium loading capacity.

This is the first truck of this kind in Japan. This particular truck features the 2,199 c.c. Diesel engine, a four-cylinder unit having a bore of 79.4 mm and a stroke of 111.1 mm. Its power output is 61HP at 3,600 rpm and the peak torque is 14.0 kgm at 2,200 rpm. A gasoline engine of a similar specification can be had in place of the Diesel engine. The compression ratio of the Diesel engine is 19:1, an unusually high figure.

The engine is equipped with a four-speed transmission gear box of full-synchromesh arrangement.

The frame of this truck is of a most conventional ladder-type with the longitudinal sills positioned perfectly parallel. The rear box is spaciously dimensioned with a loading capacity of 2,500 kg.

Crankshaft with cast-in balancing weights for damping engine vibration.

Light-type Diesel engine with a four-speed transmission gear box, developing 61 HP.

The driver's cab is styled in the latest fashion admitting three persons.

A notable mechanical feature is the special servo-assisted brake system called "Hydromaster," actuated and intensified by boost pressure of the engine. By virtue of this special arrangement, the brake pressure is increased by 200% at the same pedal pressure.

Another intresting feature of construction developed by this company is the employment of leaf spring of the near-constant spring constant. By dint of this special spring, stiffness of the spring remains constant regardless of the loading conditions.

ISUZU LIGHT TRUCK "ELF"

A synchromesh-type transmission gear box and suspension-type brake and clutch pedals for easier operation.

The Isuzu ELF is a name given to a small-size truck having a loading capacity of 2,000 kg introduced to the market quite recently.

This new-comer features the 1,491 c.c. gasoline engine, a four cylinder power unit having a bore of 78 mm and a stroke of 78 mm.

Its power output is 60 HP at 4,600 rpm and the peak torque is 11 kgm at 2,200 rpm. The engine is characterized by a high standard of performance by employment of overhead valves of high volumetric efficiency and wedge type combustion chamber of high combustion efficiency.

The engine is installed underneath the driver's seat, an example of cab-over engine arrangement rarely found in Japanese vehicles.

Removal of a seat cushion at the center ensures easy accessibility to all parts of the engine.

Special attention has accordingly been paid to achieve better insulation to heat and vibration inside the driver's cab. Vigorous cooling air current is available from the center of the front floor and seats are made of special sound-absorbing materials.

For servicing and maintenance, the seat is easily detached to give a free access to engine components. The cab is typical of the recent trend of styling of forward-control layouts, commanding a wide range of vision.

The controlling equipment bears close resemblance to the conventional cars, with suspension-type control pedals, hydraulic clutch control system, remote-controlling type gear shift lever, self-cancelling winker control and shapely horn ring.

The main leaves of the rear suspension spring, in the same manner as the front, are made in a semi-elliptic form and cylindrical rubber springs are mounted as the auxiliary springs.

MAZDA 3-WHEELED TRUCK "HBR"

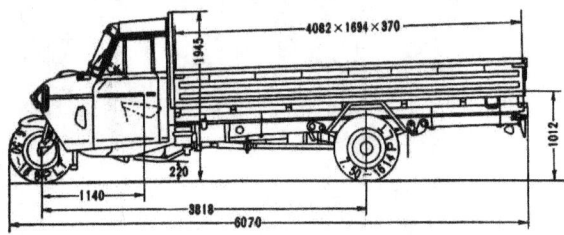

Three-wheeled trucks are Japanese speciality in the field of automotive vehicles. The production and circulation of these particular vehicles constitute the leading percentage in the statistics of recent years.

The Mazda HBR three-wheeled truck is one of the Mazda range of trucks, well-known for its comprehensive specifications.

This particular truck is powered by a massive 1,400 c.c. overhead valve vee twin engine developing 42HP at 3,500 rpm. The engine is equipped with a four-speed transmission gear box with synchromesh gears on the second, third and fourth speeds, eliminating necessity of double clutch operation.

Gear-shifting is performed by means of a gear shift lever attached on the steering column. The starting of the engine is made by the push-button type electric starter.

Power generated by the engine is transmitted to the rear-axle through the differential gear unit of ample dimensions equipped with Hypoid gears.

Engine mounting is made on the rubber pads in order to absorb vibrations generated by the engine. Ignition advance is performed not only by a centrifugally operated automatic device, but also by a vacuum operated ingenious method.

Engine is located underneath the seat affording increased area for accommodation of goods —an arrangement rarely found in the competitive vehicles in Japan.

A flexible rubber coupling is inserted between the power output end of the engine and the front end of the propeller shaft to absorb vibration and misalignment of center lines of both parties.

The clutch is provided with the Japan's first oil pressure control system, ensuring exactness of operation and longer life of clutch component parts.

The front-wheel is suspended by a powerful front fork provided with efficient spring and hydraulic shock-absorbers.

A new hydraulically operated vibration damper is added to the rear-wheel suspension system. This ingenious gadget is so designed and constructed that both upward and downward shocks can be absorbed, giving a reasonable riding comfort irrespective of loads.

The driver's cabin of improved comfort and ease of driving is provided with a fully upholstered bench with spacious area for accommodating two persons alongside the driver.

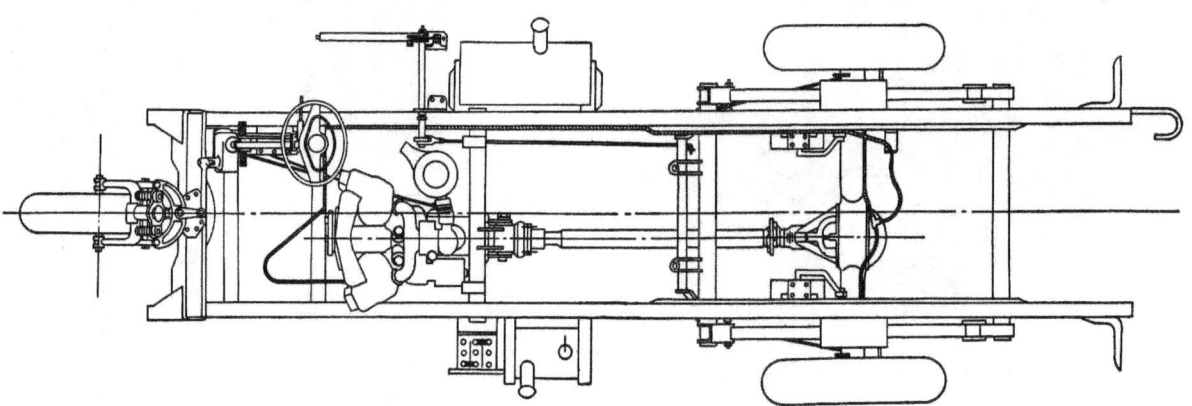

A curved safety glass of veneered type is used for the windshield glass affording a wide range of vision and driving safety. Left-side door can be locked from inside and the right-side door can be locked from outside, preventing unauthorized interference with the key, while the vehicle is kept unattended for a long period of time.

The driver's seat located on the top of the engine compartment is filled with noise and heat insulating materials.

Styling is in tune with contemporary four-wheeled truck trends and the spacious rear body has a loading capacity of 2,000 kg fit either for long hauls or short door-to-door delivery.

DAIHATSU "MIDGET DKA"

An overwhelming popularity has recently been created in the community specialized in light-weight transportation and the Daihatsu Midget is the model which enjoys the largest sales amount in Japan.

This particularly simple and compact three-wheeled truck is powered by a two-stroke, single-cylinder, air-cooled 250 c.c. engine developing 10HP with the compression ratio of 9.2. The engine equipped with a three-speed transmission gear box is started by an electric starter. It can with a rear window.

As the Midget is provided with the most limited dimensions, it is particularly fitted for making a turn with a minimum radius of turning or threading through the congested areas for door-to-door delivery of light goods.

The whole structure is well balanced and the height of the center of gravity is reduced to a minimum, aiming at excellent manoeuvability and balance. It maintains pronounced road holding even if an abrupt turn is made at a higher speed with considerable load.

A chameleon-type speedometer provided with warning lamps of different colors is mounted for prevention of over-speed driving.

The load carrying capacity of this midget truck is 300 kg and the maximum speed under this load is about 65 km/h. It can easily negotiate the hill of 1/5 inclination. The front

also be started by a kickstarter.

Power generated by the engine is transmitted to the half-floating rear axle through the differential gear unit of the conventional type.

The single front-wheel is suspended by a short swing-arm provided with telescopic front fork and the rear-wheels are suspended by leaf spring suspension system.

The driver's cabin is constructed by a shapely front shield and rear panel with canvas top. It is entirely separated from the load carrying space with a simple partition built by a canvas sheet panoramic windshield provided with an electrically operated wiper and Vinyl top accommodate good weather protection to the man at the steering wheel.

Wheels of small diameter 5.00-9 are intentionally mounted and thanks to this small-size tires exceptionally sharp cornering can be effected.

Reduced overall dimensions and special weight-saving policy contributed to originate a vehicle of outstanding lightness, resulting to unusual economy of operational and maintenance costs.

MIDGET-TYPE TRUCKS

Production of the heavy-duty trucks as well as light-type trucks dates back to the later part of the third decade of this century and the product vehicles cover a wide range of specifications, including heavy trucks and dump trucks of more than 10 ton loading capacities

Kurogane Baby Tokyu Kurogane Motor product

Cony 360 Aichi Machine product

Humbee Mitsui Precision product

Mitsubishi Pet Leo Mitsubishi Reorganized product

powered by engines up to the piston displacement of 7,000 c.c. and power output of 230 HP.

Production of these trucks ranks at the highest of all motored vehicles in Japan.

On the other hand, in recent years, the so-called midget-type trucks and vans, the smallest type of load-carrying vehicles powered by an engine having a piston displacement of less than 360 c.c., have been introduced to the market in increasing numbers.

The following midget-type trucks were displayed in the Tokyo Motor Show 1959.

Showa Minica Showa Works product

Suzulight Suzuki Motor product

Cony Aichi Machine product

Mazda Toyo Kogyo product

Notable Mechanical Features

Mopeds, Motorcycles & Motor Scooters

Motorcycles

In the field of motorcycles, numerous engineering achievements rank high in the international standard.

For example, a 125 c.c. two-stroke engine developes 15 HP at 9,200 rpm and a 250 c.c. four-stroke engine 20.3 HP at 9,000 rpm.

Two cylinder arrangement for light-type motorcycle is gaining overwhelming popularity, aiming at higher power output and smoother operation. The most pronounced tendency is the predominant adaptation of the electric self-starters for the engines of lower range of output; approximately 63% of existing motorcycles are equipped with this ingenious electric unit. In line with this technical trend, the battery ignition and automatic ignition timers are being met with universal acclaim.

Another technical development worthy of note is the employment of torque converter and shaft drive transmission.

The former contributes much to the ease of operation, increased gradability and fuel consumption economy; the latter tends to prevent chain detachments as well as switching-over to cantilever-type wheel mounting.

Rapid changes are being made in the frame construction, such as one-piece pressed-steel frame embodying extensive shielding and a deeply valanced rear mudguard is obtaining unanimous preference.

Motor Scooters

Examination of Japanese scooters in recent years indicates that there is a feeling of confidence throughout the industry and that the time has passed when models groped their way to the market.

The Japanese scooters cover now a wide range of piston displacement of engines, from 40 c.c. to 240 c.c.

The development work in the field of scooter is directed toward improving structural strength, riding comfort and power transmission efficiencies.

A new scooter provided with a monocoque body has been introduced aiming at reducing vehicle weights and at affording greater stiffness. The front fender of this scooter is blended into the leg shield with a shapely curve.

As per improvement of riding comfort, a scooter is available which is incorporated with air-suspension system, providing the rider with unusually smooth ride. On a certain scooter, the chain-drive has been replaced by the shaft-drive in order to eliminate noise and increase mechanical efficiency. A torque converter is likely to be more popular for its excellent advantages.

Maximum speed of the scooter reached above 100 km/h and the engine revolution is rising proportionally. The adoptation of the torque converter contributes much to achieve higher car speed at comparatively lower engine rovolution.

Sealed-beam headlamp is finding its way in increasing numbers.

HONDA "SUPER CUB"

The Super Cub represents a sport and touring moped and scooterette powered by a four-stroke, ohv, single cylinder, air-cooled, 49 c.c. engine developing 4.5 HP at 9,500 rpm.

The specific power output ranks at the top of Japanese mopeds and motorcycles.

The high standard of performance of the engine contributes to an exceptionally vivid acceleration, marvellous gradability and astounding maximum speed.

The engine is equipped with a three-speed gear change mechanism actuated by an automatic centrifugal clutch, affording an instantaneous start of the engine. Speed change can easily be performed simply by pressing down the speed change lever with a right foot, eliminating the necessity of gripping the clutch lever by a left hand.

Emphasis has been placed on the silencing of the engine exhaust noise by means of employing an extra spacious exhaust silencer.

The proportion of the volume of silencer to the piston displacement is approximately 13:1 for conventional motorcycles, however, for the Super Cub this particular proportion is increased to 23:1.

Special attention has been paid to the improved lubrication of the important component parts of the engine and power train. The four-stroke engine, unlike the two-stroke engine, supplies lubricant in a more positive manner to the location where it is needed most.

Considerable thought has been concentrated to save the vehicle weight for better economy and easier handling.

Frame of this moped is built up from shapely steel pressings and embodies the fuel tank, providing a degree of enclosure with minimum extra weight.

By virtue of this weight-reducing effort, the weight of the Super Cub turned out only 55 kg, permitting an easy handling even for a woman driver.

Outstanding mechanical features are wheel suspension systems; the front wheel is suspended by a pivoted-type front fork provided with hydraulic shock-absorbers and the rear wheel is supported by swing-arms equipped with telescopic shock-absorbers, affording a high standard of riding comfort and a high-speed operation overcoming irregularities in the road surface.

Mountings on the Super Cub include a rear-view mirror and a powerful headlamp uncommon to a moped.

On the rightside handle bar is fitted an electric switch assigned to open the electric circuit fed by the direct current magneto, when electric current for the headlamp, winker and horn is fed from a 6 V storage battery.

A brisk change-over from the normal beam to the dipped beam on the headlamp can easily be done by actuating the electrical switch fixed on the rightside handle bar.

Engine equipped with a selfstarting motor can be brought into life by a simple depression on a starting button.

HONDA "DREAM CS76"

The Honda Dream is the highlight of the Honda Motor's 1960 programme. The machine has passed the most strict inspection of the technical staff of the Honda Engineering Laboratory with respect to quality of materials, high-grade workmanship and first-class performance.

The Dream is powered by a four-cycle, two-cylinder, ohv, 247 c.c. engine developing 20 HP at 8,400 rpm, the compression ratio being 9:1.

The engine is equipped with a four-speed transmission gear box. The valves located at the top of the cylinder head are operated by an overhead camshaft through a chain, best-suited means of power transmission for the high-speed operating engines for its simplicity of construction and ease of adjustment. The cylinder is provided with a hemispherical combustion chamber permitting unusually high specific power output.

Special attention has been paid to the improved lubrication of the engine components. Oil is fed to the crankcase in required quantity by means of a gear pump from the oil tank located at the top of the frame. After passing through all the lubricating points of the engine, the oil is returned to the tank by way of an oil filter.

Unlike other conventional motorcycles, the new Dream CS76 has been admirably tailored with sturdy but lively appearance.

The entire styling has been planned so as to give a sleek and flowing impression with well-proportioned and located headlamp, front fork, front and rear fender, pressed-steel handle bar, fuel tank, fanciest exhaust pipe cover, and dual seat.

In tune with the general trend of the motorcycle, a pressed-steel frame is employed as the back-bone of the main structure. Compared with the original tubular type of frames, the existing frame strikes the observer with more beauty and strength.

This paricular pressed-steel frame is fabricated by employment of a specially engineered process called STRESSPIN process. It is applied to the curved parts and on the other hand, the square parts are treated differently. Especially, for those parts where heavy loads are applied, the recently developed electric seam-welding processes are widely adopted to ensure improved dependability and longevity.

Thus, the frame of new engineering and superior workmanship provides trustworthy mounting for powerful engine and other important functional units.

A quick-starting push-botton type starting motor is a remarkable mechanical feature, eliminating completely the starting trouble accompanied by kickstarters. The engine can be started instantaneously by releasing the clutch, irrespective of the gear position. The starter-motor is so constructed and located that it is absolutely impervious to water and dirt.

The front-wheel suspension is of pivot-type leading link system.

The rear-wheel suspension is of pivot type cushion system. Extensive pressed-steel box below the dual seat accommodates the battery and rectifier. Accessories of the most comprehensive range are equipped, contributing to make the Dream fit for both city drive and off-highway trip.

YAMAHA "250S"

The Yamaha 250S has a de luxe specification, including two carburettors, five-speed transmission gear box, tachometer integral with speedometer and comprehensive tool kit.

The machine is powered by a two-stroke, two cylinder, air-cooled 250 c.c. engine developing 14.5 HP at 6,000 rpm. The engine is equipped with two carburettors—this is Yamaha's one of the many firsts in Japan—aiming at a higher performance at high-speed operation. Power production is particularly smooth and fluid. By dint of two carburettors connected directly with the engine cylinder, uniform distribution of

The machine is designed and constructed so as to give the rider a natural and relaxed pose. The values of caster and trail at higher speeds are appropriately determined, effecting a high standard of riding comfort and an excellent manoeuvability.

The Japan's first combination tachometer and speedometer, indicating engine revolution and running speed in a single meter, contributes to safe operation of the machine.

The most common and dependable type of steel tube frame is employed for this machine. however, a special attention has been paid for maintaining its rigidity not only in longitudinal direction, but also in the traverse direction. It also gives substantial mounting for the engine by means of supporting points located at the extreme ends of the cross member of the frame.

The front wheel is suspended by an orthodox type telescopic front fork and the rear wheel by swing arms cushioned by a telescopic hydraulic shock-absorber.

Extensive pressed-steel box below the dual seat

fuel is obtained, providing the engine with a high volumetric efficiency.

The transmission system embodies again the Japan's first five-speed gear box, affording a free selection of the best gear in conjunction with the road conditions and traffic situations. The acceleration is markedly vivid.

Strenuous efforts have been exercised for reducing the weight of the engine and light alloys are used in generous quantities.

The crank-case is made of magnesium alloy featuring lightness of weight and high strength.

accommodates the battery with transparent covering to prevent moisture and dirt.

Generous tool accommodation is another notable feature of this machine including, in addition to the common range of tools, a tirelever, grease-gun, air pump, etc., guaranteeing emergency repairs on the travels of long distance.

The manufacturer of the Yamaha 250S maintains an exhaustive stock of kit parts for racing enthusiasts, accordingly, these parts are available for purchase subject to application from the customer.

LILAC "LANCER MARK LS38"

To most Japanese motorists the name LILAC immediately brings to mind an exhilarating shaft-driven sport machine.

The particular machine is powered by a four-stroke, ohv, 247 c.c. engine with two cylinders in V arrangement, developing 20.3 HP at 8,000 rpm.

The basic idea underlying the design and construction of the machine is to offer a machine of combined advantages of a sport machine and a practical machine.

In addition to the traditional feature involving power transmission by shaft, the introduction of the parallel-vee engine became another distinctive features of this machine.

The vee-twin is, in accordance with modern practice, mounted in the frame so that the cylinders project sideways and receive an excellent cooling.

Another interesting feature of the engine is that two separate carburettors are employed for better fuel distribution and improved volumetric efficiency.

The specific power output has thus been increased to 81 HP/1 (compression ratio being 8.2:1), and the torque values turned out flatter.

Starting of the engine is made by a self-starting generating dynamo and the kickstarting is also available.

A four-speed transmission gear box with synchromesh is provided with a pilot lamp located on the handle bar indicating the position of neutral and the third gear.

The main structure of the machine is incorporated with steel tubes of elliptic cross-section, a single tank rail and two down-tubes being principal stress members.

The neat style of telescopic oleo-fork, is employed for the front wheel suspension and swing arms of ample dimension are provided for the rear suspension. Extra soft cushioning of the dual seat is assured by telescopic hydraulic shock-absorbers.

Dismounting of the wheels has exceptionally been facilitated by an ingenious method and the rear wheel can be detached only by removing the rear axle. The propeller shaft for driving the rear axle is contained in a rear fork. All the moving parts are perfectly enclosed, a feature entirely different from the conventional chain-driven motorcycles.

Full-width hubs are fitted to both front and rear wheels.

Some remarkable mechanical features are incorporated on this particularly sporty model; a flasher lamp is attached on either side of the headlamp in the front and a flasher lamp for the rear is integrated with the tail-lamp.

Especially, the front flasher lamps are coordinated with a buzzer, eliminating completely the possible hazzard occurred in connection with the failure of returning the flasher lamp. This is a newly developed arrangement in Japan.

The tool box fixed at the rear of the rear fender, another first attempt in Japan.

4-stroke engine

with speedometer

plate

RABBIT "SUPER FLOW"

Already well established in Japan, the latest Rabbit Super Flow 601 is a welcome addition to the market. Few of its competitors can equal its high-speed performance and pronounced ease of driving.

The machine is powered by a two-stroke, single cylinder, air-cooled 200 c.c. engine developing 11 HP at 5,500 rpm.

The bore and stroke is 65 mm×60 mm, an over-square engine indicating that much emphasis is placed on the performance at a higher speed.

In order to achieve smooth operation and driving economy, a special hydraulically operated torque converter is embodied in the power train, ensuring at the same time brisk starting and lively acceleration.

To most scooters and motorcycles gradual application of the power was very difficult to secure, because of the uneven contact of the clutch facing, however, this difficulty has completely been removed by the employment of the torque converter.

As far as the maximum speed is concerned, the Rabbit Super Flow 601 is one of a few scooters capable of producing 100 km/h speed.

Dependability and endurance of the torque converter is specially worthy of note, it is sufficient to replace converter oil at every 3,000 km for continued satisfactory operation. No refilling is necessary. Aluminium casing provided with fins of large cooling area prevents heating of the torque converter.

The engine starting is quick and sure by means of push-button type starter dynamo, eliminating starting trouble accompanied by the kickstarter.

The machine is admirably tailored, permitting the hands and wrists to assume a natural and relaxed pose that engenders in the rider a feeling of confidence.

Special efforts have been used for better riding comfort and absence of fatigue and the world's first air-suspension system is mounted. The so-called diaphragm type air-suspension system is composed of a steel cylinder and a rubber bag containing compressed air of 1.8 atmospheric pressure. Relatively large deflections obtainable with this suspension system provides the machine with the most effective vibration damping characteristics.

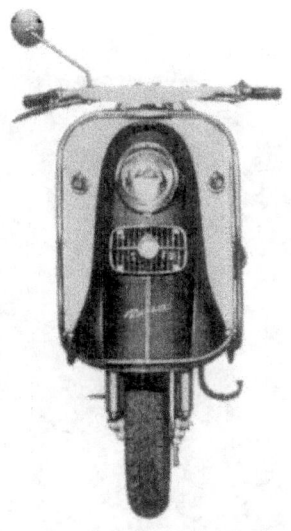

Frame is of composite tubular and pressed steel construction. The wide weathershield forms part of the main structure. The front-wheel suspension is by telescopic shock-absorber and the rear-wheel suspension by canti-lever type unit combined with the air-suspension system.

Conventional headlamp has been replaced by the sealed-beam headlamp embodied in the upper part of the front shield, a notable feature of reducing the muscular effort when moving the handlebar for steering.

The Rabbit Super Flow S601 is a luxury scooter well suited to suburban pottering, formidable hill-climbing and long distance touring.

The machine is equipped with comprehensive range of accessories to make the machine a tireless and trustworthy means of transportation.

Pandora

Yamaha Scooter

Yamaguchi Auto-Pet

Gasuden FMC

Colleda Ace 250 c.c.

Queen Sunlight

NISSAN PATROL

A 125HP engine powered Jeep-type vehicle can offer roominess, good performance and a high degree of power.

Both front and rear wheels are driven positively by individual propeller shafts, affording dependable operation even on the roughest off-highway activities. An optional winch with capacity of 1,500 kg and wire length of 45 m is available.

On a simple and robust ladder-type frame is mounted a pressed-steel constructed body with accommodating of two persons and 250 kg goods or six passengers.

Parallel troop seats providing seating for four-passengers can be folded up to secure ample loading area for goods up to 250 kg.

Front axle as well as rear axle is driven by engine power transmitted by the propeller shaft through the transfer case of the transmission system.

The P-type engine with a power output of 125 HP developes a maximum torque of 29 kgm. Four-speed transmission gear box with synchromesh engagement eliminates necessity of double clutching.

The vast versatility of usefulness of the vehicle is indicated by its ability of passing through water up to the depth of 700 mm. The electrical parts, inlet and exhaust pipes are all waterproof.

Outstanding mechanical features are waterproof engine, transmission gear box provided with all synchromesh four-speed gears, transfer case for front-wheel drive, adjustable front-seats and reclinable seat-backs, electrical system of 12 V., and sealed-beam type headlamps.

Principal applications of this vehicle are liason work in mountain districts and on rough terrain, transportation of goods and fire-fighting men, police patrol and snow removing work.

Over the back roads in a TOYOTA LAND CRUISER

BY M. A. ARVIN

By courtesy of the MOTOR LIFE, a noted monthly issued by Quinn Publications, Hollywood, this article has been reprinted from the September number, 1959.

For travel thrills there's nothing like a husky vehicle on primitive roads

Twenty-five miles away from us an asphalt strip was hot from the desert heat and the friction of thousands of screaming tires. It's the world's longest drag strip. Every week-end it operates at full capacity. On Friday nights and Saturday during the day, it runs from Los Angeles to Las Vegas. On Sunday it runs from Las Vegas to Los Angeles. Unaffectionately it's known as Highway 91. It typifies modern America in a hurry to play.

But as I said, I was twenty-five miles away from this frantic race and pace on a delightfully miserable road. I was behind the wheel of a Toyota Land Cruiser trying to get to Vegas on a dirt road.

I had carefully checked the maps and found we could make it via off-the-beaten-path dirt roads if we started from Lucerne Valley, some miles from Los Angeles.

The Toyota Land Cruiser is a much larger jeep than U.S. Jeeps, so we had plenty of room to carry suitcases, clothes, food, water, and extra gas.

We had no specific timetable except we figured it should take a day and a half of daytime driving. Most people make the run in five or six hours on the highway.

On the way to Lucerne Valley, we discovered a dirt road that falls off the top of the Sierra Madre Mountains straight down to the desert valley. Dropping rapidly through a scenic canyon, we got our "sea legs" for the rest of the trip. The Land Cruiser behaved marvellously; however, my wife did learn to appreciate the grab bar on the dash as we bumped our way down the mountain.

Back on the pavement, we cruised happily at sixty. Much more speed was available but we were in no hurry.

At Lucerne Valley we said good-bye to the pavement and drove off into what was unknown to us. We climbed the mountains and crossed desert valleys. The air was clear and you could see for hundreds of miles. The mountains took on the colors of the minerals and their jagged shapes were beautiful in their ugliness. For a hundred miles we bumped along not seeing a living soul.

We were quite enthusiastic about the Toyota. Its big 236-cubic-inch engine, which closely resembles the Chevy six, gave us no need for constant shifting of the four-speed box. Its fourwheel drive was easily engaged by a flip of a single lever and there was no need to stop or go into a compound gear which was handy when suddenly rounding a curve and finding a need for four-wheel drive.

The map shows three kinds of dirt roads—poor dirt roads, just plain dirt roads, and improved dirt road. We were coming to a stretch known as the Devil's Playground. We were looking forward to getting there, not only for its intriguing name but the map showed the road through this section as being improved. After bumping along on the back of our laps we would welcome some rest. Our improved dirt road turned out to be about as unimproved a road as you can find. In fact there was no road at all. The Devil's Playground was a series of steep and dunes. The road had simply disappeared. We could see where it took up again about a quarter of a mile away, but in between there was nothing but sand dunes. For staunch jeepers this would have been no obstacle. In fact sand dunes are considered fun, but we were not equipped with big enough tires for sand dunes travel. Most jeepers use big 8.00×13 tires. If they have a big six or V-8 engine they can go almost anywhere. The Toyota had the power, but it wasn't worth the risk of getting stuck in the middle of nowhere.

We turned back with thoughts of telling the map makers that things aren't what they used to be in the Devil's Playground. Our only choice, if we wanted to keep heading for Las Vegas, was to double back eighteen miles and then take off on a "poor road" which would connect to the highway to Las Vegas. This time the map was right. We travelled through the Mojave River sink which was all loose sand. We let the air down on the tires and charged on. The trucks in the "road" fanned out in many directions but I didn't dare slow down to make any decisions. We bounced furiously with complete concentration on not losing our momentum.

All of a sudden we came to an oasis in the form of a board road. All that was left intact and above the sand was a stretch eight feet long, but it was solid and it gave us a chance to catch our breath. People say that the only remnants of a board road are in the Yuma, Arizona, sand dunes. We were happy that they were wrong, However, it was getting dark so we couldn't enjoy our island too long.

Finally we got to the highway. While stopped at a service station to put air back in the tires, the station attendant bragged how a friend of his had used the same road a few days ago and only got stuck twice. We modestly told him that

TEST DATA

Test car: Toyota Land Cruiser FJ25
Body type: 4-passenger
Basic price: $2930
Engine: ohv inline 6
Displacement: 236.65 cubic inches
Bore and stroke: 3.5 in. × 4.0 in.
Compression ratio: 7.2 to 1
Horsepower per cubic inch: 51
Torque: 207 foot lbs. at 2,000 rpm
Weight: (curb) 3142 lbs.
Transmission: 4-speed, 4-wheel drive. Final axle ratio 4.11
Dimensions: overall length 153 in., width 65 in., height 72 in. Wheelbase 90 in. Tread 54.7 front, 53.2 rear
Springs: semi-elliptic
Tires: 6.00 × 16, 6 ply
Top speed: approximately 80 mph
Minimum ground clearance: 8¼ in.
Maximum side stability: right 45°, left 43° 50'
Power Take-Offs: Front, rear

the Toyota made it without getting stuck once. Immediately, the Toyota gained a new admirer.

Admitting defeat in making it all the way to Las Vegas on a dirt road, we continued the next day using some paved and some dirt roads. We saw some magnificent country that probably far less than one percent of the paved people will ever see. We also were made to admire the Toyota as a rugged, roomy roamer and considering its extra features it has a reasonable base price of $2930.

There's not an area of this big country of ours that doesn't have an ample supply of rugged back roads. If you are looking for excitement and fun on your next trip, take the dirt trails.

At the 1st Tokyo Motor Show in 1954, the interior of the entrance was set up with a stage. It was crowded every day with people who were anxious to enjoy hitsongs sung by popular singers.

TOKYO MOTOR SHOW

Perhaps the greatest annual event in the Japanese automobile calendar is the Tokyo Motor Show. This Show has been held annually since 1954 under the joint cooperation of practically all manufacturers of the Japanese motor industry.

The 6th Tokyo Motor Show was held in the exhibition buildings at the Harumi Fair Ground on October 24 to November 4, 1959. On display were more than 300 of the latest model cars, trucks, buses, three-wheelers, motorcycles and motor scooters together with many hundreds of parts, accessories and other allied products.

The exhibits were displayed in three buildings, classified into three groups: (1) passenger vehicles (cars, buses, motorcycles and motor scooters), (2) transport and cargo vehicles (trucks, three-wheelers and special purpose vehicles) and (3) parts, accessories and other allied products.

With the rapid growth of car registrations, great crowds thronged every inch of the floors everyday during the show. Total attendance was nearly 700,000 including many foreign visitors. The show received visits from about 100 members of the G. A. T. T. (General Agreement of Tariff and Trade) who were in Tokyo for a conference.

On Sundays and on a national holiday, there were as many as 100,000 visitors a day. Among the visitors were a large number of car-enthusiastic students and joyful children accompanying parents. So many people rushed to the show site that the police board mobilized a special team to control the congestion of traffic.

An attraction of the 6th Show was the offer by lottery of 25 vehicles, including 20 motorcycles and motor scooters to the paid attendance. This was the first attempt, but seems to have gained public favor.

The first Tokyo Motor Show was held at the

Hibiya Park Plaza in April, 1954. As no suitable facilities were available for so many vehicles and products, up to 1957 the show was held at the Hibiya Park Plaza every spring. In 1958, the show moved its site to the Korakuen Stadium and was held in the autumn.

With the permanent buildings constructed at the Harumi Fair Ground, the Tokyo Motor Show became a full-scale indoor exhibition for the first time in 1959.

The Tokyo Motor Show has contributed a great deal to not only manufacturers but also to the public in general. It is at this Show that people can take a general view of practically all the latest products of the Japanese motor industry and make a comparison of different makes of products.

Manufacturers can also make good use of the common media for public introduction of their up-to-date models. It is the best stage both for the public and manufacturers.

The Tokyo Motor Show has been held on a national—not international—scale and no foreign makes of vehicles have been displayed. It is expected, however, that the time will come very soon when foreign cars occupy places at the Tokyo Motor Show.

The photos in bird's-eye view are the Tokyo Motor Shows in 1955 (top) and 1956 (center) held at Hibiya Park Plaza. In 1956, various kinds of auto parts and accessories were displayed in the larger, round tent. The Show in 1957 (bottom) was set up at the same park with different design. The passenger cars found in the color plate were displayed on turning platforms, and mannequin girls introduced details of the cars.

The 5th Tokyo Motor Show was held at Korakuen Stadium situated in the center of Tokyo. On the diamond adjoining the Stadium, the final round of Japan series was being held, and the Show had 200,000 visitors a day. Since the 2nd Show in 1955, the Crown Prince has visited the Show every year, except 1959, the year when he was occupied with the affairs of his wedding ceremony.

The 6th Tokyo Motor Show was held at Harumi Fair Ground in the autumn of 1959. The 30 meters high arch in front of the entrance (above) was a gluede laminated wooden arch, constructed by the Hokkaido Mill of Mitsui Lumber Industry, Ltd. The Show occupied the 1st, 2nd and 3rd Halls. The 2nd Hall is of a mammoth dome with 100 meter in diameter. The 3rd Hall is named Swan Hall, a floating building on the water, and auto parts and accessories were displayed there.

In the 1st Hall (above), utilizing a former airplane shed, trucks of various sizes from 350 kg to 15 tons were exhibited. In the 2nd Hall (right and left) cars were displayed in the center surrounded by buses, motorcycles and motor scooters, classified in group by makers. On Sunday, the number of visitors exceeded 100,000, and the avenue from Ginza street to Harumi were thronged by cars, and police officers were mobilized for controling traffic congestion.

The interior of the dome presented a beautiful sight bathing the sun beams through the skylight in the center of the ceiling. The show had nearly 700,000 visitors in total including a great number of foreigners. The members of GATT (below) inspected the display warmly for as long as two hours.

NOTES

Principal Automobile Makers in Japan

On the following pages, principal automobile makers in Japan are introduced in compliance with their requests. A brief history, president's name, head office, export division, plant, etc. of each company are described together with addresses. Main products, brand names and the company's mark are also introduced.

A complete list of the manufacturers of automobiles, auto-bodies and automobile parts who are the members of respective Associations is put at the end of this book.

―― In Alphabetical Order ――

Aichi Machine Industry Co., Ltd.
Daihatsu Kogyo Kabushiki Kaisha
Fuji Heavy Industries, Ltd.
Fuji Precision Machinery Co , Ltd.
Hino Motors, Ltd.
Hirano Seisakusho, Ltd.
Honda Motor Co., Ltd.
Isuzu Motor Co., Ltd.
Marusho Motorcycle Industrial Co., Ltd.
Meguro Manufacturing Co., Ltd.
Minsei Diesel Engineering Co., Ltd.
Mitsubishi Heavy Industries, Reorganized, Co., Ltd.
Mitsubishi Nippon Heavy-Industries, Ltd.
Mitsui Precision Machinery & Engineering Co., Ltd.
Nissan Motor Co., Ltd.
Ryowa Motor Sales Co., Ltd.
Shin Meiwa Industry Co., Ltd.
Showa Works, Ltd.
Suzuki Motor Co., Ltd.
Tokyo Hatsudoki Co., Ltd.
Tokyu Kurogane Motor Co., Ltd.
Toyo Kogyo Co., Ltd.
Toyota Motor Co., Ltd.
Yamaguchi Bicycle Manufacturing Co., Ltd.
Yamaha Motorcycle Co., Ltd.

AICHI MACHINE INDUSTRY CO., LTD.

This company was formed in result of reorganization of the Aichi Aircraft Co. (alias Aichi Kigyo Kaisha) which had been engaged in the manufacture of aircraft for the Japanese Navy before the war. Its line today is production and sales of mostly three wheelers and light motor vehicles, producing monthly 400 three-wheelers, 1,000 light four-wheelers and 1,000 farm gasoline engines.

Nagoya Main Plant

Giant Stand at 6th Tokyo Motor Show

President
Tokuichiro Gomei
Head Office
1, 6-chome, Ichibancho, Atsuta-ku, Nagoya
Telephone: (66) 0151
Cable Address: GIANT NAGOYA
Export Department
In the Head Office
Branch Offices
Tokyo Branch—Nagoya-Shokokan Bldg.,
5, Nishi 4-chome, Ginza, Chuo-ku, Tokyo
Kanagawa Office—54, 2-chome, Ogimachi,
Naka-ku, Yokohama
Fukui Office—Inuishimomachi, Fukui
Shikoku Office—6, 6-chome, Kameicho, Takamatsu
Plant
1, 6-chome, Ichibancho, Atsuta-ku, Nagoya
Main Products
Three-wheelers "GIANT" & "CONY"

Cony 360
Cony AA 29
Giant AA 24LHS
Giant AA 24T

CONY 360

102

DAIHATSU KOGYO KABUSHIKI KAISHA

This company was founded in March, 1907, to make internal combustion engine under the title of the Hatsudoki Seizo Kaisha (Engine Mfg. Co., Ltd.) which was changed to the present name in 1951.

Although the first three-wheeler was made in 1930, it was in 1957 when the company embarked in large scale in the new field of light three- and four-wheeled trucks which have been growing steadily in sales.

The capital of this company at present amounts to ¥3,000 million, and the average annual sales are about ¥20,000 million. The number of employees totals about 4,000.

The output of the company for the year ending April 30, 1959, is as follows:

Three-wheeled trucks	45,468 units
Light four-wheeled trucks	1,156 units
Diesel engines	37,609 HP

President
Yuji Koishi

Head Office
3, 2-chome, Daini Higashi, Oyodo-ku, Osaka
Telephone: (45) 2551
Cable Address: DAIHATSU OSAKA

Export Department
In the Head Office & Tokyo Office

Business Offices
Tokyo Office—7, 2-chome, Honcho, Nihonbashi, Chuo-ku, Tokyo
Fukuoko Office—Babashinmachi, Fukuoka
Sapporo Branch—7, Nishi-3-chome, Minami-Shichijo, Sapporo
Nagoya Branch—33, 2-chome, Oikemachi, Naka-ku, Nagoya

Plants
Ikeda Plant—1,170, Momozonocho, Ikeda City, Osaka Pref.
Tokyo Plant—48, 1-chome, Minami-Rokugo, Ota-ku, Tokyo
Shimonoseki Plant—17, Higashi-Yamatocho, Shimonoseki City

Main Products
Three-wheelers "DAIHATSU" & "MIDGET"
Four-wheeled truck "VESTA"

Daihatsu Vesta FPOL
Daihatsu Vesta FPO
Daihatsu Vacuum Car FPOE
Daihatsu FPOD
Daihatsu Midget DK-2 Standard
Daihatsu Midget MPA Handy Wagon
Daihatsu Midget DK-2 Station Wagon
Daihatsu Midget Light Van
Daihatsu Midget DK-2 Canvas Van
Daihatsu Midget DK-2 Panel Van
Daihatsu Midget MPA Mail Van
Daihatsu SKC-7
Daihatsu PL-7
Daihatsu PF 8-TL
Daihatsu PM10
Daihatsu PO13-T
Daihatsu Dump Truck PO 8-D
Daihatsu Fire Engine
Daihatsu Pack Master
Daihatsu Tractor & Trailer

DAIHATSU
MIDGET
VESTA

Osaka Main Plant

Assembly Line of 3-wheeler

Smaller Truck "MIDGET"

FUJI HEAVY INDUSTRY, LTD.

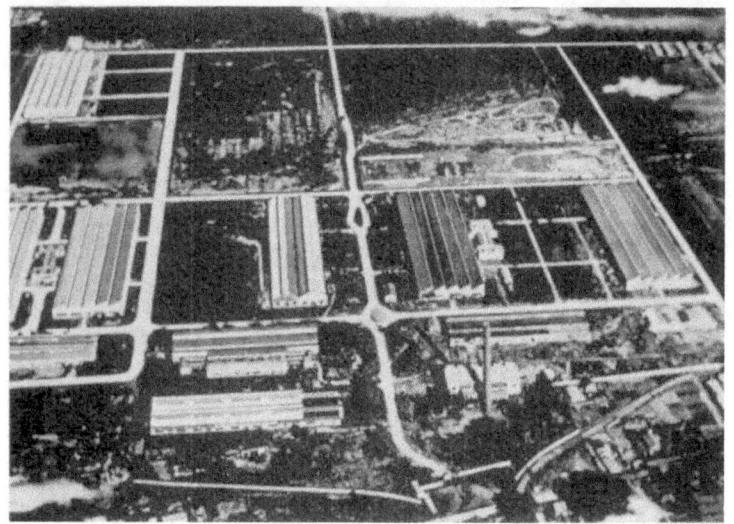

Omiya Plant

Isezaki Plant

The history of this firm dates back to 1917, the year when a laboratory on aircraft was founded at Ohta-machi, Gunma Pref. by the late Mr. Chikuhei Nakajima.

A rapid growth was made by the company under the title of Nakajima Aircraft Industry, Ltd. during the period between 1931 to 1940 as an aircraft maker. After Japan's surrender, Nakajima Aircraft was dissolved to form twelve separate new firms, but Fuji Heavy Industries, Ltd. was formed on July 15, 1953 as a joint venture of some of these five new firms with the capital of ¥50 million fully paid. On April 1, 1955, these five companies were amalgamated with paid-up capital increased to ¥830.5 million.

President
Takao Yoshida
Head Office
18, 2-chome, Marunouchi, Chiyoda-ku, Tokyo
Telephone: (281) 3551
Cable Address: FUJIHEAVY TOKYO
Export Department
In the Head Office
Business Offices
Tokyo Office—10, Toranomon, Minato-ku, Tokyo
Osaka Office—Gosho Bldg., 25, 2-chome, Nakanoshima, Kita-ku, Osaka
Sapporo Branch—Sassho Bldg., 2, Nishi 4-chome, Kitaichijo, Sapporo
Sendai Branch—Tohoseimei Bldg., 35, Minamicho, Sendai
Nagoya Branch—Shin Nagoya Bldg., 19, 3-chome, Hirokojidori, Nakamura-ku, Nagoya
Hiroshima Branch—Hatasho Bldg., 44, Ebisumachi, Hiroshima
Fukuoka Branch—National Bldg., 26, Tsujinodo, Fukuoka
Plants
Mitaka Plant—1,439, Osawa, Mitaka City, Tokyo
Omiya Plant—1, Kamomiyacho, Omiya City, Saitama Pref.
Ota Plant—747, Ota, Ota City, Gunma Pref.
Isezaki Plant—100, Suehirocho, Isezaki City, Gunma Pref.
108, Asahimachi, Isezaki City, Gunma Pref.
Utsunomiya Plant—680, Nishiharamachi, Utsunomiya City
Main Products
Motor scooter "RABBIT", small-sized car "SUBARU 360"

Subaru 360
Rabbit Minor S-201
Rabbit Junior S-82S
Rabbit Superflow S-601

SUBARU 360 at 6th Tokyo Motor Show

FUJI PRECISION MACHINERY CO., LTD.

Formed in July, 1950, this company started production of precision equipments such as sewing machine, farm diesel engine and projector (cinema) at Tokyo and Hamamatsu factories which were formerly operated by the now defunct Nakajima Aircraft Industry, Ltd.

Next year (1951), the company added to its product list 1,500 c.c. engines for "Prince" cars and marked its first step into motor industry.

Since 1952, the company reopened its activity as an aircraft maker by taking up repair and overhauling of aircraft engines, and in 1953, started production of jet engine parts as one of the member of Japan Jet Engine Mfg. Co., Ltd.

In the same year, the company started pilot production of rockets, and paved the way for the company to build "Kappa" rocket which played an important part in research by scientists in the International Earth Observation Year.

In April, 1954, the company absorbed by purchase Prince Motor Co., Ltd. and began to put the Prince cars on production stream.

In April, 1957, the company introduced into the market "Skyline" model and established a firm standing in the motor industry.

Ogikubo Plant

Mitaka Plant

President
Ino Dan
Head Office
88, Shukumachi, Suginami-ku, Tokyo
Telephone: (398) 1911
Export Department
Bridgestone Bldg., 1, 1-chome, Kyobashi, Chuo-ku, Tokyo
Telephone: (561) 6256
Cable Address: PRINCEAUTOEX TOKYO
Plants
Ogikubo Plant—33, Shukumachi, Suginami-ku, Tokyo
Mitaka Plant—997, Kamirenjaku, Mitaka City, Tokyo
Main Products
Passenger car "PRINCE" Skyline de Luxe & Standard; Trucks "PRINCE" New Miler & Clipper; Light van "PRINCE" Skyway

Prince Gloria BLSI
Prince Skyline Deluxe ALSID
Prince skyline ALSIE (Export Model)
Prince Skyline Standard ALSIS
Prince Micro Bus AQVH-B
Prince Skyway Light Van ALVG
Prince Route Van AQVH
Prince New Miler Light Van ARVE
Prince Skyway Pack-Up ALPE
Prince Clipper AQTI
Prince New Miler ARTH
Prince Clipper Vacuum CAR
Prince New Miler Vacuum Car
Prince Clipper

PRINCE SKYLINE at 6th Tokyo Motor Show

HINO MOTORS, LTD.

Hino Main Plant

Embarked in 1917 as a pioneer in the automotive industry, the company by 1942 had become Japan's leading specialized manufacturer of diesel-powered vehicles. The company's first truck, the 4-ton "Chiyoda," produced in 1917 at its Ohmori Plant, was the very first of the kind built in Japan. In 1940 the plant was moved to the present site in Hino, suburbs of Tokyo, for expansion required, and ever since the plant facilities have been constantly improved to meet the up-to date requirement.

Right after World War II, in line with the Japanese Government policy, Hino developed Japan's first large-sized trailer buses and trucks. Later in 1950, the company succeeded in making large-sized buses, trucks and various other heavy-duty motor vehicles. In 1952 the company started the manufacture of French "Renault" passenger car.

Engine Shop

President
Shoji Okubo
Head Office
Hino Bldg., 4, Tori 2-chome, Nihonbashi, Chuo-ku, Tokyo
Telephone : (201) 0441
Export Division
Hino Motor Sales, Ltd.—Hino Bldg., 4, Tori 2-chome,
Nihonbashi, Chuo-ku, Tokyo
Telephone : (201) 0441
Cable Address : HINODIECO TOKYO
Business Office
Hino Bldg., 4, Tori 2-chome, Nihonbashi, Chuo-ku, Tokyo
Plant
7,319, Hino-machi, Minamitama-gun, Tokyo
Main Products
"HINO" Diesel buses, trucks, dump trucks, tank lorries, tractor-trailer trucks, trolly buses & other utility vehicles.
"HINO" Diesel engines for construction, marine & stationary equipment. "HINO RENAULT" car

HINO COMMERCE at 6th Tokyo Motor Show

Renault Hino PA
Hino BD
Hino BG
Hino Bus Chassis BG
Hino Commerce Mini Bus
Hino Commerce Van
Hino TH
Hino TE
Hino TA
Hino ZG
Hino ZH

HIRANO SEISAKUSHO, LTD.

Established in 1920 as a loom maker, the company has supplied hundreds of thousand units of HIRANO LOOM to home and overseas markets such as Hongkong, Pakistan, Near and Middle East and Latin American countries.

After World War II, the company commenced production of motor scooter, gasoline engines, etc. The company had a long established technical background and excellent engineers in pre-war days, and promptly succeeded especially in the production of motor scooters.

The company produces at present four types of motor scooters—175 c.c., 125 c.c., 78 c.c. and 50 c.c. models.

Nagoya Main Plant

HIRANO POPET at 6th Tokyo Motor Show

President
Seijiro Aoyama
Head Office
1, Tamafunecho, Nakagawa-ku, Nagoya
Telephone : (66) 0141
Export Department
In the Head Office
Cable Address : HIRANOLOOM NAGOYA
In the Tokyo Branch
Telephone : (571) 6870–6872
Cable Address : HIRANOLOOM TOKYO
Business Offices
Tokyo Branch—3, Nishi 7-chome, Ginza, Chuo-ku, Tokyo
Osaka Office—22, Shiochodori, Minami-ku, Osaka
Plants
39, 2-chome, Showabashidori, Nakagawa-ku, Nagoya
Main Products
Motor scooters "TOP MANLEE"

Hirano Popet
Hirano Pop Manlee FN 125
Hirano Pop Manlee FN 175

HONDA MOTOR CO., LTD.

Hamamatsu Plant

Saitama Plant

HONDA DREAM at 6th Tokyo Motor Show

This company was established in 1948 and succeeded the property and technical personnel of Honda Technological Laboratory which were specialized in research of internal combustion engine vehicles.

Started production of "Dream" motorcycles in August, 1949, and its output now amounts to 5,500 units monthly. In September, 1952, the company commenced production of farm engines.

"Benly" motorcycle was introduced to the market in June, 1953, and this type is at present the main product of this company selling 7,500 units each month. Motorcycle "Super Cub," put in production stream in August, 1957, is now being produced at 10,000 units monthly.

In April, 1959, "Benly Super Sports" and "Farm Engine F150" were put on production line. In June, U.S. Honda was opened in Los Angels, Cal. In June, 1959, the company's motorcycle joined T. T. Race for the first time and awarded "Maker Prize."

President
Soichiro Honda
Head Office
7, 5-chome, Yaesu, Chuo-ku, Tokyo
Telephone: (281) 7331
Export Department
In the Head Office
Cable Address: HONDAMOTOR TOKYO
Branch Offices
Tokyo Branch—7, 5-chome, Yaesu, Chuo-ku, Tokyo
Nagoya Branch—9, 3-chome, Tokodori, Showa-ku, Nagoya
Osaka Branch—3, 12-chome, Minamiogimachi, Kita-ku, Osaka
Kyushu Branch—80, 1-chome, Daimyocho, Fukuoka
Hokkaido Branch—Hokken Bldg., 2, Nishi 3-chome, Kitaichijo, Sapporo
Sendai Branch—Yasuda Bldg., 51, Higashi 4-bancho, Sendai
Plants
Saitama Works—4,560, Niikura, Yamatomachi, Saitama Pref.
Hamamatsu Works—34, Aoicho, Hamamatsu City, Shizuoka Pref.
Technological Laboratory—1,319, Shirako, Yamatomachi, Saitama Pref.
Main Products
Motorcycles "DREAM", "BENLY" & "SUPER CUB"

Honda Super Cub C-100
Honda Benly C-92
Honka Dream CS-71

ISUZU MOTOR CO., LTD.

This company was formed in 1949 under the present name by Tokyo Motor Industry, Ltd. This Tokyo Motor was incorporated in 1937, combining the motor divisions of the two companies, Ishikawajima Shipbuilding and Engineering Co., Ltd. and Tokyo Gas and Electric Engineering Co., Ltd. who started production of motor vehicles as early as in 1916.

The company has been specialized in production of trucks and buses ranging from 5 to 6 tons. But in the spring of 1959, larger (8 tons) trucks and buses were put on production line, and later in the fall of the same year a group of smaller (2 tons) trucks and buses were added. Thus, the company is now in a position to supply motor vehicles of all sizes and types.

The company's annual output now exceeds 50% of all diesel motor vehicles yearly produced in Japan, and its products are exported to more than 30 different overseas countries.

President
Goro Sannomiya
Head Office
2,691, Oi-Sakashitacho, Shinagawa-ku, Tokyo
Telephone : (761) 0121, 2121
Cable Address : ISUZU TOKYO
Export Department
In the Head Office
Branch Offices
Osaka Branch—Umeda Bldg., 7, Umeda, Kita-ku, Osaka
Kyushu Branch—Nissanseimeikan, 23, Gofukucho, Fukuoka
Tohoku Branch—Shin Sendai Bldg., 175, 4-chome, Omachi, Sendai
Nagoya Branch Shin Nagoya Bldg., 19, 3-chome, Hirokoji Nishidori, Nakamura-ku, Nagoya
Hokkaido Branch Sasseki Bldg., 8, Nishi 3-chome, Minami-ichijo, Sapporo
Plants
Kawasaki Works—5,931, Shimotonomachi, Daishigawara, -Kawasaki City, Kanagawa Pref.
Tsurumi Works—4, 2-chome, Suehirocho, Tsurumi-ku, Yokohama
Sueyoshi Works—765, Shimo-sueyoshicho, Tsurumi-ku, Yokohama
Omori Works—2,691, Oi-sakashitacho, Shinagawa-ku, Tokyo
Main Products
"ISUZU" & "FLF" Buses, trucks, dump trucks, fire engines & other utility vehicles. "ISUZU" Diesel & gasoline engines for generating, farm, construction & marine equipment

Hillman Minx de Luxe
Isuzu BA 540
Isuzu BC 150
Isuzu BX 550
Isuzu BB 550 Bus Chassis
Isuzu BX 540 Bus Chassis
Isuzu Elf Micro Bus TL 221
Isuzu Elf TL 251
Isuzu TX 550
Isuzu TX 640-W
Isuzu TW 540
Isuzu TD 150
Isuzu Fire Fighting TX 440
Isuzu TD 140
Iszu TS 540

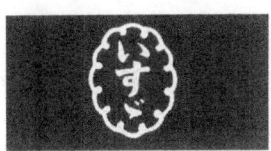 

Kawasaki Plant

Assembly Line

HILLMAN MINX at 6th Tokyo Motor Show

MARUSHO MOTORCYCLE INDUSTRIAL CO., LTD.

Since its formation in May, 1948, the company has made steady progress as a motorcycle maker. The annual production at present totals 1,000 units, that is 250 c.c. model 600 units and 125 c.c. model 400 units.

The company is now hurrying expansion of its production facilities, which are expected to be completed by April, 1960. By this expansion, the company's output will be increased to total 2,300 units per year, namely 300 c.c. model 300 units, 250 c.c. model 1,000 units and 125 c.c. model 1,000 units. The company now produces six different models of motorcycles.

Main Plant

Assembly Line

President
Masashi Ito
Head Office
2, 2-chome, Takaracho, Chuo-ku, Tokyo
Telephone : (561) 1491–6
Cable Address : LILACMOTOR TOKYO
Export Department
In the Head Office
Branch Offices
Tokyo Branch—2, 2-chome, Takaracho, Chuo-ku, Tokyo
Nagoya Branch—83, Shimomaezu, Naka-ku, Nagoya
Osaka Branch—38, Satsumabori-Higashinomachi, Nishi-ku, Osaka
Kyushu Branch—25, Myorakuji, Fukuoka
Plant
413, Moritamachi, Hamamatsu City, Shizuoka Pref.
Main Products
Motorcycles "LILAC"

Lilac CS 28
Lilac LS 16
Lilac LS 38

LILAC at 6th Tokyo Motor Show

MEGURO MANUFACTURING CO., LTD.

This company was established in 1924, as a pioneer in Japan's motorcycle industry. The list of products includes motorcycles, engines and parts, etc., but at present the company is concentrating its activity in the production of the Meguro motorcycles.

The General Headquarters of the Occupation Forces bought about 200 Meguro motorcycles; this figure represents 98% of the total motorcycle purchases they made in Japan. Meguro motorcycles are available in six models, ranging from 125 c.c. to 650 c.c. and total monthly output is 1,500 to 1,800 units.

As regular customers, the company has the National and Metropolitan Police, Asahi Newspaper, etc.

President
Nobuji Murata
Head Office
575, 3-chome, Osaki-Honcho, Shinagawa-ku, Tokyo
Telephone : (491) 3191
Export Department
In the Head Office
Plants
Main Plant—575, 3-chome, Osaki-Honcho, Shinagawa-ku, Tokyo
Karasuyama Plant—495, Karasuyamamachi, Nasu-gun, Tochigi Pref.
Main Products
Motorcycles "MEGURO"

Meguro Cadet CA
Meguro Junior S 5
Meguro YA
Meguro Stamina Z 7

MEGURO STAND at 6th Tokyo Motor Show

MEGURO STAMINA for Patrol

MEGURO CADET at 6th Tokyo Motor Show

MINSEI DIESEL ENGINEERING CO., LTD.

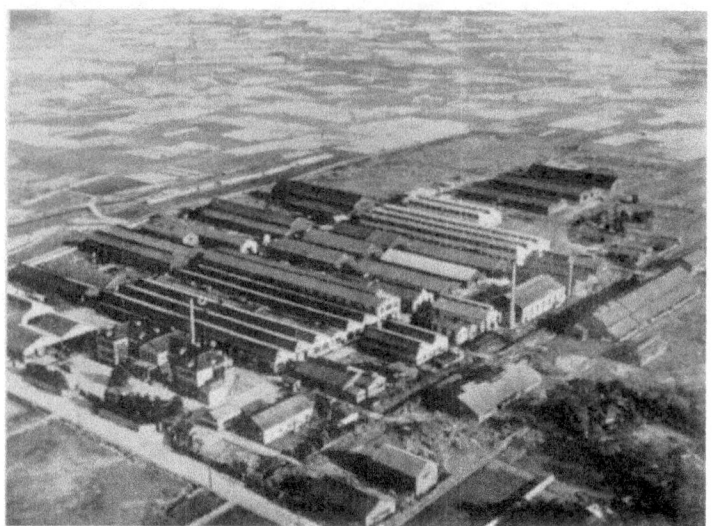

Kawaguchi Main Plant

Assembly Line

MINSEI STAND at 6th Tokyo Motor Show

The company was organized in 1935, under the name of Nippon Diesel Engineering Co., Ltd. In 1946, the company built "Condor" bus BR-31, the first integral and rear-engined bus in Japan.

After several years of intense researches and development works, the company produced, in 1955, a new excellent engine Model UD.

In 1956, the largest bus in Japan (equipped with 230 b.h.p. engine, developing maximum speed up to 120 km/h) was completed. In 1957, rear-engined bus, adopting air-suspension system, was built by the company.

Nissan-Minsei Diesel Sales Co., Ltd. was formed in July, 1955, under joint capital of Nissan Motor Co., Ltd. and Minsei Diesel Engineering Co., Ltd.

President
Yoshiyasu Watanabe
Head Office
253, Yaheicho, Kawaguchi City, Saitama Pref.
Telephone : Kawaguchi (082) 3131
Export Division
Export Department, Nissan-Minsei Diesel Sales Co., Ltd.
Kobundo Bldg., 4, 4-chome, Kanda Surugadai,
Chiyoda-ku, Tokyo
Telephone : (251) 2191-5
Cable Address : NISMINDS TOKYO
Business Office
Nissan-Minsei Diesel Sales Co., Ltd.
2, 2-chome, Kanda Tsukasacho, Chiyoda-ku, Tokyo
And its 58 agents throughout Japan
Plant
253, Yaheicho, Kawaguchi City, Saitama Pref.
Main Products
"MINSEI" Diesel trucks, buses & engines

Minsei B80
Minsei "Condor" RF 91
Minsei "Condor" 6RFL-101 A
Minsei RX 102
Minsei T80 (truck)
Minsei T80 (tank lorry)
Minsei Discharging Tower Vehicle T80-S
Minsei T80-S

MITSUBISHI HEAVY INDUSTRIES, REORGANIZED, CO., LTD.

This company manufactures bus body, Jeep and motor scooter at its Nagoya Works and three- and four-wheelers at its Mizushima Works.

The Nagoya Works was built as the main plant of the Mitsubishi Internal Combustion Engine Mfg. Co., which was afterward made Mitsubishi Aircraft Industries, Ltd., and produced aircraft and aircraft engine. After World War II, the company embarked in motor vehicle field.

The Mizushima Works was constructed in 1940, as an expansion plan of Mitsubishi Aircraft Industries, and after the war started production of three-wheeled motor vehicles. "Jupiter" medium truck and "Leo" light three-wheeler were introduced to the market in April, 1959, by this company.

Steady increase has been seen in the output of motor vehicles, and the output represents 23% of all products made by this company. Motor scooters rank the top followed by three-wheelers, Jeeps and bus bodies.

The completion of pilot product of light car "Mitsubishi 500" was announced in October, 1959, and this new car will be put in the market in the beginning of 1960.

Nagoya Main Plant

Jeep Assembly Line

President
Yoshito Yoshida
Head Office
10, 2-chome, Marunouchi, Chiyoda-ku, Tokyo
Telephone: (211) 3411
Cable Address: HISHIJU TOKYO
Export Department
In the Head Office
Business Offices
Tokyo Office—Motorcar Marketing Department
in the Head Office
Osaka Office—Daiichi-Seimei Bldg., 2, Umeda, Kita-ku, Osaka
Plants
Nagoya Works—2, Oemachi, Minato-ku, Nagoya
Mizushima Works—87, Mizushima-Takasagocho,
Kurashiki City, Okayama Pref.
Kyoto Works—1, Uzumasa-Tatsumicho, Ukyo-ku, Kyoto
Main Products
Bus & car bodies, "MITSUBISHI Jeep", trucks "JUPITER",
three-wheelers "MITSUBISHI TM" & "PET LEO",
small-sized car "MITSUBISHI 500"

Mitsubishi 500
Mitsubishi Pet Leo Standard LT10
Mitsubishi Pet Leo Light Van LT11
Mitsubishi Pet Leo Canvas Van LT10
Mitsubishi TM 15-F
Mitsubishi TM 18-BH
Mitsubishi "Jupiter" T10-DA·T11-GA
Mitsubishi "Jupiter" T11-GBH
Mitsubishi "Jupiter" T22-DBH
Mitsubishi "Jeep" CJ-3B-J10
Mitsubishi "Jeep" CJ-3B-J3
Mitsubishi "Jeep" CJ-3B-J10
Mitsubishi "Jupiter" T22 D-D
Silver Pigeon C-300
Silver Pigeon C-200
Silver Pigeon C-110

MITSUBISHI 500 at 6th Tokyo Motor Show

Kawasaki Main Plant

MITSUBISHI FUSO Bus for Chile

MITSUBISHI FUSO TRUCK at 6th Tokyo Motor Show

MITSUBISHI NIPPON HEAVY INDUSTRIES, LTD.

This company is one of the manufacturing companies formed in result of the dissolution of the Mitsubishi Heavy Industries, Ltd., the largest heavy industrial enterprise in this country, taking over from the latter top class engineers and the most modern production facilities.

In addition to buses, trucks and heavy-duty vehicles as shown elsewhere in this book, the company can boast of a vast fields of activities, including manufacture of all types of diesel engine, boiler and other industrial machinery as well as building and repairing of ocean going vessels.

Its products, motor-vehicles and construction machinery, are highly evaluated by their users for their excellent performance and for high economy.

A big shipment of 600 buses was made to Chile a couple of years ago, and the company's Overseas Department is booking export orders from buyers in Central and Latin American countries as well as Egypt, Spain and other countries.

President
Toshiki Sakurai
Head Office
4, 2-chome, Marunouchi, Chiyoda-ku, Tokyo
Telephone : (281) 2351
Cable Address : BISHINIPPON TOKYO
Telex : TK2282 BISIJUKO
Export Department
In the Head Office
Business Offices
Mitsubishi Fuso Motors, Ltd. (Home Agency)
15, 4-chome, Honshiba, Minato-ku, Tokyo
Its branch offices & sales agents throughout Japan
Plants
Tokyo Works—321, Shimo-marukomachi, Ota-ku, Tokyo
Maruko Plant—In the Tokyo Works
Kawasaki Plant—526, Kashimada, Kawasaki City, Kanagawa Pref.
Oi Plant—5,600, Oi-morimaecho, Shinagawa-ku, Tokyo
Main Products
" MITSUBISHI FUSO " buses, trucks, dump & tractor trucks, tank lorries, truck crane, tractor shovel, " MITSUBISHI " bulldozers, motor graders & scrapers, snow plow & other utility vehihcles. Diesel engines for vehicles & construction machines

Mitsubishi Fuso　B520
Mitsubishi Fuso　R710
Mitsubishi Fuso　T33
Mitsubishi Fuso　T320-D
Mitsubishi Fuso　W11-D
Mitsubishi Fuso　T52
Mitsubishi Fuso Concrete Mixer　T320
Mitsubishi Fuso Truck Tractor　W21
Mitsubishi Fuso Truck Tractor　T350
Mitsubishi Fuso Truck Crane　T360
Mitsubishi Fuso Truck Crane　W25A
Mitsubishi Motor Scraper　WTS
Mitsubishi Motor Grader　LGII
Mitsubishi Tractor Shovel　BS30
Mitsubishi Bulldozer　BE10
Mitsubishi Bulldozer　BF

 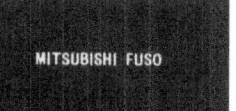

MITSUI PRECISION MACHINERY & ENG. CO., LTD.

Founded in December, 1928, under the name of Tsugami Seisakusho, the company was later reorganized and named Mitsui Precision Machinery & Eng. Co., Ltd.

The main line was the manufacture of high precision engineering machinery, guages and tools, but after the end of World War II, the company newly added manufacture of three-wheeled trucks, various types of compressors and refrigerators in its line.

Owing to their novel design and powerful engines, the company's "Orient" brand three-wheeler and "Humbee" light three-wheeler are enjoying an extensive popularity in spite of competition from older brands, along with the active sales in other high precision machinery.

President
Masanobu Matsukata
Head Office
3, 3-chome, Muromachi, Nihonbashi, Chuo-ku, Tokyo
Telephone: (241) 2251, 2261, 3261, 2351
Export Division
Export Department, Hino Motor Sales, Ltd.
4, Tori 2-chome, Nihonbashi, Chuo-ku, Tokyo
Cable Address: HINODECO TOKYO
Telephone: (201) 0441
Business Office
Orient Divsion, Hino Motor Sales, Ltd.
4, Tori 2-chome, Nihonbashi, Chuo-ku, Tokyo
Plant
Okegawa Plant —101, Okegawa, Okegawamachi, Kita-adachi-gun, Saitama Pref.
Main Products
Three wheeled trucks "ORIENT" & "HUMBEE"

Humbee EF 11
Humbee Light Van EF11
Humbee Surry EF11

Okekawa Main Plant

Assembly Line

HUMBEE at 6th Tokyo Motor Show

Yokohama Main Plant

Assembly Line of Truck

DATSUN BLUEBIRD at 6th Tokyo Motor Show

NISSAN MOTOR CO., LTD.

This company was incorporated on December 26, 1933 in Yokohama and commenced the production of Datsun cars. In twenty seven years since, the company has grown into the top-ranking motor manufacturer with its paid-up capital amounting to ¥6,930 million.

The list of its products includes "Nissan" trucks and buses, "Datsun" cars, etc. The company's monthly output averages about 7,500 units in total including all different types.

In December, 1952, an agreement for assembly and manufacture of Austin Motor Vehicles (A-40 Somerset Saloon) was concluded between the company and the Austin Motor Company, England.

In December, 1957, an agreement for assembly and manufacture of Nissan vehicles was made between the Yue Loong Engineering Company in Formosa and the company.

In July, 1958, distributor agreements were concluded between the Luby Datsun Distributors, Ltd. of New York and the Western Datsun Distributors, Ltd. of Los Angeles and the company respectively.

Its main works are located at Yokohama, Tsurumi and Yoshiwara. The number of employees totals 8,335 and the annual sales of the company amount to about ¥50,000 million.

President
Katsuji Kawamata
Head Office
2, Takaracho, Kanagawa-ku, Yokohama
Telephone : (44) 2331
Export Department
Otemachi Bldg., 4, 1-chome, Otemachi, Chiyoda-ku, Tokyo
Cable Address : NISMO TOKYO
Telephone : (201) 5831
Business Office
Same as Export Department
Plants
Yokohama Plant—Shinkoyasu, Yokohama
Yoshiwara Plant—Yoshiwara City, Shizuoka Pref.
Main Products
"NISSAN" Trucks & Buses (standard-sized, gasoline & diesel),
Carriers & Patrols (4-wheel drive),
Junior Trucks (medium-sized, gasoline),
"DATSUN" Cars & Trucks (small-sized, gasoline)

Datsun Bluebird P310-U
Datsun Sports Car S211
Austin A50 de Luxe
Nissan UG 690
Nissan Junior Micro Buz KC 42
Datsun 4-Door Station Wagon WP 211
Datson 2-door Station Wagon VG 221
Datsun Ranch Sedan UP 221
Datsun Pick-Up PG 222-U
Nissan Junior Caball C 43
Nissan Junior B 42 Nissan G 680
Nissan UG 680 Nissan TG 680
Nissan F 680 Nissan Junior FRB 42
Nissan Patrol Station Wagon W 4W65
Nissan Patrol 4W 66 Nissan Carrier 4W 73
Nissan DG 680 Nissan DUG 680

RYOWA MOTOR SALES CO., LTD.

This is an exclusive distributor of "Mitsubishi Jeep," medium-size truck "Jupiter" and a small-size car "Mitsubishi 500" manufactured by Mitsubishi Heavy Industries, Reorganized, ltd. who began production of Jeeps under agreement with Willy, since 1953.

The company has sold so far more than 20,000 Jeeps to Self-Defence Force and U.S. Army stationed in Japan.

In 1958, Mitsubishi purchased from Willys the right to produce Jeep, and since then this company shipped a large number of Jeeps to overseas markets.

In addition to "Mitsubishi Jeep," Ryowa is the exclusive exporter of "Jupiter" truck and a new small car "Mitsubishi 500" made by the Mitsubishi.

President
Ei Hiramatsu
Head Office
Otemachi Bldg., 4, 1-chome, Otemachi, Chiyoda-ku, Tokyo
Telephone: (201) 7551
Export Department
In the Head Office
Branch Offices
Nagoya Branch—Nagoya Works, Mitsubishi Heavy Industries, Reorganized, Co., Ltd.
2, Oemachi, Minato-ku, Nagoya
Mizushima Branch—Mizushima Works, Mitsubishi Heavy Industries, Reorganized, Co., Ltd.
87, Mizushima Takasagomachi, Kurashiki City, Okayama Pref.
Sales
Trucks "MITSUBISHI JUPITER" & "MITSUBISHI JEEP"
Car "MITSUBISHI 500"

Mitsubishi 500
Mitsubishi " Jupiter " T10-DA · T11-GA
Mitsubishi " Jupiter " T11-GHB
Mitsubishi " Jupiter " T22-DBH
Mitsubishi " Jupiter " T22D-D
Mitsubishi " Jeep " CJ3B-J10
Mitsubishi " Jeep " CJ3B-J3
Mitsubishi " Jeep " Fire Engine CJ3B-J10

Nagoya Works Ohe Plant

MITSUBISHI-JEEP

MITSUBISHI 500 at 6th Tokyo Motor Show

SHIN MEIWA INDUSTRY CO., LTD.

Nishinomiya Plant

Engine Test

SHIN MEIWA STAND at 6th Tokyo Motor Show

This company was formed in 1949, under the present title for making motorcycles, farm petroleum engines, etc., taking over the technical personnel and production facilities of the now defunct Kawanishi Aircraft Industry, Ltd.

Line of Business:
"Pointer" motorcycles
Dumpers and other special vehicles
"Pointer" pumps
Repair work mainly of Defence Force vehicles
Overhauling of aircraft engines, etc.

President
Shigeru Furukawa
Head Office
125, Kami-Naruomachi, Nishinomiya City, Hyogo Pref.
Telephone: Nishinomiya (4) 331
Export Department
10, Unagidani Nishinomachi, Minami-ku, Osaka
Business Offices
Osaka Office—Same as Export Department
Tokyo Office—Higashi-Nihon Pointer Office,
39, Shiba-Kurumamachi, Minato-ku, Tokyo
Nagoya Office—Naka-Nihon Pointer Office,
13, Higashi-Kadomachi, Naka-ku, Nagoya
Sapporo Office—Hokkaido Pointer Office,
Higashi 2-chome, Kitashijo, Sapporo
Plant
Naruo Plant—72, 1-chome, Takasucho, Nishinomiya City, Hyogo Pref.
Main Products
Motorcycles "POINTER"

Pointer Junior PF-III
Pointer Senior PSB-II
Pointer Comet PCB-II
Pointer Ace PAT-II

SHOWA WORKS, LTD.

Established in 1939, the company is one of a few motorcycle manufacturers and pioneer of light motorcycles. Following the introduction of "Showa 100 c.c. LA" light motorcycle, the company has made many original improvements in its products including adoption of Dyna-starter for 125 c.c. model, hydraulic shock absorbers, etc, and mass production of 250 c.c. 2 cycle single cylinder engine.

The company produces extensive types of motorcycles ranging from "50 c.c. Echo" to "650 c.c. Hosk" under a strict quality control system.

President
Yoshio Kojima
Head Office
178, Matsunaga, Numazu City, Shizuoka Pref.
Telephone: Numazu 5111-5
Export Department
9, 1-chome, Kanda Tsukasacho, Chiyoda-ku, Tokyo
Cable Address: CHANHO TOKYO
Telephone: (231) 4176-9
Business Office
Osaka Office—20, 3-chome, Edobori-Kitadori, Nishi-ku, Osaka
Plants
Numazu Works—178, Matsunaga, Numazu City, Shizuoka Pref.
Tokyo Works—2,431, Midorigaoka, Meguro-ku, Tokyo
Main Products
Motorcycles "CRUISER", "LIGHT CRUISER" & "SHOWA HOSK"

Light Cruiser SL-III
Marien 125
Cruiser SC-II
Hosk 350 FA
Hosk 500 Twin DB
Hosk 500 Single GA

Numazu Plant

Assembly Line

SHOWA STAND at 6th Tokyo Motor Show

SUZUKI MOTOR CO., LTD.

Hamamatsu Plant

This company is derived from Suzuki Loom Manufacturing Company established in 1909.

The company began production of motorcycle engine in 1952, and started production of light four-wheeled "Suzulight" which received applause by motor market. In May, 1958, the company introduced new product "Suzumoped" 50 c.c.

The main plant consists of about 30 separate factories built in extensive site covering 165,000 square meters. The monthly output is reported to average:

- a) "Minifree" 50 c.c. bike engines — 3,000 units
- b) "Suzumoped" 50 c.c. — 5,000 units
- c) "Colleda" 125 c.c. & 250 c.c. — 6,000 units
- d) "Suzulight" light four wheelers — 200 units

Grinding Shop

President
Shunzo Suzuki
Head Office
300, Takatsuka, Kamimura, Hamana-gun, Shizuoka Pref.
Telephone: Hamamatsu (2) 8111
Cable Address: SUZUKIORI HAMAMATSU
Export Department
In the Head Office
Branch Office
Tokyo Branch—1, 5-chome, Shinbashi, Shiba, Minato-ku, Tokyo
Plant
300, Takatsuka, Kamimura, Hamana-gun, Shizuoka Pref.
Main Products
Motorcycles "COLLEDA", "SUZUMOPED" & "MINIFREE", 4-wheeled van "SUZULIGHT"

SUZULIGHT at 6th Tokyo Motor Show

Suzulight TL
Suzuki Sel PET
Colleda Seltwin SB
Colleda ST-6A
Colleda 250 TM-2
Colleda Twin Ace TA

COLLEDA
SUZUMOPED
SUZULIGHT

TOKYO HATSUDOKI CO., LTD.

It is forty years since this company started making small two and four cycle high speed engines at Osaki, Tokyo, in 1922, under the title of Takata Motor Laboratory.

In two-cycle engines, the company has held a unique position in the industry with its long established background and can boast of its products unrivalled in performance by any product in the world. Because of this highly dependable engine, the company has an extensive and regular market for its TOHATSU motorcycles, minor-type fire engines, farm engines, outboard engines, hoist pumps, electric generators, etc. Total sales of motorcycles recorded over one million units since its first product was sent to the market in 1948.

Shimura I, II, and Okaya Plants

President
Daisuke Akashi
Head Office
11, 2-chome, Kyobashi, Chuo-ku, Tokyo
Telephone: (561) 6251-5, 0451-5
Cable Address: TOHATSU TOKYO
Export Department
In the Head Office
Branch Offices
Fukuoka Branch—52, Nakashomachi, Fukuoka
Takamatsu Branch—6, 1-chome, Tenjinmae, Takamatsu
Hiroshima Branch—233, Nishikicho, Hiroshima
Osaka Branch—63, 3-chome, Sonezaki-shinchi, Kita-ku, Osaka
Nagoya Branch—20, 3-chome, Oikemachi, Naka-ku, Nagoya
Tokyo Branch—11, 2-chome, Kyobashi, Chuo-ku, Tokyo
Sendai Branch—7, Higashi Ichibancho, Sendai
Sapporo Branch—Mitsuya Bldg., Nishi 3-chome,
Kitaichijo, Sapporo
Plants
Shimura Plant—1st Plant: 5, 1-chome, Shimuracho,
Itabashi-ku, Tokyo
2nd plant: 3, 4-chome, Shimuracho, Itabashi-ku, Tokyo
Okaya Plant—830, Imai, Okaya City, Nagano Pref.
Main Products
Motorcycles "TOHATSU"

Tohatsu New Birdy GB
Tohatsu Arrow LA
Tohatsu Arrow LB
Tohatsu Hurry TA

Assembly Line

TOHATSU at 6th Tokyo Motor Show

TOKYU KUROGANE MOTOR CO., LTD.

Assembly Line at Kamata Plant

Infrared Lamp Room at Omori Plant

KUROGANE BABY at 6th Tokyo Motor Show

This company is the successor to Nippon Jidosha Co., Ltd., who commenced production of "New Era" three-wheeler in 1928, at its motor factory, Ohmori, Tokyo. This three-wheeler was renamed "Kurogane-go" in 1937.

In 1942 the company possessed five factories at Ohmori, Kamata, Kawasaki, Samukawa and Amagasaki and had produced, besides three-wheelers, vehicles for special purposes up to the termination of the war.

After World War II, the company reopened production in 1949 under the new title of Japan Internal Combustion Engine Mfg. Co., Ltd. Its capital was increased to ¥400 million in 1956.

In 1957, the company purchased Ohta Motors Co., Ltd. and started production of light three- and four-wheeled trucks with the capital increased to ¥500 million.

In June, 1959, the name of the company was changed to Tokyu Kurogane Motor Co., Ltd. Since November, 1959, the company put its light four-wheeled truck "Kurogane Baby" on production stream.

President
Hisao Kinoshita
Head Office
30, Akasaka Tameikecho, Minato-ku, Tokyo
Telephone : (481) 8141, 8341
Export Department
In the Head Office
Business Offices
Tokyu Kurogane Motor Sales Co., Ltd.—
1,260, Kamimeguro, Meguro-ku, Tokyo
Kansai Kurogane Sales Co., Ltd.—
31, Isemachi Kita-ku, Osaka
Plants
Kamata Plant—177, Furuichimachi, Ota-ku, Tokyo
Omori Plant—58, 3-chome, Omori, Ota-ku, Tokyo
Kawasaki Plant—345, 4-chome, Tsukagoshi, Kawasaki City, Kanagawa Pref.
Samukawa Plant—600, 2-chome, Okada, Samukawa-machi, Koza-gun, Kanagawa Pref.
Products
Small-sized Three- & Four-wheelers "KUROGANE"

Kurogane Light Van NCV
Kurogane Nova KN-1500
Kurogane NB
Kurogane Baby Canvas Wagon KB-360
Kurogane Baby Carrier KB-360
Kurogane Baby Commercial KB-360
Kurogane NBD
Kurogane KW 8
Kurogane KY10

TOYO KOGYO CO., LTD.

This company was founded on January 30, 1920, with the capital of ¥500,000. At present, the factory covers in floor space 180,000 sq. meters and is built in the newest design in the site extending 460,000 sq. meters.

The company's product extends about thirty varieties including ½ and 2 ton three wheelers, 1 and 2 ton four-wheeled trucks, light vans, three- and four-wheeled dump trucks, vacuum cars, pick-ups and fire fighters.

The monthly output is 6,000 units on average. The company produces all parts at its own factory except rubber products, some electric parts, bearings, etc.

The total sales during the six months ending April 30, 1959, amounted to about ¥9,200 million. A rapid increase in sales is expected for the present term owing to the highly popular demand for the light three-wheelers put on the market since May.

Hiroshima Main Plant

Assembly Line of 3-wheeler

President
Tsuneji Matsuda
Head Office
6,047, Shinchi, Fuchumachi, Aki-gun, Hiroshima Pref.
Telephone: Hiroshima Minami (4) 4141
Cable Address: TOYOKO HIROSHIMA
Export Department
In the Head Office
Branch Offices
Tokyo Branch — 6, 3-chome, Edobashi, Nihonbashi, Chuo-ku, Tokyo
Osaka Branch — 5, 5-chome, Minami Kyuhojimachi, Higashi-ku, Osaka
Plant
6,047, Shinchi, Fuchumachi, Aki-gun, Hiroshima Pref.
Main Products
"MAZDA" trucks, dump trucks, vacuum cars, light van & three-wheelers

TOYO KOGYO STAND at 6th Tokyo Motor Show

Mazda D 1100 · DTA 81
Mazda D 1500 · DUA 12S
Mazda K 360 · KTBA 43
Mazda T 600 · TEA 46
Mazda MBR 81
Mazda T1100 · TTA 81
Mazda HBR 12S
Mazda T1500 · TUA 12S

TOYOTA MOTOR CO., LTD.

Toyota Main Plant

Toyopet Assembly Line

TOYOPET CROWN at 6th Tokyo Motor Show

This company was formed in 1937, detaching from the Toyota Automatic Loom Works, the maker of the world-famous power looms and spinning machinery. Next year, it completed the construction of its main plant at Toyota City and started production of automotive vehicles with equipments of whole range from processing to assembly. The plant occupied 150 acre site at the time, but it now expanded to a compound of 520 acres. Furthermore, the company recently completed Motomachi Plant at which passenger cars are solely manufactured.

Accelerated by rationalization and modernization, the productivity of the plants has been magnificently enhanced, and monthly output is expected to reach 10,000 units.

Toyota Motor Sales Co., Ltd., the sales division of the company is, in overseas countries, represented by sixty firms in more than forty different countries. American Toyota was incorporated in 1958 at Los Angeles to promote Toyota motor vehicles to the U.S.

President
Taizo Ishida
Head Office
1, Toyotacho, Toyota City, Aichi Pref.
Telephone: Toyota 0120
Export Division
Toyota Motor Sales Co., Ltd.
3, 2-chome, Hatchobori, Chuo-ku, Tokyo
Cable Address: JIDOSHA TOKYO
Telephone: (551) 7111
Sales Division
Toyota Motor Sales Co., Ltd.
(Head Office) 2, 2-chome, Hijiecho, Nakamura-ku, Nagoya
(Tokyo Office) Same as the Export Division
(Osaka Office) Hankyu-Koku Bldg., 31, Kadotacho,
Kita-ku, Osaka
(Bangkok Branch) No. 180, Suriwogse Road,
Bangkok, Thailand
Plants
1, Toyotacho, Toyota City, Aichi Pref.
1, Motomachi, Toyota City, Aichi Pref.
Main Products
TOYOPET Cars & Trucks, TOYOTA Buses, Trucks, Fire Engines
Dump & Fork-lift Trucks, Land Cruiser, TOYO ACE Trucks

Toyopet Crown Custom RS 22-L
Toyopet Crown Deluxe RS 21
Toyopet Crown RS 20   Toyopet Corona PT 10
Toyota DR 10 · DR 15   Toyota DB 85
Toyopet Crown Custom Wagon RS 27-LG
Toyopet Masterline Light Van RS 26-V
Toyopet Coronaline PT 16-V
Toyopet Route Van RK 85-V
Toyo-Ace Light Van PK 20-V
Toyopet Masterline Pick-Up RS 26
Toyopet Masterline Utility RS 26-P
Toyopet Stout RK 30   Toyopet Stout RK 35-B
Toyopet Dyna RK 85   Toyo-Ace PK 20
Toyota FA 80 · 95-H   Toyota DA 80 · 95
Toyota Cargo Truck FW 10 · DW 10
Toyota FA 80   Toyota FA 74
Toyota FC 74   Toyota FJ 24
Toyota Land Cruiser Wagon FJ 28
Toyota Land Cruiser Hardtop FJ 25-D
Toyota Land Cruiser Canvastop FJ 2
Toyota Weapon Carrier FQ 10
Toyota DH 90

TOYOTA
TOYOPET
TOYO-ACE

YAMAGUCHI BICYCLE MFG. CO., LTD.

Founded in 1914 as a bicycle maker, the company has made a marvelous growth as one of the biggest bicycle and motorbicycle manufacturers in this country in result of ceaseless effort made by the management for improvement of its manufacturing techniques.

Mr. Shigehiko Yamaguchi, president, made several visits to the U.S. and European countries for the study of the newest trend of the industry and brought home to his plants production system by automation and cost reducing, and at the same time, adopted the system of modern scientific management. He is also collecting basic data to make ready for cultivating overseas market and is regarded as one of the leaders in the industry.

Kawaguchi Main Plant

President
Shigehiko Yamaguchi
Head Office
135, Takecho, Daito-ku, Tokyo
Telephone: (831) 9241-5, 9251-5
Sales Network
100 Sales Companies & 10,000 Agents throughout Japan
Plants
Kawaguchi Plant—184, 1-chome, Sakaecho, Kawaguchi City, Saitama Pref.
Mukojima Plant—60, Nishi 4-chome, Azumacho, Sumida-ku, Tokyo
Tanashi Plant—Kamihoya, Hayamachi, Kitatama-gun, Tokyo
Main Products
Motorcycles "YAMAGUCHI" De Luxe, Sel Super, Special Super & Auto-Pet.

YAMAGUCHI CYCLE CENTER

Yamaguchi Auto-Pet BP-50
Yamaguchi Auto-Pet
Yamaguchi Super Twin 125
Yamaguchi Sel Super 350
Yamaguchi Deluxe 800S

YAMAGUCHI STAND at 6th Tokyo Motor Show

 YAMAGUCHI MOTOR

YAMAHA MOTORCYCLE CO., LTD.

Machine Shop

YAMAHA 250

YAMAHA Scooter at 6th Tokyo Motor Show

This company is the motorcycle division of Nippon Gakki Co. (Musical Instrument Co.) organized as a separate firm on July 1, 1955. "Yamaha 125" was introduced into the market in February, 1955, followed by "Yamaha 130" in June.

"Yamaha 175" (March, 1956) and "Yamaha 250" (May, 1956) were successively sent to the market and their monthly production reached 1,500 units.

By winning brilliant victories in many home and international races, the name of the company became well-known in the trade, home and abroad, during only three years or so.

In 1958, Yamaha International Industries was formed at Los Angeles, U.S.A. and Yamaha de Mexico at Mexico City, to distribute Yamaha motorcycles to local dealers.

In February, 1959, "Yamaha YAIII" and "250 YDII" were introduced to the market, and in July "Yamaha Sports 250S" followed. The company's monthly output now reaches 6,000 units including all different models.

President
Genichi Kawakami
Head Office
250, Nakazawacho, Hamamatsu City, Shizuoka Pref.
Telephone : Hamamatsu (2) 2111
Export Division
Export Department, Nihon Gakki Seizo K. K.,
250, Nakazawacho, Hamamatsu City, Shizuoka Pref.
Telephone : Hamamatsu (2) 2111
Business Offices
Tokyo Sales Office—1, 7-chome Ginza, Chuo-ku, Tokyo
Osaka Sales Office—39, 2-chome, Shinsaibashisuji,
Minami-ku, Osaka
Nagoya Sales Office—1, 3-chome, Sakaecho,
Naka-ku, Nagoya
Kyushu Sales Office—1, 3-chome, Kamimiseyacho, Fukuoka
Hokkaido Sales Office—12, Nishi 4-chome,
Minami Sanjo, Sapporo
Sendai Sales Office—182, 4-chome, Omachi, Sendai
Plant
1,280, Kitakawahara, Nakanojo, Hamakitacho,
Hamana-gun, Shizuoka Pref.
Main Products
Motorcycles "YAMAHA" & "YAMAHA SPORTS"

Yamaha Scooter
Yamaha 125
Yamaha 250
Yamaha 250 S Standard
Yamaha 250 S Racer
Yamaha 250 S Scrambler

AUTO PARTS

Pistonring

TEIKOKU PISTON RING CO., LTD.

Established in December, 1939 at Osaka as a maker of pistonrings for marine and automobile engines, the company later became specialized in manufacture of pistonring for aircraft engines at its Okaya Plant in December, 1940.

Since October, 1945, the company increased line, in addition to its main items, pistonrings for automobile and marine engines, etc., to include cylinder sleeves and liners, castings and metal platings.

The company's present monthly capacity is as follows:
Pistonrings	600,000 pcs
Cylinder sleeves & liners	100,000 pcs
Brake drums	20,000 pcs

The company's "Porous" chrome plated liners are known to excel in abrasion resistance and saving in lubricant, and are finding extensive market for use with small automotive engines and medium and large diesel marine engines.

President
Toshikazu Mikami
Head Office
7, 3-chome, Yaesu, Chuo-ku, Tokyo
Telephone: (271) 2826
Cable Address: TEIKOKUPIS TOKYO
Export Department
In the Head Office
Business Offices
Tokyo Office—In the Head Office
Osaka Office—28, 1-chome, Asahimachi, Kita-ku, Osaka
Nagoya Office—221, 1-chome, Sasajimacho,
Nakamura-ku, Nagoya
Plant
Okaya Plant—753, Okaya City, Nagano Pref.
Main Products
Pistonring, cyliner liner, brake drum

Electric furnace in Okaya Plant

Piston sleeve testing

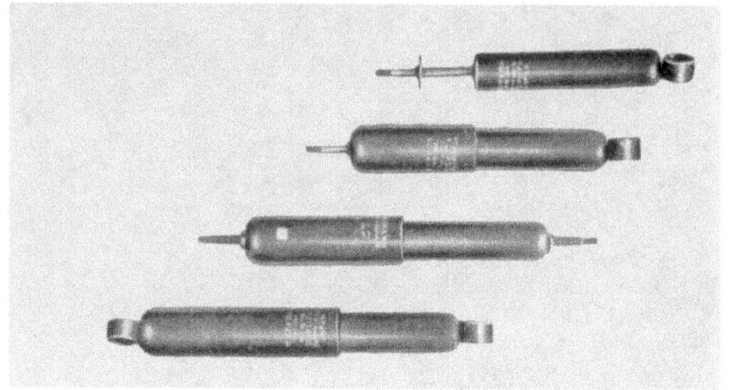

Shock absorbers

The interior of Kayaba Industry's plant

Oil pressure jacks

AUTO PARTS

Shock Absorber & Jack

KAYABA INDUSTRY CO., LTD.

This company embarked in motor industry after World War II, taking over technical personnel and production facilities, specialized in oil pressure equipments, from Kayaba Seisakusho, Ltd., well-known in the war time as the top-ranking maker of shock absorbers for aircraft.

The company holds its important position in motor industry as a supplier of oil pressure shock absorber, oil pressure jacks for automobiles. In addition to shock absorber and oil pressure jacks, the company makes power steering equipments, oleo forks for motorcycles and three-wheelers, oil cushion units, etc.

In recent years, a great increase has been made in the sales of oil pressure equipment, owing to the extensive uses in motor vehicles for special purposes, such as dump trucks and concrete mixer trucks, etc.

President
Ryozo Asano
Head Office
1, 1-chome, Shibaura, Minato-ku, Tokyo
Telephone: (451) 5141, 8156
Cable Address: KYBKOGYO TOKYO
Export Department
In the Head Office
Business Offices
Nagoya Office—Nikkei Bldg., 8, 3-chome, Sakuracho, Naka-ku, Nagoya
Osaka Office—Mansei Bldg., 46, 4-chome, Kitahama, Higashi-ku, Osaka
Plants
Tokyo Plant—1, 1-chome, Shibaura, Minato-ku, Tokyo
Gifu Plant—505, Tsuchida Kanimachi, Kani-gun, Gifu Pref.
Main Products
Shock absorber, oil cushion unit, oleo fork, power steering, levelling valve, oil jack, etc.

261 ADVANCE DESIGNED MODELS

Illustrated with
Principal Specifications and Features

Passenger car	131
Bus	141
Light Commercial Vehicle	151
Light Truck	158
Heavy-Duty Truck	168
Tank Lorry	174
Fire Engine	177
Jeep Type	180
Dump Truck	184
Construction Equipment	194
Three-Wheeler	199
Motor Scooter	213
Motorcycle	218

PASSENGER CAR

Japanese-made passenger cars are with a seating capacity of 4 or 6 persons and equipped with an engine from 360 c.c. to 1,500 c.c.
It is almost a quarter century since production of passenger cars was commenced aiming at durability and economy. Passenger cars presently manufactured in Japan are so comfortable and durable as to effectively meet the demands both at home and abroad. This is represented in the fact that orders of overseas countries for Japanese passenger cars are markedly increasing.

TOYOPET CROWN CUSTOM RS22L

Overall Length: 4,365 mm.　Overall Width: 1,695 mm.　Overall Height: 1,529 mm. Wheelbase: 2,530 mm.　Vehicle Weight: 1,194 kg.　No. of Seats: 6　Engine: Gasoline, pushrod ohv,　4 cycle　4 cyl　1,453 cc　65 HP　4,500 rpm　122 km/h.　Clutch: Single dry plate with torsional rubber dampers.　Transmission: Synchromesh second and top speeds, remote control, gears of helical type.　No. of Speeds: forward 3, reverse 1　Gear Ratio: 1st 3.647, 2nd 1.807, top direct, reverse 4.863.　Tire: front 6.40–13, 4P　rear 6.40–13, 4P

Most luxuriously built passenger car featuring overdrive transmission and ball joint front suspension, affording higher standard of riding comfort and safer drive on the road.

TOYOTA MOTOR PRODUCT

TOYOPET CROWN RS20

Overall Length: 4,365 mm. Overall Width: 1,695 mm.　Overall Height: 1,550 mm. Wheelbase: 2,530 mm.　Vehicle Weight: 1,225 kg.　No. of Seats: 6　Engine: 4 cycle 4 cyl 1,453 cc 60 HP 4,500 rpm 110 km/h.　Clutch: Single dry plate with torsional rubber dampers.　Transmission: Synchromesh.　No. of Speeds: forward 3, revese 1　Gear Ratio: 5.286　Tire: front 6.40–15, 4P　rear 6.40 15, 4P

One of the most popular passenger cars in Japan. This popularity was created by the generous accommodation of passengers and pronounced ease of driving and maintenance.

TOYOTA MOTOR PRODUCT

TOYOPET CROWN DELUXE RS21

Overall Length: 4,365 mm. Overall Width: 1,695 mm. Overall Height: 1,540 mm. Wheelbase: 2,530 mm. Vehicle Weight: 1,250 kg. No. of Seats: 6 Engine: 4 cycle 4 cyl 1,453 cc 62 HP 4,500 rpm 110 km/h. Clutch: Dry single plate with torsional rubber dampers Transmission: Synchromesh. No. of Speeds: Forward 3, reverse 1 Gear Ratio: 5.286 Tire: front 7.00—14, 4P rear 7.00—14, 4P

This small passenger car is designed and manufactured to meet requirements for low fuel consumption and ease of driving. It affords excellent riding comfort. Modernized oriental flavor is a basic thought given to the body design.

TOYOTA MOTOR PRODUCT

TOYOPET CORONA PT10

Overall Length: 3,910 mm. Overall Width: 1,470 mm.
Overall Height: 1,555 mm. Wheelbase: 2,400 mm.
Vehicle Weight: 985 kg. No. of Seats: 5 Engine: 4 cycle 4 cyl 997 cc 45 HP 5,000 rpm 105 km/h. Clutch: Single dry plate with torsional rubber dampers. Transmission: Synchromesh. No. of Speeds: forward 3, reverse 1 Gear Ratio: 5.714 Tire: front 5.60—14, 4P rear 5.60—14, 4P

Japan's most compactly built passenger car. Its frame is a special "built-in" frame featuring generous inside dimensions. Three-leaf rear suspension affords better riding comfort.

TOYOTA MOTOR PRODUCT

Datsun Bluebird in front of the Diet Library.

DATSUN BLUEBIRD P310-U

Overall Length: 3,890 mm. Overall Width: 1,496 mm. Overall Height: 1,460 mm. Wheelbase: 2,280 mm. Vehicle Weight: 850 kg. No. of Seats: 5 Engine: Gasoline, water-cooled, in-line, 4 cycle 4 cyl 1,189 cc 48 HP 4,800 rpm 123 km/h. Clutch: Dry, single disc. Transmission: Synchromesh. No. of Speeds: forward 3, reverse 1 Gear Ratio: 4.625 Tire: front 5.60—13, 4P rear 5.60—13, 4P.

This most admirably tailored passenger car is best fitted for exportation because of its longer wheelbase, wider track and lower floor. Coil spring suspension and generous inside dimensions added more fitness for family use.

NISSAN MOTOR PRODUCT

DATSUN SPORTS CAR S211

Overall Length: 3,985 mm. Overall Width: 1,455 mm. Overall Height: 1,350 mm. Wheelbase: 2,220 mm. Vehicle Weight: 810 kg. No. of Seats: 4 Engine: Gasoline, water-cooled, in-line, 4 cycle 4 cyl 988 cc 34 HP 4,400 rpm 115 km/h. Clutch: Dry, single disc. Transmission: Synchromesh. No. of Speeds: forward 4, reverse 1 Gear Ratio: 4.875 Tire: front 5.20—14, 4P rear 5.20—14, 4 P

The choice of Datsun models is becoming wider by the addition of this particular our-seater model. On top of outstanding performance, exceptional road-holding and highest degree of safety in common with all Datsun range, this model features the glass-fibre-reinforced polyester body shell. Unusual lightness in weight, high insulating property against heat, corrosion and noise are outstanding qualities.

NISSAN MOTOR PRODUCT

PRINCE SKYLINE DELUXE ALSID

Overall Length: 4,280 mm. Overall Width: 1,675 mm. Overall Height: 1,535 mm. Wheelbase 2,535 mm. Vehicle Weight: 1,330 kg. No. of Seats: 6 Engine: Water-cooled, ohv, gasoline, 4 cycle 4 cyl 1,484 cc 70 HP 4,800 rpm 130 km/h. Clutch: Single dry plate. Transmission: Synchromesh, selective rotation, remote control.   No. of Speeds: forward 4, reverse 1   Gear Ratio: 1st 4.18, 2nd 2.87, 3rd 1.59, 4th 1.00, reverse 5.50 Tire: front 6.40—14, 4P. rear 6.40—14, 4P.

Introduction of De Dion rear axle and back-bone tray type frame contributed much to improve riding comfort and high-speed stability as well as car life.
FUJI PRECISION PRODUCT

PRINCE SKYLINE ALSIE   EXPORT MODEL

Overall Length: 4,360 mm. Overall Width: 1,675 mm. Overall Height: 1,535 mm. Wheelbase: 2,535 mm. Vehicle Weight: 1,310 mm.   No. of Seats: 6   Engine: Water-cooled, ohv, gasoline, 4 cycle 4 cyl 1,484 cc 73 HP 4,800 rpm 130 km/h. Clutch: Hydraulically actuated, single dry plate. Transmission: Remote control, synchromesh, selective sliding.   No. of Speeds: forward 4, reverse 1   Gear Ratio: 1st 4.18, 2nd 2.87, 3rd 1.59, 4th 1.00, reverse 5.50 Tire: Front 6.40—14, 4P. rear 6.40—14, 4P.

An export model of the PRINCE SKYLINE. Introduction of De Dion rear axle and back-bone tray type rame contributed to enhance riding comfort and high-speed stability as well as car life.
FUJI PRECISION PRODUCT

PRINCE SKYLINE STANDARD ALSIS

Overall Length: 4,290 mm.   Overall Width: 1,675 mm.
Overall Height: 1,535 mm.   Wheelbase: 2,535 mm.
Vehicle Weight: 1,310 kg.   No. of Seats: 6   Engine:
Water-cooled, ohv, gasoline, 4 cycle 4 cyl 1,484 cc
70 HP 4,800 rpm 130 km/h.   Clutch: Single dry plate.
Transmission: Synchromesh, selective rotation.   No. of
Speeds: forward 4, reverse 1   Gear Ratio: 1st 4.18,
2nd 2.87, 3rd 1.59, 4th 1.00, reverse 5.50   Tire: front
6.40—14, 6P.   rear 6.40—14, 6P.

Power plant and other functional parts are exactly the same as the SKYLINE DELUXE. This particular STANDARD model is characterised by a silver belt line running along the side panel, giving the car an impression of European styling.

FUJI PRECISION PRODUCT

PRINCE GLORIA BLSI

Overall Length: 4,360 mm.   Overall Width: 1,675 mm.
Overall Height: 1,535 mm.   Wheelbase: 2,535 mm.
Vehicle Weight: 1,340 kg.   No. of Seats: 6   Engine:
Water-cooled, ohv, gasoline, 4 cycle 4 cyl 1,862 cc
80 HP 4,800 rpm 135 km/h.   Clutch: Hydraulically actuated, single dry plate.   Transmission: Remote control, synchromesh, selective sliding.   No. of Speeds: forward 4, reverse 1   Gear Ratio: 1st 4.18, 2nd 2.64, 3rd 1.59, 4th 1.00, reverse 5.50   Tire: front tubeless 6.40—14, 4P.   rear tubeless 5.40—14, 4P.

The largest and most luxuriously equipped passenger car powered by the most powerful engine in Japan. Firmly cushioned for posture ease, seats are at the perfect height for pure riding pleasure.

FUJI PRECISION PRODUCT

SUBARU 360

Overall Length: 2,990 mm.   Overall Width: 1,300 mm.   Overall Height: 1,380 mm.   Wheelbase: 1,800 mm.
Vehicle Weight: 385 kg.   No. of Seats: 4   Engine: Forced air cooling, 2 cycle 2 cyl 356 cc 16 HP 4,500 rpm
83.0 km/h.   Clutch: Single dry plate.   Transmission: Constant mesh, selective sliding gear.   No. of Speeds:
forward 3, reverse 1   Tire: 4.50—10, 2P.

A revolutionary new passenger car powered by the smallest engine in Japan. Two-stroke air cooled engine mounted in the rear, glass-fibre-reinforced polyester roof and light alloy front and engine covers are main features of this car of practical value.   **FUJI HEAVY PRODUCT**

SMALLER CAR

Passenger cars are classified in the Japanese laws by the size of engine as follows:

   360 c.c. and under   Mini cars
   Over 360 c.c. to 1,500 c.c. Small cars
   Over 1,500 c.c.   Cars

Driving licenses and vehicle taxes (imposed on the vehicle owners) vary according to the categories classified.

Of the vehicles shown here, "Subaru 360" has an engine of 356 c.c., "Mitsubishi 500" 493 c.c. and "Mikasa" 585 c.c. These cars are among the group of the smallest cars currently manufactured in Japan, and are very popular as most suitable cars for owner-drivers.

MITSUBISHI 500
Overall Length: 3,140 mm. Overall Width: 1,390 mm. Overall Height 1,380 mm. Wheelbase: 2,060 mm. Vehicle Weight: 490 kg. No. of Seats: 4 Engine: Forced air cooling, 4 cycle 2 cyl 493 cc 20 HP 90 km/h. Clutch: Single dry plate. Transmission: Synchromesh second and top speeds. No. of Speeds: forward 3 reverse 1 Gear Ratio: 1st 3.417, 2nd 1.789, 3rd 1.120, reverse 3.417 Tire: 5.20–12, 2PR

Fundamental thoughts underlying design of this Japan's prospective "people's car" are light-weight construction, excellent road-holding capacity, easiness of driving and lower driving and maintenance costs. **MITSUBISHI REORGANIZED PRODUCT**

MIKASA TOURING
Overall Length: 3,810 mm. Overall Width: 1,400 mm. Overall Height: 1,365 mm. Wheelbase: 2,100 mm. Vehicle Weight: 610 kg. No. of Seats: 4 Engine: Forced air cooling, horizontal opposed, ohv, 4 cycle 2 cyl 585 cc 20 HP 4,000 rpm 90 km/h. Transmission: Torque converter. No. of Speeds: forward 2, reverse 1 Tire: front 5.00–15, 4P rear 5.00–15, 4P

A passenger car of the most unique design. It is equipped with a fluid torque converter with two-speed and reverse gearbox. Front mounted and front drive engine contributes to unusual compactness of the whole vehicle. **OKAMURA PRODUCT**

Japan Makes of 'Austin' 'Hillman Minx' & 'Renault'

Under contract with foreign manufacturers, three makes of cars are currently manufactured in Japan. They are Austin, Hillman Minx and Renault. Nissan Motor commenced the assembly of Austin in 1952; Isuzu Motor, Hillman Minx in 1953; and Hino Motors, Renault in 1952. At present, they are manufactured with domestic parts in entirety. All of these cars produced are supplied to the domestic market.

AUSTIN A50 DE LUXE
Overall Length: 4,120 mm. Overall Width: 1,580 mm. Overall Height: 1,590 mm. Wheelbase: 2,520 mm. Vehicle Weight: 1,085 kg. No. of Seats: 6 Engine: Gasoline ohv, 4 cycle 4 cyl 1,489 cc 57 HP 130 km/h. Transmission: Synchromesh. No. of Speeds: forward 4 reverse 1 Tire: 5.60—15, 6 P

HILLMAN MINX DE LUXE
Overall Length: 4,125 mm. Overall Width: 1,555 mm. Overall Height: 1,511 mm. Wheelbase: 2,438 mm. Vehicle Weight: 1,065 kg. No. of Seats: 6 Engine: Water-cooled, 4 cycle 4 cyl 1,494 cc 62 HP 138 km/h. Transmission: Cynchromesh, 2nd, 3rd & top speeds. No. of Speeds: forward 4, reverse 1 Tire: 5.60—15, 6 P

RENAULT HINO PA
Overall Length: 3,845 mm. Overall Width: 1,435 mm. Overall Height: 1,440 mm. Wheelbase: 2,100 mm. Vehicle Weight: Standard 625 kg. Deluxe 640 kg. No. of Seats: 4 Engine: 4 cycle 4 cyl 748 cc 21 HP 4,000 rpm 100 km/h. Clutch: Single dry plate. Transmission: Synchromesh. No. of Speeds: forward 3 revese 1 Tire: front 5.00—15 rear 5.00—15

BUS

Buses are one of the most important export items in the Japanese motor industry. As mentioned elsewhere in this publication, Japanese-made buses are now running in various countries all over the world.

A high popularity of Japanese buses abroad is attributable to their economical costs and high quality. Usually, buses cannot be built on mass-production systems, because of the nature of the products themselves, and of the fact that customers order by choice various types from bus manufacturers. Such facts have placed the Japanese manufacturers in a more competitive position.

Another contributing factor is that the Japanese bus manufacturers have, since the end of the war, made the fullest possible use of Japanese aircraft technology whose excellence had been noted throughout the world.

A number of types of buses are manufactured in Japan: "Bonnet", "Cab-over", "Rear-engined", "Under-floor engined" and "Micro" buses. Large-sized buses have a seating capacity of as many as 50, while micro buses have some 13 seats. Worthy of brief mention is air suspension systems, which are used into many of the recent buses to offer more comfortable riding.

Most of the Japanese buses are equipped with diesel engines. In recent years they have increased to such an extent that more than 90% of the Japanese bus production is accounted for by diesel-driven buses. Incidentally, Japan ranks among the world's top bus manufacturing countries.

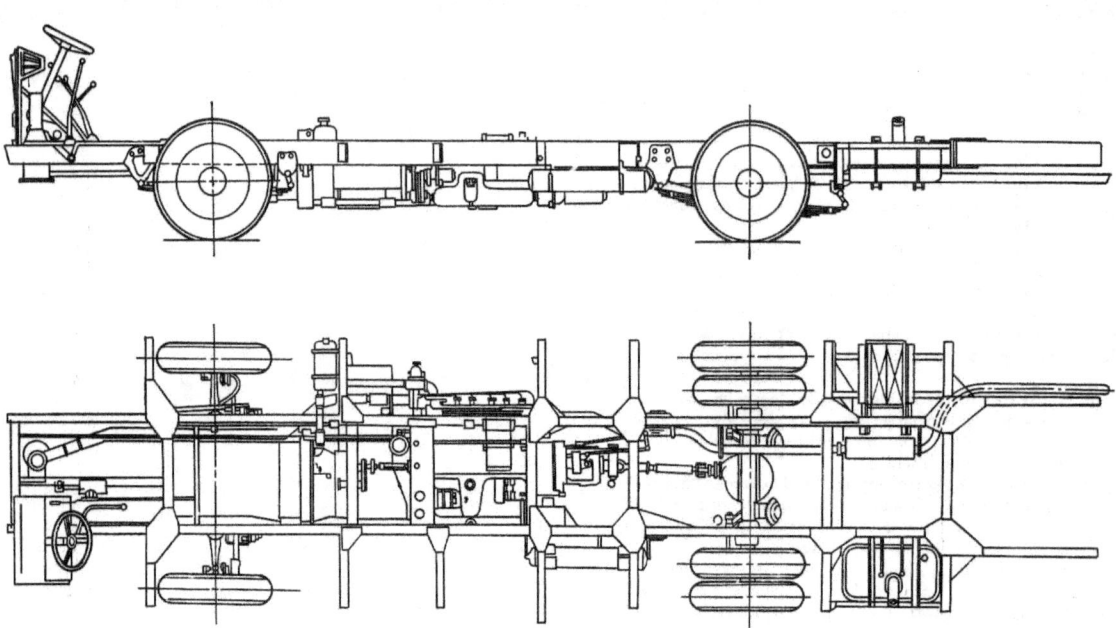

HINO BG BUS CHASSIS

Overall Length : 10,040 mm.   Overall Width : 2,395 mm.   Overall Height : 1,865 mm.   Wheelbase : 5,500 mm.   Vehicle Weight : 4,830 kg.   Engine : 4 cycle   6 cyl   7,698 cc   150 HP   2,400 rpm   97 km/h.   Clutch : Single plate dry disc.   Transmission : Selective sliding gear.   No. of Speeds : forward 5 reverse 1   Gear Ratio : 1st 5.407 : 1, 2nd 3.083 : 1, 3rd 1.722 : 1, 4th 1.000 : 1, 5th 0.806 : 1, reverse 6.489 : 1   Tire : front 11.00—20 rear 11.00—20

The horizontal HINO Diesel engine with output of 150 HP is installed under the floor. Floor area of the passenger space is generously dimensioned. Lively acceleration and safe stop is ensured by the air brake.

HINO MOTORS PRODUCT

HINO BD
UNDER FLOOR ENGINE

Overall Length: 10,020 mm. Overall Width: 2,450 mm. Overall Height: 3,080 mm. Wheelbase: 4,800 mm. Vehicle Weight: 7,830 kg. No. of Seats: 45 Engine: 4 cycle 6 cyl 7,698 cc 150 HP 2,400 rpm 75 km/h. Clutch: Single plate, dry disc. Transmission: Selective sliding gear. No. of Speeds: forward 4 reverse 1 Gear Ratio: 1st 5.407:1, 2nd 3.083:1, 3rd 1.722:1, 4th 1.000:1, reverse 6.489:1 Tire: front 9.00—20 rear 9.00—20

A 150 HP Diesel engine is mounted under the floor in the horizontal cylinder arrangement. Compared with the HINO bus of BG model, radius of turning circle is reduced, ensuring easiness of driving and increased comfort.

HINO MOTORS PRODUCT

HINO BG
UNDER FLOOR ENGINE

Overall Length: 10,450 mm. Overall Width: 2,525 mm. Overall Height: 3,100 mm. Wheelbase: 5,500 mm. Vehicle Weight: 8,600 kg. No. of Seats: 45 Engine: 4 cycle 6 cyl 7,698 cc 150 HP 2,400 rpm 97 km/h. Clutch: Single plate, dry disc. Transmission: Selective sliding gear. No. of Speeds: forward 5 reverse 1 Gear Ratio: 1st 5.407:1, 2nd 3.083:1, 3rd 1.722:1, 4th 1.000:1, 5th 0.806:1, reverse 6.489:1 Tire: front 11.00—20 rear 11.00—20

This bus chassis is meant for exportation to the various countries where complete body can be mounted to suit individual requirements. It can be broken down into small sections allowing easy reassembly.

HINO MOTORS PRODUCT

MINSEI "CONDOR" RF91

Overall Length: 9,660 mm. Overall Width: 2,450 mm. Overall Height: 3,000 mm. Wheelbase: 5,000 mm. Vehicle Weight: 7,330 kg. No. of Seats: 67 (41+24+2) Engine: 2 cycle 4 cyl 4,941 cc 155 HP 2,000 rpm 73 km/h. Clutch: Single dry plate. Transmission: Conventional. No. of Speeds: forward 4 reverse 1 Gear Ratio: 1st 5.82, 2nd 2.92, 3rd 1.91, 4th 1.00, reverse 7.12 Tire: 9.00—20, 14P

The first bus in Japan ever equipped with pneumatic suspension system. This particular bus is powered by a rear mounted supercharged 2-stroke Diesel engine with the maximum output of 155 HP.

MINSEI DIESEL PRODUCT

MINSEI B80

Overall Length: 9,913 mm. Overall Width: 2,450 mm. Overall Height: 2,850 mm. Wheelbase: 5,000 mm. Vehicle Weight: 6,760 kg. No. of Seats: 62 (37+23+2) Engine: 2 cycle 4 cyl 4,941 cc 155 HP 2,000 rpm 71 km/h. Clutch: Single dry plate. Transmission: Conventional. No. of Speeds: forward 4 reverse 1 Gear Ratio: 1st 5.82, 2nd 2.92, 3rd 1.91, 4th 1.00, reverse 7.12 Tire: front 9.00—20, 14P rear 9.00—20, 14P

A 155 HP engine is mounted for extra power ensuring increased acceleration and greater comfort. Considerable thought is given to the safety of drive.

MINSEI DIESEL PRODUCT

MINSEI RX102

Overall Length: 10,210 mm. Overall Width: 2,440 mm. Overall Height: 2,970 mm. Wheelbase: 5,000 mm. Vehicle Weight: 7,770kg. No. of Seats: 70 (45+23+2) Engine: 2 cycle 4 cyl 4,941 cc 155 HP 2,000 rpm 71 km/h. Clutch: Single dry plate. Transmission: Conventional. No. of Speeds: forward 4 reverse 1 Gear Ratio: 1st 5.82, 2nd 2.92, 3rd 1.91, 4th 1.00, reverse 7.12 Tire: front 9.00—20, 14P rear 9.00—20, 14P

Simplification of body construction is the fundamental thought underlying the design of this bus and the body is integral with the frame. The fuel consumption is reasonable for the size, riding comfort and accommodation of passengers.

MINSEI DIESEL PROCUCT

MINSEI "CONDOR" 6RFL-101A

Overall Length: 10,890 mm. Overall Width: 2,450 mm. Overall Height: 3,000 mm. Wheelbase: 5,500 mm. Vehicle Weight: 8,500 kg. No. of Seats: 77 (49+26+2) Engine: 2 cycle 6 cyl 7,412 cc 230 HP 2,000 rpm 120 km/h. Clutch: Single dry plate. Transmission: Conventional. No. of Speeds: forward 5 reverse 1 Gear Ratio: 1st 5.011, 2nd 3.016, 3rd 1.937, 4th 1.000, 5th 0.794, reverse 4.524 Tire: front 10.00−20, 14P rear 10.00−20, 14P

Specially constructed for long distance and high speed transportation on the speed way. The most powerful Diesel engine, 230 HP and pneumatic suspension system are outstanding features. It can cover 1,500 km in a day at the maximum velocity of 120 km/h.

MINSEI DIESEL PRODUCT

ISUZU BC150 REAR ENGINE WITH AIR SUSPENSION

Overall Length: 10,400 mm. Overall Width: 2,490 mm. Overall Height: 3,015 mm. Wheelbase: 5,335 mm.
Vehicle Weight: 8,235 kg. No. of Seats: 49+2 Engine: Diesel, 4 cycle 6 cyl 10,179 cc 180 HP 2,300 rpm
101 km/h. Clutch: Single dry plate with rubber damper. Transmission: Synchromesh, partially sliding, w/overdrive. No. of Speeds: forward 5 reverse 1 Gear Ratio: 5.29 (37/7) Tire: front 9.00—20, 14P rear 9.00 20, 14P

The latest trends in Diesel bus design are exemplified by this bus driven by a rear mounted turbo-charged 180 HP Diesel engine, the construction of the body being of the unitary construction.

ISUZU MOTOR PRODUCT

ISUZU BA540 REAR ENGINE WITH AIR SUSPENSION

Overall Length: 9,200 mm. Overall Width: 2,450 mm. Overall Height: 2,960 mm. Wheelbase: 4,200 mm.
Vehicle Weight: 6,830 kg. No. of Seats: 41+2 Engine: Diesel, 4 cycle 6 cyl 6,126 cc 125 HP 2,600 rpm
103 km/h. Clutch: Single dry plate with rubber damper. Transmisssion: Synchromesh, partially sliding, w/overdrive. No. of Speeds: forward 5 reverse 1 Gear Ratio: 5.57 (39/7) Tire: front 8.25 20, 14P rear 8.25—20, 14P

This bus is specially provided with smaller turning radius, so that any narrow roads can be negotiated. Body is of the unitary construction. A Diesel engine of 125 HP is mounted lengthwise in the rear. Both pneumatic and leaf spring suspension are available on request.

ISUZU MOTOR PRODUCT

ISUZU BB550 BUS CHASSIS
REAR ENGINE

Overall Length: 8,881 mm. Overall Width: 2,352 mm. Overall Height: 1,760 mm. Wheelbase: 5,000 mm. Vehicle Weight: 3,325 kg (chassis only). No. of Seats: 39+1 Engine: Diesel, 4 cycle 6 cyl 6,126 cc 125 HP 2,600 rpm 103 km/h. Clutch: Single dry plate with rubber damper. Transmission: Synchromesh, partially sliding, w/ overdrive. No. of Speeds: forward 5 reverse 1 Gear Ratio: 5.57 (39/7) Tire: front 8.25–20, 14P rear 8.25–20, 14P

This rear engine bus chassis is separatable from its frame. Dimensions are approximately the same as the BS model. The chassis lends itself to be transported on land or sea without breaking down.
ISUZU MOTOR PRODUCT

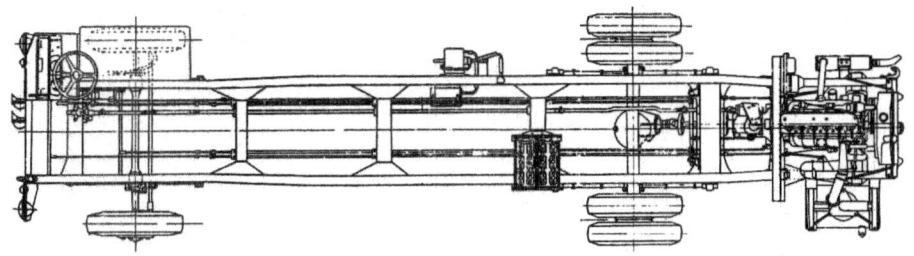
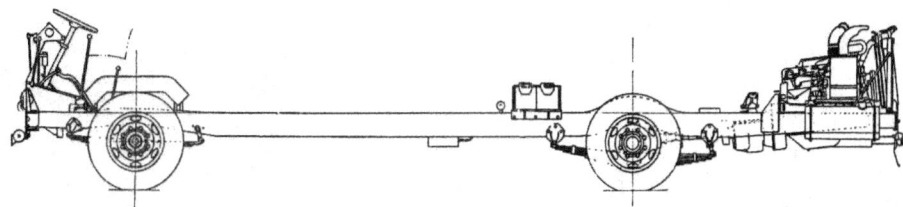

ISUZU BX550

Overall Length: 9,505 mm. Overall Width: 2,450 mm. Overall Height: 2,965 mm. Wheelbase: 5,200 mm. Vehicle Weight: 6,035 kg. No. of Seats: 37+2 Engine: Diesel, 4 cycle 6 cyl 6,126 cc 125 HP 2,600 rpm 80 km/h. Clutch: Single dry plate with rubber damper. Transmission: Synchromesh, partially sliding. No. of Speeds: forward 4 reverse 1 Gear Ratio: 5.57 (39/7) Tire: front 8.25–20, 14P rear 8.25–20, 14P

This particular bus is powered by 125 HP Diesel engine. Designed and constructed for transportation of intermediate distances. Features economical driving for passenger accommodation.
ISUZU MOTOR PRODUCT

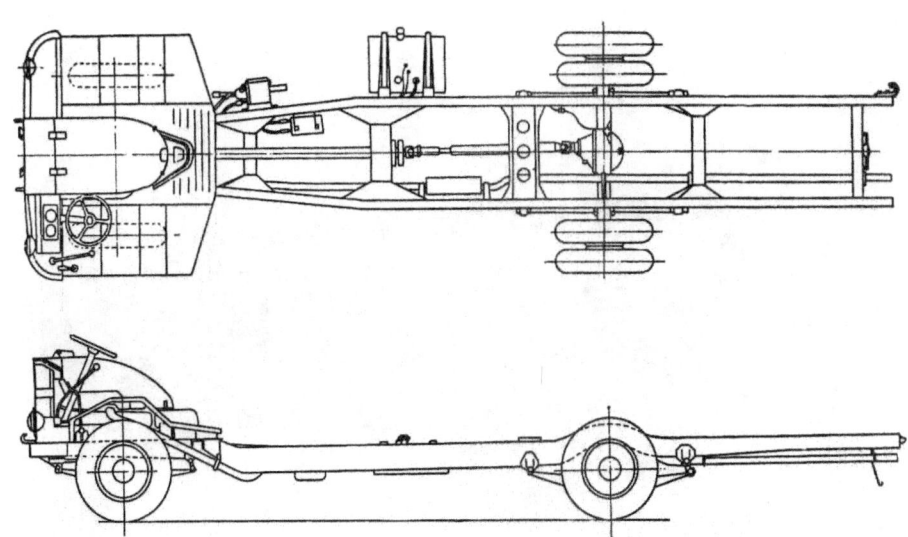

ISUZU BX540 BUS CHASSIS

Overall Length: 8,610 mm. Overall Width: 2,400 mm. Overall Height: 1,820 mm. Wheelbase: 4,800 mm. Vehicle Weight: 3,433 kg (chassis only). No. of Seats: 35+2 Engine: Diesel, 4 cycle 6 cyl 6,126 cc 125 HP 2,600 rpm 80 km/h. Clutch: Single dry plate with rubber damper. Transmission: Synchromesh, partially sliding. No. of Speeds: forward 4 reverse 1 Gear Ratio: 5.57 (39/7) Tire: front 8.25–20, 14P rear 8.25–20, 14P

This chassis is applicable to such buses that perform scheduled trips on the predetermined route. The power plant is mounted in the far extreme front affording increased passenger accommodation. A Diesel engine of 125 HP output is installed.
ISUZU MOTOR PRODUCT

MITSUBISHI FUSO B520
DIESEL

Overall Length: 10,500 mm. Overall Width: 2,490 mm. Overall Height: approx 3,100 mm. Wheelbase: 5,600 mm. Vehicle Weight: 7,415 kg. No. of Seats: 42 (passenger 41 crew 1). Engine: Diesel, 4 cycle 6 cyl 8,550 cc 165 HP 2,300 rpm 82 km/h. Clutch: Single dry plate. Transmission: Selective sliding gear. No. of Speeds: forward 4 reverse 1 Gear Ratio: 5.125 (final drive gear). Tire: front 9.00 20, 14P (optional 10.00 20, 14P) rear 9.00 20, 14P (optional 10.00 20, 14P)

Front wheels are fitted with shock absorbers and wheels are braked with pneumatic air brake system. Power assisted steering five-speed gear box is available for extra price.

MITSUBISHI NIPPON PRODUCT

MITSUBISHI FUSO R710
DIESEL

Overall Length: 10,430 mm. Overall Width: 2,490 mm. Overall Height: approx 3,070 mm. Wheelbase: 5,400 mm. Vehicle Weight: 8,260 kg. No. of Seats: 46 (passenger 45, crew 1). Engine: Diesel, 4 cycle 6 cyl 8,550 cc 165 HP 2,300 rpm 85 km/h. Clutch: Single dry plate. Transmission: Selective sliding gear, remote control. No. of Speeds: forward 4 reverse 1 Gear Ratio: 5.125 (final drive gear). Tire: front 10.00 20, 14P rear 10.00 20, 14P

The engine is mounted in the rear of the body with the crankshaft located parallel to the longitudinal axis of the vehicle. Brake system is intensified by pneumatic pressure. Power-assisted steering five speed gear box is available for extra price.

MITSUBISHI NIPPON PRODUCT

TOYOTA DR10 (DR15) DIESEL

Overall Length : 9,170 mm. Overall Width : 2,490 mm. Overall Height : 2,990 mm. Wheelbase : 5,000 mm (4,200 mm). Vehicle Weight : 6,000 kg (6,010 kg). No. of Seats : 68 (68) or 67 (66) Engine : 4 cycle 6 cyl 6,494 cc 130 HP 2,600 rpm 78 km/h. Clutch : Single dry plate with torsional rubber dampers. Transmission : Synchromesh. No. of Speeds : forward 4 reverse 1 Gear Ratio : 5.83 Tire : front 8.25—20, 14P rear 8.25—20, 14P

The chassis of this bus is incorporated with the first antiroll-damper in Japan for preventing rolling at high speeds and contributing much to the improvement of the riding comfort. Two different wheelbases are available alternatively.

TOYOTA MOTOR PRODUCT

TOYOTA DB85 DIESEL

Overall Length : 8,225 mm. Overall Width : 2,445 mm. Overall Height : 2,955 mm. Wheelbase : 4,360 mm. Vehicle Weight : 5,265 kg. No. of Seats : 48 or 49 Engine : 4 cycle 6 cyl 6,494 cc 130 HP 2,600 rpm 75 km/h. Clutch : Single dry plate with torsional rubber dampers. Transmission : Synchromesh. No. of Speeds : forward 4, reverse 1 Gear Ratio : 5.83 Tire : front 7.50—20, 12P rear 7.50—20, 12P

Low floor construction embodies in chassis design and well positioned torsional damper bring about excellent riding comfort. There is a choise of two alternative seat arrangements, one double seats all facing forward, the other seats facing three directions.

TOYOTA MOTOR PRODUCT

NISSAN UG690
DIESEL

Overall Length : 9,040 mm. Overall Width : 2,485 mm. Overall Height : 2,930 mm. Wheelbase : 5,000 mm. Vehicle Weight : 5,740 kg. No. of Seats : 35 Engine : Diesel, water-cooled, in-line, direct. 2 cycle 3 cyl 3,706 cc 120 HP 2,200 rpm 84 km/h. Clutch : Dry, single disc. Transmission : Synchromesh. No. of Speeds : forward 5, reverse 1 Gear Ratio : 5.57 Tire : front 7.50—20, 12P rear 7.50—20, 12P double

This particular model is powered by the UD3 Diesel engine. It accommodates 56 passengers when seated on all forward-facing seats and 57 passengers when seated on three-direction seats.

NISSAN MOTOR PRODUCT

HINO COMMERCE MINI BUS

Overall Length: 3,930 mm. Overall Width: 1,690 mm. Overall Height: 1,880 mm. Wheelbase: 2,100 mm. Vehicle Weight: 1,675 kg. No. of Seats: 11 Engine: 4 cycle 4 cyl 836 cc 28 HP 4,600 rpm 82 km/h. Clutch: Single dry plate. Transmission: Synchromesh, second, third and top speeds. Gear Ratio: Spiral bevel gear 5.71 Tire: front 5.50—14, 6PR rear 5.50—14, 6PR

The Hino "Minibus" is provided with a seating capacity of eleven passengers. Radius of turning circle is 4.6 m. All four wheels are independently suspended and the front wheels are driving wheels. The bus is easy to operate for all purposes with minimum costs of operation and maintenance. **HINO MOTORS PRODUCT**

NISSAN JUNIOR MICRO BUS KC42

Overall Length: 4,590 mm. Overall Width: 1,675 mm. Overall Height: 1,990 mm. Wheelbase: 2,390 mm. Vehicle Weight: 1,830 kg. No. of Seats: 13 Engine: Gasoline, water-cooled, in-line, 4 cycle 4 cyl 1,489 cc 57 HP 4,400 rpm 88 km/h. Clutch: Dry, single disc. Transmission: Synchromesh. No. of Speeds: forward 4, reverse 1 Gear Ratio: 6.83 Tire: front 7.00—15, 6P rear 7.00—15, 6P

A small bus provided with 13 passenger seats. The bus features unlimited use of intensified glass for the windows, wide and twostepped foot board, vinyl-covered seats and trunk compartment in the extreme rear.
NISSAN MOTOR PRODUCT

ISUZU ELF MICRO BUS TL221

Overall Length: 4,335 mm. Overall Width: 1,690 mm. Overall Height: 1,970 mm. Wheelbase: 2,180 mm. Vehicle Weight: 1,660 kg. No. of Seats: 12 Engine: Gasoline, 4 cycle 4 cyl 1,491 cc 60 HP 4,600 rpm 100 km/h. Clutch: Single dry plate with rubber damper. Transmission: Synchromesh, partially sliding. No. of Speeds: forward 4, reverse 1 Gear Ratio: 6.83 (41/6) Tire: front 7.00—15, 6P rear 7.00—15, 6P

Cab-over type engine mounting permits ample space for accommodating 12 passengers in spite of limited overall dimensions. A gasoline engine of 60 HP can be replaced by a Diesel engine of the equivalent output.
ISUZU MOTOR PRODUCT

PRINCE MICRO BUS AQVH-B

Overall Length: 4,690 mm. Overall Width: 1,695 mm. Overall Height: 1,990 mm. Wheelbase: 2,345 mm. Vehicle Weight 1,880 kg. No. of Seats: 14 Engine: Water-cooled, ohv, gasoline, 4 cycle 4 cyl 1,484 cc 70 HP 4,800 rpm 105 km/h. Clutch: Single dry plate. Transmission: Synchromesh, selective rotation. No. of Speeds: forward 4 reverse 1 Gear Ratio: 1st 5.19, 2nd 3.03, 3rd 1.70, 4th 1.00, reverse 5.97 Tire: front 6.50—16, 6P rear 6.50—16, 8P

The Prince Microbus takes 14 passengers, the largest number of passengers in the class of buses subject to the same driving permit. It can be applied for sight-seeing, commuting and school children transportation.
FUJI PRECISION PRODUCT

LIGHT COMMERCIAL VEHICLE

Of all types of vehicles, commercial cars are probably most convenient to carry small baggages as well as passengers. As chassis are identical to those for cars, comfortable riding is offered.

With the development of commerce and industry in Japan and abroad, this type of vehicles have been very popular. One of the greatest customers for the cars are merchants dealing with such goods as watches, glasses, radio and TV sets, medicines, clothes, etc.

A reason for the rapid rise of commercial cars is the fact, that this type of vehicles are classified, in the Japanese laws, as "trucks", on which no commodity tax and a lower rate of vehicle tax are imposed.

On the other hand, these vehicles are not permitted by the traffic laws to run at the same speed with passenger cars. Such a handicap, however, is trifle, so long as the current traffic congestion in the main cities prevents all vehicles from running at high speed.

SUZULIGHT TL

Overall Length: 2,990 mm. Overall Width: 1,295 mm. Overall Height: 1,380 mm. Wheelbase: 2,050 mm. Vehicle Weight: 490 kg. No. of Seats: 4 Engine: Forced air-cooled, 2 cycle 2 cyl 360 cc 20 HP 5,300 rpm 80 km/h. Clutch: Single dry disk. Transmission: Four-speed gear box with constant mesh. No. of Speeds: forward 3 reverse 1 Gear Ratio: 1st 4.58, 2nd 2.09, 3rd 1.17, reverse 4.58 Tire: front 4.50—12, 4P rear 4.50—12, 4P

One of the few examples of front-driven light vans in Japan. Other outstanding features are ball joint suspension system, air-cooled 2-stroke engine of line arrangement, leaf springs of greater width, etc.

SUZUKI MOTOR PRODUCT

DATSUN RANCH SEDAN UP221

Overall Length: 4,105 mm. Overall Width: 1,466 mm. Overall Height: 1,550 mm. Wheelbase: 2,220 mm. Vehicle Weight: 985 kg. No. of Seats: 5, payload 400 kg. Engine: Gasoline, water-cooled, in-line, 4 cycle 4 cyl 1,189 cc 48 HP 4,800 rpm 103 km/h. Clutch: Dry, single disc. Transmission: Synchromesh. No. of Speeds: forward, 4 reverse 1 Gear Ratio: 5.57 Tire: front 5.50–15, 6P rear 5.50–15, 6P

This multi-purpose car takes 5 passengers and 400 kg load. Rear cargo body is covered by a special plastic material, Vinylon, by means of fasteners, ensuring better weather protection and admirable external appearance.

NISSAN MOTOR PRODUCT

DATSUN STATION WAGON WP211 4-DOOR

Overall Length: 3,870 mm. Overall Width: 1,466 mm. Overall Height: 1,530 mm. Wheelbase: 2,220 mm. Vehicle Weight: 1,005 kg. No. of Seats 4 Engine: Gasoline, water-cooled, in-line. 4 cycle 4 cyl 1,189 cc 48 HP 4,800 rpm 113 km/h. Clutch: Dry, single disc. Transmission: Synchromesh. No. of Speeds: forward 4 reverse 1 Gear Ratio: 4.88 Tire: front 5.00–15, 4P rear 5.00–15, 4P

This small commercial vehicle is designed and constructed to achieve combined objects of passenger transportation and goods haulage. It is wellknown for its front adjustable seats and rear foldable seats. **NISSAN MOTOR PRODUCT**

MIKASA MARK II

Overall Length: 3,755 mm. Overall Width: 1,380 mm. Overall Height: 1,540 mm. Wheelbase: 2,100 mm. Vehicle Weight: 610 kg. No. of Seats: 2 Engine: Air-cooled, horizontal opposed, 4 cycle 2 cyl 585 cc 18 HP 73 km/h. Transmission: Torque converter. No. of Speeds: forward 3, reverse 1 Tire: front 5.00–15, 4P rear 5.00–15, 4P

The MARK II is a box-type light van developing the same performance as the MARK I. Large interior space is fit for transporting bulky goods.

OKAMURA PRODUCT

DATSUN STATION WAGON VG221 2-DOOR

Overall Length: 4,195 mm. Overall Width: 1,490 mm. Overall Height: 1,575 mm. Wheelbase: 2,520 mm. Vehicle Weight: 1,020 kg. No. of Seats: 5, payload 300 kg. Engine: Gasoline, water-cooled, in-line, 4 cycle 4 cyl 988 cc 37 HP 4,600 rpm 90 km/h. Clutch: Dry, single disc. Transmission: Synchromesh. No. of Speeds: forward 4, reverse 1 Gear Ratio: 5.86 Tire: front 5.50—15, 6P rear 5.50—15, 6P

The interior is equipped with rear seats of especially ample dimensions and at the same time provided with adequate loading area. Much thought was given to the comfort and convenience of the man at the wheel.

NISSAN MOTOR PRODUCT

DATSUN PICK-UP PG222-U

Overall Length: 4,105 mm. Overall Width: 1,480 mm. Overall Height: 1,560 mm. Wheelbase: 2,520 mm. Vehicle Weight: 920 kg. No. of Seats: 2, payload 250, 500, 1,100 kg. Engine: Gasoline, water-cooled, in-line, 4 cycle 6 cyl 1,189 cc 48 HP 4,800 rpm 110 km/h. Clutch: Dry, single disc. Transmission: Synchromesh. No. of Speeds: forward 4, reverse 1 Gear Ratio: 5.13 Tire: front 5.60—15, 6P rear 5.60—15, 6P

These light trucks are built in three different load carrying capacities, 250, 500 and 1,100 kg. Front seat is regulatable, affording reasonable riding comfort. High standard of manoeuvrability, smaller radius of turning circle and easiness of driving are principal features.

NISSAN MOTOR PRODUCT

MIKASA MARK I

Overall Length: 3,850 mm. Overall Width: 1,400 mm. Overall Height: 1,450 mm. Wheelbase: 2,100 mm. Vehicle Weight: 610 kg. No. of Seats: 4 Engine: Air-cooled, horizontal opposed, 4 cycle 2 cyl 585 cc 18 HP 73 km/h. Transmission: Torque converter. No. of Speeds: forward 2, reverse 1 Tire: front 5.00—15, 4P rear 5.00—15, 4P

This is the first small commercial vehicle in the world which has ever been equipped with a torque converter. Easiness of driving, longevity of engine and power train and economy of operation are some of the derivatives of this outstanding feature.

OKAMURA PRODUCT

TOYOPET CROWN CUSTOM WAGON RS27-LG 4-DOOR
Overall Length: 4,415 mm. Overall Width: 1,680 mm. Overall Height: 1,570 mm. Wheelbase: 2,530 mm. Vehicle Weight: 1,520 kg. No. of Seats: 3 or 6 Engine: Gasoline, 4 cycle 4 cyl 1,453 cc 65 HP 4,500 rpm 110 km/h. Clutch: Single dry plate with torsional rubber dampers. Transmission: Synchromesh second and top speeds. No. of Speeds: forward 3, reverse 1 Gear Ratio: 4.875 Tire: front 6.40—13, 4P, rear 6.40—13, 4P, T-500 white sidewall.

This particular station-wagon is specially provided with four doors for the ease of entrance and exit. The rear end is so constructed that it accommodates wide opening vertically in two directions.

TOYOTA MOTOR PRODUCT

TOYOPET MASTERLINE PICK-UP RS26
Overall Length: 4,380 mm. Overall Width: 1,680 mm. Overall Height: 1,605 mm. Wheelbase: 2,530 mm. Vehicle Weight: 1,170 kg. No. of Seats: 6 Engine: Gasoline, 4 cycle 4 cyl 1,453 cc 60 HP 4,500 rpm 100 km/h. Clutch: Single dry plate with torsional rubber dampers. Transmission: Synchromesh, second and top speeds. No. of Speeds: forward 3, reverse 1 Gear Ratio: 5.286 Tire: front 6.00—15, 6P rear 6.00—15, 6P

Front driver's cab has been well blended into the lines of cargo body of modern styling. Special attention has been given for enlarged view and increased riding comfort.

TOYOTA MOTOR PRODUCT

TOYOPET MASTERLINE UTILITY RS26-P
Overall Length: 4,380 mm. Overall Width: 1,680 mm. Overall Height: 1,605 mm. Wheelbase: 2,530 mm. Vehicle Weight: 1,220 kg. No. of Seats: 6 Engine: Gasoline, pushrod ohv, 4 cycle 4 cyl 1,453 cc 60 HP 4,500 rpm 100 km/h. Clutch: Single dry plate with torsional rubber dampers. Transmission: Synchromesh, second and top speeds, remote control, helical. No. of Speeds: forward 3, reverse 1 Gear Ratio: 5.286 Tire: front 6.00—15, 6P rear 6.00—15, 6P

This particular vehicle is a perfect combination of the advantages of both small truck and passenger car. Loading area totals 1 m². Fit for passenger transportation, routing and delivery of goods.

TOYOTA MOTOR PRODUCT

TOYOPET MASTERLINE WAGON RS26-V

Overall Length: 4,380 mm. Overall Width: 1,680 mm. Overall Height: 1,605 mm. Wheelbase: 2,530 mm. Vehicle Weight: 1,260 kg. No. of Seats & Capacity: 6+ 400 kg or 3+500 kg. Engine: 4 cycle 4 cyl 1,453 cc 60 HP 4,500 rpm 100 km/h. Clutch: Single dry plate with torsional rubber dampers. Transmission: Synchromesh. No. of Speeds: forward 3, reverse 1 Gear Ratio: 5.286 Tire: front 6.00—15, 6PLT rear 6.00—15, 6PLT

This commercial car features graceful styling originated from the passenger car. Special attention has been given to allow wide opening in the rear for loading and unloading.

TOYOTA MOTOR PRODUCT

TOYOPET CORONALINE PT16-V

Overall Length: 3,970 mm. Overall Width: 1,475 mm. Overall Height: 1,575 mm. Wheelbase: 2,400 mm. Vehicle Weight: 1,025 kg. No. of Seats & Capacity: 5+300 kg or 2+500 kg. Engine: 4 cycle 4 cyl 997 cc 45 HP 5,000 rpm 100 km/h. Clutch: Single dry plate with torsional rubber dampers. Transmission: Synchromesh. No. of Speeds: forward 3, reverse 1 Gear Ratio: 6.167 Tire: front 5.50—14, 6P rear 5.50—14, 6P

The car is a happy combination of merits of both midget passenger cars and small trucks. Original amazing riding comfort and ease of driving of the passenger car are perfectly maintained.

TOYOTA MOTOR PRODUCT

TOYOPET ROUTE VAN RK85-V

Overall Length: 4,675 mm. Overall Width: 1,680 mm. Overall Height: 1,990 mm. Wheelbase: 2,750 mm. Vehicle Weight: 1,620 kg. No. of Seats: 3 Engine: Gasoline, pushrod ohv, 4 cycle 4 cyl 1,453 cc 60HP 4,500 rpm 100 km/h. Clutch: Single dry plate with torsional rubber dampers. Transmission: Synchromesh, second, third and top speeds, remote control, helical. No. of Speeds: forward 4, reverse 1 Gear Ratio: 6.167 Tire: front 7.00—15, 6P rear 7.50—15, 10P

Under-seat engine permits spacious leg-room and shifting of controls forward for more cargo loading. The RK85V offers a winning combination of high-finish sales-promotion car and utility truck.

TOYOTA MOTOR PRODUCT

TOYO-ACE LIGHT VAN PK20-V

Overall Length: 4,280 mm. Overall Width: 1,690 mm. Overall Height: 1,940 mm. Wheelbase: 2,500 mm. Vehicle Weight: 1,360 kg. No. of Seats & Capacity: 3+1,000 kg. Engine: 4 cycle 4 cyl 997 cc 45 HP 5,000 rpm 90 km/h. Clutch: Single dry plate with torsional rubber dampers. Transmission: Synchromesh. No. of Speeds: forward 4, reverse 1 Gear Ratio: 7.167 Tire: front 6.00—15, 6PLT rear 6.00—15, 8PLT

Specially designed for damage-free transportation of delicate and bulky items. By installing a broadcasting unit, the vehicle will serve the purpose of a sales promotion van also.

TOYOTA MOTOR PRODUCT

PRINCE SKYWAY LIGHT VAN ALVG

Overall Length: 4,420 mm. Overall Width: 1,680 mm. Overall Height: 1,590 mm. Wheelbase: 2,535 mm. Vehicle Weight: 1,410 kg. No. of Seats: 6 Engine: Water-cooled, ohv, gasoline, 4 cycle 4 cyl 1,484 cc 70 HP 4,800 rpm 115 km/h. Clutch: Single dry plate. Transmission: Synchromesh, selective rotation. No. of Speeds: forward 4, reverse 1 Gear Ratio: 1st 5.15, 2nd 3.03, 3rd 1.70, 4th 1.00, Reverse 5.97 Tire: front 5.50—15, 6P rear 6.00—15, 8P

Transfer and movement of freight and goods on the passenger car is the fundamental thought of the design of this particular universal vehicle. Front roller-mounted adjustable seats and rear foldable seats are one of the outstanding features.

FUJI PRECISION PRODUCT

PRINCE NEW MILER LIGHT VAN ARVF

Overall Length: 4,690 mm. Overall Width: 1,680 mm. Overall Height: 1,790 mm. Wheelbase: 2,800 mm. Vehicle Weight: 1,600 kg. No. of Seats: 6 Engine: Water-cooled, ohv, gasoline, 4 cycle 4 cyl 1,484 cc 70 HP 4,800 rpm 110 km/h. Clutch: Single dry plate. Transmission: Synchromesh, selective rotation. No. of Speeds: forward 4, reverse 1 Gear Ratio: 1st 5.19, 2nd 3.03, 3rd 1.70, 4th 1.00, reverse 5.97 Tire: front 6.50—16, 6P rear 6.50—16, 8P

A robust chassis of the PRINCE NEW MILER TRUCK is used in common for mounting a light van body admitting 6 passengers and 500 kg load. By a simple modification it is possible to carry 3 passengers and 1,000 kg load.

FUJI PRECISION PRODUCT

HINO COMMERCE VAN

Overall Length: 3,930 mm. Overall Width: 1,690 mm. Overall Height: 1,880 mm. Wheelbase: 2,100 mm. Vehicle Weight: 1,625 kg. No. of Seats & Capacity: 2+500 kg. Engine: 4 cycle 4 cyl 836 cc 28 HP 4,600 rpm 82 km/h. Clutch: Single dry plate. Transmission: Synchromesh, second, third and top speeds. Gear Ratio: Spiral bevel gear. Tire: front 5.50—14, 6PR rear 5.50—14, 6PR

The note-worthy features of the Hino Commerce are the ample dimension of inside loading area, extreme low level of the floor and ample opening width of doors. The vehicle is intended for transportation of both passengers and goods.

HINO MOTORS PRODUCT

PRINCE SKYWAY PICK-UP ALPE

Overall Length: 4,420 mm.　Overall Width: 1,680 mm.　Overall Height: 1,575 mm.　Wheelbase: 2,535 mm.
Vehicle Weight: 1,375 kg.　No. of Seats: 6　Engine: Water-cooled, ohv, gasoline, 4 cycle 4 cyl 1,484 cc 70 HP
4,800 rpm 115 km/h.　Clutch: Single dry plate.　Transmission: Synchromesh, selective rotation.　No. of Speeds:
forward 4, reverse 1　Gear Ratio: 1st 5.19, 2nd 3.03, 3rd 1.70, 4th 1.00, reverse 5.97　Tire: front 5.50 15, 6P
rear 6.00 15, 8P

*Combination of passenger car and truck taking 6 passengers and 500 kg load, retaining high standard of comfort.
Available for use as the service cars, delivery cars and liason cars.*

FUJI PRECISION PRODUCT

PRINCE ROUTE VAN AQVH

Overall Length: 4,690 mm.　Overall Width: 1,695 mm.　Overall Height: 1,990 mm. Wheelbase: 2,345 mm.　Vehicle Weight: 1,760 kg.　No. of Seats: 3　Engine: Water-cooled, ohv, gasoline, 4 cycle 4 cyl 1,484 cc 70 HP 4,800 rpm 107 km/h. Clutch: Single dry plate.　Transmission: Synchromesh, selective rotation.　No. of Speeds: forward 4, reverse 1　Gear Ratio: 1st 5.19, 2nd 3.03, 3rd 1.70, 4th 1.00, reverse 5.97　Tire: front 6.50 16, 6P rear 6.50 16, 8P

This medium-sized commercial vehicle is provided with the greatest loading area in the equivalent vehicles in Japan, accommodating 3 passengers and 1,250 kg load. The body can be used for carrying 6 passengers and 850 kg load by a slight modification.

FUJI PRECISION PRODUCT

KUROGANE NCV

Overall Length: 4,210 mm.　Overall Width: 1,690 mm.　Overall Height: 1,940 mm. Wheelbase: 2,350 mm.　Vehicle Weight: 1,510 kg.　No. of Saetes & Capacity: 3+ 1,000 kg. 6+750 kg.　Engine: 4 cycle 4 cyl 1,046 cc 42 HP 4,700 rpm 90 km/n. Clutch: Single dry plate.　Transmission: Constant mesh.　No. of Speeds: forward 4, reverse 1　Gear Ratio: 1st 4.896, 2nd 2.881, 3rd 1.755, 4th 1.000　Tire: front 6.00-15, 6P rear 6.50 -15, 8P

This is a multi-purpose light vehicle of all-steel construction. It can be used as a 6 passenger light van, delivery van, sales promotion car and service car.

TOKYU KUROGANE MOTOR PRODUCT

LIGHT TRUCK

In contrast to heavy-duty trucks, light trucks are suited to carry light goods from 1 ton to 2 tons. In addition to goods of such weight, the vehicles have seating accommodations for 2 or 3 persons. Light trucks are running on Japanese narrow roads in ever-increasing numbers. Smaller 3-wheeled trucks which carry goods of less than ½ ton are also becoming very popular in Japan.

Datsun truck seen parked in front of a cathedral in Barcelona, Spain.

NISSAN JUNIOR CABALL C43

Overall Length: 4,580 mm. Overall Width: 1,675 mm. Overall Height: 1,990 mm. Wheelbase: 2,390 mm. Vehicle Weight: 1,505 kg. No. of Seats: 3, payload 2,000 kg. Engine: Gasoline, water-cooled, in-line, 4 cycle 4 cyl 1,489 cc 57 HP 4,400 rpm 88 km/h. Clutch: Dry, single disc. Transmission: Synchromesh. No. of Speeds: forward 4, reverse 1 Gear Ratio: 6.83 Tire: front 7.00—15, 6P rerr 7.00—15, 10P

Notable mechanical features is a double-barrel carburettor to produce higher performance of the engine. The truck offers very roomy accommodation for three passengers and 2,000 kg load.

NISSAN MOTOR PRODUCT

NISSAN JUNIOR B42

Overall Length: 4,610 mm. Overall Width: 1,675 mm. Overall Height: 1,830 mm. Wheelbase: 2,610 mm. Vehicle Weight: 1,510 kg. No. of Seats: 3, payload 1,750 kg. Engine: Gasoline, water-cooled, in-line, 4 cycle 4 cyl 1,489 cc 57 HP 4,400 rpm 90 km/h. Clutch: Dry, single disc. Transmission: Synchromesh. No. of Speeds: forward 4, reverse 1 Gear Ratio: 6.83 Tire: 7.00—16, 6P rear 7.00—16, 12P

A double-barrel carburettor is mounted for better fuel economy and livelier acceleration. Introduction of high compression ratio contributed to high output, high torque and strong tractive force.

NISSAN MOTOR PRODUCT

ISUZU ELF TL251

Overall Length: 4,690 mm. Overall Width: 1,690 mm. Overall Height: 1,985 mm. Wheelbase: 2,460 mm. Vehicle Weight: 1,530 kg. No. of Seats & Capacity: 3+2,000 kg. Engine: Gasoline, 4 cycle 4 cyl 1,491 cc 60 HP 4,600 rpm 100 km/h. Clutch: Single dry plate with rubber damper Transmission: Synchromesh, partially sliding. No. of Speeds: forward 4, reverse 1 Gear Ratio: 6.83 (41/6) Tire: front 7.00—15, 6P rear 7.00—15, 12P

Designed and constructed either for long hauls and short door-to-door delivery. Powerful 60 HP engine and the longest ever known rear body are mounted for transporting materials of unusual lengths.

ISUZU MOTOR PRODUCT

MITSUBISHI "JUPITER" T10-DA (T11-GA)

Overall Length: 5,370 mm.　Overall Width: 1,850 mm.　Overall Height: 1,950 mm (gasoline)　1,940 mm (diesel). Wheelbase: 3,310 mm.　Vehicle Weight: 1,750 kg.　No. of Seats & Capacity: 3+2,000 kg (diesel) 3,000 kg (gasoline). Engine: Gasoline or diesel,　4 cycle　4 cyl　2,199 cc　75 HP　4,000 rpm　95 m/kh (gasoline), 62 HP 3,600 rpm　80 km/h (diesel).　Clutch: Single disc, dry, hydraulic operation.　Transmission: Synchromesh.　No. of Speeds: forward 4, reverse 1　Gear Ratio: 6.333　Tire: front 7.00—16,8P (gasoline), 6.50—16, 8P (diesel) rear 7.00—16, 8P (gasoline), 6.50—16, 8P (diesel)

Low floor construction affords easy loading. Payload: 2,000 kg for Diesel engine; 3,000 kg for gasoline engine. This powerful truck features the pneumatically intensified oilbrake and synchromesh transmission.

MITSUBISHI REORGANIZED PRODUCT

MITSUBISHI "JUPITER" T11-GBH

Overall Length: 6,400 mm.　Overall Width: 1,900 mm.　Overall Height: 1,970 mm.　Wheelbase: 3,860 mm. Vehicle Weight: 2,000 kg.　No. of Seats & Capacity: 3+3,000 kg.　Engine: Gasoline, 4 cycle　4 cyl　2,199 cc 75 HP　4,000 rpm　95 km/h.　Clutch: Single disc, dry, hydraulic operation.　Transmission: Synchromesh.　No. of Speeds: forward 4 reverse 1　Gear Ratio: 6.333　Tire: front 7.00—16, 8P rear: 7.00—16, 8P dual

This particular truck represents a medium-sized truck of high floor construction, provided with a rear body 4 m long. Driver's cab is glazed with the panoramic window affording an excellent visibility.

MITSUBISHI REORGANIZED PRODUCT

MITSUBISHI "JUPITER" T22-DBH

Overall Length: 6,540 mm. Overall Width: 1,900 mm. Overall Height: 1,970 mm. Wheelbase: 3,860 mm. Vehicle Weight: 2,100 kg.　No. of Seats & Capacity: 3+ 3,000 kg.　Engine: Diesel, 4 cycle　6 cyl　3,300 cc　85 HP 3,500 rpm　91 km/h.　Clutch: Single disc, dry, hydraulic operation.　Transmission: 4 speeds, synchromesh, remote control.　No. of Speeds: forward 4, reverse 1　Gear Ratio: 5.5　Tire: front 7.00—16, 10P rear 7.00—16, 10P dual

The KE-36 Diesel engine is available with model T22 DBH in 3,000 kg payload. The six-cylinder engine squeezes more energy from every drop of fuel, giving higher horse power out-put, 85 HP at 3,500 rpm. with greater fuel economy.

MITSUBISHI REORGANIZED PRODUCT

TOYOPET STOUT RK30

Overall Length: 4,285 mm. Overall Width: 1,685 mm. Overall Height: 1,700 mm. Wheelbase: 2,515 mm. Vehicle Weight: 1,345 kg. No. of Seats: 3 Engine: 4 cycle 4 cyl 1,453 cc 60 HP 4,500 rpm 100 km/h. Clutch: Single dry plate with torsional rubber dampers. Transmission: Synchromesh No. of Speeds: forward 4, reverse 1 Gear Ratio: 6.167 Tire: front 7.00—15, 6PLT rear 7.00—15, 10PLT

Designed to fulfil the double purpose of transportation of goods and passengers as well. Improved in many details as synchromesh gears in higher speeds, remote control steering system, front seat accommodating three persons, etc.

TOYOTA MOTOR PRODUCT

TOYOPET STOUT RK35-B

Overall Length: 4,675 mm. Overall Width: 1,685 mm. Overall Height: 1,700 mm. Wheelbase: 2,740 mm. Vehicle Weight: 1,380 kg. No. of Seats & Capacity: 3+1,750 kg. Engine: 4 cycle 4 cyl 1,453 cc 60 HP 4,500 rpm 105 km/h. Clutch: Single dry plate with torsional rubber dampers. Transmission: Synchromesh. No. of Speeds: forward 4, reverse 1 Gear Ratio: 6.167 Tire: front 7.00—15, 6PLT rear 7.50—15, 10 PLT

Strenuous efforts have been exercised to produce a pleasing appearance as a vehicle of versatile purpose. Powerful engine is installed to stand rough usage under hard working conditions.

TOYOTA MOTOR PRODUCT

PRINCE NEW MILER ARTH

Overall Length: 4,680 mm. Overall Width: 1,695 mm. Overall Height: 1,775 mm. Wheelbase: 2,800 mm. Vehicle Weight: 1,590 kg. No. of Seats: 3 Engine: Water-cooled, ohv, gasoline, 4 cycle 4 cyl 1,484 cc 70 HP 4,800 rpm 108 km/h. Clutch: Single dry plate. Transmission: Synchromesh, selective rotation. No. of Speeds: forward 4, reverse 1 Gear Ratio: 1st 5.19, 2nd 3.03, 3rd 1.70, 4th 1.00, reverse 5.97 Tire: front 7.00 16, 6P rear 7.00 16, 12P

Represents a medium-sized bonnet-type truck with an exceptionally spacious loading area. Notable features are high-performance engine and low floor chassis. Good forward visibility and reasonable riding comfort are other notable features.

FUJI PRECISION PRODUCT

TOYOPET DYNA RK85

Overall Length: 4,665 mm. Overall Width: 1,680 mm. Overall Height: 1,980 mm. Wheelbase: 2,740 mm. Vehicle Weight: 1,440 kg. No. of Seats: 3 Engine: 4 cycle 4 cyl 1,453 cc 60 HP 4,500 rpm 105 km/h. Clutch: Single dry plate with torsional rubber dampers. Transmission: Synchromesh. No. of Speeds: forward 4, reverse 1 Gear Ratio: 6.167 Tire: front 7.00—15, 6 PLT rear 7.50—15, 10 PLT

An outstanding feature of this light truck is an exceptionally long cargo body afforded by the semi-cabover arrangement of the engine. Single piece glass windshield contributes to wider range of vision.

TOYOTA MOTOR PRODUCT

TOYO-ACE PK20

Overall Length: 4,260 mm. Overall Width: 1,690 mm. Overall Height: 1,895 mm. Wheelbase: 2,500 mm. Vehicle Weight: 1,175 kg. No. of Seats & Capacity: 3+1,000 kg. (1,250 kg.) Engine: 4 cycle 4 cyl 997 cc 45 HP 5,000 rpm 90 km/h. Clutch: Single dry plate with torsional rubber dampers. Transmission: Synchromesh. No. of Speeds: forward 4, reverse 1 Gear Ratio: 7.167 Tire: front 6.00—15, 6 P rear 6.00—15, 8P

A modern method of approach for body design is indicated by this cab-over construction. Loading area of rear body is increased beyond the conventional proportion. Much attention is paid to improve riding comfort.

TOYOTA MOTOR PRODUCT

PRINCE CLIPPER AQTI

Overall Length: 4,690 mm. Overall Width: 1,695 mm. Overall Height: 1,975 mm. Wheelbase: 2,345 mm. Vehicle Weight: 1,630 kg. No. of Seats: 3 Engine: Water-cooled, ohv, gasoline, 4 cycle, 4 cyl 1,484 cc 70 HP 4,800 rpm 105 km/h. Clutch: Single dry plate. Transmission: Synchromesh, selective rotation. No. of Speeds: forward 4 reverse 1 Gear Ratio: 1st 5.19, 2nd 3.03, 3rd 1.70, 4th 1.00, reverse 5.97 Tire: front 7.00—16, 6P rear 7.00—16, 10P

This particular light truck was provided, for the first time in Japan, with the under-seat engine. Results of this epoch-making arrangement are spacious room for carrying three persons and 2,000 kg load. Other important features are heavy-duty duplex brakes.

FUJI PRECISION PRODUCT

KUROGANE NOVA KN1500

Overall Length: 4,690 mm.　　Overall Width: 1,690 mm.　　Overall Height: 1,765 mm.　　Wheelbase: 2,850 mm.
Vehicle Weight: 1,650 kg.　　No. of Seats: 3　　Engine: 4 cycle　　4 cyl　1,488 cc　62 HP　4,700 rpm　95 km/h.
Clutch: Dry, single disc.　　Transmission: Shynchromesh.　　No. of Speeds: forward 4, reverse 1　　Gear Ratio:
1st 5.218, 2nd 3.083, 3rd 1.713, 4th 1.000, reverse 6.377　Tire: front 7.00—16, 6 PLT　rear 7.50—16, 12 PLT
   This particular light truck is powered by 12 HP engine, giving accommodation to three passengers and 2,000 kg load. Emphasis has been placed for obtaining increased riding comfort as well as high performance.
TOKYU KUROGANE MOTOR PRODUCT

KUROGANE BABY CARRIER KB360

Overall Length: 2,990 mm. Overall Width: 1,278 mm.　　Overall Height: 1,665 mm. Wheelbase: 1,750 mm.　　Vehicle Weight: 480 kg.　No. of Seats: 2 (4)　　Engine: 4 cycle　2 cyl　356 cc　18 HP　4,500 rpm 70 km/h.　Clutch: Single dry plate.　Transmission: Selective constant mesh　No. of Speeds: forward 3, reverse 1　Gear Ratio: 1st 24.84, 2nd 15.92, 3rd 7.66 reverse 33.12 Tire: front. 4.50—12, 4P　rear 4.50—12, 4P
  Recent introduction of the smallest class of trucks. Fourstroke two-cylinder water-cooled engine mounted in the rear, takes 350 kg of load. Simplest body construction comprising pipes, angles and other common shapes. Available for business trips and for short haulage.
TOKYU KUROGANE MOTOR PRODUCT

KUROGANE BABY CANVAS WAGON KB360

Overall Length: 2,990 mm. Overall Width: 1,278 mm. Overall Height: 1,665 mm. Wheelbase 1,750 mm. Vehicle Weight: 480 kg. No. of Seats: 2 (4) Engine: 4 cycle 2 cyl 356 cc 18 HP 4,500 rpm 70 km/h. Clutch: Single dry plate. Transmission: Selective constant mesh No. of Speeds: forward 3, reverse 1 Gear Ratio: 1st 24.84, 2nd 15.92, 3rd 7.66, reverse 33.12 Tire: front 4.50—12, 4PLT rear 4.50—12, 4 PLT

Designed and constructed for accommodation of four persons and some quantity of goods in addition. Fit for family picnics and trips.

TOKYU KUROGANE MOTOR PRODUCT

KUROGANE NB

Overall Length: 4,675 mm. Overall Width: 1,690 mm. Overall Height: 1,975 mm. Wheelbase: 2,700 mm. Vehicle Weight: 1,630 kg. No. of Seats: 3 Engine: 4 cycle 4 cyl 1,488 cc 62 HP 4,700 rpm 95 km/h. Clutch: Dry, single disc. Transmission: Shynchromesh. No. of Speeds: forward 4, reverse 1 Gear Ratio: 1st 5.218, 2nd 3.083, 3rd 1.713, 4th 1.000, reverse 6.377 Tire: front 7.00—15, 6 PLT rear 7.50—15, 10 PLT

Maximum allowable interior dimensions were given to the rear body. Side boards and tail gate can easily be hinged down to afford convenient loading and emptying.

TOKYU KUROGANE MOTOR PRODUCT

KUROGANE BABY COMMERCIAL KB360

Overall Length: 2,990 mm. Overall Width: 1,278 mm. Overall Height: 1,665 mm. Wheelbase: 1,750 mm. Vehicle Weight: 480 mm. No. of Seats: 2 (4) Engine: 4 cycle 2 cyl 356 cc 18 HP 4,500 rpm 70 km/h. Clutch: Single dry plate. Transmission: Selective constant mesh. No. of Speeds: forward 3, reverse 1 Gear Ratio: 1st 24.84, 2nd 15.92, 3rd 7.66, reverse 33.12 Tire: front 4.50—12, 4P rear 4.50—12, 4P

On this vehicle, loads are completely covered by taupauline preventing any possible damages during transportation. Reasonable riding comfort afforded by light weight construction.

TOKYU KUROGANE MOTOR PRODUCT

MAZDA D1100 (DTA81)

Overall Length: 4,290 mm. Overall Width: 1,690 mm. Overall Height: 1,910 mm. Wheelbase: 2,500 mm. Vehicle Weight: 1,375 kg. No. of Seats: 3 Engine: Water-cooled, ohv, 4 cycle 4 cyl 1,139 cc. 46 HP 4,600 rpm 87 km/h. Clutch: Single dry plate, foot-operated, hydraulic. Transmission: Synchromesh. No. of Speeds: forward 4, reverse 1 Gear Ratio: low 5.28, 2nd 2.92, 3rd 1.72, top 1.00, reverse 7.05 Tire: front 6.00—16, 6 PLT rear 6.00—16, 8 PLT

Excellent riding comfort equivalent to a passenger car and pleasing external appearance have been sought. Engine is powerful enough to haul 1,000 kg load.

TOYO KOGYO PRODUCT

DAIHATSU VESTA FPOL

Overall Length: 4,690 mm. Overall Width: 1,690 mm. Overall Height: 1,980 mm. Wheelbase: 2,600 mm. Vehicle Weight: 1,780 kg. No. of Seats: 3 Engine: 4 cycle V-2 cyl 1,478 cc 53 HP 3,600 rpm 85km/h. Clutch: Single dry plate. Transmission: Synchromesh 2.3, Selective sliding 1.R. No. of Speeds: forward 6, reverse 2 Gear Ratio: forward 6.833, 9.737, 13.441, 19.055, 26.321, 37.507 reverse 33.837, 48.218 Tire: front 6.00—16, 8 PLT rear 6.00—16, 8 PLT

Notable features are two-cylinder V-type water-cooled engine, rear body of generous load carrying capacity and strong chassis fabricated with 6 mm thick steel plates. Dual tires are used.

DAIHATSU KOGYO PRODUCT

CONY 360

Overall Length: 2,985 mm. Overall Width: 1,285 mm. Overall Height: 1,515 mm. Wheelbase: 1,955 mm. Vehicle Weight: 575 kg. No. of Seats: 2 Engine: Air-cooled, gasoline, 4 cycle 2 cyl 359 cc 16 HP 4,800 rpm 66 km/h. Clutch: Single dry plate. Transmission: Constant mesh No. of Speeds: forward 3 reverse 1 Gear Ratio: forward 4.38, 2.16, 1.14 reverse 4.77 Tire: front 5.50—13, 4 P (SLP) or 5.20—13, 6 P (ELP) rear 5.50—13, 4P (SLP) or 5.20—13, 6P (ELP)

This midget-type four-wheeled truck, having a loading capacity of 350 kg, is powered by a four-stroke, horizontally opposed two-cylinder, fan-cooled engine, developed by a well-known three-wheeled truck manufacturer which had been producing GIANT for considerable period of time. The driver's cabin is equipped with separate seats accommodating two persons.

AICHI MACHINE PRODUCT

MAZDA D1500 (DUA12S)

Overall Length: 4,690 mm. Overall Width: 1,690 mm. Overall Height: 1,940 mm. Wheelbase: 2,800 mm. Vehicle Weight: 1,620 kg. No. of Seats: 3 Engine: Water-cooled, ohv, 4 cycle 4 cyl 1,484 cc 60 HP 4,600 rpm 95 km/h. Clutch: Single dry plate, foot-operated, hydraulic. Transmission: Synchromesh. No. of Speeds: forward 4, reverse 1 Gear Ratio: low 5.28, 2nd 2.92, 3rd 1.72, top 1.00, reverse 7.05 Tire: front 6.00—16, 6PLT reverse 7.50—16, 10PLT

Engine is of water-cooled, 4-stroke, overhead-valve-type provided with synchromesh transmission gear box. Rear body is of robust constuction, capable of hauling 2,000 kg load at high speeds.

TOYO KOGYO PRODUCT

IHATSU VESTA FPO

Overall Length: 4,690 mm. Overall Width: 1,690 mm. Overall Height: 1,980 mm. Wheelbase: 2,600 mm. Vehicle Weight: 1,760 kg. No. of Seats: 3 Engine: 4 cycle V-2 cyl 1,478 cc 53 HP 3,600 rpm 85 km/h. Clutch: Single dry plate. Transmission: Synchromesh 2.3, selective sliding 1.R. No. of Speeds: forward 6, reverse 2 Gear Ratio: forward 6.833, 9.737, 13.441, 19.055, 26.321, 37.507 reverse 33.837, 48.218 Tire: front 6.00—16, 8 PLT rear 6.00—16, 8 PLT double

Powerful two-cylinder V-type water-cooled engine assures satisfactory tractive force. Rear body is of the low floor construction contributing to easy loading. Dual tires are used.

DAIHATSU KOGYO PRODUCT

PADDLE PD33

Overall Length: 2,990 mm. Overall Width: 1,280 mm. Overall Height: 1,430 mm. Wheelbase: 1,950 mm. Vehicle Weight: 515 kg. No. of Seats: 2 Engine: 4 cycle 2 cyl 359 cc 15 HP 4,000 rpm 60 km/h. Clutch: Single plate. Transmission: Constant mesh. No. of Speeds: forward 4 reverse 1 Gear Ratio: forward 3.875, 2.131, 1.389, 1.000, reverse 4.810 Tire: front 4.00—16, 4P rear: 4.00—16, 6P

This new light truck features compact water-cooled engine with two cylinders arranged in vertical twin type. Four speed transmission gear box is coupled directly to the engine; Easiness of driving and economy of driving costs are outstanding features.

MITAKA FUJI PRODUCT

HEAVY-DUTY TRUCK

This group of trucks are suitable for hauling heavy loads to distant places, e.g. from producing districts to markets. The construction of bodies vary according to the kinds of loads such as steel sheets, gravel, lumber, cement, agricultural products, etc.
Dump trucks under this group range in carrying capacity from 2 tons to 10 tons and are built durable and strong enough to stand the heaviest work.
Special types of trucks such as cargo trucks and trailer trucks are also built to meet customers' requirements.

MITSUBISHI FUSO T33
DIESEL

Overall Length: 8,190 mm. Overall Width: 2,480 mm. Overall Height: approx 2,500 mm. Wheelbase: 4,800 mm. Vehicle Weight: 5,775 kg. No. of Seats: 3, loading capacity 8,000 kg. Engine: Diesel, 4 cycle 6 cyl 8,550 cc 165 HP 2,300 rpm 77 km/h. Clutch: Single dry plate. Transmission: Selective sliding. No. of Speeds: forward 4, reverse 1 Gear Ratio: 5.667 (final drive gear) Tire: front 10.00—20, 14P rear 10.00—20, 14 p

This heavy duty Diesel truck is featured by the air-servo oil brake to ensure hard driving on rough terrain. Power-assisted steering five speed transmission is available.

MITSUBISHI NIPPON PRODUCT

NISSAN UG680
DIESEL

Overall Length: 7,355 mm. Overall Width: 2,275 mm. Overall Height: 2,335 mm. Wheelbase: 4,200 mm. Vehicle Weight: 4,240 kg. No. of Seats: 3, payload 6,000 kg. Engine: Diesel, water-cooled, in-line, direct, 2 cycle 3 cyl 3,706 cc 120 HP 2,200 rpm 80 km/h. Clutch: Dry, single disc. Transmission: Synchromesh. No. of Speeds: forward 5, reverse 1. Gear Ratio: 6.17 Tire: front 8.25—20, 14 P rear 8.25—20, 14 P double

The UD 3 Diesel engine designed and constructed for longer durability and maximum economy is mounted on this heavy-duty truck. Generously dimensioned Hypoid differential gear is mounted on the rear axle.

NISSAN MOTOR PRODUCT

MINSEI T80

Overall Length: 8,190 mm. Overall Width: 2,480 mm. Overall Height: 2,500 mm. Wheelbase: 4,800 mm. Vehicle Weight: 5,610 kg. No. of Seats: 3 Engine: 2 cycle 4 cyl 4,941 cc 155 HP 2,000 rpm 81 km/h. Clutch: Single dry plate. Transmission: Conventional. No. of Speeds: forward 4, reverse 1 Gear Ratio: 1st 5.82, 2nd 2.92, 3rd 1.91, 4th 1.00, reverse 7.12 Tire: front 10.00 20, 14 P rear 10.00—20, 14 P

The engine power has recently been raised to 155 HP. Maximum rigidity is given to frame construction. It is fit for long distance transportation of heavy loads.

MINSEI DIESEL PRODUCT

NISSAN G680

Overall Length: 7,355 mm. Overall Width: 2,275 mm. Overall Height: 2,330 mm. Wheelbase: 4,200 mm. Vehicle Weight: 3,785 kg. No. of Seats: 3, payload 6,000 kg. Engine: Gasoline, water-cooled, in-line, 4 cycle 6 cyl 3,956 cc 125 HP 3,400 rpm 92 km/h. Clutch: Dry, single disc. Transmission: Synchromesh. No. of Speeds: forward 5, reverse 1 Gear Ratio: 6.83, optional 6.17 Tire: front 8.25—20, 14 P rear 8.25—20, 14 P double

First heavy-duty truck in Japan mounted with the four head lamps. The driver's cab is fitted with panoramic window ensuring high standard of visibility. Body of dynamic styling and strength affords carrying capacity of 6,000 kg.

NISSAN MOTOR PRODUCT

ISUZU TX550

Overall Length: 7,490 mm. Overall Width: 2,340 mm. Overall Height: 2,430 mm. Wheelbase: 4,300 mm. Vehicle Weight: 4,425 kg. No. of Seats & Capacity: 3+ 6,000 kg. Engine: Diesel, 4 cycle 6 cyl 6,126 cc. 125 HP 2,600 rpm 103 km/h. Clutch: Single dry plate with rubber damper. Transmission: Synchromesh, partially sliding, w/overdrive No. of Speeds: forward 5 reverse 1 Gear Ratio: 5.57 (39/7) Tire: front 8.25—20, 14 P rear 8.25—20, 14 P

This 6,000 kg carrying heavy-duty truck is provided with rear cargo body as long as 4.6 m. It is fit for long distance transportation of heavy and bulky loads. An overdrive is installed in the transmission gear box.

ISUZU MOTOR PRODUCT

ISUZU TW540

SIX-WHEEL-DRIVE VEHICLE

Overall Length: 7,345 mm. Overall Width: 2,340 mm. Overall Height: 2,440 mm. Wheelbase: 4,000 mm. Vehicle Weight: 5,765 kg. No. of Seats & Capacity: 3+ 6,000 kg. Engine: Diesel, 4 cycle 6 cyl 6,126 cc 125 HP 2,600 rpm 65 km/h. Clutch: Single dry plate with rubber damper. Transmission: Synchromesh, partially sliding. No. of Speeds: forward 4 reverse 1 Gear Ratio: 6.5 (39/6) Tire: front 7.50—20, 12 P rear 7.50—20, 12 P

High-performance Diesel engine with the output of 125 HP is installed for driving six wheels separately. It is suited for rough usage under hard working condition on mountain districts, uneven terrains and sandy grounds.

ISUZU MOTOR PRODUCT

ISUZU TX640-W

Overall Length: 7,000 mm. Overall Width: 2,340 mm. Overall Height: 2,410 mm. Wheelbase: 4,000 mm. Vehicle Weight: 4,095 kg. No. of Seats & Capacity: 3+ 5,000 kg. Engine: 4 cycle 6 cyl 5,654 cc. 145 HP 3,000 rpm 88 km/h. Clutch: Single dry plate with rubber damper. Transmission: Synchromesh, partially sliding. No. of Speeds: forward 4 reverse 1 Gear Ratio: 5.57 (39/7) Tire: front 7.50—20, 12 P rear 7.50—20, 12 P

This powerful truck is powered either by 145 HP gasoline engine or 125 HP Diesel engine. A specially long rear body of 4.6 m is mounted for accommodating load of unusual lengths.

ISUZU MOTOR PRODUCT

TOYOTA DA80 (95)
DIESEL

Overall Length: 7,105 mm. (7,405 mm.) Overall Width: 2,400 mm. (2,400 mm.) Overall Height: 2,285 mm. (2,310 mm.) Wheelbase: 4,200 mm. (4,200 mm.) Vehicle Weight: 4,130 kg. (4,420 kg.) No. of Seats & Capacity: 3+5,000 kg. (3+6,000 kg.) Engine: 4 cycle 6 cyl 5,890 cc (6,494cc) 110 (130) HP 2,600 rpm 75 (95) km/h. Clutch: Single dry plate with torsional rubber dampers. Transmission: Synchromesh, 2, 3, 4 speeds, helical. No. of Speeds: forward 4 reverse 1 Gear Ratio: 5.83 (1st 6.78, 2nd 4.79) Tire: front 7.50-20, 12 P (8.25-20, 14 P) rear 7.50-20, 12 P (8.25-20, 14 P)

This heavy-duty truck is powered by compact and high-performance Diesel engine. Ample dimensions are given to rear cargo body, provided with an unusual length of 4.25 m. The Hypoid differential gear, synchromesh gear transmission and two-speed rear axle are outstanding functional features.

TOYOTA MOTOR PRODUCT

HINO TH
WITH CAB

Overall Length: 7,810 mm. Overall Width: 2,395 mm. Overall Height: 2,440 mm. Wheelbase: 4,800 mm. Vehicle Weight: 4,690 kg. Engine: 4 cycle 6 cyl 7,698cc 150 HP 2,400 rpm 80 km/h. Clutch: Single plate, dry disc. Transmisson: Selective sliding spur gear with 1 overdrive gear. No. of Speeds: forward (standard) 4 (optional) 5 reverse 1 Gear Ratio: 1st 5.41, 2nd 3.08, 3rd 1.72 4th 1.00, reverse 6.49 Tire: front 11.00—20 rear 11.00—20

This multi-purpose truck chassis is powered by a 150 HP Diesel engine. It is designed and constructed to suit heavy trucks of maximum payload and for long distance transportation. A special air brake system affords positive and safe operation.

HINO MOTORS PRODUCT

HINO TE

Overall Length: 7,525 mm. Overall Width: 2,030 mm. Overall Height: 2,230 mm. Wheelbase: 4,300 mm. Vehicle Weight: 11,585 kg. No. of Seats & Capacity: 2+6,500 kg. Engine: 4 cycle 6 cyl 7,014 cc. 135 HP 2,500 rpm 93 km/h. Clutch: Single dry plate. Transmission: Selective sliding, helical & spur gear. No. of Speeds: forward 5 reverse 1 Gear Ratio: worm & gear 26:1 Tire: front 9.20—20, 14 P (optional 8.25—20, 14 P) rear 9.20—20, 14 P (optional 8.25—20, 14 P)

This truck is powered by a 150 HP Diesel engine specially designed for economical operation. Rigidly built chassis accommodating a loading capacity of 6,500 kg is provided with a particularly short radius of turning circle. Wheels are equipped with pneumatic power-assisted brakes.

HINO MOTORS PRODUCT

TOYOTA FA80 (95-H)

Overall Length: 7,105 mm. (7,405 mm.) Overall Width: 2,400 mm. Overall Height: 2,285 mm (2,310 mm.) Wheelbase: 4,200 mm. (4,400 mm.) Vehicle Weight: 3,735 kg. (4,025 kg.) No. of Seats & Capacity: 3+5,000 kg. (3+6,000 kg.) Engine: 4 cycle 6 cyl 3,878 cc. 125 HP 3,600 rpm 90 km/h (110 km/h). Clutch: Single dry plate with torsional rubber dampers. Transmission: Synchromesh. No. of Speeds: forward 4, reverse 1 Gear Ratio: 6.67 (1st 7.64, 2nd 5.60) Tire: front 7.50-20, 12 P (8.25-20, 14 P) rear 7.50-20, 12 P (8.25-20, 14 P)

Powerful and economical gasoline engine is mounted for accommodation of 6,000 kg load. The Hypoid differential gear and two-speed rear axle are outstanding mechanical features. Eight speed transmission gear box is mounted.
TOYOTA MOTOR PRODUCT

TOYOTA FW10
CARGO TRUCK 6×6

Overall Length: 6,507 mm. Overall Width: 2,255 mm. Overall Height: 2,790 mm. Wheelbase: 4,000 mm. Vehicle Weight: 4,690 kg. No. of Seats & Capacity: 2+5,000 kg. Engine: 4 cycle 6 cyl 3,878 cc. 125 HP 3,600 rpm 82 km/h. Clutch: Single dry plate with torsional rubber dampers. Transmission: Synchromesh. No. of Speeds: forward 4, reverse 1 Gear Ratio: 6.667 Tire: front 7.50-20, 10 P rear 7.50-20, 10 P

Designed and constructed to meet the heaviest requirement as the military vehicle, complete with Hotchkiss-drive, full-floating front axle, synchromesh transmission gear box and auxiliary transmission. A winch is mounted in the front and receives engine power through power-takeoff.
TOYOTA MOTOR PRODUCT

TOYOTA DW10
CARGO TRUCK 6×6

Overall Length: 6,507 mm. Overall Width: 2,255 mm. Overall Height: 2,790 mm. Wheelbase: 4,000 mm. Vehicle Weight: 4,980 kg. No. of Seats & Capacity: 2+5,000 kg. Engine: 4 cycle 6 cyl 5,890 cc. 110 HP 2,600 rpm 76 km/h. Clutch: Single dry plate with torsional rubber dampers. Transmission: Synchromesh. No. of Speeds: forward 4 reverse 1 Gear Ratio: 5.83 Tire: 7.50-20, 10 P rear 7.50-20, 10 P

An unique six-wheel-drive truck of rugged reliability. A power-takeoff is provided on the frame for driving a winch, giving the widest range of application.
TOYOTA MOTOR PRODUCT

TANK LORRY

ISUZU TD150

Overall Length: 8,155 mm. Overall Width: 2,470 mm. Overall Height: 2,800 mm. Wheelbase: 4,800 mm. Vehicle Weight: 7,225 kg. No. of Seats & Capacity: 3+9,000 l. Engine: Diesel, 4 cycle 6 cyl 10,179 cc 180 HP 2,300 rpm 106 km/h. Clutch: Single dry plate with rubber damper. Transmission: Synchromesh, partially sliding, w/overdrive. No. of Speeds: forward 5 reverse 1 Gear Ratio: 5.57 (39/7) Tire: front 10.00—20, 14 P rear 10.00—20, 14 P

A Diesel engine of 180 HP is mounted. The capacity of the tank, totalling 9,000 l, is the largest of the same type of vehicles. The chassis of 8,000 kg truck has been converted to install the tank. **ISUZU MOTOR PRODUCT**

NISSAN TG680

Overall Length: 7,080 mm.　Overall Width: 2,350 mm.　Overall Height: 2,400 mm.　Wheelbase: 4,200 mm.　Vehicle Weight: 5,095 kg.　No. of Seats: 3.　Capacity: 7,000 l.　Engine: Gasoline, water-cooled, in-line, 4 cycle 6 cyl　3,956 cc　125HP　3,400 rpm　92 km/h.　Clutch: Dry, single disc.　Transmission: Synchromesh.　No. of Speeds: forward 5, reverse 1　Gear Ratio: 6.83　Tire: front 8.25—20, 14 P　rear 8.25—20, 14 P double

This particular lorry is powered by the Nissan high-torque and high-output engine. The 6,000 kg truck chassis has been converted to support the tank with a capacity of 7,000 l. Applicable for transporting milk.

NISSAN MOTOR PRODUCT

MINSEI T80

Overall Length: 8,377 mm.　Overall Width: 2,400 mm.　Overall Height: 2,600 mm.　Wheelbase: 4,800 mm.　Vehicle Weight: 7,320 kg.　No. of Seats: 3　Engine: 2 cycle　4 cyl　4,941 cc　155HP　2,000 rpm　71 km/h.　Clutch: Single dry plate.　Transmission: Conventional.　No. of Speeds: forward 4 reverse 1　Gear Ratio: 1st 5.82, 2nd 2.92, 3rd 1.91, 4th 1.00 reverse 7.12　Tire: front 10.00—20, 14 P　rear 10.00—20, 14 P

Intensive development work has been done in order to give extra strength to power train, axles and wheels. A powerful Diesel engine is mounted to comply with the requirement for transporting a large amount of fuel to a great distance.

MINSEI DIESEL PRODUCT

TOYOTA FA80

Overall Length: 7,105 mm.　Overall Width: 2,400 mm.　Overall Height: 2,285 mm.　Wheelbase: 4,200 mm.　Vehicle Weight: 4,795 kg.　No. of Seats & Capacity: 3+7000 l.　Engine: Gasoline, ohv, 4 cycle 6 cyl 3,878 cc　125 HP 3,600 rpm　85 km/h.　Clutch: Single dry plate with torsional rubber dampers.　Transmission: Synchromesh, 2nd, 3rd and top speeds, helical.　No. of Speeds: forward 4 reverse 1　Gear Ratio: 6.67　Tire: front 7.50—20, 12 P rear 7.50—20, 12 P

Constructed strongly enough to transport 6,000 l of liquid to a great distance in safety. Incorporated with a powerful pump available for filling and emptying the tank within the shortest length of time.　**TOYOTA MOTOR PRODUCT**

PRINCE NEW MILER VACUUM CAR

Overall Length: 4,560 mm. Overall Width: 1,680 mm. Overall Height: 1,870 mm. Wheelbase: 2,800 mm. Vehicle Weight: 2,205 kg. No. of Seats: 3 Engine: Water-cooled, ohv, gasoline, 4 cycle 4 cyl 1,484 cc 70 HP 4,800 rpm 108 km/h. Clutch: Single dry plate. Transmission: Synchromesh, selective rotation. No. of Speeds: forward 4 reverse 1 Gear Ratio: 1st 5.19, 2nd 3.03, 3rd 1.70, 4th 1.00, reverse 5.97 Tire: front 7.00—16, 6 P rear 7.50—16, 12 P

The prince New-miler chassis has been converted for mounting a strong vacuum suction plant fit for city sewage cleaning purposes. The tank has a capacity of 1,800 l. Maximum suction head: 8 m; maximum pressure: 2.5 kg/cm²; vacuum intensity: 711 mm.Hg.

FUJI PRECISION PRODUCT

PRINCE CLIPPER VACUUM CAR

Overall Length: 4,540 mm. Overall Width: 1,695 mm. Overall Height: 1,980 mm. Wheelbase: 2,345 mm. Vehicle Weight: 2,255 kg. No. of Seats: 3 Engine: Water-cooled, ohv, gasoline, 4 cycle 4 cyl 1,484 cc 70 HP 4,800 rpm 105 km/h. Clutch: Single dry plate. Transmission: Synchromesh, selective rotation. No. of Speeds: forward 4 reverse 1 Gear Ratio: 1st 5.19, 2nd 3.03, 3rd 1.70, 4th 1.00, reverse 5.97 Tire: front 7.00—16, 8P rear 7.00—16, 12 P

The Prince Clipper chassis has been converted for mounting a strong vacuum suction plant fit for city sewage cleaning purposes. The tank has a capacity of 1,800 l. Maximum suction head: 8 m; maximum pressure: 2.5 kg/cm²; Vacuum intensity: 711 mm.Hg.

FUJI PRECISION PRODUCT

DAIHATSU VACCUM CAR FPOE

Overall Length: 4,660 mm. Overall Width: 1,690 mm. Overall Height: 1,950 mm. Wheelbase: 2,600 mm. Vehicle Weight: 2,340 kg. No. of Seats: 3 Engine: 4 cycle V-2 cyl 1,478 cc 53 HP 3,600 rpm 85 km/h. Clutch: Single dry plate. Transmission: Synchromech gear 2.3, selective sliding gear 1.R. No. of Speeds: forward 6 reverse 2 Gear Ratio: foward 6.833, 9.737, 13.441, 19.055, 26.321, 37.507 reverse 33.837, 48.218 Tire: front 6.00—16, 6 PLT 6.00—16, 8 PLT double

Notable features are roomy driver's cab allowing three persons, double transmission mechanism and short radius of turning circle. This particular car is available for use as a cess-pool emptier. The tank has a capacity of 1,800 l.

DAIHATSU KOGYO PRODUCT

FIRE ENGINE

TOYOTA FJ24

Overall Length: 4,200 mm. Overall Width: 1,700 mm. Overall Height: 1,813 mm. Wheelbase: 2,430 mm. Vehicle Weight: 2,160 kg. Engine: 4 cycle 6 cyl 3,878 cc 125 HP 3,600 rpm 99 km/h. Clutch: Single dry plate with torsional rubber dampers. Transmission: Synchromesh. No. of Speeds: forward 4, reverse 1 Gear Ratio: 4.11 Tire: front 6.50—16, 6 P rear 6.50—16, 8 p

This vehicle represents a comparatively smaller type of fire fighters, available for primary stage of fire extinguishing operations. Easy to manoeuvre and fit for threading through gconested areas.

TOYOTA MOTOR PRODUCT

MITSUBISHI "JEEP" CJ3B-J10

Overall Length: 3,539 mm. Overall Width: 1,450 mm. Overall Height: 1,580 mm. Wheelbase: 2,032 mm. Vehicle Weight: 1,540 kg. No. of Seats: 4 Engine: Water-cooled, F-head, 4 cycle 4 cyl 2,199 cc 75 HP 4,000 rpm 95 km/h. Clutch: Vacuum, dry, single disc. Transmission: Synchromesh. No. of Speeds: forward 3, reverse 1 Gear Ratio: 5.375 Tire: front 6.50—16 rear 6.50—16

"Jeep" fire engine of four-wheel drive can rush to any places whether congested or isolated, getting over rough terrain or steep slope or through water, mud, snow or sand. The short radius of turning circle enables the "Jeep" to approach fire area threading through the crowded traffic area.

MITSUBISHI REORGANIZED PRODUCT

TOYOTA FC74

Overall Length: 5,495 mm. Overall Width: 2,185 mm. Overall Height: 2,250 mm. Wheelbase: 3,000 mm. Vehicle Weight: 3,865 kg. Engine: Gasoline, pushrod ohv, 4 cycle 6 cyl 3,878 cc 125 HP 3,600 rpm 85 km/h. Clutch: Single dry plate with torsional rubber dampers. Transmission: Synchromesh, second, third, and top speeds, helical. No. of Speeds: forward 4, reverse 1 Gear Ratio: 1st 7.06, 2nd 3.58, 3rd 1.97, top direct, reverse 6.78 Tire: front 7.00—20, 10 P rear 7.00—20, 10 P

High standard of practicability, including readiness of starting, easiness of driving, etc., is effected by this 110 HP fire engine. Powerful pump assures the most active and lasting fire fighting operations.

TOYOTA MOTOR PRODUCT

NISSAN JUNIOR FRB42

Overall Length: 4,680 mm. Overall Width: 1,760 mm. Overall Height: 2,000 mm. Wheelbase: 2,620 mm. Vehicle Weight: 2,595 kg. No. of Seats: 8 Engine: Gasoline, water-cooled, in-line, 4 cycle 6 cyl 3,956 cc 125 HP 3,400 rpm 110 km/h. Clutch: Dry, single disc. Transmission: Synchromesh. No. of Speeds: forward 4, reverse 1 Gear Ratio 3.91 Tire: front 7.00—16, 6 P rear 7.00—16, 12 P

Regardless of its reduced vehicle dimensions, this special vehicle is powered by an engine with the power output of 125 HP. High standard of performance, such as maximum velocity, gradability, etc., ensures positive practicability both in the crowded part of the city and in the off-highway district.

NISSAN MOTOR PRODUCT

NISSAN F680

Overall Length: 7,210 mm. Overall Width: 2,240 mm. Overall Height: 2,400 mm. Wheelbase: 4,200 mm. Vehicle Weight: 4,820 kg. No. of Seats: 6 Engine: Gasoline, water-cooled, 4 cycle 6 cyl 3,956 cc 125 HP 3,400 rpm 92 km/h. Clutch: Dry, single disc. Transmission: Synchromesh. No. of Speeds: forward 5, reverse 1 Gear Ratio: 6.83 Tire: front 8.25—20, 14 P rear 8.25—20, 14 P double

High-performance engine with power output of 125 HP is mounted on this particular fire fighter. A common chassis can interchangeably be used for a tanked chemical fire extinguisher, injector equipped emergency fire engine, fire-auto with extension ladder, etc.

NISSAN MOTOR PRODUCT

TOYOTA FA74

Overall Length: 7,105 mm. Overall Width: 2,400 mm. Overall Height: 2,285 mm. Wheelbase: 4,200 mm. Vehicle Weight: 4,715 kg. Engine: 4 cycle 6 cyl 3,878 cc 125 HP 3,600 rpm 85 km/h. Clutch: Single dry plate with torsional rubber dampers. Transmission: Synchromesh. No. of Speeds: forward 4, reverse 1 Gear Ratio: 6.67 Tire: front 7.50—20, 12 P rear 7.50—20, 12 P

This particular vehicle is equipped with a tank with a capacity of 2,500—3,000 l and injectors. The tank contains water or chemical agent. It is best applicable for preliminary fire fighting activity.

TOYOTA MOTOR PRODUCT

MINSEI T80-S   DISCHARGING TOWER VEHICLE

Overall Length: 9,723 mm. Overall Width: 2,500 mm. Overall Height: 3,000 mm. Wheelbase: 4,800 mm. Vehicle Weight: 9,800 kg (gross) No. of Seats: 3 Engine: Diesel, 2 cycle 4 cyl 4,941 cc 155 HP 2,000 rpm. 71 km/h. Clutch: Single dry, plate. Transmission: Conventional. No. of Speeds: forward 4, reverse 1 Gear Ratio: 1st 5.82, 2nd 2.92, 3rd 1.91, 4th 1.00 reverse 7.12 Tire: front 9.00—20, 14 P rear 9.00—20, 14 P

The Minsei "Carrier" chassis is used for mounting a water pump of high discharging capacity: it can stand continued service under rugged conditions.

MINSEI DIESEL PRODUCT

ISUZU TX440 FIRE FIGHTING

Overall Length: 6,648 mm. Overall Width: 2,109 mm. Overall Height: 1,910 mm. Wheelbase: 4,000 mm. Vehicle Weight: 5,835 kg. No. of Seats & Capacity: 3+ 3,000 l. Engine: 4 cycle 6 cyl 5,654 cc 145 HP 3,000 rpm 88 km/h. Clutch: Single dry plate with rubber damper. Transmission: Synchro-mesh, partially sliding. No. of Speeds: forward 4, reverse 1 Gear Ratio: 5.57 (39/7) Tire: front 7.50—20, 12 P rear 7.50—20, 12 P

A gasoline engine of improved power output developing 145 HP is mounted on the chassis. A water pump is provided with a delivery quantity of 1,000 gal. per min. with a pressure of 20 psi.

ISUZU MOTOR PRODUCT

MITSUBISHI "JEEP" CJ3B-J10

Overall Length : 3,566 mm.　　Overall Width : 1,684 mm.
Overall Height : 1,973 mm.　　Wheelbase : 2,032 mm.
Vehicle Weight : 1,180 kg. (diesel)　1,130 kg. (gasoline)
No. of Seats : 6　Engine: gasoline or diesel,　4 cycle
4 cyl 2,199 cc 75HP 4,000 rpm 95 km/h (gasoline) 60 HP
3,500 rpm 85 km/h (diesel)　Clutch: Dry, single disc.
Transmission : Synchromesh.　No. of Speeds : forward 3,
reverse 1　Gear Ratio : 5.375　Tire : front 6.00—16, 6 p
rear 6.00—16, 6 P

Comfortable full-width seat provides additional seating capacity to three people, if necessary. Double-fold seats give easy access to cargo and rear passenger area.

MITSUBISHI REORGANIZED PRODUCT

MITSUBISHI "JEEP" CJ3B-J3

Overall Length : 3,388 mm.　　Overall Width : 1,688 mm.
Overall Height : 1,895 mm.　　Wheelbase : 2,032 mm.
Vehicle Weight : 1,170 kg. (diesel)　1,056 kg. (gasoline)
No. of Seats : 4　Engine: gasoline or diesel,　4 cycle
4 cyl 2,199 cc 75 HP　4,000 rpm　95 km/h (gasoline)
60 HP 3,500 rpm 85 km/h (diesel) Clutch : Dry, single disc.
Transmission : Synchromesh.　No. of Speeds : forward 3
reverse 1　Gear Ratio : 5.375　Tire : 6.00—16, 6 P
rear 6.00—16, 6 P

The "JEEP" F-head engine (Model JH-4) has achieved world-wide recognition for reliability and stamina. The new "JEEP" Diesel engine (Model KE-31) has been designed primarily to provide an alternative means of power for the "JEEP" gasoline engine.

MITSUBISHI REORGANIZED PRODUCT

TOYOTA LAND CRUISER FJ21
CANVAS TOP

Overall Length : 3,843 mm.　　Overall Width : 1,665 mm.
Overall Height : 1,850 mm.　　Wheelbase : 2,285 mm.
Vehicle Weight : 1,450 kg.　No. of Seats : 6　Engine :
gasoline, ohv,　4 cycle 6 cyl 3,878 cc　125 HP　3,600
rpm 110 km/h.　Clutch : Single dry plate with torsional
rubber dampers.　Transmission : Synchromesh, third and
top speeds.　No. of Speeds : forward 4, reverse 1　Gear
Ratio : 4.11　Tire : front 6.00—16, 6 P　rear 6.00—16,
6 P

An all-purpose truck of four-wheel drive. Longer and shorter wheelbases are available for choice. This type of truck is applicable for road construction and other general contractors' work.

TOYOTA MOTOR PRODUCT

JEEP TYPE

4-WHEEL DRIVE VEHICLE

This unique type of vehicle is used for general purposes in our industrial life. With a 4-wheel drive mechanism, it can even go up stone-steps and run through shallow water.

Mitsubishi Jeep at work.

Toyota's Land Cruiser in Thailand.

TOYOTA WEAPON CARRIER FQ10

Overall Length: 5,100 mm. Overall Width: 2,057 mm. Overall Height: 2,320 mm. Wheelbase: 3,000 mm. Vehicle Weight: 2,810 kg. No. of Seats: 2 Engine: Gasoline, ohv, 4 cycle 6 cyl 3,878 cc 125 HP 3,600 rpm 85 km/h. Clutch: Single dry plate with torsional rubber dampers. Transmission: Synchromesh, second, third, and top speeds, helical. No. of Speeds: forward 4, reverse 1 Gear Ratio: 6.667 Tire: front 7.50—20, 8 P rear 7.50—20, 8P

A four-wheel drive truck of the widest range of application. Two different wheel-bases are available. The vehicle is used for dam construction work, general contractors work, agricultural work, etc.

TOYOTA MOTOR PRODUCT

TOYOTA LAND CRUISER FJ25-D
HARDTOP

Overall Length: 3,843 mm. Overall Width: 1,665 mm. Overall Height: 1,900 mm. Wheelbase: 2,285 mm. Vehicle Weight: 1,500 kg. No. of Seats & Capacity: 6+2,000 kg. Engine: Gasoline, 4 cycle 6 cyl 3,878 cc 125 HP 3,600 rpm 110 km/h. Clutch: Single dry plate with torsional rubber dampers. Transmission: Synchromesh, third and top speeds. No. of Speeds: forward 4 reverse 1 Gear Ratio: 4.11 Tire: front 6.00—16, 6 P rear 6.00—16, 6 P

They have developed a new glass-fibre-reinforced roof material for heat insulation and noise silencing. Body is of build-up type and it is easily detachable from the chassis.

TOYOTA MOTOR PRODUCT

TOYOTA LAND CRUISER FJ 28 WAGON

Overall Length: 4,365 mm. Overall Width: 1,690 mm. Overall Height: 1,860 mm. Wheelbase: 2,430 mm. Vehicle Weight: 1,700 kg. No. of Seats: 5 Engine: Gasoline, pushrod ohv, 4 cycle 6 cyl 3,878 cc 125 HP 3,600 rpm 110 km/h. Clutch: Single dry plate with torsional rubber dampers. Transmission: Synchromesh, third and top speeds, helical. No. of Speeds: forward 4, reverse 1 Gear Ratio: 4.11 Tire: front 6.50—16, 6 P rear 6.50—16, 8 P

This particular vehicle is good for transporting passengers and goods in remote places. Two different wheel-bases are available.

TOYOTA MOTOR PRODUCT

NISSAN CARRIER 4W73

Overall Length : 4,760 mm. Overall Width : 2,045 mm. Overall Height : 2,320 mm. Wheelbase : 2,800 mm. Vehicle Weight : 2,730 kg. No. of Seats : 10 Engine : Gasoline, water-cooled, in-line, 4 cycle 6 cyl 3,956 cc 125 HP 3,400 rpm 84 km/h. Clutch : Dry, single disc. Transmission : Synchromesh. No. of Speeds : forward 4, reverse 1 Gear Ratio : 6.14 Tire : front 7.50—20, 8 P rear 7.50—20, 10 P

Specially built all-wheel drive truck of versatile purposes. Bench seats located in the luggage space can be folded up. The luggage space is covered with detachable canvas awning.

NISSAN MOTOR PRODUCT

NISSAN PATROL 4W66

Overall Length : 3,540 mm. Overall Width : 1,700 mm. Overall Height : 1,945 mm. Wheelbase : 2,210 mm. Vehicle Weight : 1,550 kg. No. of Seats : 6 Engine : Gasoline, water-cooled, in-line, 4 cycle 6 cyl 3,956 cc 125 HP 3,400 rpm 117 km/h. Clutch : Dry, single disc. Transmission : Synchromesh. No. of Speeds : forward 4, reverse 1 Gear Ratio : 4.09 Tire : front 6.50—16, 6 P rear 6.50—16, 6 P

A strongly built all-wheel drive truck powered by an engine with the output of 125 HP, capable of carrying two passengers and 250 kg load. Arrangement of rear seats turns the luggage space into passenger space for additional four persons. Rear doors open outward for easy entrance and exit.

NISSAN MOTOR PRODUCT

NISSAN PATROL W4W65
STATION WAGON

Overall Length : 4,270 mm. Overall Width : 1,700 mm. Overall Height : 1,950 mm. Wheelbase : 2,510 mm. Vehicle Weight : 1,780 kg. No. of Seats : 8 Engine : Gasoline, water-cooled, 4 cycle 6 cyl 3,956 cc 105 HP 3,400 rpm 106 km/h. Clutch : Dry, single disc. Transmission : Synchromesh. No. of Speeds : forward 4, reverse 1 Gear Ratio : 4.09 Tire : front 6.50—16, 6 P rear 6.50—16, 6 P

Designed for rough usage on uneven terrain with four-wheel drive arrangement. It is provided with seats for eight persons all facing forward. The body is of all-steel construction.

NISSAN MOTOR PRODUCT

Isuzu dump truck in action.

DUMP TRUCK

Mitsubishi Fuso's construction vehicles.
Left: Bulldozer　　　Right: Rakedozer

NISSAN DG680

Overall Length: 6,655 mm. Overall Width: 2,380 mm. Overall Height: 2,400 mm. Wheelbase: 4,200 mm. Vehicle Weight: 4,525 kg. No. of Seats: 3, payload 6,000 kg. Engine: Gasoline, water-cooled, in-line, 4 cycle 6 cyl 3,956 cc 125 HP 3,400 rpm 92 km/h. Clutch: Dry, single disc. Transmission: Synchromesh. No. of Speeds: forward 5, reverse 1 Gear Ratio: 6.83 Tire: front 8.25-20, 14 P rear 6.25-20, 14 P double

This strongly built dump truck is mounted with a gasoline engine of high performance. Outstanding mechanical features are the synchromesh transmission gear box and the differential gear unit with a Hypoid gear of large dimensions.

NISSAN MOTOR PRODUCT

NISSAN DIESEL DUG680

Overall Length: 6,655 mm. Overall Width: 2,380 mm. Overall Height: 2,400 mm. Wheelbase: 4,200 mm. Vehicle Weight: 4,980 kg. No. of Seats: 3, payload 6,000 kg. Engine: Diesel, water-cooled, in-line, direct, 2 cycle 3 cyl 3,706 cc 120 HP 2,200 rpm 60 km/h. Clutch: Dry, single disc Transmission: Synchromesh. No. of Speeds: forward 5, reverse 1 Gear Ratio: 6.17 Tire: front 8.25-20, 14 P rear 8.25-20, 14 P double

The Nissan UD3 Diesel engine is mounted on this 6,000 kg loading capacity dump truck. Outstanding mechanical features are the synchromesh transmission gear box and the differential gear unit with a Hypoid gear of large dimensions.

NISSAN MOTOR PRODUCT

MINSEI T80-S

Overall Length: 7,713 mm. Overall Width: 2,380 mm. Overall Height: 2,570 mm. Wheelbase: 4,800 mm. Vehicle Weight: 6,620 kg. No. of Seats: 3 Engine: 2 cycle 4 cyl 4,941 cc 155 HP 2,000 rpm 81 km/h. Clutch: Single dry plate. Transmission: Conventional. No. of Speeds: forward 4, reverse 1 Gear Ratio: 1st 5.82, 2nd 2.92, 3rd 1.91, 4th 1.00 reverse 7.12 Tire: front 10.00−20, 14 P rear 10.00−20, 14 P

Strong construction to withstand the severest punishment on the rough road. The vehicle is powered by a 155 HP Diesel engine which has recently been powered up. Short wheelbase allows small radius of turning circle.

MINSEI DIESEL PRODUCT

HINO ZH

	(rear)	(3-way)
Overall Length:	7,100 mm.	7,000 mm.
Overall Width:	2,345 mm.	2,460 mm.
Overall Height:	2,720 mm.	2,640 mm.
Wheelbase:	1,820 mm.	1,820 mm.
Vehicle Weight:	6,655 kg.	6,670 kg.

Engine: 4 cycle 6 cyl 7,698 cc 150 HP 2,400 rpm 46 km/h. Clutch: Single plate, dry disc. Transmission: Selective sliding gear. No. of Speeds: forward 4, reverse 1 Tire: front 11.00 20, rear 11.00 20

Designed for increased engine power and reduced service attention. Dependable 150 HP Diesel engine is installed. Specially constructed chassis can be used interchangeable with vehicles for other type of work.

HINO MOTORS PRODUCT

HINO ZG

Overall Length: 6,363 mm. Overall Width: 3,000 mm. Overall Height: 3,200 mm. Wheelbase: 3,600 mm. Vehicle Weight: 13,310 kg. Engine: 4 cycle 6 cyl 10,857 cc 175 HP 2,000 rpm 46 km/h. Clutch: Single plate, dry disc. Transmission: Constant mesh, selective sliding gear. No. of Speeds: forward 6, reverse 1 Gear Ratio: 1st 6.983:1, 2nd 4.324:1, 3rd 2.632:1, 4th 1.633:1, 5th 1.000:1, 6th 0.615:1 Tire: front 12.00—24 rear 14.00—24

Special attention is paid to manoeuvrability of this heavy vehicle, providing power-assisted steering system. Radius of turning circle has also been reduced to a minimum. It is equipped with six-speed forward and reverse gear box.

HINO MOTORS PRODUCT

HINO TA

	(rear)	(side)	(3-way)
Overall Length:	7,085 mm.	7,370 mm.	7,105 mm.
Overall Width:	2,455 mm.	2,490 mm.	2,440 mm.
Overall Height:	(approx) 2,610 mm.	(approx) 2,630 mm.	(approx) 2,630 mm.
Wheelbase:	4,200 mm.	4,200 mm.	4,200 mm.
Vehicle Weight:	6,620 kg.	7,450 kg.	7,000 kg.

Engine: 4 cycle 6 cyl 7,698 cc 150 HP 2,400 rpm 80 km/h. Clutch: Single plate, dry disc. Transmission: Selective sliding gear. No. of Speeds: forward (standard) 4, (optional) 5, reverse 1 Tire: front 11.00—20, rear 11.00—20

Exclusive HINO 150 HP Diesel engine embodies the results of intensive development work on minimizing of power wastage, effecting high power output and remarkably low fuel consumption.

HINO MOTORS PRODUCT

TOYOTA DA90

Overall Length: 6,770 mm. Overall Width: 2,350 mm. Overall Height: 2,300 mm. Wheelbase: 4,200 mm. Vehicle Weight: 9,665 kg. No. of Seats & Capacity: 3+5,000 kg. Engine: Diesel 4 cycle 6 cyl 6,494 cc 130 HP 2,600 rpm 80 km/h. Clutch: Single dry plate with torsional rubber dampers. Transmission: Synchromesh, 2nd, 3rd and top speeds, helical. No. of Speeds: forward 4, reverse 1 Gear Ratio: 5.83 Tire: front 8.25—20, 14 P rear 8.25—20, 14 P

Designed for extra strength and improved practicability specifically required for the dump trucks. Rear bodies are built for rear dumping, side dumping and three-way dumping.

TOYOTA MOTOR PRODUCT

MITSUBISHI FUSO T52

Overall Length: 5,370 mm. Overall Width: 2,500 mm. Overall Height: 2,900 mm. Wheelbase: 2,700 mm. Vehicle Weight: 6,950 kg. Loading Capacity: 7,000 kg. Engine: Diesel, 4 cycle 6 cyl 8,550 cc 145 HP 2,000 rpm 48 km/h. Clutch: Single dry plate. Transmission: Selective sliding gear. No. of Speeds: forward 5, reverse 3 Gear Ratio: 10.153 (final drive gear) Tire: front 10.00 20, 14 P rear 12.00 20, 16 P

The chassis is mounted with scoop and loading vessel with a capacity of 4.0 m³. "Non-spin" differential gear unit is a notable feature. Applicable for rugged off-highway constructional work. Power-assisted steering system is available as optional equipment.

MITSUBISHI NIPPON PRODUCT

MITSUBISHI FUSO T320-D

Overall Length: 7,170 mm.　　Overall Width: 2,460 mm. Overall Height: 2,560 mm. Wheelbase: 4,300 mm. Vehicle Weight: 6,765 kg. Loading Capacity: 7,000 kg. Engine: Diesel,　4 cycle　6 cyl　8,550 cc　165 HP　2,300 rpm 77 km/h. Clutch: Single dry plate. Transmission: Selective sliding gear. No. of Speeds: forward 4, reverse 1 Gear Ratio: 5.667 (final drive gear) Tire: front 10.00—20, 14 PR　rear 10.00—20, 14 PR

The chassis is mounted with a loading vessel with a capacity of 4.0 m³, two side boards and a tail gate can be dropped down. It is a rational combination of advantages of both conventional trucks and dump trucks with respect to manoeuvrability and exact steering. Higher loading capacity available for short radius of turning circle.

MITSUBISHI NIPPON PRODUCT

MITSUBISHI FUSO W11-D

Overall Length: 7,035 mm.　　Overall Width: 2,450 mm. Overall Height: 2,800 mm.　　Wheelbase: 4,000 mm. Vehicle Weight: 9,520 kg. Loading Capacity: 10,000 kg. Engine: Diesel, 4 cycle 6 cyl 8,550 cc 145 HP 2,000 rpm 53 km/h. Clutch: Single dry plate. Transmission: Selective sliding gear.　No. of Speeds: forward 8, reverse 2 Gear Ratio: 8.7 (final drive gear)　Tire: front 9.00 20, 14 P rear 9.00 20, 14 P

6×6 all-wheel drive dump truck with the carrying capacity of 10,000 kg. Designed for both road and cross-country operation. Applicable also for long distance transportation.

MITSUBISHI NIPPON PRODUCT

ISUZU TS540

Overall Length: 6,375 mm. Overall Width: 2,355 mm. Overall Height: 2,490 mm. Wheelbase: 4,000 mm. Vehicle Weight: 5,530 kg. No. of Seats: 3 Loading Capacity: 5,000 kg. Engine: Diesel, 4 cycle 6 cyl 6,126 cc 125 HP 2,600 rpm 69 km/h. Clutch: Single dry plate with rubber damper. Transmission: Synchromesh, partially sliding. No. of Speeds: forward 4, reverse 1 Gear Ratio: 6.5 (39/6) Tire: front 8.25—20, 14 P rear 8.25—20, 14 P

This 5,000 kg capacity dump truck is powered by the HINO Diesel engine. To cope with hard working conditions, it is designed as four-wheel drive.

ISUZU MOTOR PRODUCT

ISUZU TD140

Overall Length: 7,030 mm. Overall Width: 2,455 mm. Overall Height: 2,585 mm. Wheelbase: 4,200 mm. Vehicle Weight: 6,505 kg. No. of Seats: 3 Loading Capacity: 7,000 kg. Engine: Diesel, 4 cycl 6 cyl 10,179 cc 180 HP 2,300 rpm 75 km/h. Clutch: Single dry plate with rubber damper. Transmission: Synchromesh, partially sliding. No. of Speeds: forward 5, reverse 1 Gear Ratio: 5.57 (39/7) Tire: front 9.00—20, 14 P rear 9.00—20, 14 P

Output of the Diesel engine has been raised to 180 HP with the result of improved performance. Increase of load carrying capacity and road transport speed have been effected by the employment of this powerful engine.

ISUZU MOTOR PRODUCT

Dump truck at work, behind of which is a "Shonan" train of the Tokaido Main Line.

LIGHT DUMP TRUCK

MITSUBISHI "JUPITER" T22D-D

Overall Length : 5,280 mm. Overall Width : 2,020 mm. Overall Height : 1,990 mm. Wheelbase : 3,310 mm. Vehicle Weight : 2,470 kg. No. of Seats : 3 Loading Capacity : 3,000 kg. Engine : Diesel, 4 cycle 6 cyl 3,300 cc 85 HP 3,500 rpm 91 km/h. Clutch : Single disc, dry hydraulic operation. Transmission : Synchromesh, remote control. No. of Speeds : forward 4, reverse 1 Gear Ratio : 5.5 Tire : front 7.00—16, 10 P rear 7.00—16, 10 P

The "Jupiter" Dump Truck, now available with either gasoline 2,500 kg (75 HP) or Diesel 2,000 kg (62 HP) and 3,000 kg (85 HP) payload, can do its pick-up delivery work in so many types of operation.

MITSUBISHI REORGANIZED PRODUCT

KUROGANE NBD

Overall Length : 5,075 mm. Overall Width : 1,740 mm. Overall Height : 1,885 mm. Wheelbase : 3,215 mm. Vehicle Weight : 1,945 kg. No. of Seats : 2 Engine : 4 cycle 4 cyl 1,488 cc 62 HP 4,700 rpm 85 km/h. Clutch : Dry, single disc. Transmission : Synchromesh. No. of Speeds : forward 4, reverse 1 Gear Ratio : 1st 5.218, 2nd 3.083, 3rd 1.713, 4th 1.000, reverse 6.377 Tire : front 6.50–16, 10 PLT rear 7.50–16, 14 PLT

Designed and constructed to meet even the severest requirement for use in the mountainous districts and rough terrain. Applicable for road construction and transportation of sand, ore and other heavy items.

TOKYU KUROGANE MOTOR PRODUCT

Small vehicles are favorite types with the Japanese motor industry and light dump trucks are no exception. Light dump trucks with a hauling capacity of 1—2 ton are most suitable to carry small quantity of materials.

PRINCE CLIPPER

Overall Length: 4,400 mm. Overall Width: 1,695 mm. Overall Height: 1,980 mm. Wheelbase: 2,345 mm. Vehicle Weight: 2,030 kg. No. of Seats: 3 Engine: Water-cooled, ohv, gasoline, 4 cycle 4 cyl 1,484 cc 70 HP 4,800 rpm 105 km/h. Clutch: Single dry plate. Transmission: Synchromesh, selective rotation. No. of Speeds: forward 4, reverse 1 Gear Ratio: 1st 5.19, 2nd 3.03, 3rd 1.70, 4th 1.00, reverse 5.97 Tire: front 7.00—16, 8 P rear 7.00—16, 12 P

This particular vehicle is applicable for comparatively lower dumping loads. The rear body accommodates 1,700 kg load. Emphasis has been placed for better manoeuvrability and operational economy.

FUJI PRECISION PRODUCT

DAIHASTU VESTA FPOD

Overall Length: 4,560 mm. Overall Width: 1,690 mm. Overall Height: 1,980 mm. Wheelbase: 2,600 mm. Vehicle Weight: 1,980 kg. No. of Seats: 3 Engine: 4 cycle V-2 cyl 1,478 cc 53 HP 3,600 rpm 85 km/h. Clutch: Single dry plate. Transmission: Synchromesh gear 2.3, selective sliding gear 1.R No. of Speeds: forward 6, reverse 2 Gear Ratio: forward 6.833, 9.737, 13.441 19.055, 26.321, 37.507 Reverse 33.837,48.218 Tire: front 6.00—16, 6 PLT rear 6.00—16, 8 PLT

Unusual strength of the whole structure is indicated by the use of steel plate of 6 mm thick, thickest of this class of dump trucks. Tilting motion of the rear body is performed by the link mechanisms.

DAIHATSU KOGYO PRODUCT

CONSTRUCTION EQUIPMENT

MITSUBISHI FUSO CONCRETE MIXER T320

Overall Length: 7,890 mm. Overall Width: 2,460 mm. Overall Height: approx. 3,100 mm. Wheelbase: 4,300 mm. Vehicle Weight: 8,320 kg. Loading Capacity: 5,500 kg. Engine: Diesel, 4 cycle 6 cyl 8,550 cc 165 HP 2,300 rpm 77 km/h. Clutch: Single dry plate. Transmission: Selective sliding gear. No. of Speeds: forward 4, reverse 1 Gear Ratio: 5.667 (final drive gear) Tire: front 10.00—20, 14 P rear 10.00—20, 14 P

A mixing plant with a mixing capacity of 2,3 m³ is accommodated on the strongly built chassis. A separate engine developing 75 HP is mounted to obtain better mixing.   **MITSUBISHI NIPPON PRODUCT**

MITSUBISHI FUSO TRUCK TRACTOR T350

Overall Length: 5,860 mm. Overall Width: 2,450 mm. Overall Height: approx. 2,450 mm. Wheelbase: 3,450 mm. Vehicle Weight: 5,225 kg. Loading Capacity: 8,000 kg. (5th wheel) Towing Capacity: 19,310 kg. Engine: Diesel, 4 cycle 6 cyl 8,550 cc 165 HP 2,300 rpm 53 km/h. Clutch: Single dry plate. Transmission: Selective sliding gear. No. of Speeds: forward 4, reverse 1 Gear Ratio: 7.994 (final drive gear) Tire: front 9.00—20, 14 P rear 9.00—20, 14 P

Out of four wheels supporting the tractor, two wheels are driving wheels. This particular tractor is capable of towing a trailer with a loading capacity of 12.000 kg.   **MITSUBISHI NIPPON PRODUCT**

MITSUBISHI FUSO TRUCK TRACTOR W21

Overall Length: 7,135 mm. Overall Width: 2,500 mm. Overall Height: 2,850 mm. Wheelbase: 4,700 mm. Vehicle Weight: 9,590 kg. Loading Capacity: 9,000 kg. (5th wheel) Towing Capacity: 20,000 kg. Engine: Diesel, 4 cycle 6 cyl 13,741 cc 200 HP 2,000 rpm 55 km/h. Clutch: Single dry plate. Transmission: Selective sliding gear, w/transfer case. No. of Speeds: forward 10, reverse 2 Gear Ratio: 9.667 (final drive gear) Tire: front 11.00—20, 14 P rear 11.00—20, 14 P

The tractor is of the all-wheel drive type and equipped with a winch. It is designed and constructed to tow a low-bed semi-trailer with a loading capacity of 20,000 kg over rough terrain. **MITSUBISHI NIPPON PRODUCT**

MITSUBISHI MOTOR SCRAPER WTS

Overall Length: 10,780 mm. Overall Width: 2,710 mm. Overall Height: 2,860 mm. (to the top o exhaust pipe) Wheelbase: 3,000 mm. (tractor) Vehicle Weight: 14,500 kg. Bowl Capacity: 4.5 m^3. Engine: Diesel, 4 cycle 6 cyl 8,550 cc 130 HP 2,000 rpm 32.6 km/h. Clutch: Dry multi-plate. Transmission: Selective sliding gears. No. of Speeds: forward 4, reverse 4 Gear Ratio: 11.3 Tire: front 14.00—24, 10 P rear 18.00—25, 16 P Scraper 18.00—25, 16 P

A special purpose vehicle comprising a four-wheeled tractor good for medium and long distance haulage and a two-wheeled scraper. Maximum speed is conveniently high with a record of 32.6 km/h. **MITSUBISHI NIPPON PRODUCT**

MITSUBISHI BULLDOZER BF

Overall Length: 5,470 mm. Overall Width: 3,860 mm. Overall Height: 2,800 mm. (to the top of exhaust pipe) Length of Ground Contact: 2,500 mm. Vehicle Weight: 16,300 kg. Blade: Length×Height 3,860 mm.×950 mm. Engine: Diesel, 4 cycle 4 cyl 14,140 cc 140 HP, 250 rpm 9.9 km/h. Clutch: Single dry plate. Transmission: Selective sliding gears. No. of Speeds: forward 5, reverse 4 Gear Ratio: 25.7

Mounted with an engine of ample dimension and of high surplus power output. The framing of the bulldozer is particularly robust.

MITSUBISHI NIPPON PRODUCT

MITSUBISHI TRACTOR SHOVEL BS30

Overall Length: 5,350 mm. Overall Width: 2,200 mm. Overall Height: 2,710 mm. (to the top of exhaust pipe) Length of Ground Contact: 2,615 mm. Vehicle Weight: 13,000 kg. Bucket Capacity: 1.8 m³. Engine: Diesel, 4 cycle 6 cyl 8,550 cc 115 HP 1,800 rpm 10.9 km/h. Clutch: Dry multi-plate. Transmission: Selective sliding gears. No. of Speeds: forward 4, reverse 4 Gear Ratio: 33.2

A heavy-duty hydraulic lifting mechanism fed by a hydraulic pump driven by the MITSUBISHI DB31C Diesel engine is particularly suited for heavy excavation work as well as loading work.

MITSUBISHI NIPPON PRODUCT

MITSUBISHI MOTOR GRADER LGII

Overall Length: 7,970 mm.　Overall Width: 2,316 mm.　Overall Height: 2,808 mm.　Wheelbase: 5,850 mm.　Vehicle Weight: 11,500 kg.　Blade-Length×Height: 3,710 mm.×530 mm.　Engine: Diesel, 4 cycle　6 cyl　8,550 cc　115 HP　1,800 rpm　33.7 km/h.　Clutch: Dry dual plates.　Transmission: Selective sliding gears.　No. of Speeds: forward 6, reverse 2　Gear Ratio: 22.7　Tire: front 14.00—24, 10 P　rear 14.00—24, 10 P

Powered by the MITSUBISHI DB31C Diesel engine and equipped with the geared-type tandem drive unit. To ensure increased braking performance, brakes are installed on all four wheels in the rear. Power-assisted steering can be installed as an optional equipment.　**MITSUBISHI NIPPON PRODUCT**

MITSUBISHI BULLDOZER BE10

Overall Length: 6,480 mm.　Overall Width: 4,140 mm.　Overall Height: To the top of exhaust pipe 3,000 mm.　Length of Ground Contact: 2,840 mm.　Vehicle Weight: 24,500 kg.　Blade Length×Height: 4,140 mm. ×1,150 mm.　Engine: Diesel, 4 cycle　6 cyl　21,200 cc　210 HP　1,250 rpm　11.8 km/h.　Clutch: 3 elements 1 stage torque converter.　Transmission: Planetary gears with hydraulic clutches.　No. of Speeds: forward 3, reverse 3　Gear Ratio: 35.1

Departing from the standard direct-coupled type, an optional type with a torque converter is available also. The vehicle is strongly built, capable of licking any kind of difficult jobs.

MITSUBISHI NIPPON PRODUCT

MITSUBISHI FUSO TRUCK CRANE T360

Overall Length: 10,758 mm.　Overall Width: 2,500 mm.
Overall Height: Approx. 3,300 mm.　Wheelbase 4,600 mm.
Vehicle Weight: 13,120 kg.　Crane Capacity: 7,250 kg.
(loading radius 3 m).　Engine: Diesel, 4 cycle　6 cyl
8,550 cc　165 HP　2,300 rpm　77 km/h.　Clutch: Single dry plate.　Transmission: Selective sliding gear.　No. of Speeds: forward 4, reverse 1　Gear Ratio: 5.667 (final drive gear)　Tire: front 10.00—20, 14 P　rear 10.00—20, 14 P

This is an ingenious combination of the Mitsubishi 4×2, 7,000 kg truck chassis and the P & H 55 TC crane unit. Output of engine is 165 HP and hoisting capacity is 7,250 kg.

MITSUBISHI NIPPON PRODUCT

MITSUBISHI FUSO TRUCK CRANE W25A

Overall Length: 13,080 mm.　Overall Width: 2,800 mm.
Overall Height: 3,750 mm.　Wheelbase: 4,700 mm.
Vehicle Weight: 30,050 kg.　Crane Capacity: 22,500 kg.
Engine: Diesel, 4 cycle　6 cyl　13,741 cc　200 HP　2,000 rpm
54 km/h.　Clutch: Single dry plate.　Transmission: Selective sliding gear.　No. of Speeds: forward 5, reverse 1
Gear Ratio: 9.667 (final drive gear)　Tire: front 12.00—20, 16 P　rear 12.00—20, 16 P

This particular truck crane represents the greatest of its kind in Japan with a lifting capacity of 22,500 kg. Quite a number of different operations can be performed by fixing various attachments, shovel, cramshell, etc.

MITSUBISHI NIPPON PRODUCT

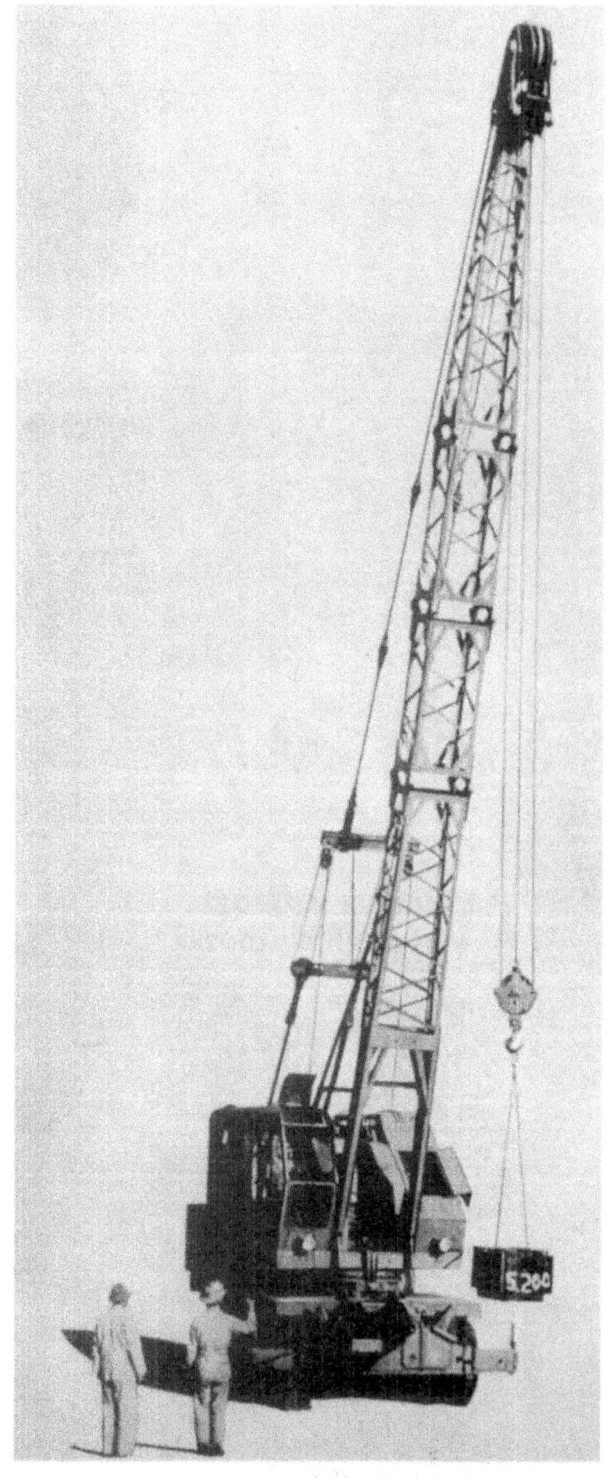

THREE-WHEELER

The first three-wheeled vehicle designed as a small delivery truck was manufactured in Japan around 1926. In those days no driving license was required and a considerable number of trucks came into use.

Three-wheeled vehicles today have been perfected after many years of researches and developments to cope with the narrow and steep road conditions existing in Japan.

The largest three-wheeled truck has a loading capacity of two tons. Some of recent models have round steering wheel, self-starter, remote gear-shift control and other features comparable to ordinary four-wheeled vehicles.

In the list of Japanese three-wheeled vehicles are enumerated not only trucks but also fire engines, dump trucks, ambulances, tank lorries, etc. At present, more than 600,000 three-wheeled vehicles are running on the Japanese roads. At any rate, three-wheeled vehicles are the products quite peculiar to Japan.

DAIHATSU MIDGET DK-2 STANDARD

Overall Length: 2,540 mm.　Overall Width: 1,206 mm. Overall Height: 1,515 mm.　Wheelbase: 1,680 mm. Vehicle Weight: 318 kg.　No. of Seats: 1　Engine: 2 cycle 1 cyl 249 cc 10 HP 65 km/h. Clutch: Single dry plate.　Transmission: Selective sliding gear.　No. of Speeds: forward 3, reverse 1　Gear Ratio: forward 6.375, 11.095, 19.615, reverse 28.528　Tire: front 5.00—9, 4 P　rear 5.00—9, 6 P

The Midget is provided with the most unique body construction affording high standard of strength and rigidity. The radius of turning circle (2,100 mm) is the shortest of all the light type three wheelers. Both kickstarter and electric starter available. The canvas tarpaulin serves the purpose of the "moving sign."

DAIHATSU KOGYO PRODUCT

DAIHATSU MIDGET MPA HANDYWAGON

Overall Length: 2,675 mm. Overall Width: 1,290 mm. Overall Height: 1,510 mm. Wheelbase: 1,740 mm. Vehicle Weight: 405 kg. No. of Seats: 2 Engine: 2 cycle 1 cyl 249 cc 10 HP 4,500 rpm 65 km/h. Clutch: Single dry plate. Transmission: Selective sliding gear. No. of Speeds: forward 3, reverse 1 Gear Ratio: forward 6.571, 11.434, 20.220, reverse 29.407 Tire: front 5.00—9, 4 P rear 5.00—9, 4 P

A tarpaulin-protected multiple-purpose vehicle. It is best suited for delivery trips of miscellaneous merchandises and industrial materials. Easy to handle and economical to drive, specific fuel consumption being 23 km/l.

DAIHATSU KOGYO PRODUCT

DAIHATSU MIDGET DK-2 STATION WAGON

Overall Length: 2,670 mm. Overall Width: 1,240 mm. Overall Height: 1,650 mm. Wheelbase: 1,680 mm. Vehicle Weight: 385 kg. No. of Seats: 5 Engine: 2 cycle 1 cyl 249 cc 10 HP 4,500 rpm 65 km/h. Clutch: Single dry plate. Transmission: Selective sliding gear. No. of Speeds: torward 3, reverse 1 Gear Ratio: forward 6.375, 11.095, 19.615, reverse 28.528 Tire: front 5.00—9, 4 P rear 5.00—9, 4 P

A newly introduced station wagon of limited overall dimensions, affording an accommodation to five persons. Best weather protection is effected by hermetically sealed tarpaulin.

DAIHATSU KOGYO PRODUCT

DAIHATSU MIDGET DK-2 LIGHT VAN

Overall Length: 2,550 mm. Overall Width: 1,290 mm. Overall Height: 1,500 mm. Wheelbase: 1,680 mm. Vehicle Weight: 343 kg. No. of Seats: 1 Engine: 2 cycle 1 cyl 249 cc 10 HP 4,500 rpm 65 km/h. Clutch: Single dry plate. Transmission: Selective sliding gear. No. of Speeds: forward 3, reverse 1 Gear Ratio: forward 6.571, 11.434, 20.220, reverse 29.407 Tire: front 5.00—9, 4 P rear 5.00—9, 6 P

Designed and constructed upon the basic plan of affording better weather protection and increased insulation. The loading space is hermetically sealed by the all-metal structure. Available loading space is 1.2 m³ for foods, textile materials, valuable goods, etc.

DAIHATSU KOGYO PRODUCT

DAIHATSU MIDGET DK-2 CANVAS VAN

Overall Length: 2,540 mm. Overall Width: 1,206 mm.
Overall Height: 1,500 mm. Wheelbase: 1,680 mm.
Vehicle Weight: 318 kg. No. of Seats: 1 Engine:
2 cycle 1 cyl 249 cc 10 HP 4,500 rpm 65 km/h. Clutch:
Single dry plate. Transmission: Selective sliding gear.
No. of Speeds: Forward 3, reverse 1 Gear Ratio: forward 6.375, 11.095, 19.615, reverse 28.528 Tire: front 5.00—9, 4 P rear 5.00—9, 6 P

Rear part of this particular light-type three-wheeled truck is incorporated with awning of tarpaulin. Electric starting unit affords improved readiness for starting. Fuel consumption, by virtue of the light weight of the truck is as low as 28 km/l.

DAIHATSU KOGYO PRODUCT

DAIHATSU MIDGET MPA PANEL VAN

Overall Length: 2,720 mm. Overall Width: 1,290 mm.
Overall Height: 1,510 mm. Wheelbase: 1,740 mm.
Vehicle Weight: 410 kg. No. of Seats: 2 Engine:
2 cycle 1 cyl 249 cc 10 HP 4,500 rpm 65 km/h. Clutch:
Single dry plate. Transmission: Selective sliding gear.
No. of Speeds: forward 3, reverse 1 Gear Ratio: forward 6.571, 11.434, 20.220, reverse 29.407 Tire: front 5.00—9, 4P rear 5.00—9, 4P

This particularly light truck is designed and constructed with the main aim at better weather protection and increased insulation. The loading space is hermetically sealed by the all-metal structure. Available loading area is 1.1 m³.

DAIHATSU KOGYO PRODUCT

DAIHATSU MIDGET DK-2 MAIL VAN

Overall Length: 2,550 mm. Overall Width: 1,290 mm.
Overall Height: 1,500 mm. Wheelbase: 1,680 mm.
Vehicle Weight: 345 kg. No. of Seats: 1 Engine:
2 cycle 1 cyl 249 cc 10 HP 4,500 rpm 65 km/h. Clutch:
Single dry plate. Transmission: Selective sliding gear.
No. of Speeds: forward 3, reverse 1 Gear Ratio: forward 6.571, 11.434, 20.220, reverse 29.407 Tire: front 5.00—9, 4 P rear 5.00—9, 6 P

Following recent trends in small car body design, Daihatsu engineers have aimed at greater stiffness and improved weather protection. This particular mail van is provided with a completely sealed metallic van body with a loading space of 1.2 m³.

DAIHATSU KOGYO PRODUCT

DAIHATSU SKC-7

Overall Length : 3,855 mm. Overall Width : 1,630 mm.
Overall Height : 1,860 mm. Wheelbase : 2,440 mm.
Vehicle Weight : 1,770 mm. No. of Seats : 2 Engine :
4 cycle 9° V-2 cyl 751 cc 22 HP 3,700 rpm 63 km/h.
Clutch : Single disc, coil spring. Transmission : Selective
sliding gear, constant mesh, silent. No. of Speeds : forward 4, reverse 1 Gear Ratio : forward 7.833, 12.909, 21.627, 37.598, reverse 51.024 Tire : front 5.50 16, 6 PLT rear 6.00–16, 6 PLT

This three-wheeled truck with a loading capacity of 750 kg is powered by an air-cooled, V-2 cylinder engine provided with a special hemispherical combustion chamber. First to use in Japan the Hypoid differential gears in the power train.
DAIHATSU KOGYO PRODUCT

DAIHATSU PL-7

Overall Length : 4,030 mm. Overall Width : 1,710 mm.
Overall Height : 1,830 mm. Wheelbase : 2,630 mm.
Vehicle Weight : 1,025 kg. No. of Seats : 2 Engine :
4 cycle 90° V-2 cyl 751 cc 25 HP 3,800 rpm 70 km/h.
Clutch : Single disc, coil spring. Transmission : Constant mesh, silent. No. of Speeds : forward 4, reverse 1 Gear Ratio : forward 7.833, 12.909, 21.627, 37.598, reverse 51.024 Tire : front 5.50–16, 6 PTL rear 6.50–16, 8 PLT

This particular three-wheeled truck has been designed and constructed to offer a new means of transportation, featuring better fuel economy, ease of driving and lower cost of maintenance. **DAIHATSU KOGYO PRODUCT**

DAIHATSU PF8-TL

Overall Length : 4,420 mm. Overall Width : 1,730 mm.
Overall Height : 1,855 mm. Wheelbase : 2,835 mm.
Vehicle Weight : 2,610 kg. No. of Seats : 2 Engine :
4 cycle 90°V-2 cyl 1,005 cc 33 HP 4,000 rpm 75 km/h.
Clutch : Single disc, coil spring. Transmission : Constant mesh, silent. No. of Speeds : forward 4, reverse 1 Gear Ratio : forward 7.667, 12.352, 21.414, 35.038, reverse 46.715 Tire : front 5.50–16, 6 PLT rear 7.00–16, 8 PLT

To achieve the object of easy loading and emptying, the chassis is designed as a low level arrangement. Two side boards and a tail gate of the rear body can easily be dropped down. **DAIHATSU KOGYO PRODUCT**

DAIHATSU PM-10

Overall Length: 5,110 mm. Overall Width: 1,710 mm. Overall Height: 1,855 mm. Wheelbase: 3,205 mm. Vehicle Weight: 2,885 kg. No. of Seats: 2 Engine: 4 cycle 90°·V 2 cyl 1,135 cc 35 HP 3,700 rpm 70 km/h. Clutch: Single disc, coil spring. Transmission: Constant mesh, silent. No. of Speeds: forward 4, reverse 1 Gear Ratio: forward 8.168, 13.157, 22.810, 37.323, reverse 49.762 Tire: front 6.00—16, 6 PLT rear 7.00—16, 10 PLT

Ample dimensions have been given to the loading space on the rear body. Outstanding features are low costs of driving and maintenance.

DAIHATSU KOGYO PRODUCT

DAIHATSU PO13-T

Overall Length: 6,065 mm. Overall Width: 1,825 mm. Overall Height: 1,850 mm. Wheelbase: 3,830 mm. Vehicle Weight: 1,710 kg. No. of Seats: 2 Engine: 4 cycle 90°V-2 cyl 1,478 cc 45 HP 3,600 rpm 75 km/h. Clutch: Single disc, coil spring. Transmission: Constant mesh, silent. No. of Speeds: forward 6, reverse 2 Gear Ratio: forward 7.667, 10.925, 14.521, 20.693, 28.299, 40.326, reverse 38.028, 54.190 Tire: front 6.50—16, 8 PLT rear 7.50—16, 12 PLT or 7.50—16, 14 PLT

This powerful three-wheeled two-tonner is powered by water-cooled V-2 cylinder engine. The rear body is provided with adequate lengths for carrying materials of unusual lengths. Two side boards and tail gate of the rear body can easily hinged down.

DAIHATSU KOGYO PRODUCT

DAIHATSU DUMP TRUCK PO8-D

Overall Length: 4,285 mm. Overall Width: 1,710 mm. Overall Height: 1,820 mm. Wheelbase: 2,935 mm. Vehicle Weight: 3,825 mm. No. of Seats: 2 Engine: 4 cycle 90°V-2 cyl 1,480 cc 45 HP 3,600 rpm 75 km/h. Clutch: Single disc, coil spring. Transmission: Constant mesh, silent. No. of Speeds: forward 6, reverse 2 Gear Ratio: forward 7.667, 10.925, 14.521, 20.693, 28.299, 40.326, reverse 38.028, 54.190 Tire: front 6.00—16, 8 PLT rear 7.50—16, 14 PLT

The hydraulically operated body tilting mechanism features the tail gate that opens in two different ways. Maximum tilting angle of rear body; 60°: Tipping time of up stroke: 15 second. Tipping time of down-stroke: 14 seconds. Loading capacity 2,000 kg.

DAIHATSU KOGYO PRODUCT

DAIHATSU FIRE ENGINE

Overall Length: 5,265 mm. Overall Width: 1,800 mm.
Overall Height: 1,800 mm. Wheelbase: 3,290 mm.
Vehicle Weight: 2,400 kg. No. of Seats: 2 Engine:
4 cycle 90°V-2 cyl 1,478 cc 45 HP 3,600 rpm 75 km/h.
Clutch: Single disc, coil spring. Transmission: Constant mesh, silent. No. of Speeds: forward 6, reverse 2 Gear Ratio: forward 7.667, 10.925, 14.521, 20.693, 28.299, 40.326, reverse 38.028, 54.196 Tire: front 6.50—16, 8 PLT rear 7.50—16, 12 PLT

An engine designed for exclusive use for fire fighting engine and a pump with a discharge capacity of 2.08 m³/min. are mounted on the truck chassis. Water tank contains 1,000 l of water. **DAIHATSU KOGYO PRODUCT**

DAIHATSU PACK-MASTER

Overall Length: 4,690 mm. Overall Width: 1,690 mm.
Overall Height: 1,990 mm. Wheelbase: 2,600 mm
Vehicle Weight: 2,700 kg. No. of Seats: 3 Engine:
4 cycle V-2 cyl 1,478 cc 53 HP 3,600 rpm 85 km/h.
Clutch: Single dry plate. Transmission: Synchromesh gear 2, 3, selective sliding gear 1.R. No. of Speeds: forward 6, reverse 2 Gear Ratio: forward 6.833, 9.737, 13.441, 19.055, 26.321, 37.507, reverse 33.837, 48.218 Tire: front 6.00—16, 8 PLT rear 6.00—16, 8 PLT double

This special purpose vehicle is available for use in the field of disposal of city waste materials. A special hydraulic packing unit compresses the materials into compact blocks. They are dumped out most efficiently from the vehicle. Loading capacity of the vehicle is 2,000 kg.
DAIHATSU KOGYO PRODUCT

DAIHATSU TRACTOR & TRAILER

Overall Length: 7,710 mm. Overall Width: 2,285 mm. Overall Height: 1,980 mm. Wheelbase: tractor 2,945 mm. trailer 3,000 mm. Vehicle Weight: 3,157 kg. No. of Seats: 2 Engine:: 4 cycle 90°V-2 cyl 1,478 cc 48 HP 3,600 rpm 62 km/h. Clutch: Single disc, coil spring. Transmission: Constant mesh, silent. No. of Speeds: forward 6, reverse 2 Gear Ratio: forward 7.667, 10.925, 14.521, 20.693, 28.299, 40.326, reverse 38.028, 54.190 Tire: front KNMA 6.50—16, 10 P (I) rear 7.00—12, 12 P (I) TNM 6.50—16, 10 P (I) double

This rapid-loading type semi-trailer features a special automatic coupler. Available for a choice of tractive forces, 2,500 kg, 5,000 kg and 6,000 kg. It can stand the highest towing speed of 63 km/h. **DAIHATSU KOGYO PRODUCT**

MAZDA K360 KTBA43

Overall Length: 2,975 mm. Overall Width: 1,280 mm. Overall Height: 1,430 mm. Wheelbase: 2,060 mm. Vehicle Weight: 485 kg. No. of Seats: 2 Engine: Forced air cooling by fan, 760° V, ohv, 4 cycle 2 cyl 356 cc 11 HP 4,300 rpm 65 km/h. Clutch: Single dry plate, foot-operated, hydraulic. Transmission: Constant mesh. No. of Speeds: forward 3 reverse 1 Gear Ratio: low 3.53, 2nd 1.89, top 1.00, reverse: 4.32 Tire: front 5.20—12, 4 PR rear 5.20—12, 6 PR

This midget truck embodies the results of intensive development work on independently-working dual mechanical and hydraulic brake systems, selfstarting motor, veneered safety windshield glass, circular steering wheel and spacious two-seat driver's cabin. **TOYO KOGYO PRODUCT**

MAZDA T600 TEA45

Overall Length: 3,125 mm. Overall Width: 1,280 mm. Overall Height: 1,450 mm. Wheelbase: 2,060 mm. Vehicle Weight: 510 kg. No. of Seats: 2 Engine: forced air cooling by fan, 76° V, ohv, 4 cycle 2 cyl 577 cc. 20 HP 4,300 rpm 75 km/h. Clutch: Single dry plate, foot-operated, hydraulic. Transmission: Constant mesh. No. of Speeds: forward 3 reverse 1 Gear Ratio: low 3.53, 2nd 1.89 top 1.00 reverse 4.32 Tire: front 5.00—13, 4 PRLT rear 5.20—13, 6 PRLT

Notable mechanical features of this particula truck are limited overall dimensions, high power output of engine, circular steering wheel, two lamps assuring safe night driving, rapid-starting motor, dual brake systems, hydraulic vibration dampers preventing damage of load. **TOYO KOGYO PRODUCT**

MAZDA MBR81

Overall Length: 4,360 mm. Overall Width: 1,685 mm. Overall Height: 1,890 mm. Wheelbase: 2,830 mm. Vehicle Weight: 1,260 kg. No. of Seats: 3 Engine: forced air cooling by fan, 76° V, ohv, 4 cycle 2 cyl 1,005 cc 31.5 HP 3,700 rpm 74 km/h. Clutch: Single dry plate, foot-operated, hydraulic. Transmission: Synchromesh. No. of Speeds: forward 4, reverse 1 Gear Ratio: low 5.30, 2nd 2.97, 3rd 1.73, top 1.00 reverse 7.07 Tire: front 6.00—16, 6 PR rear 6.50—16, 8 PR

Powered by the under-seat-type Autocle engine featuring a special device capable of maintaining the operating temperature of engine at constant. Other outstanding mechanical features are hydraulic shock absorber, hydraulic clutch and rubber flexible coupling on the propeller shaft. **TOYO KOGYO PRODUCT**

MAZDA T1100 TTA81

Overall Length: 4,360 mm. Overall Width: 1,685 mm. Overall Height: 1,920 mm. Wheelbase: 2,830 mm. Vehicle Weight: 1,315 kg. No. of Seats: 3 Engine: Water-cooled, ohv, 4 cycle 4 cyl 1,139 cc 46 HP 4,600 rpm 87 km/h. Clutch: Single dry plate, foot-operated, hydraulic. Transmission: Synchromesh. No. of Speeds: forward 4 reverse 1 Gear Ratio: low 5.30, 2nd 2.97, 3rd 1.73, top 1.00, reverse 7.07 Tire: front 6.00—16, 8 PLT rear 6.50—16, 8 PLT

Engine has recently been redesigned to change over to water cooling system. Wet cylinder sleeves are installed. Whole range includes 1,000 kg, 1,250 kg and 1,500 kg capacities. Side boards and rear gate can be hinged down quickly. **TOYO KOGYO PRODUCT**

MAZDA HBR12-S

Overall Length: 5,122 mm. Overall Width: 1,834 mm. Overall Height: 1,946 mm. Wheelbase: 3,356 mm. Vehicle Weight: 1,597 kg. No. of Seats: 3 Engine: Forced air cooling by fan, 76°V, ohv, 4 cycle 2 cyl 1,400 cc 42 HP 3,500 rpm 77 km/h. Clutch: Single dry plate, foot-operated, hydraulic. Transmission: Synchromesh. No. of Speeds: forward 4, reverse 1 Gear Ratio: low 5.30, 2nd 2.97, 3rd 1.73 top 1.00, reverse 7.07 Tire: front 6.50—16, 8 PR rear 7.50—16, 12 PR

The rear body devoid of fender projection permits free loading of long materials and bulky goods with a maximum loading efficiency. The rear body accommodating 2,000 kg load, are composed of two side boards and a tail gate. Other types of rear body with respect to dimensions and forms are available. **TOYO KOGYO PRODUCT**

MAZDA T1500 TUA12-S

Overall Length: 5,120 mm. Overall Width: 1,840 mm. Overall Height: 1,920 mm. Wheelbase: 3,270 mm. Vehicle Weight: 1,640 kg. No. of Seats: 3 Engine: Water-cooled, ohv, 4 cycle 4 cyl 1,484 cc 60 HP 4,600 rpm 92 km/h. Clutch: Single dry plate, foot-operated, hydraulic. Transmission: Synchromesh. No. of Speeds: forward 4 reverse 1 Gear Ratio: low 5.30, 2nd 2.97, 3rd 1.73, top 1.00, reverse 7.07 Tire: front 6.50—16, 8 PLT rear 7.50—16, 14 PLT

Rear body is incorporated with flat floor ensuring vibration-free transportation of long or bulky goods. Side boards and rear gate can quickly be hinged down for easy loading. Odd sizes of rear bodies are available. **TOYO KOGYO PRODUCT**

MITSUBISHI PET LEO LT10
STANDARD

Overall Length: 2,830 mm. Overall Width: 1,280 mm. Overall Height: 1,520 mm. Wheelbase: 1,910 mm. Vehicle Weight: 350 kg. No. of Seats: 2 Engine: 4 cycle 1 cyl 310 cc 13 HP 4,700 rpm 72 km/h. Clutch: Single dry plate. Transmission: Synchromesh, selective sliding gear. No. of Speeds: forward 3 reverse 1 Gear Ratio: 1st 3.00, 2nd 1.789, 3rd 1.038, reverse 4.333 Tire: front 5.00-9, 4 PR rear 5.00-9, 6 PR

No other midget class truck is equipped with synchromesh transmission gear box. Engine is of the unique under-seat arrangement. Special shockabsorbing and stabilizing device on both front and rear wheels afford high standard of riding comfort.

MITSUBISHI REORGANIZED PRODUCT

MITSUBISHI PET LEO LT11
LIGHT VAN

Overall Length: 2,830 mm. Overall Width: 1,280 mm. Overall Height: 1,520 mm. Wheelbase: 1,910 mm. Vehicle Weight: 400 kg. No. of Seats: 2 Engine: 4 cycle 1 cyl 310 cc 13 HP 4,700 rpm 72 km/h. Clutch: Single dry plate. Transmission: Synchromesh, selective sliding gear. No. of Speeds: forward 3 revers 1 Gear Ratio: 1st 3.00, 2nd 1.789, 3rd 1.038, reverse 4.333 Tire: front 5.00-9, 4 PR rear 5.00-9, 6 PR

Rear body bears a resemblance to a common panel delivery van. Driver's cabin is of all-steel construction and is completely sealed for better weather protection. Front windshield glass is panoramic, affording an excellent visibility.

MITSUBISHI REORGANIZED PRODUCT

MITSUBISHI PET LEO LT10
CANVAS VAN

Overall Length: 2,830 mm. Overall Width: 1,280 mm. Overall Height: 1,520 mm. Wheelbase: 1,910 mm. Vehicle Weight: 350 kg. No. of Seats: 2 Engine: 4 cycle 1 cyl 310 cc 13 HP 4,700 rpm 72 km/h. Clutch: Single dry plate. Transmission: Synchromesh, selective sliding gear. No. of Speeds: forward 3 reverse 1 Gear Ratio: 1st 3.00, 2nd 1.789, 3rd 1.038, reverse 4.333 Tire: front 5.00-9, 4 PR rear 5.00-9, 6 PR

A four-stroke horizontal, fan-cooled, 310 c.c. engine is mounted under the driver's seat. Considerable thought has been given to achieve increased manoeuvrability, excellent weather protection and operational economy.

MITSUBISHI REORGANIZED PRODUCT

MITSUBISHI TM15F

Overall Length: 4,130 mm. Overall Width: 1,640 mm. Overall Height: 1,780 mm. Wheelbase: 2,765 mm. Vehicle Weight: 980 kg. No. of Seats: 2 Engine: 4 cycle 2 cyl 1,145 cc 36 HP 3,700 rpm 78 km/h. Clutch: Single dry plate. Transmission: Selective sliding gear. No. of Speeds: forward 4 reverse 1 Gear Ratio: 1st 4.199, 2nd 2.510, 3rd 1.534, 4th 1.000, reverse 4.199 Tire: front 5.50—16, 6 PRLT rear 6.50—16, 6 PRLT

This 1,000 kg capacity three-wheeled truck features excellent performance, including short radius of turning circle. Reasonable riding comfort on account of ingenious front suspension is traditional. Another model of truck accommodating 1,250 kg is available.

MITSUBISHI REORGANIZED PRODUCT

MITSUBISHI TM18BH

Overall Length: 5,120 mm. Overall Width: 1,840 mm. Overall Height: 1,810 mm. Wheelbase: 3,350 mm. Vehicle Weight: 1,320 kg. No. of Seats: 2 Engine: 4 cycle 2 cyl 1,489 cc 47 HP 3,500 rpm 80 km/h. Clutch: Single dry plate. Transmission: Selective sliding gear. No. of Speeds: forward 4 reverse 1 Gear Ratio: 1st 5.056, 2nd 3.022, 3rd 1.700, 4th 1.000, reverse 5.056 Tire: front 6.50—16, 6 PRLT rear 7.50—16, 12 PRLT

The driver's cabin is sealed and heated in winter time for comfortable driving. Rear body is mounted in high level arrangement with a loading capacity of 2,000 kg. Notable mechanical features are dependable front suspension, special RBA rear spring suspension and hydraulic shock absorbers.

MITSUBISHI REORGANIZED PRODUCT

HOPE STAR

Overall Length: 2,985 mm. Overall Width: 1,270 mm. Overall Height: 1,635 mm. Wheelbase: 1,960 mm. Vehicle Weight: 420 kg. No. of Seats: 2 Engine: 2 cycle 2 cyl 350 cc 15 HP 60 km/h. Clutch: Transmission: Synchromesh. No. of Speeds: forward 3, reverse 1 Tire: front 4.50—14, 4 P rear 4.50—14, 6 P

A fan-cooled, double-piston, two-stroke engine powers this particular midget three-wheeled truck. Driver's cabin is provided with facilities for easy drive for lady drivers. Loading capacity of the rear body is 300 kg.

HOPE JIDOSHA PRODUCT

HUMBEE EF11

Overall Length: 2,690 mm. Overall Width: 1,220 mm. Overall Height: 1,500 mm. Wheelbase: 1,825 mm. Vehicle Weight: 365 kg. No. of Seats: 1 Engine: 2 cycle 1 cyl 285 cc 11.5 HP 4,200 rpm 70 km/h. Clutch: Single plate, dry disc. Transmission: Selective sliding gear. No. of Speeds: forward 3, reverse 1 Gear Ratio: 1st 3.11, 2nd 1.84, 3rd 1.00, revease 4.07 Tire: front 5.00—9, 4 P rear 5.00—9, 6 P

A two-stroke single cylinder engine is mounted. Steering can be performed by a bar handle. Designed and constructed most simply, so as to achieve the easiest driving and maintenance.
MITSUI PRECISION PRODUCT

HUMBEE EF11 LIGHT VAN

Overall Length: 2,680 mm. Overall Width: 1,220 mm. Overall Height: 1,500 mm. Wheelbase: 1,825 mm. Vehicle Weight: 335 kg. No. of Seats & Capacity: 1+350 kg. Engine: 2 cycle 1 cyl 285 cc 11.5 HP 4,200 rpm 70 km/h. Clutch: Single dry plate. Transmission: Selective sliding gear. No. of Speeds: forward 3 reverse 1 Gear Ratio: Tire: front 5.00—9, 4 PRLT rear 5.00—9, 6 PRLT

This particular vehicle was designed and constructed to provide a means of door-to-door transportation of light loads ——a light three-wheeled van applicable to versatile uses.
The body is made of polyester, a special plastic material, light in weight, stiff and impervious to corrosive attack.
MITSUI PRECISION PRODUCT

HUMBEE EF11 SURREY

Overall Length: 2,825 mm. Overall Width: 1,250 mm. Overall Height: 1,625 mm. Wheelbase: 1,825 mm. Vehicle Weight: 360 kg. No. of Seats & Capacity: 3+300 kg. Engine: 2 cycle 1 cyl 285 cc 11.5 HP 4,200 rpm 70 km/h. Clutch: Single dry plate. Transmission: Selective sliding gear. No. of Speeds: forward 3 reverse 1 Tire: front 5.00—9, 4 PRLT rear 5.00—9, 4 PRLT

A most unconventionally designed car of versatile usefulness, accommodating three passengers, if it is used as a passenger car. A plastic body shell is mounted on the Humbee standard chassis. When it is used as a small truck, it has a loading capacity of 340 kg. Loading and emptying are done through the rear door.
MITSUI PRECISION PRODUCT

CONY AA27

Overall Length: 2,940 mm.   Overall Width: 1,235 mm.
Overall Height: 1,515 mm.   Wheelbase: 2,050 mm.   Vehicle Weight: 470 kg.   No. of Seats: 2   Engine: Horizontal opposed, forced air-cooling, gasoline. 4 cycle 2 cyl 359 cc 16 HP 4,800 rpm 68 km/h.   Clutch: Single dry plate.   Transmission: Selective sliding mesh gear.   No. of Speeds: forward 3 reverse 1   Tire: front 4.00--16, 6P rear 4.00 —16, 6P

This midget truck is powered by a four-stroke, horizontally opposed, two cylinder engine, bearing a close resemblance to the world-renowned Volkswagen engine arrangement. Notable mechanical features are circular steering wheel, electric starter, roomy driver's cabin accommodating two persons

AICHI MACHINE PRODUCT

GIANT AA24-LHS

Overall Length: 5,185 mm.   Overall Width: 1,830 mm.   Overall Height: 1,830 mm.   Wheelbase: 3,235 mm.   Vehicle Weight: 1,825 kg.   No. of Seats: 3   Engine: Horizontal opposed, water-cooling, gasoline, 4 cycle 4 cyl 1,488 cc   58 HP 4,500 rpm 70 km/h.   Clutch: Single dry plate.   Transmission: Selective sliding mesh gear.   No. of Speeds: forward 4 reverse 1   Tire: front 6.50—16, 8P rear 7.50—16, 14P

The Giant's water-cooled, horizontally-opposed four cylinder engine is dynamically well-balanced and supplies ample power free from noise and vibration. A circular steering wheel and panoramic windshield feature the roomy driver's cabin accommodating three persons.   **AICHI MACHINE PRODUCT**

GIANT AA24-T

Overall Length: 3,810 mm.   Overall Width: 1,910 mm.   Overall Height: 1,740 mm.   Wheelbase: 2,865 mm.   Vehicle Weight: 1,540 kg.   No. of Seats: 2   Engine: Horizontal opposed, water-cooling, gasoline, 4 cycle 4 cyl 1,488 cc   58.4 HP, 500 rpm 69.3 km/h.   Clutch: Single dry plate.   Transmission: Selective sliding mesh gear.   No. of Speeds: forward 5, reverse 1   Tire: front 6.50—16, 10P rear 7.00—12, 12P

Designed and constructed specially for transporting unusually long materials. Features the shortest radius of turning circle.

AICHI MACHINE PRODUCT

KUROGANE KW8

Overall Length: 4,355 mm. Overall Width: 1,740 mm. Overall Height: 1,780 mm. Wheelbase: 2,730 mm. Vehicle Weight: 1,255 kg. No. of Seats: 2 Engine: 4 cycle 4 cyl 1,046 cc 42 HP 4,700 rpm 90 km/h. Clutch: Single dry plate. Transmission: Selective, constant mesh. No. of Speeds: forward 4 reverse 1 Gear Ratio: 1st 4.896, 2nd 2.881, 3rd 1.755, 4th 1.000, reverse 6.644 Tire: front 5.50—16, 6 PLT rear 6.50—16, 8 PLT

The four-cylinder water-cooled engine is powerful and well-suited to the robust overall chassis arrangement. A considerable amount of work has been done on the improvement of the front fork and increase of rigidity of the frame structure.
TOKYU KUROGANE MOTOR PRODUCT

KUROGANE KY10

Overall Length: 5,075 mm. Overall Width: 1,740 mm. Overall Height: 1,885 mm. Wheelbase: 3,215 mm. Vehicle Weight: 1,600 mm. No. of Seats: 2 Engine: 4 cycle 4 cyl 1,488 cc 62 HP 4,700 rpm 85 km/h. Clutch: Dry, single disc. Transmission: Synchromesh. No. of Speeds: forward 4, reverse 1 Gear Ratio: 1st 5.216, 2nd 3.083 3rd 1.713, 4th 1.000 reverse 6.377 Tire: front 6.50—16, 8 PLT rear 7.50—16, 12 PLT

This particular three-wheeled truck is specialized by a 62 HP engine, the most powerful of the same type of vehicle. By virtue of this advantage, the truck is best adapted to transportation of loads of unusual lengths and bulkiness.
TOKYU KUROGANE MOTOR PRODUCT

MUSASHI MF21

Overall Length: 2,815 mm. Overall Width: 1,265 mm. Overall Height: 1,650 mm. Wheelbase: 1,050 mm. Vehicle Weight: 462 kg. No. of Seats: 1 Engine: 4 cycle 2 cyl 359 cc 15 HP 4,000 rpm 60 km/h. Clutch: Single plate. Transmission: Constant mesh. No. of Speeds: forward 4, reverse 1 Gear Ratio: forward 3.875, 2.131, 1.389, 1.000, reverse 4.810 Tire: front 4.00—16, 4 P rear 4.00—16, 4 P

A water-cooled, vertical twin cylinder, 359 cc engine, developing 15 HP is mounted only on this particular vehicle. Other outstanding mechanical feature is the directly-coupled and elastically-supported four speed transmission gear box.
MITAKA FUJI PRODUCT

MOTOR SCOOTER

SILVER PIGEON C-300

Overall Length : 1,860 mm.　Overall Width : 660 mm.
Overall Height : 1,000 mm.　Wheelbase : 1,360 mm.
Vehicle Weight : 110 kg.　No. of Seats : 2　Engine :
2 cycle　1 cyl　123 cc　5.5 HP　5,400 rpm　70 km/h.
Clutch : Centrifugal friction plate.　Transmission : Automatic.　No. of Speeds : N/A　Gear Ratio : 3.5 : 1　Tire :
front 4.00—8, 2 P　rear 4.00—8, 4 P (tubeless)

A new two-stroke engine mounted scooter introduced by a well-known manufacturing company of the four-stroke engines. Notable mechanical features are front wheel brake, two-stage exhaust silencer and automatic transmission. Dry weight is only 110 kg, a remarkable light weight construction.
MITSUBISHI REORGANIZED PRODUCT

SILVER PIGEON C-200

Overall Length : 1,900 mm.　Overall Width : 710 mm.
Overall Height : 1,000 mm.　Wheelbase : 1,390 mm.
Vehicle Weight : 140 kg.　No. of Seats : 2　Engine :
4 cycle　1 cyl　124 cc　5.5 HP　6,000 rpm　72 km/h.
Clutch : Centrifugal friction plate.　Transmission : Automatic.　No. of Speeds : N/A　Gear Ratio : 4 : 1　Tire :
front 4.00—8, 2 P　rear 4.00—8, 4 P (tubeless)

A single cylinder, o.h.v. 124 c.c. engine is provided with a wedge-shaped combustion chamber, affording the highest efficiency for all range of revolutions. Centrifugal clutch automatic transmission and quick-acting brake system are outstanding features.
MITSUBISHI REORGANIZED PRODUCT

SILVER PIGEON C-110

Overall Length : 1,910 mm.　Overall Width : 755 mm.
Overall Height : 955 mm.　Wheelbase : 1,400 mm.　Vehicle Weight : 155 kg (empty)　No. of Seats : 2　Engine :
4 cycle 1 cyl 175 cc 8.5 HP 6,000 rpm 83 km/h. Clutch :
Centrifugal friction plate. Transmission : Automatic. No.
of Speeds : N/A　Gear Ratio : 3.5 : 1　Tire : front 4.00—8,
2 P　rear 4.00—8, 4 p (tubeless)

One of the representative motor scooters in Japan, featuring a centrifugal clutch-type automatic stepless speed-change mechanism actuated by a hand grip and the secondary power transmission by a shaft. Considerable thought has been given to elimination of vibration and noise.
MITSUBISHI REORGANIZED PRODUCT

RABBIT MINOR S-201

Overall Length : 1,800 mm. Overall Width : 680 mm. Overall Height : 990 mm. Wheelbase : 1,190 mm. Vehicle Weight : 75 kg (dry) No. of Seats : 1 Engine : 2 cycle 1 cyl 90 cc 5HP 6,200 rpm 75 km/h. Transmission : Helical gear. Tire : front 2.50—15, 2P rear 2.50—15, 4P

Advantages of both motorcycle and motor scooter are happily combined for the achievement of excellent liveliness and pronounced power. High specific output, 56 HP/l, indicates a high standard of high-speed performance.

FUJI HEAVY PRODUCT

RABBIT JUNIOR S-82S

Overall Length : 1,830 mm. Overall Width : 720 mm. Overall Height : 960 mm. Wheelbase : 1,310 mm. Vehicle Weight : 117 kg (wet) No. of Seats : 1~2 Engine : 2 cycle 1 cyl 123 cc 6.2 HP 5,600 rpm 75 km/h. Transmission : Grip control. Tire : 4.00—8, 4P

The engine is designed and constructed for higher torque figures in the lower range of revolutions. Performance in the higher range of revolution reveals reasonable too. Better riding comfort is aimed by means of front rubber suspension and rear swing arm.

FUJI HEAVY PRODUCT

RABBIT SUPERFLOW S-601

Overall Length : 1,900 mm. Overall Width : 750 mm. Overall Height : 1,000 mm. Wheelbase : 1,330 mm. Vehicle Weight : 150 kg (dry) No. of Seats : 2 Engine : 2 cycle 1 cyl 200 cc 11 HP 100 km/h. Transmission : Hydraulic torque converter. Tire : 4.00—8, 4P

The first Japanese-made motor scooter which has successfully broken the speed record of 100 km/h. The first motor scooter in the world which is equipped with a pneumatic suspension system. Power transmission is made by chains running in oil bath contained in a hermetically sealed casing.

FUJI HEAVY PRODUCT

YAMAHA SCOOTER

Overall Length: 1,770 mm.   Overall Width: 930 mm.
Overall Height: 660 mm. Wheelbase: 1,260 mm. Vehicle Weight: 123 kg.   No. of Seats: 2   Engine: Forced air cooling, gasaline, 2 cycle 1 cyl 175.1 cc 10 HP 5,800 rpm 90 km/h.   No. of Speeds: automatic. Tire: front 3.5.—10, 2 P rear 3.50—10, 4 P

The engineering staff of the company has successfully developed a new motor scooter characterized by outstanding reduction of dry weight. Furthermore, the engine of this scooter is equipped with a torque converter and two-speed transmission gear box.

YAMAHA MOTORCYCLE PRODUCT

PANDORA TS-1

Overall Length: 1,850 mm.   Overall Width: 780 mm.
Overall Height: 950 mm.   Wheelbase: 1,320 mm.
Vehicle Weight: 120 kg. No. of Seats: 1   Engine: 2 cycle 1 cyl 123 cc 6.5 HP 5,200 rpm, 77 km/h Clutch: Automatic centrifugal.   Transmission: V-belt automatic change. No. of Speeds: Stepless.   Gear Ratio: 3.12: 1~1:1   Tire: front 4.00—8   rear 4.00—8

First self-starting engine on a scooter powered by the 125 c.c. class engine. A headlamp is embedded in a steering handle casing, affording a better view at the turning corner. The external appearance of the rear is reminiscent of a deluxe car.   **TOSHO MOTOR PRODUCT**

HIRANO POPET

Overall Length: 1,740 mm. Overall Width: 630 mm. Overall Height: 940 mm. Wheelbase: 1,210 mm. Vehicle Weight: 60 kg. No. of Seats: 1 Engine: 2 cycle 1 cyl 50 cc 2½ HP 5,500 rpm. 54 km/h. Clutch: Automatic centrifugal. Transmission: Automatic. No. of Speeds: non. Tire: front 18- 2½, 4 P rear 18—2½, 4 P

A happy combination of advantages of both scooter and motored bicycle. This particularly small two-wheeled vehicle is mounted with a winker light, speedometer, leg shield and other standard equipment commonly found on a larger scooter.

HIRANO PRODUCT

HIRANO POP MANLEE FN125

Overall Length: 1,950 mm. Overall Width: 680 mm. Overall Height: 990 mm. Wheelbase: 1,390 mm. Vehicle Weight: 126 kg. No. of Seats: 1 Engine: 2 cycle 1 cyl 125 cc 6 HP 5,500 rpm 70 km/h. Clutch: Automatic centrifugal Transmission: Automatic. No. of Speeds: non. Tire: front 3½—10, 2 P rear 3½—10, 4 P tubeless

Fully mechanized scooterettes featuring the self-starting dynamo and automatic transmission gear system. Front telescopic shock-absorber and enlarged tire diameter of 18″ improved markedly the riding comfort. It is designed for economical drive for both short door-to-door and long-distance trips.

HIRANO PRODUCT

HIRANO POP MANLEE FN175

Overall Length: 1,950 mm. Overall Width: 680 mm. Overall Height: 990 mm. Wheelbase: 1,390 mm. Vehicle Weight: 140 kg. No. of Seats: 2 Engine: 2 cycle 1 cyl 175 cc 9 HP 5,600 rpm 80 km/h. Clutch: Automatic centrifugal. Transmission: Automatic. No. of Speeds: non. Tire: front 3½—10, 2 P rear 3½—10, 4 p tubeless

The power plant incorporated on this particular scooter can easily be started and operated by a self-starting motor of a push-button type and an automatic speed-change mechanism.

HIRANO PRODUCT

MOTORCYCLE

MOPED &
125 c.c. and under

Mopeds of 50 c.c. class are much in vogue in Japan. Being economical and suitable to sports mopeds are now largely used in replacement of bicycles.

HONDA SUPER CUB C-100

Overall Length: 1,780 mm.   Overall Width: 575 mm. Overall Height: 945 mm. Wheelbase: 1,180 mm. Vehicle Weight: 55 kg. No. of Seats: 1   Engine: Air-cooled, ohv, 4 cycle 1 cyl 49 cc 4.5 HP 9,500 rpm 75 km/h. Clutch: Multi-plate, wet, centrifugal automatic. Transmission: Three-speed gear box, foot control. No. of Speeds: forward 3 Gear Ratio: 1st 2.69, 2nd 1.45, 3rd 0.96. Tire: front 2.25—17 rear 2.25—17.

The machine of high standard of performance is powered by an engine equipped with a three-speed gear change mechanism actuated by an automatic centrifugal clutch. The machine is pronouncedly economical to drive, consuming only 1.1 l per 100 km. The weight of the machine is extremely light and it is easily handled by ladies and children.

HONDA MOTOR PRODUCT

MIYAPET II

Overall Length: 1,850 mm.   Overall Width: 635 mm. Overall Height: 920 mm. Wheelbase: 1,180 mm. Vehicle Weight: 65 kg. No. of Seats: 1   Engine: 2 cycle 1 cyl 48 cc 2.8 HP 6,500 rpm 65 km/h. Clutch: Multi-plate, wet. Transmission: 2 speed, foot control. No. of Speeds: forward 2 Gear Ratio: top 1.615, low 2.78 Tire: front 22—2.25, 2 P rear 22—2.25, 4 P

The design is particular clean and specifies a pressed-steel shell frame with fuel tank embodies in the main beam. A bottom-links are featured for the front fork and a plunger-type springing for the rear axle. Well-balanced rear fender as well as engine cover afford perfect protection for water and dust. Fit for a woman rider.

MIYATA WORKS PRODUCT

YAMAGUCHI AUTO-PET BP-50

Overall Length: 1,800 mm.   Overall Width: 615 mm. Overall Height: 880 mm. Wheelbase: 1,160 mm. Vehicle Weight: 62.5 kg. No. of Seats: 1   Engine: Air-cooled, with self-starter, 2 cycle 1 cyl 50 cc 3 HP 7,000 rpm 65 km/h. Transmission: Constant mesh. No. of Speeds: forward 3 Tire: front 22—2.25 rear 22—2.25

An engine-driven two-wheeler of the smallest dimensions. It can be operated with utmost ease comparable with a common bicycle. Outstanding features are admirable safety and riding comfort on rough roads. A two-stroke 50c.c. engine is equipped with a self-starting generating dynamo, affording quick and sure starting of the engine.

YAMAGUCHI BICYCLE PRODUCT

YAMAGUCHI AUTO-PET

Overall Length: 1,800 mm. Overall Width: 615 mm
Overall Height: 880 mm. Wheelbase: 1,160 mm. Vehicle Weight: 54.5 kg. No. of Seats: 1 Engine: Air cooling, 2 cycle 1 cyl 50 cc 2.8 HP 6,500 rpm 65 km/h. Clutch: Multi-plate, wet. Transmission: Constant mesh, with integrating-type speedchange. No. of Speeds: forward 3   Gear Ratio: low 38.72: 1, 2nd 19.81: 1, top 13.35: 1 Tire: front 22 2¼, rear 22 2¼

Styled in the most orthodoxical fashion of a motorcycle and can be operated at ease. Outstanding mechanical features are wet multi-disc type clutch, constant-mesh three-speed transmission gear box, bottom-link front fork, swing-arm rear suspension, etc.

YAMAGUCHI BICYCLE PRODUCT

MILLION SUNLIGHT

Overall Length: 1,780 mm.   Overall Width: 620 mm. Overall Height: 900 mm. Wheelbase: 1,120 mm. Vehicle Weight: 48 kg.   No. of Seats: 1   Engine: 2 cycle 1 cyl 49 cc 2.5 HP 5,800 rpm. 50 km/h.   Clutch: Automatic.   Transmission: Automatic speed change. Gear Ratio: 1.11–2.8 automatic non-stage Tire: front 22–2.25 rear 22–2.25

The design is particularly clean and specifies a tubular steel frame with water-proof covering over the power plant. The engine is equipped with a self-starting generating dynamo assuring an easy and instantaneous starting.

ITAGAKI PRODUCT

ECHO SE

Overall Length: 1,745 mm.   Overall Width: 600 mm. Overall Height: 915 mm. Wheelbase: 1,125 mm. Vehicle Weight: 49.5 kg.   No. of Seats: 1   Engine: 2 cycle 1 cyl 49.9 cc 2.5 HP 5,500 rpm 55 km/h. Clutch: Automatic centrifugal. Transmission: V-belt automatic change. No. of Speeds: Stepless. Gear Ratio: 5.36: 1~ 1: 1 Tire: front 22–2.25. rear 22–2.25

Japan's first pull-rope type hand-starting engine ensures the easiest operation for a woman driver. The moped is equipped with brakes on both front and rear wheels. An ingenious novelty is an automatic transmission system, affording easy speed change by means of handlebar control.

TOSHO MOTOR PRODUCT

SUZUKI SEL PET

Overall Length: 1,870 mm.   Overall Width: 630 mm. Overall Height: 940 mm. Wheelbase: 1,170 mm. Vehicle Weight: 54 kg.   No. of Seats: 1   Engine: Air-cooled 2 cycle 1 cyl 49.9 cc 1.5 HP 4,000 rpm 45km/h. Clutch: Multiple dry disk Transmission: Primary V-belt, finally chain.   Tire: front 24–2 rear 24–2

The moped has a sturdy back-bone-type frame of pressed-steel construction and is powered by a 50 c.c. two-stroke engine. Pedalling gear is retained for starting and emergency propulsion. Operation of the clutch lever turns a bicycle into a self-propelling machine. Fuel consumption as low as 70 km/l is worthy of note.

SUZUKI MOTOR PRODUCT

HONDA BENLY C-92

Overall Length: 1,910 mm.   Overall Width: 640 mm.
Overall Height: 945 mm. Wheelbase: 1,265 mm. Vehicle Weight: 120 kg. No. of Seats: 1 Engine: Air cooling, ohc, 4 cycle 2 cyl 123 cc 11.5 HP 9,500 rpm 115 km/h. Clutch: Wet multple-disk. Transmission: Constant mesh, rotary change. No. of Speeds: forward 4 Gear Ratio: 1st 2.97, 2nd 1.83, 3rd 1.35, 4th 1.00 Tire: front 3.00—16 rear 3.00—16

Of all the motorcycles produced in Japan, this particular model enjoys the greatest production. The Benly is featured by the excellent performance of the power plant and the lowness of driving costs. The standard of finish and of detail workmanship is uncommonly high.

HONDA MOTOR PRODUCT

MEGURO CADET CA

Overall Length: 1,925 mm.   Overall Width: 700 mm.
Overall Height: 960 mm. Wheelbase: 1,275 mm. Vehicle Weight: 124 kg. No. of Seats: 1 Engine: 4 cycle 1 cyl 123 cc 7.5 HP 6,700 rpm 85 km/h. No. of Speeds: forward 4 Gear Ratio: low 1:3.12, 2nd 1:2.10, 3rd 1:1.43, top 1:1. Tire: front 2.75—17, 4 P rear 2.75—17, 4 P

This motorcycle is powered by a four-stroke, single cylinder engine, affording an exceptionally trouble-free and economical operation. A special decompressor and self-starting dynamo contribute to an instantaneous starting even in the coldest season at the temperature of −20°C.

MEGURO PRODUCT

COLLEDA SELTWIN SB

Overall Length: 1,975 mm.   Overall Width: 700 mm.
Overall Height: 930 mm. Wheelbase: 1,280 mm. Vehicle Weight: 118 kg. No. of Seats: 2 Engine: Air-cooled, 2 cycle 2 cyl 125 cc 8.5 HP 7,000 rpm 100 km/h. Clutch: Multiple wet disk. Transmission: 4 speed, foot-operated with constant mesh. No. of Speeds: forward 4 Gear Ratio: low 1:2.8, 2nd 1:1.6, 3rd 1:1.1, top 1:08 Tire: front 2.75—17, 4 P rear 2.75—17, 4 P

A 125 c.c. two-stroke, two-cylinder, parallel-twin engine claims to have succeeded in damping out the individual power impulses of the engine, insuring smooth power delivery. A high compression ratio contributing to the development of high power output of 10 HP is worthy of note.

SUZUKI MOTOR PRODUCT

COLLEDA ST-6A

Overall Length: 2,000 mm.   Overall Width: 740 mm.
Overall Height: 1,000 mm. Wheelbase: 1,280 mm. Vehicle Weight: 119 kg. No. of Seats: 2 Engine: Air-cooled, 2 cycle 1 cyl 123 cc 7 HP 6,000 rpm 85 km/h. Clutch: Multiple wet disk. Transmission: 3 speed, foot-operated. No. of Speeds: forward 3 Gear Ratio: low 1:2.85, 2nd 1:1.5, high 1:1 Tire: front 24—2.75, 4 P rear 24—2.75, 4 P

Designed and constructed for a machine of universal popularity. A quick-responding dynamo rendered helpful service for achievement of the above aim. One of the outstanding technical novelties is the "chameleon" type speedometer. A powerful 35 W head lamp produces an intense beam.

SUZUKI MOTOR PRODUCT

YAMAHA 125
Overall Length: 1,870 mm. Overall Width: 705 mm. Overall Height: 937 mm. Wheelbase: 1,245 mm. Vehicle Weight: 106 kg. No. of Seats: 1 Engine: 2 stoke, 2 cycle 1 cyl 123 cc 6.8 HP 6,000 rpm 85 km/h. Clutch: Multi-plate. Transmission: Foot-operated, 4 speed gear box and chain. No. of Speeds: forward 4 Gear Ratio: low 1:21.42, 2nd 1:13.09, 3rd 1:8.92, 4th 1:7.00 Tire: front 3.00—16, 2 P rear 3.00—16, 4 P

A two-stroke 125 c.c. engine is equipped with a self-starting generating dynamo for easy starting. The machine has a pressed-steel spine frame of monocoque construction.
YAMAHA MOTORCYCLE PRODUCT

LILAC CS28
Overall Length: 1,940 mm. Overall Width: 650 mm. Overall Height: 920 mm. Wheelbase: 1,300 mm. Vehicle Weight: 126 kg. No. of Seats: 1 Engine: 4 cycle 2 cyl 124.6 cc 10.5 HP 8,000 rpm 110 km/h. Clutch: Single dry plate. Transmission: Constant mesh. No. of Speeds: forward 4 Gear Ratio: low 5.16:1, 2nd 3.63:1, 3rd 2.74:1 top 2.07:1 Tire: front 22—2.75, 2 P rear 22—2.75, 4 P

A 124.6 c.c. overhead-valve, vee-twin engine is mounted on a composite pressed-steel and tubular frame. Quick starting can easily be effected by the self-starting generator dynamo. A shaft-drive system is employed for transmitting power of the engine to the rear wheel.
MARUSHO MOTORCYCLE PRODUCT

ASAHI LA DELUXE II
Overall Length: 2,015 mm. Overall Width: 700 mm. Overall Height: 970 mm. Wheelbase: 1,265 mm. Vehicle Weight: 112 kg. No. of Seats: 1 Engine: 2 cycle 1 cyl 123 cc 7.5 HP 6,000 rpm 90 km/h. Clutch: Multi-plate, wet. Transmission: 3 speed, positive stop, foot control. No. of Speeds: forward 3 Gear Ratio: top 1, 2nd 1.59, low 2.59 Tire: front 24—2.75, 2 P rear 24—2.75, 4 P

The frame is of composite construction of ample strength and rigidity with steel pipe and steel pressing welded together. A push on the starting button on the handle bar brings the engine quickly into life. The front fork features telescopic suspension system.
MIYATA WORKS PRODUCT

TSUBASA FIGHTER
Overall Length: 1,870 mm. Overall Width: 750 mm. Overall Height: 880 mm. Wheelbase: 1,250 mm. Vehicle Weight: 116 mm. No. of Seats: 1 Eng'ne: 2 cycle 1 cyl 123 cc 7.7 HP 5,500 rpm 70 km/h. Clutch: Multiple plate, wet. Transmission: Constant mesh. No. of Speeds: forward 4 Gear Ratio: bottom 3.31:1, 2nd 2.11:1, 3rd 1.44:1, top 1.07:1 Tire: front 22—2.75 rear 22—2.75

Unusual mechanical features are self-starting generator dynamo, pressed-steel unit-construction frame, special swing-arm springing with preventive device for elongation of driving chain, stable front fork of rocking-arm pattern.
TSUBASA INDUSTRY PRODUCT

TOHATSU NEW BIRDY GB

Overall Length : 1,835 mm.   Overall Width : 640 mm.
Overall Height : 955 mm. Wheelbase : 1,180 mm. Vehicle Weight : 80 kg. No. of Seats : 1 Engine : 2 cycle 1 cyl 90 cc 4.8 HP 5,300 rpm 80 km/h. Transmission : Automatic. Gear Ratio : highest 1 : 1.82, lowest 1 : 3.65 Tire : front 22—2.25 rear 22—2.25

Notable mechanical features are a two-stroke, 90 c.c. engine and an automatic stepless speed-change mechanism. Every operation can be performed with one hand only. Employment of a cover over the carburettor contributed to eliminate fuel smears on the driver's cloth.

TOKYO HATSUDOKI PRODUCT

TOHATSU ARROW LA

Overall Length : 1,890 mm.   Overall Width : 685 mm.
Overall Height : 965 mm. Wheelbase : 1,235 mm. Vehicle Weight : 130 kg. No. of Seats : 1 Engine : 2 cycle 1 cyl 123 cc 8.0 HP 5,500 rpm 95 km/h. Clutch : 3 plates, wet. Transmission : 3 speed, foot operated. No. of Speeds : forward 3 reverse nil. Gear Ratio : high 1 : 1, 2nd 1 : 1.56, low 1 : 2.77 Tire : front 22—2.75 rear 22—2.75

Outstanding mechanical features are three-speed, constant mesh, rotary-type transmission gear unit, self-starting generator dynamo, Chameleon-type speedometer (based on the fundamental principle of changing color of needle on the dial in conjunction with speed) and two-step adjustable rear cushion.

TOKYO HATSUDOKI PRODUCT

TOHATSU ARROW LB

Overall Length : 1,990 mm.   Overall Width : 720 mm.
Overall Height : 930 mm. Wheelbase : 1,250 mm. Vehicle Weight : 112 kg. No. of Seats : 1 Engine : 2 cycle 1 cyl 123 cc 6.5 HP 5,000 rpm 85 km/h. Clutch : Single dry disk. Transmission : 3 speed, foot operated. No. of Speeds : forward 3 reverse nil. Gear Ratio : high 1 : 1, 2nd 1 : 1.56, low 1 : 2.77 Tire : front 24—2.75 rear 24—2.75

Features are a constant-mesh, foot-operated, rotary-type transmission gear system. The machine is designed and constructed for transportation of goods. Generous dimensions of the rear seat cushion permit loading of heavy goods. Costs of operation and maintenance are low.

TOKYO HATSUDOKI PRODUCT

GASUDEN BC-D

Overall Length : 1,950 mm.   Overall Width : 776 mm.
Overall Height : 940 mm. Wheelbase : 1,270 mm. Vehicle Weight : 110 kg. No. of Seats : 2 Engine : 2 cycle 1 cyl 122 cc 5.5 HP 5,000 rpm 85 km/h. Clutch : Moulded-cork, wet, multi-plate. Transmission : Synchromesh, gradual sliding. No. of Speeds : forward 3 reverse none. Gear Ratio : 1st 21.2 : 1, 2nd 11.8 : 1, 3rd 8.1 : 1 Tire : front 22—2.75, 2 P rear 22—2.75, 4 P

Quick response of the starter dynamo rendered the kickstart lever utterly unnecessary. The power transmission mechanism is an ingenious novelty, featuring a patented three-speed, progressively sliding, constantmesh gear system.

FUJI MOTOR PRODUCT

QUEEN SUNLIGHT JUNIOR
Overall Length: 1,770 mm.　　Overall Width: 612 mm.
Overall Height: 937 mm.　Wheelbase: 1,180 mm.　Vehicle Weight: 70 kg.　No. of Seats: 1　Engine: 2 cycle 1 cyl 80 cc　4 HP　5,800 rpm　60 km/h.　Clutch: Automatic centrifugal.　Transmission: Primary transmission, V-belt (242/1″)　Tire: front 20—2.25　rear 20—2.25

A sister machine of the Itagaki Queen Sunlight. It is designed and constructed to achieve the object of excellent starting acceleration and high-speed stability.
ITAGAKI PRODUCT

ROYAL SUNLIGHT
Overall Length: 1,910 mm.　　Overall Width: 650 mm.
Overall Height: 960 mm.　Wheelbase: 1,290.　Vehicle Weight: 114 kg.　No. of Seats: 1　Engine: 2 cycle 1 cyl 124 cc　6.8 HP　5,800 rpm　80 km/h.　Clutch: Automatic centrifugal.　Transmission: Primary transmission, V-belt (242/1″)　Tire: front 3.00—15　rear 3.00—15

The frame pressing embodies extensive shielding, a deeply valanced rear mudguard, a special leg-shield. Japan's first example of completely covered motorcycle.
ITAGAKI PRODUCT

QUEEN SUNLIGHT
Overall Length: 1,910 mm.　　Overall Width: 650 mm.
Overall Height: 950 mm.　Wheelbase: 1,290 mm.　Vehicle Weight: 105 kg.　No. of Seats: 1　Engine: 2 cycle 1 cyl 124 cc　6.8 HP　5,800 rpm　80 km/h.　Clutch: Automatic centrifugal.　Transmission: Primary transmission, V-belt (242/1″)　Tire: front 20—2.75　rear 20—2.75

The outside apperance of this particular machine bears close resemblance to a motor scooter. The engine of two-stroke, 124 c.c. piston displacement and developing 6.8 HP is mounted with an automatic clutch and automatic speed change mechanism.
ITAGAKI PRODUCT

ROAD KING
Overall Length: 1,848 mm.　　Overall Width: 650 mm.
Overall Height: 910 mm.　Wheelbase: 1,240 mm.　Vehicle Weight: 110 kg.　No. of Seats: 1　Engine: 2 cycle 1 cyl 123 cc　7.3 HP　90 km/h.　Transmission: Constant mesh.　No. of Speeds: forward 4　Tire: front 22—2.75, 2 P　rear 22—2.75, 4 P

A spine-type pressed-steel frame affords rigid support to the powerful engine which is equipped with the self-starting dynamo. By virtue of the pressed-steel construction, the machine reveals high strength and sturdiness contributing much to the elongation of durability life.
FUJI KIKAI PRODUCT

MEIHATSU ACE

Overall Length : 1,950 mm.　　Overall Width : 760 mm. Overall Height : 940 mm.　Wheelbase : 1,275 mm.　Vehicle Weight : 105 kg.　No. of Seats : 1　Engine : 2 cycle 2 cyl 123.5 cc　6 HP　5,5000 rpm 85 km/h.　Clutch : Multi-plate wet.　Transmission : Three speed, constant mesh.　No. of Speeds : forward 3　Gear Ratio : bottom 23.04, 2nd 13.37, top 8.20　Tire : front 22—2.75, 4 P　rear 22—2.75, 4 P

The machine is equipped with the Dyna-starter affording easy starting. The front fork is of bottom-link type. The machine has a 125 c.c. two-stroke engine in unit with a three-speed gear-box. Special attention has been paid for ease of disassembly and repair of the engine and transmission.

KAWASAKI MEIHATSU PRODUCT

MEIHATSU SUPER

Overall Length : 1,950 mm.　　Overall Width : 760 mm. Overall Height : 940 mm.　Wheelbase : 1,275 mm.　Vehicle Weight : 110 kg.　No. of Seats : 1　Engine : 2 cycle 2 cyl 123.5 cc　6 HP　5,500 rpm　85 km/h.　Clutch : Multi-plate, wet.　Transmission : three speed, constant mesh.　No. of Speeds : forward 3　Gear Ratio : bottom 23.04, 2nd 13.37, top 8.20　Tire : front 22-2.75, 4 P　rear 22 2.75, 4 P

Easily detachable unit construction is employed for the transmission gear casing. Secondary chain is of double-chain design of a high mechanical efficiency. By removal of a spindle, contact of the wheel and the brake drum is disengaged, affording easy removal of the wheel.

KAWASAKI MEIHATSU PRODUCT

YAMAGUCHI SUPER TWIN 125

Overall Length : 1,910 mm.　　Overall Width : 650 mm. Overall Height : 950 mm.　Wheelbase 1,250 mm.　Vehicle Weight : 120 kg.　No. of Seats : 1　Engine : Air-cooled, in-line, with self-starter, 2 cycle　2 cyl　125 cc　10.5 HP 8,000 rpm　105 km/h. Clutch : Multi-plates, wet.　Transmission : Constant mesh.　No. of Speeds : forward 4 Tire : front 3.00—16　rear 3.00—16

Improved engine performance by constant-meshing four-speed transmission gear box equipped with the integrating-type speed-change system. The frame is of pressed-steel construction and the luggage carrier is of unitary construction with the rear fender. Rigid foot-rests are worthy of note.

YAMAGUCHI BICYCLE PRODUCT

YAMAGUCHI SEL SUPER 350

Overall Length : 1,950 mm.　　Overall Width : 650 mm. Overall Height : 920 mm.　Wheelbase : 1,275 mm.　Vehicle Weight : 113.6 kg.　No. of Seats : 1　Engine : Air-cooled, 2 cycle 1 cyl 125 cc　7.0 HP 5,800 rpm 90 km/h.　Clutch : Multi-plate, wet.　Transmission : Constant mesh.　No. of Speeds : forward 4　Gear Ratio : low 24.91 : 1, 2nd 15.68 : 1, 3rd 11.07 : 1, top 8.04 : 1　Tire : front 3.00—16 rear 300—16P

A two-stroke-engine-powered machine with comprehensive specifications and brisk performance. Important proportions and principal dimensions have been determined by thorough experimentation so as to make the rider assume a natural and relaxed pose. Starting is easy by a self-starter motor.

YAMAGUCHI BICYCLE PRODUCT

LIGHT CRUISER SL-III

Overall Length: 2,000 mm. Overall Width: 680 mm. Overall Height: 930 mm. Wheelbase: 1,286 mm. Vehicle Weight: 115 kg. Engine: Air cooling, 2 cycle 1 cyl 125 cc 8 HP 90 km/h. Transmission: Constant mesh, three speed, foot-operated (left). Tire: front 24—2.75 rear 24—2.75

The Dyna-starter mounted on this particular machine is a happy combination of advantages of a self-starting motor and an electric generator. Its construction is simple and functioning is dependable. A gentle push on the button brings the engine to life instantaneously.

SHOWA PRODUCT

MARIEN 125

Overall Length: 1,880 mm. Overall Width: 650 mm. Overall Height: 950 mm. Wheelbase: 1,295 mm. Vehicle Weight: 120 kg. No. of Seats: 1 Engine: Forced air cooling, 2 cycle 1 cyl 123 cc 8 HP 6,200 rpm 80 km/h. Transmission: Hydraulic torque converter, constant mesh. Tire: front 3.00—14, 4 P rear 3.00—14, 4 P

This machine embodies combined advantages of a motorcycle and a motor scooter. Wheels are all of disc wheel type and the rear wheel is equipped with air suspension system. Engine power is transmitted by a transmission shaft through a torque converter. **SHOWA PRODUCT**

POINTER JUNIOR PF-III

Overall Length: 1,930 mm. Overall Width: 740 mm. Overall Height: 940 mm. Wheelbase: 1,230 mm. Vehicle Weight: 92 kg. No. of Seats: 1 Engine: Air-cooled, 2 cycle 1 cyl 89 cc 4.3 HP 6,000 rpm 65 km/h. Clutch: Double plates, wet. Transmission: Constant mesh. No. of Speeds: forward 2 Gear Ratio: low 18.105, top 10.65 Tire: front 24—2.50 rear 24—2.50

Much thought has been poured to create a machine of light weight and excellent practicability. Housing of the engine is integral with the casing of two-speed transmission gear box. By virtue of the light-weightedness of the whole structure, operational and maintenance costs can be reduced to a minimum. **SHIN MEIWA PRODUCT**

POINTER SENIOR PSB-II

Overall Length: 1,935 mm. Overall Width: 755 mm. Overall Height: 955 mm. Weelbase: 1,255 mm. Vehicle Weight: 125 kg. No. of Seats: 2 Engine: Air-cooled, 2 cycle 1 cyl 123 cc 7.5 HP 6,000 rpm 90 km/h. Clutch: Multi-plate, wet. Transmission: Constant mesh. No. of Speeds: forward 4 Gear Ratio: low 22.99, 2nd 14.46, 3rd 10.20, top 7.83 Tire: front 22—3.00 rear 22—3.00.

A two-stroke engine is mounted on a robust pressed-steel frame. Power generated by the engine is transmitted to the rear wheel through the four-speed rotary-type transmission gear system. Noiseless operation of the engine is worthy of note. The front wheel suspension incorporates the Neidhart torsion rubber cushioning. Easy starting is effected by the self-starting generator dynamo.

SHIN MEIWA PRODUCT

QUEEN ROCKET 125F

Overall Length: 1,925 mm.　　Overall Width: 700 mm.
Overall Height: 950 mm.　Wheelbase: 1,250 mm.　Vehicle Weight: 102 kg.　No. of Seats: 2　Engine: With self-starter, 2 cycle 1 cyl 123.2cc 7.8 HP 5,400 rpm 85 km/h. Clutch: Wet.　Transmission: 3 speeds, constant mesh. No. of Speeds: forward 3　Gear Ratio: 1st 1:2.85, 2nd 1:1.55, 3rd 1:1　Tire: front 22—2.75, 2 P rear 22—2.75, 4 P

The frame is of tubular spine construction. The engine is started by a self-starting generating dynamo provided with an inside rotor. The front wheel is sprung by a telescopic front fork and the rear wheel by a swing arm.

ROCKET PRODUCT

IMC YB-II

Overall Length: 1,988 mm.　　Overall Width: 788 mm.
Overall Height: 881 mm.　Wheelbase: 1,275 mm.　Vehicle Weight: 102 kg.　No. of Seats: 2　Engine: 2 cycle 1 cyl 122 cc 6 HP 5,000 rpm 87 km/h.　Clutch: Multi-plate, wet.　Transmission: Three speeds, constant mesh.　No. of Speeds: forward 3　Gear Ratio: bottom 3.26, 2nd 1.38, top 1.24　Tire: front 2.75—24 rear 2.75—24

A single-cylinder, two-stroke engine is equipped with a self-starting generating dynamo. The transmission gear mechanism is of three speed constant-mesh type provided with a patented shifting device. Long stroke hydraulic vibration dampers are mounted both in front and rear. Generously dimensioned exhaust silencer and thick rubber vibration damper for the rear wheel are notable features.

ITO MOTOR PRODUCT

KATAKURA AUTO K-60

Overall Length: 1,985 mm.　　Overall Width: 750 mm.
Overall Height: 900 mm.　Wheelbase: 1,270 mm.　Vehicle Weight: 110 kg.　No. of Seats: 2　Engine: 2 cycle 1 cyl 125 cc 7.5 HP 5,800 rpm 90 km/h.　Clutch: Wet plates. Transmission: Constant mesh.　No. of Speeds: forward 4 Gear Ratio: 1st 7.58:1, 2nd 4.77:1, 3rd 3.36:1, 4th 2.44:1　Tire: front 3—16, 4 P rear 3—16, 4 P

This starter-dynamo-equipped machine guarantees low costs of operation and maintenance. Outstanding advantages are high standard of performance, including gradability, excellent high speed stability and admirable riding comfort.

KATAKURA CYCLE PRODUCT

EMURO DELUXE ED-110

Overall Length: 1,870 mm.　　Overall Width: 730 mm.
Overall Height: 920 mm.　Wheelbase: 1,250 mm.　Vehicle Weight: 110 kg.　No. of Seats: 1　Engine: 2 cycle 1 cyl 123 cc 6.75 HP 4,800 rpm 80 km/h.　Clutch: Cork, multi-plate, wet.　Transmission: Three speeds, foot-operated, constant mesh.　No. of Speeds: forward 3　Gear Ratio: 2.235, 3.059, 6.837　Tire: front 22—2.75 rear 22—2.75

Emphasis is placed on the front and rear springing to damp out oscillation, especially the trailing-link front fork is an unusual feature. Other notable mechanical feature is the anti-seizure device of the engine cylinder wall.

HEALTH MOTOR PRODUCT

TOYOMOTOR FHA

Overall Length : 2,010 mm.　　Overall Width : 740 mm.
Overall Height : 1,000 mm.　　Wheelbase : 1,320 mm.
Vehicle Weight : 121 kg.　No. of Seats : 2.　Engine :
2 cycle 1,236 cc 6.5 HP 80 km/h. No. of Speeds : forward 4

Outstanding mechanical features are engine equipped with self-starting dynamo generator, four-speed transmission gear box operated by ball-shifting principle, engine casing integral with transmission gear casing, semi-sealed type headlamp, driving hub of pressed-steel construction, and pipe frame integral with carrier.

TOYOMOTOR PRODUCT

126 c.c. and over

Motorcycles currently manufactured are equipped with 4-cycle or 2-cycle engines. The former burns gasoline and the latter, a mixture of gasoline and mobil oil.

The largest models produced in Japan at present have a piston displacement of 800 c.c. and attain the speed of 135 km per hour. They are used mainly by police boards, newspaper companies and other special customers.

Recent trends are that motorcycles have been equipped with modified engines and accessories and that more importance has been attached to styling and color.

COLLEDA 250 TM-2

Overall Length : 1,980 mm.　　Overall Width : 730 mm.
Overall Height : 960 mm. Wheelbase : 1,280 mm. Vehicle Weight : 110 kg. No. of Seats : 2 Engine : Air-cooled, 2 cycle 2 cyl 247 cc 15 HP 6,000 rpm 120 km/h. Clutch : Multiple wet disk. Transmission : 4 speeds, foot-operated. No. of Speeds : forward 4　Gear Ratio : low 1 : 2.8, 2nd 1 : 1.6, 3rd 1 : 1.1, high 1 : 0.8　Tire : front 3—18, 4 P rear 3—18, 4 P

The machine is powered by a 247 c.c. two-stroke, parallel-twin engine with comprehensive specifications and brisk performance. Much attention has been paid for giving the rider a feeling of confidence in a rough ride.

SUZUKI MOTOR PRODUCT

COLLEDA TWIN ACE TA

Overall Length : 2,030 mm.　　Overall Width : 690 mm.
Overall Height : 950 mm. Wheelbase : 1,320 mm. Vehicle Weight : 148 kg. No. of Seats : 2　Engine : Air-cooled, 2 cycle 2 cyl 246 cc 18 HP 7,000 rpm 130 km/h. Clutch : Multiple wet disk. No. of Speeds : forward 4　Gear Ratio : low 1 : 2.8, 2nd 1 : 1.5, 3rd 1 : 1.04, top 1 : 0.7 Tire : front 3.25—16, 4 P　rear 3.25—16, 4 P

Japan's first hydraulic brake system features this machine, affording simultaneous braking action on both wheels. Thus the driver can bring the machine to the safest stop. A powerful engine fed by two carburettors guarantees high standard of performance and economical operation.

SUZUKI MOTOR PRODUCT

HONDA DREAM CS71

Overall Length: 1,990 mm. Overall Width: 670 mm. Overall Height: 980 mm. Wheelbase: 1,310 mm. Vehicle Weight: 143 kg. No. of Seats: 2 Engine: Air cooling, ohc, 4 cycle 2 cyl 247 cc 20 HP 8,400 rpm 135 km/h. Clutch: Wet, multiple-disk. Transmission: Constant mesh, rotary change. No. of Speeds: forward 4 Gear Ratio: 1st 3.72, 2nd 1.89, 3rd 1.38, 4th 1.00 Tire: front 3.25—16 rear 3.25—16

The most orthodox in conception is the Dream CS-71 with a high-compression and high-torque engine. The engine is equipped with a four-speed rotary speed-change mechanism; both primary and second speeds are chain-driven. Automatic ignition advancer ensures smooth and noiseless operation of the engine. The frame is of pressed-steel back-bone construction.

HONDA MOTOR PRODUCT

MEGURO JUNIOR S5

Overall Length: 2,110 mm. Overall Width: 750 mm. Overall Height: 1,010 mm. Wheelbase: 1,370 mm. Vehicle Weight: 158 kg. No. of Seats: 2 Engine: ohv, 4 cycle 1 cyl 248 cc 11.5 HP 5,200 rpm 100 km/h. Clutch: Multiple dry plate. Transmission: Rotary foot change. No. of Speeds: forward 4 Gear Ratio: low 2.976, 2nd 2.082, 3rd 1.461, top 1.00 Tire: front 3.00-18, 4 P rear 3.25 18, 4P

Styled in best British fashion, this machine features low center of gravity and remarkable stability, affording high performance even in a rough ride. The engine operates trouble-free and gives high torque figure in the lower revolution range.

MEGURO PRODUCT

MEGURO YA

Overall Length: 2,055 mm. Overall Width: 720 mm. Overall Height: 1,000 mm. Wheelbase: 1,350 mm. Vehicle Weight: 162 kg. No. of Seats: 2 Engine: ohc, 4 cycle 1 cyl 325 cc 19.5 HP 5,500 rpm 120 km/h. Clutch: Multiple dry plate. Transmission: Rotary foot change. No. of Speeds: forward 4 Gear Ratio: low 2.976, 2nd 2.082, 3rd 1.461, top 1.00 Tire: front 3.00-18, 4 P rear 3.25-18, 4 P

This model retains a light and sporting build with the exhaust pipe and silencer raised to a middle position. The engine, single cylinder 3.25 c.c. is amply studded with light-alloy cooling fins. **MEGURO PRODUCT**

MEGURO STAMINA Z7

Overall Length: 2,270 mm. Overall Width: 820 mm. Overall Height: 1,090 mm. Wheelbase: 1,440 mm. Vehicle Weight: 204 kg. No. of Seats: 2 Engine: ohv, 4 cycle 1 cyl 498 cc 20.2 HP 4,400 rpm 120 km/h. Clutch: Multiple dry plate. Transmission: Rotary foot change. No. of Speeds: forward 4 Gear Ratio: low 2.926, 2nd 2.070, 3rd 1.425, top 1.00 Tire: front 3.25—19, 4 P rear 3.50—19, 4 P

To cope with the greater power output, the patented Sendite Metal is employed in the engine. High accelerating ability of the engine affords quick response from a crawl to the maximum speed.

MEGURO PRODUCT

YAMAHA 250

Overall Length: 1,900 mm.　　Overall Width: 740 mm.
Overall Height: 955 mm.　Wheelbase: 1,270 mm.　Vehicle Weight: 140 kg.　No. of Seats: 2　Engine: 2 stroke, 2 cycle 2 cyl 247 cc 14.5 HP 6,000 rpm 115 km/h.　Clutch: Multi-plate.　Transmission: Foot-operated (left)　No. of Speeds: forward 4　Gear Ratio: low 1:25.601, 2nd 1:14.631, 3rd 1:10.917, top 1:8.420　Tire: front 3.25—16, 2 P rear 3.25—16, 4 P

The machine is powered by the self-starting, two-stroke, parallel-twin cylinder engine and constructed with robust steel pipe frame. Ease of control encourages high speed racing and low speed traffic threading.

YAMAHA MOTORCYCLE PRODUCT

YAMAHA 250S (STANDARD)

Overall Length: 1,980 mm.　　Overall Width: 615 mm.
Overall Height: 950 mm.　Wheelbase: 1,285 mm.　Vehicle Weight: 138 kg.　No. of Seats: 2　Engine: 2 stroke, 2 cycle 2 cyl 246 cc 20 HP 7,500 rpm 140 km/h.　Clutch: Multi-plate.　Transmission: Foot-operated, 5 speed gear box & chain.　No. of Speeds: forward 5　Tire: front 3.00–18, 2 P rear 3.00–18, 4 P

The machine is powered by a two-stroke, two-cylinder engine developing 20 HP. It is equipped with two carburettors and five-speed transmission gear box. The machine is best fitted for highspeed operation, capable of standing the speed of above 140 km/h. Lightweight principle has been adopted by generous use of lightalloys.

YAMAHA MOTORCYCLE PRODUCT

YAMAHA 250S (SCRAMBLER)

Overall Length: 1,980 mm.　　Overall Width: 615 mm.
Overall Height: 950 mm.　Wheelbase: 1,285 mm.　Vehicle Weight: 138 kg.　No. of Seats: 2　Engine: 2 cycle 2 cyl 246 cc 20 HP 7,500 rpm 140 km/h.　Clutch: Constant mesh.　Transmission: Foot-operated, 5 speed gear box & chain.　No. of Speeds: forward 5　Tire: front 3.00–18, 2 P rear 3.00–18, 4 P

This throughout new machine is powered by a two-stroke, parallel-twin engine developing 15 HP. It is equipped with five-speed transmission gear system, affording free selection of the most appropriate gear. The machine is fit for driving over rough terrain and formidable inclination. The maximum speed is 135 km/h.

YAMAHA MOTORCYCLE PRODUCT

YAMAHA 250S (RACER)

Overall Length: 1,980 mm.　　Overall Width: 615 mm.
Overall Height: 950 mm.　Wheelbase: 1,285 mm.　Vehicle Weight: 138 kg.　No. of Seats: 2　Engine: 2 cycle 2 cyl 246 cc 20 HP 7,500 rpm 140 km/h.　Clutch: Constant mesh.　Transmission: Foot-operated, 5 speed gear box & chain.　No. of Speeds: forward 5　Tire: front 3.00 18, 2 P rear 3.00 18, 4 P

This lively racing machine features outstanding vivid acceleration, unusually high maximum speed (160 km/h) and pronounced road holding capacity. Drastically up-raised exhaust muffler cover appeals to high-speed enthusiasts.

YAMAHA MOTORCYCLE PRODUCT

RIKUO FB

Overall Length: 2,120 mm. Overall Width: 800 mm.
Overall Height: 1,100 mm. Wheelbase: 1,375 mm.
Vehicle Weight: 175 kg. No. of Seats: 2 Engine: ohv, 4 cycle 1 cyl 247 cc 12 HP 100 km/h. Transmission: Constant mesh, endless rotary cam, conducted by foot lever. No. of Speeds: forward 4 Tire: front 3.25—18, 2 p rear 3.25—18, 4 P

An orthodox shaft-driven machine featuring low center of gravity and admirable road-holding. Outstanding mechanical features are dynamo with automatic ignition advancer, foot-operated, rotary-type, four-speed transmission gear box. The machine is well-known for lively riding comfort and easiness of cleaning and maintenance.
RIKUO MOTORCYCLE PRODUCT

RIKUO AC

Overall Length: 2,120 mm. Overall Width: 800 mm.
Overall Height: 1,050 mm. Wheelbase: 1,400 mm. Vehicle Weight: 180 kg. No. of Seats: 2 Engine: 4 cycle 1 cyl 34.5 cc 20 HP 5,200 rpm 120 km/h. Clutch: Single dry disc, operated by hand lever. Transmission: Changed with endless rotary cam, conducted by foot lever. No. of Speeds: forward 4 Gear Ratio: 6.3:1 at top speed. Tire: front 3.00—18, 4 P rear 3.25—18, 4 P

This particular machine represents a shaft-driven motorcycle equipped with high-strength bevel gears, featuring low center of gravity and admirable roadholding. The powerful engine permits highspeed and formidable climbing. A foot-operated rotary-type, four-speed transmission gear box is mounted.
RIKUO MOTORCYCLE PRODUCT

RIKUO RT

Overall Length: 2,350 mm. Overall Width: 925 mm.
Overall Height: 1,030 mm. Wheelbase: 1,500 mm. Vehicle Weight: 235 kg. No. of Seats: 2 Engine: V, Side valve, 4 cycle 2 cyl 747 cc 25 HP 130 km/h. Transmission: Constant mesh, endless rotary cam conducted by foot lever. No. of Speeds: Forward 4 Tire: front 16—5.00, 4 P rear 16—5.00, 4 P

Featuring a massive and robust construction characteristic of the Harley-Davidson range, the Rikuo RT rates as a most interesting addition to the heavy motorcycles available in Japan. The original Harley-Davidson design has been modified to suit Japanese riders. Its continued high speed and durability are worthy of note. Notable mechanical features are dry-sump lubricating system, automatic ignition advancer and foot-operated, rotary-type, four-speed transmission gear box.
RIKUO MOTORCYCLE PRODUCT

TOHATSU HURRY TA

Overall Length: 1,980 mm. Overall Width: 620 mm.
Overall Height: 1,010 mm. Wheelbase: 1,315 mm. Vehicle Weight: 155 kg. No. of Seats: 2 Engine: 2 cycle 1 cyl 249 cc 18.0 HP 5,800 rpm 120 km/h. Clutch: 3 plates, wet. Transmission: 4 speed, foot-operated. No. of Speeds: forward 4, reverse nil. Gear Ratio: High 1:1, 2nd 1:1.28, 3rd 1:1.88, low 1:3.09 Tire: front 16—3.25 rear 16—3.25

Quick starting can easily be effected by the electric starter actuated by a push-button switch. The machine is admirably tailored with pressed steel frame giving impression of high standard of performance and stability.
TOKYO HATSUDOKI PRODUCT

YAMAGUCHI DELUXE 800S

Overall Length: 1,930 mm.　　Overall Width: 700 mm.
Overall Height: 900 mm.　Wheelbase: 1,300 mm.　Vehicle Weight: 130 kg.　No. of Seats: 2　Engine: Air cooling, 2 cycle　1 cyl　200 cc　11.9 HP　5,400 rpm　110 km/h. Clutch: Multi-plate, wet.　Transmission: Constant mesh No. of Speeds: forward 4　Gear Ratio: low 20.38 : 1, 2nd 12.74 : 1, 3rd 8.92 : 1, top 6.49 : 1　Tire: front 3.00—16, rear 3.00—16

New specification includes numerous features designed to appeal to the sport machine loving rider. The two-stroke engine with a piston displacement of 200 c.c. developing 11.9 HP is mounted with a monobloc carburettor for higher power output and livelier acceleration.

YAMAGUCHI BICYCLE PRODUCT

KATAKURA AUTO 202

Overall Length: 1,955 mm.　　Overall Width: 730 mm. Overall Height: 920 mm.　Wheelbase: 1,260 mm.　Vehicle Weight: 116 kg.　No. of Seats: 2　Engine: 2 cycle 1 cyl　200 cc　10.8 HP　5,500 rpm　110 km/h.　Clutch: Wet plates.　Transmission: Constant mesh.　No. of Speeds: forward 4　Gear Ratio: 1st 7.58 : 1, 2nd 4.56 : 1, 3rd 3.07 : 1, 4th 2.31 : 1　Tire: front 3—16, 4 P　rear 3—16, 4 P

In general the machine follows orthodox design practice aiming at high standard of performance and gradability. The machine is powered by a two-stroke, single cylinder engine of 200 c.c. piston displacement.

KATAKURA CYCLE PRODUCT

TSUBASA FALCON

Overall Length: 2,077 mm.　　Overall Width: 840 mm. Overall Height: 955 mm.　Wheelbase: 1,373 mm.　Vehicle Weight: 170 kg.　No. of Seats: 2　Engine: 4 cycle 1 cyl　247 cc　12 HP　6,500 rpm　35 km/h.　Clutch: Single dry plate.　Transmission: Sliding.　No. of Speeds: forward 4　Gear Ratio: bottom 4.39 : 1, 2nd 2.92 : 1, 3rd 2.00 : 1, top 1.57 : 1　Tire: front 3.00—18, 2 P　rear 3.25—18, 4 P

An easy starting is effected by a self-starting generating dynamo. The engine is engineered for long durability. Special attention has been paid for high standard of riding comfort. Equipped with a four-speed transmission gear box provided with direct return to neutral position from any speed by means of a stroke of a foot. Powerful 45 W headlamp beam guarantees safe night drive.

TSUBASA INDUSTRY PRODUCT

QUEEN ROCKET 200R

Overall Length: 2,010 mm.　　Overall Width: 720 mm. Overall Height: 970 mm.　Wheelbase: 1,300 mm.　Vehicle Weight: 145 kg.　No. of Seats: 2　Engine: With self-starter, 2 cycle　1 cyl　199.5 cc　12.3 HP　5,200 rpm　110 km/h.　Clutch: Wet.　Transmission: Four speed, constant mesh.　No. of Speeds: forward 4　Gear Ratio: 1st 1 : 3.34, 2nd 1 : 1.96, 3rd 1 : 1.33, 4th 1 : 1　Tire: front 3.00—16, 2 P　rear 3.00—16, 4 P

Tubular back-bone type frame gives steady mounting to the engine giving the rider the feeling of confidence and stability. Engine is equipped with a starting-dynamo with the outside rotor in order that better balancing of engine torque can be effected.

ROCKET PRODUCT

CRUISER SC-II

Overall Length: 2,000 mm.　　Overall Width: 680 mm.
Overall Height: 960 mm.　Wheelbase: 1,290 mm.　Vehicle Weight: 150 kg.　No. of Seats: 2　　Engine: Air cooling.　2 cycle　1 cyl　250 cc　15 HP　5,500 rpm　120 km/h.　Clutch: Multi-plate, wet.　Transmission: 4 speed, constant mesh, foot operated (left)　Tire: front 3.00—18　rear 3.00—18

The model retains the original 250 c.c. single cylinder engine as the power source. The engine develops 15 HP, indicating the weightpower ratio of 10 kg/HP a sign of smooth running from the slow pottering to the highest speed. A special lubricating device is equipped for the crankshaft.

SHOWA PRODUCT

HOSK 350FA

Overall Length: 2,180 mm.　　Overall Width: 720 mm.
Overall Height: 1,060 mm.　　Wheelbase: 1,430 mm.
Vehicle Weight: 170 kg.　No. of Seats: 2　Engine: Air-cooled, ohv, 4 cycle　1 cyl　340 cc　18 HP　125 km/h. Transmission: 4 speed, constant mesh, foot change.　No. of Speeds: forward 4　Tire: front 3.00—19　rear 3.25—19

The engine and frame construction are exactly the same as the Hosk GA. The transmission system is of the Burman four-speed type. The machine is equipped with telescopic front fork and swing-arm suspension system. The frame construction formed in triangle is light in weight and stiff. The long durability life of the engine as well as the frame features this machine of pronounced practicability.

SHOWA PRODUCT

HOSK 500 SINGLE GA

Overall Length: 2,190 mm.　　Overall Width: 750 mm
Overall Height: 1,070 mm.　　Wheelbase: 1,400 mm.
Vehicle Weight: 198 kg.　No. of Seats: 2　Engine: Air-cooled, vertical, ohc, 4 cycle　1 cyl　499 cc　24.4 HP　140 km/h.　Transmission: 4 Speed, constant mesh, foot change.　No. of Speeds: forward 4　Tire: front 3.25—19　rear 3.50—19

The machine is powered by a four-stroke, o.h.v. engine equipped with hairpin valve springs, capable of standing continued high-speed operation. Ignition of engine is performed by coil-ignition system provided with dual manual and automatic ignition advancing apparatus.

SHOWA PRODUCT

HOSK 500 TWIN DB

Overall Length: 2,190 mm.　　Overall Width: 750 mm.
Overall Height: 1,090 mm.　　Wheelbase: 1,430 mm.
Vehicle Weight: 210 kg.　No. of Seats: 2　Engine: Air-cooled, in-line, ohc, 4 cycle　2 cyl　498 cc　26 HP　140 km/h.　Transmission: 4 speed, constant mesh, foot change.　No. of Speeds: forward 4　Tire: front 3.25—19　rear 3.50—19

The machine is powered by a four-stroke, parallel twin. o.h.v. engine. The camshaft is operated by a chain eliminating such mechanical loss that is caused by the reciprocating motions when a push-rods are used. Avoid acceleration and noiseless operation similar to the engine of a car feature the two-cylinder engine of this de luxe motorcycle.

SHOWA PRODUCT

LILAC LS18

Overall Length: 2,030 mm. Overall Width: 770 mm.
Overall Height: 1,000 mm. Wheelbase: 1,350 mm
Vehicle Weight: 165 kg. No. of Seats: 2 Engine:
4 cycle 2 cyl 247.2cc 18.5 HP 7,500 rpm 130 km/h.
Clutch: Single dry plate. Transmission: Constant mesh,
rotary. No. of Speeds: forward 4 Gear Ratio: low,
5.43:1, 2nd 2.95:1, 3rd 2.22:1, top 1.69:1 Tire: front
3.25—17, 2 P rear 3.25—17, 4 P

This machine represents the standard model of 250 c.c. class, styled in most conventional fashion. This practicability-conscious motorcycle is well-suited to suburban pottering and long distance touring. Basic construction is similar to the Lilac LS38.

MARUSHO MOTORCYCLE PRODUCT

LILAC LS38

Overall Length: 2,050 mm. Overall Width: 645 mm.
Overall Height: 990 mm. Wheelbase: 1,350 mm. Vehicle
Weight: 160 kg. No. of Seats: 2 Engine: 4 cycle
2 cyl 247.2 cc 20.3 HP 8,000 rpm 140 km/h
Clutch: Single dry plate. Transmission: Constant mesh,
rotary. No. of Speeds: forward 4 Gear Ratio:
low 5.43:1, 2nd 2.95:1, 3rd 2.22:1, top 1.69:1 Tire:
front 3.00—18, 4 P rear 3,00—18, 4 P

This particular machine is powered by a 247 c.c. four-stroke, V-2 engine developing 20.3 HP. The specific output of 82 HP/l ranks highest of the equivalent motorcycles. Notable features are the selfstarter, dual carburettors, four-speed rotary-type transmission and power transmission-shaft. **MARUSHO MOTORCYCLE PRODUCT**

POINTER COMET PCB-II

Overall Length: 1,935 mm. Overall Width: 755 mm.
Overall Height: 955 mm. Wheelbase: 1,255 mm. Vehicle
Weight: 135 kg. No. of Seats: 2 Engine: Air-cooled,
2 cycle 1 cyl 175 cc 11 HP 6,000 rpm 100 km/h.
Clutch: Multi-plate, wet. No. of Speeds: forward 4
Gear Ratio: low 20.16, 2nd 12.65, 3rd 8.92, top 6.85
Tire: front 3.00—16 rear 3.00—16

The model "Comet" is constructed with a frame of new design and mounted with a two-stroke, over-square engine equipped with the four-speed rotary-type transmission. Outstanding features are the Neidhart torsion rubber suspension system, the first attempt in the world and an electric starting motor. **SHIN MEIWA PRODUCT**

POINTER ACE PAT-II

Overall Length: 1,990 mm. Overall Width: 760 mm.
Overall Height: 950 mm. Wheelbase: 1,255 mm. Vehicle
Weight: 150 kg. No. of Seats: 2 Engine: Air-cooled,
2 cycle 2 cyl 247 cc 15 HP 6,000 rpm 120 km/h. Clutch:
Multi-plate, wet. Transmission: Constant mesh, rotary.
No. of Speeds: forward 4 Gear Ratio: low 17,65, 2nd
10.35, 3rd 7.36, top 5.66 Tire: front 3.25—16 rear
3.25—16

The model "Ace" is of robust, but light-weight type, powered by the two-stroke twin-cylinder engine. The engine is equipped with the rotary-type transmission and the quick-starting Dyna-starter. The world first Neidhart torsion rubber suspension system is incorpated in the front fork.

SHIN MEIWA PRODUCT

GASUDEN FB

Overall Length: 1,980 mm. Overall Width: 770 mm. Overall Height: 930 mm. Wheelbase: 1,300 mm. Vehicle Weight: 135 kg. No. of Seats: 2 Engine: 2 cycle 1 cyl 199.4 cc 10.8 HP 5,500 rpm 110 km/h. Clutch: Cork, wet, multi-plates. Transmission: Synchromesh, gradual, sliding. No. of Speeds: forward 4 Gear Ratio: 1st 7.58:1, 2nd 4.56:1, 3rd 3.07:1, 4th 2.31:1 Tire: front 2.75—17, 2 P rear 3.00—17, 4 P

The notable mechanical features are the newly-designed two-stroke, over-square engine of high speed performance and the centrifugal-type automatic ignition advancing device ensuring high standard of low speed performance. As per the frame, vibration damping elements are so designed to maintain an ample road clearance.

FUJI MOTOR PRODUCT

GASUDEN GW-5

Overall Length: 2,030 mm. Overall Width: 770 mm. Overall Height: 960 mm. Wheelbase: 1,325 mm. Vehicle Weight: 165 kg. No. of Seats: 2 Engine: 2 cycle 2 cyl 244 cc 13 HP 4,500 rpm 120 km/h. Clutch: Cork, wet, multi-plate. Transmission: Synchromesh, gradual, sliding. No. of Speeds: forward 4, reverse none. Gear Ratio: 1st 7.75:1, 2nd 4.82:1, 3rd 3.32:1, 4th 2.45:1 Tire: front 3.00—18, 2 P rear 3.25—18, 4 P

This machine is powered by a two-stroke, two cylinder engine performing alternating explosions. By virtue of this arrangement, considerable gain can be obtained in smoother engine revolution and flatter torque curve, tending to vibration-free and comfortable ride.

FUJI MOTOR PRODUCT

EMURO MIGHTY FC-610

Overall Length: 1,875 mm. Overall Width: 750 mm. Overall Height: 940 mm. Wheelbase: 1,295 mm. Vehicle Weight: 150 kg. No. of Seats: 2 Engine: 2 cycle 1 cyl 248 cc 14 HP 5,300 rpm 122 km/h. Clutch: Cork, wet, multi-plate. Transmission: Constant mesh, 4 speed, rotary, foot change. No. of Speeds: forward 4 Gear Ratio: 5.74 Tire: front 3.25—16 rear 3.25—16

Japan's first single-cylinder 250 c.c. engine mounted motorcycle. Outstanding mechanical features of the machine are the trailing-type front suspension system, anti-seizure device of cylinder wall, leakage free filler cap of fuel tank.

HEALTH MOTOR PRODUCT

EMURO EL-500

Overall Length: 2,170 mm. Overall Width: 830 mm. Overall Height: 1,000 mm. Wheelbase: 1,390 mm. Vehicle Weight: 215 kg. No. of Seats: 2 Engine: 2 cycle 2 cyl 494 cc 24.82 HP 4,800 rpm 133 km/h. Clutch: Multi-plate, wet. Transmission: Constant mesh, 4 speed, rotary, foot change. No. of Speeds: forward 4 Gear Ratio: 4.42 Tire: front 4—16 rear 4—16

Japan's first two-stroke 500 c.c. engine powered motorcycle. The engine with the generous piston displacement developing 25 HP claims to be ample in power to overcome any rough driving under the hardest conditions. Mechanical features are automatic ignition advancing mechanism of a wide range and front and rear shock absorbers.

HEALTH MOTOR PRODUCT

TOYOMOTOR FJA

Overall Length: 2,070 mm. Overall Width: 725 mm.
Overall Height: 1,000 mm. Wheelbase: 1,340 mm.
Vehicle Weight: 150 kg. No. of Seats: 2 Engine:
With self-starter, 2 cycle 216 cc 13 HP 110 km/h. No.
of Speeds: forward 4 Tire: front 3.00—18, 2P rear 3.00—18, 4 P

Designed and constructed for joy-rides and door-to-door transportation of light goods. The machine is powered by a powerful engine featuring selfstarting dynamo generator. Electric parts and headlamp function satisfactorily. Frame is of pressed-steel spine-type of maximum stiffness. Considerable effort has been poured for elegant design and styling.

TOYOMOTOR PRODUCT

MEIHATSU CROWN

Overall Length: 1,990 mm. Overall Width: 680 mm.
Overall Height: 965 mm. Wheelbase: 1,330 mm. Vehicle Weight: 160 kg. No. of Seats: 2 Engine: 2 cycle 2 cyl 247.1 cc 16 HP 6,000 rpm 120 km/h. Clutch: Multi-plate, wet. Transmission: Four speeds, constant mesh. No. of Speeds: forward 4 Gear Ratio: bottom 2.84, 2nd 1.64, 3rd 1.16, top 0.88 Tire: front 16—3.25, 4 P rear 16—3.25, 4 P

This particular motorcycle features an ingenious transmission mechanism allowing quick return from the second, third and top gears to neutral with the depressed foot pedal.

KAWASAKI MEIHATSU PRODUCT

IMC U

Overall Length: 2,045 mm. Overall Width: 740 mm.
Overall Height: 1,007 mm. Wheelbase: 1,295 mm.
Vehicle Weight: 135 kg. No. of Seats: 2 Engine: ohc, 2 cycle 1 cyl 199.4 cc 10.8 HP 5,500 rpm 100 km/h. Clutch: Multi-plate, wet. Transmission: Four speed, constant mesh. No. of Speeds: forward 4, Gear Ratio: bottom 7.58, 2nd 4.56, 3rd 3.07, top 2.31 Tire: front 3.00—18, 4 P rear 3.00—18, 4 P

By virtue of the special bore-stroke ratio, a high standard of low speed performance has been achieved. The transmission gear box is provided with four-speed gears of constant-mesh type. A special legshield can be mounted when it is required.

ITO MOTOR PRODUCT

IMC R

Overall Length: 2,330 mm. Overall Width: 822 mm.
Overall Height: 920 mm. Wheelbase: 1,346 mm.
Vehicle Weight: 165 kg. No. of Seats: 2 Engine: 2 cycle 2 cyl 243 cc 13 HP 4,500 rpm 116 km/h. Clutch: Multi-plates, wet. Transmission: Four speed, contant mesh. No. of Speeds: forward 4 Tire: front 3.00—18, 4 P rear 3.25—18, 4 P

A two-stroke, two-cylinder engine provides the machine ample power for smooth running. The engine is equipped with four-speed constantmeshing transmission gear box. The front wheel is provided with a spring-type telescopic shock-absorber and a horizontal swing arm hinged to a lug extended from the front fork.

ITO MOTOR PRODUCT

Manufacturers' List

I. **CARS, BUSES, TRUCKS & THREE-WHEELERS**
II. **MOTORCYCLES & MOTOR SCOOTERS**
III. **PARTS & ACCESSORIES**

NOTE: The manufacturers enlisted in the following pages are the members of Automotive Industrial Association, Midget Motor Manufactures' Association of Japan and Automobile Parts Manufacturers' Association. The address given there indicates the location of the export division of each concern.

1. CARS, BUSES, TRUCKS & THREE-WHEELERS

AICHI MACHINE INDUSTRY CO., LTD.
1, 6-chome, Ichiban-cho, Atsuta-ku, Nagoya
Tel. No., Cable Add.: (66) 0151 GIANT NAGOYA
Products: Three-Wheelers "GIANT" & "CONY," Four-Wheeled Truck "CONY 360"

DAIHATSU KOGYO KABUSHIKI KAISHA
3, 2-chome, Daini Higashi, Oyodo-ku, Osaka
Tel. No., Cable Add.: (45) 2551 DAIHATSU OSAKA
Products: Three-Wheelers "DAIHATSU" & "MIDGET," Four-Wheeled Truck "VESTA"

FUJI HEAVY INDUSTRIES, LTD.
18, 2-chome, Marunouchi, Chiyoda-ku, Tokyo
Tel. No., Cable Add.: (281) 3551 FUJIHEAVY TOKYO
Products: Motor Scooters "RABBIT," Small-sized Car "SUBARU 360," Motorcycles "HURRICANE"

FUJI PRECISION MACHINERY CO., LTD.
Bridgestone Bldg., 1, 1-chome, Kyobashi, Chuo-ku, Tokyo
Tel. No., Cable Add.: (561) 6256 PRINCEAUTOEX TOKYO
Products: "PRINCE" Cars, "PRINCE NEW MILER" & "CLIPPER" Trucks & Light Van

HINO MOTORS, LTD.
Hino Motor Sales Ltd., Hino Bldg., 4, Tori 2-chome, Nihonbashi, Chuo-ku, Tokyo
Tel. No., Cable Add.: (201) 0441 HINODECO TOKYO
Products: "HINO" Buses, Trucks, Dump Trucks, Tank Lorries, Tractor-trailer Trucks, Trolly Buses, "HINO RENAULT" Car

HOPE JIDOSHA CO., LTD.
13, 9-chome, Shiba Tamachi, Minato-ku, Tokyo
Tel. No.: (451) 8514
Products: Three-Wheeled Truck "HOPE STAR"

ISUZU MOTOR CO., LTD.
2691, Oi-Sakashita-cho, Shinagawa-ku, Tokyo
Tel. No., Cable Add.: (761) 0121, 2121 ISUZU TOKYO
Products: "ISUZU" & "ELF" Buses, Trucks, Dump Trucks, Fire Engines, Tank Lorries, Mixer Trucks

MINSEI DIESEL ENGINEERING CO., LTD.
Nissan-Minsei Diesel Sales Co., Ltd., Kobundo Bldg., 4, 4-chome, Kanda Surugadai, Chiyoda-ku, Tokyo
Tel. No., Cable Add.: (251) 2191-5 NISMINDS TOKYO
Products: "MINSEI" Buses, Trucks, Dump Trucks, Tank Lorries, Crane Trucks

MITAKA FUJI INDUSTRIAL CO., LTD.
481, Shimorenjyaku, Mitaka City, Tokyo
Tel. No.: (022) 5361
Products: Three-Wheeled Truck "MUSASHI"

MITSUBISHI HEAVY INDUSTRIES, REORGANIZED, CO., LTD.
10, 2-chome, Marunouchi, Chiyoda-ku, Tokyo
Tel. No., Cable Add.: (211) 3411 HISHIJU TOKYO
Products: Bus & Car Bodies, "MITSUBISHI JEEP," Trucks "MITSUBISHI JUPITER," Three-Wheelers "MITSUBISHI" & "PET LEO," Small-sized Car "MITSUBISHI 500," Motor Scooters "SILVER PIGEON"

MITSUBISHI NIPPON HEAVY-INDUSTRIES, LTD.
4, 2-chome, Marunouchi, Chiyoda-ku, Tokyo
Tel. No., Cable Add.: (281) 2351 BISHINIPPON TOKYO
Products: "MITSUBISHI FUSO" Buses, Trucks, Dump & Tractor Trucks. "MITSUBISHI" Bulldozers, Motor Graders & Scrapers

MITSUI PRECISION MACHINERY & ENG. CO., LTD.
Hino Diesel Sales Co., Ltd., 4, Tori 2-chome, Nihonbashi, Chuo-ku, Tokyo
Tel. No., Cable Add.: (201) 0441 HINODECO TOKYO
Products: Three-Wheeled Trucks "ORIENT" & "HUMBEE"

NISSAN MOTOR CO., LTD.
Otemachi Bldg., 4, 1-chome, Otemachi, Chiyoda-ku, Tokyo
Tel. No., Cable Add.: (201) 5831 NISMO TOKYO
Products: "NISSAN" Trucks & Buses, "NISSAN" Junior Trucks, "DATSUN" Cars & Trucks, "DATSUN BLUEBIRD" Car.

OKAMURA MFG. CO., LTD.
81, 2-chome, Nagata-cho, Chiyoda-ku, Tokyo
Tel. No. Cable Add.: (581) 0351 UNIONOKAMURA TOKYO
Products: "MIKASA TOURING" Sports Car, "MIKASA" Light Vans.

SUZUKI MOTOR CO., LTD.
300, Takatsuka, Kamimura, Hamana-gun, Shizuoka Pref.
Tel. No., Cable Add.: Hamamatsu (2) 8111 SUZUKIORI HAMAMATSU
Products: Motorcycles "COLLEDA," "SUZUMOPED" & "MINIFREE," 4-Wheeled Van "SUZULIGHT"

TOKYU KUROGANE MOTOR CO., LTD.
30, Akasaka Tameike-cho, Minato-ku, Tokyo
Tel. No., Cable Add.: (481) 8141, 8341 TOKYUKUROGANE TOKYO
Products: Three-Wheelers & Four-Wheelers "KUROGANE"

TOYO KOGYO CO., LTD.
6047, Shinchi Fukumachi, Aki-gun, Hiroshima Pref.
Tel. No., Cable Add.: Hiroshima Minami (4) 4141 TOYOKO HIROSHIMA
Products: "MAZDA" Trucks, Dump Trucks, Vacuum Cars, Light Van & "MAZDA" Three-Wheelers.

TOYOTA MOTOR CO., LTD.
Toyota Motor Sales Co., Ltd., 3, 2-chome, Hatchobori, Chuo-ku, Tokyo
Tel. No., Cable Add.: (551) 7111 JIDOSHA TOKYO
Products: "TOYOPET" Cars & Trucks, "TOYOTA" Buses, Trucks, Fire Engines, Dump & Fork-Lift Trucks, Land Cruiser, "TOYO-ACE" Trucks.

II. MOTORCYCLES & MOTOR SCOOTERS

FUJI HEAVY INDUSTRIES, LTD. (See I)

FUJI KIKAI CO., LTD.
1, 170, Maehata-cho, Shimura, Itabashi-ku, Tokyo
Tel. No.: (961) 6131
Products: Motorcycles "ROAD KING"

FUJI MOTORS CORPORATION
1, 5-chome, Shiba Shimbashi, Minato-ku, Tokyo
Tel. No., Cable Add.: (431) 5171 FUJIMOTOR TOKYO
Products: Motorcycles "GASUDEN"

HEALTH MOTOR INDUSTRIAL CO., LTD.
19, Kotohira-cho, Minato-ku, Tokyo
Tel. No.: (501) 9054
Products: Motorcycle "EMURO DELUXE"

HIRANO SEISAKUSHO, LTD.
1, 1-chome, Tamafune-cho, Nakagawa-ku, Nagoya
Tel. No., Cable Add.: Nagoya (66) 0141
Products: Motor Scooters "POP MANLEE"

HONDA MOTOR CO., LTD.
5, 5-chome, Yaesu, Chuo-ku, Tokyo
Tel. No., Cable Add.: (281) 7331 HONDAMOTOR TOKYO
Products: Motorcycles "HONDA DREAM" "HONDA BENLY" "HONDA SUPER CUB"

ITAGAKI CO., LTD.
980, 7-chome, Honcho, Isezaki City, Gumma Pref.
Tel. No.: (Isezaki) 1380
Products: Motorcycles "SUNLIGHT"

ITO MOTOR CO., LTD.
1-12, 2-chome, Kawaguchi-cho, Minato-ku, Nagoya
Tel. No.: Nagoya (6) 2446
Products: Motorcycles "IMC"

KATAKURA CYCLE CO., LTD.
32, 1-chome, Kyobashi, Chuo-ku, Tokyo.
Tel. No.: (831) 7572
Products: Motorcycles "KATAKURA AUTO"

KAWASAKI MEIHATSU INDUSTRY CO., LTD.
1,272, 2-chome, Kanamachi, Katsushika-ku, Tokyo
Tel. No.: (691) 1901
Products: Motorcycles "MEIHATSU"

MARUSHO MOTORCYCLE INDUSTRIAL CO., LTD.
2, 2-chome, Takara-cho, Chuo-ku, Tokyo
Tel. No., Cable Add.: (561) 1491 LILACMOTOR TOKYO
Products: Motorcycles "LILAC"

MEGURO MANUFACTURING CO., LTD.
575, 3-chome, Osaki-Honcho, Shinagawa-ku, Tokyo
Tel. No.: (491) 3191
Products: Motorcycles "MEGURO"

MITSUBISHI HEAVY INDUSTRIES, REORGANIZED, CO., LTD. (See I)

MIYATA WORKS, LTD.
19, 2-chome, Higashirokugo, Ota-ku, Tokyo
Tel. No., Cable Add.: (731) 2121 CYCLIST TOKYO
Products: Motorcycles "ASAHI," "MIYAPET"

RIKUO MOTORCYCLE CO., LTD.
287, 3-chome, Kitashinagawa, Shinagawa-ku, Tokyo
Tel. No., Cable Add.: (491) 3016 RIKUOMOTOR TOKYO
Products: Motorcycles "RIKUO"

ROCKET CO., LTD.
327, Motohama-cho, Hamamatsu City, Shizuoka Pref.
Tel. No.: Hamamatsu (2) 9530
Products: Motorcycles "QUEEN ROCKET"

SHIN MEIWA INDUSTRY CO., LTD.
125 Agenaruo-cho, Nishinomiya City, Hyogo Pref.
Tel. No.: Nishinomiya (4) 0331
Products: Motorcycles "POINTER"

SHOWA WORKS, LTD.
178, Matsunaga, Numazu City, Shizuoka Pref.
Tel. No.: (Numazu) 5111
Products: Motorcycles "CRUISER" & "HOSK"

SUZUKI MOTOR CO., LTD. (See I)

TOKYO HATSUDOKI CO., LTD.
11, 2-chome, Kyobashi, Chuo-ku, Tokyo
Tel. No., Cable Add.: (561) 6251 TOHATSU TOKYO
Products: Motorcycles "TOHATSU"

TOSHO MOTORS CO., LTD.
4, Hanabusa-cho, Kanda, Chiyada-ku, Tokyo
Tel. No.: (291) 4771
Products: Motor Scooter "PANDORA," motorcycle "ECHO"

TOYOMOTOR CO., LTD.
Shigehara, Kariya, Aichi Pref.
Tel. No.: (Kariya) 988
Products: Motorcycles "TOYOMOTOR"

TSUBASA INDUSTRY CO., LTD.
178, Tanaka, Ibaraki, Osaka Pref.
Tel. No.: Ibaraki (0262) 2885
Products: Motorcycles "TSUBASA"

YAMAGUCHI BICYCLE MFG., CO., LTD.
135, Take-cho, Daito-ku, Tokyo
Tel. No.: (831) 9261
Products: Motorcycles "YAMAGUCHI"

YAMAHA MOTORCYCLE CO., LTD.
250 Nakazawa-cho, Hamamatsu City, Shizuoka Pref.
Tel. No.: Hamamatsu (2) 2111
Products: Motorcycles & Motor Scooters "YAMAHA"

III. PARTS & ACCESSORIES

EASTERN AREA

AJIA KELMET SEISAKUSHO
828, Yaguchi-cho, Ota-ku, Tokyo
Tel. No.: (731) 2342-3
Products: Kelmet sleeve bearing

AKEBONO INDUSTRY CO., LTD.
8, 4-chome, Honcho Nihonbashi, Chuo-ku, Tokyo
Tel. No.: (661) 9606-9
Products: Brake lining, Clutch facing

K.K. AMAO SEISAKUSHO
67, 1-chome Terazima-cho, Sumida-ku, Tokyo
Tel. No.: (611) 2824
Products: Doorlock regulator

APOLLO KOGYO CO., LTD.
84, Hongo-cho, Meguro-ku, Tokyo
Tel. No.: (712) 2101-6
Products: Direction indicator

ARAI SESAKUSHO CO., LTD.
179, Horikiri-machi, Katsushika-ku, Tokyo
Tel. No.: (697) 4355-6, (691) 1849
Products: Oil seal, O-ring packing

ART KINZOKU KOGYO K.K.
1, 8-chome, Ginza Higashi, Chuo-ku, Tokyo
Tel. No.: (541) 0042, 6967
Products: Piston, Piston pin

ASAHI ASBESTOS CO., LTD.
3, 7-chome, Ginza, Chuo-ku, Tokyo
Tel. No.: (571) 9361-5
Products: Asbestos cement product, Asbestos product

ASAHI INDUSTRY CO., LTD.
1004, Tsutsumikata-cho, Ota-ku, Tokyo
Tel. No.: (751) 1449, 4477
Products: Tire pressure gauge

ASAHI SEIKO K.K.
65, Nakasawa-cho, Hamamatsu City, Shizuoka Pref.
Tel. No.: (Hamamatsu) 3118
Products: Water pump, Oil pump

K.K. ASAHI SEISAKUSHO
221, Ikejiri-cho, Setagaya-ku, Tokyo
Tel. No.: (421) 3302
Products: Oil seal

ASIA VALVE CO., LTD.
91, Ikegami Tokumochi-cho, Ota-ku, Tokyo
Tel. No.: (751) 6141-5
Products: Universal joint, Propeller engine valve

B.S.K. AUTO PARTS MFG. CO., LTD.
363, Harayama-Shinden, Urawa, Saitama Pref.
Tel. No.: (Urawa) 7106-8
Products: Clutch cover, Disc, Tie rod end, Universal joint

CHIYODA JIDOSHA KOGYO CO., LTD.
7319, Hino, Minamitama-gun, Tokyo
Tel. No.: Hachioji (2) 7131-4
Products: King pin, Shackle pin

CHUGAI PISTON CO., LTD.
11, 3-chome, Kojiya-machi, Ota-ku, Tokyo
Tel. No.: (741) 0469
Products: Piston

CHUO SEISAKUSHO CO., LTD.
25, Senjyu-Azuma-cho, Adachi-ku, Tokyo
Tel. No.: (881) 4076
Products: Contact arm, Contact point

DIA METAL CO., LTD.
29, 4-chome, Higashi Azuma-cho, Sumida-ku, Tokyo
Tel. No.: (681) 7546, 0889, 4195
Products: Grankshaft bearing, Connecting rod bearing

DAIDO JIDOSHA YOHIN SEISAKUSHO CO., LTD.
2, Akasaka-Tameike-cho, Minato-ku, Tokyo
Tel. No.: (481) 2471
Products: Auto parts & accessories

DAIEI KOGYO CO., LTD.
4-7-1, Haneda, Ota-ku, Tokyo
Tel. No.: (741) 4964, 5456
Products: Rear-shaft, Universal joint

DAIICHI MANUFACTURE COMPANY, LTD.
10, 2-chome, Kanda Tsukasa-cho, Chiyoda-ku, Tokyo
Tel. No.: (251) 2639, 4661, 6484
Products: Ignition parts, Motor switches

DAIICHI TANZO CO., LTD.
885, 1-chome, Higashi-Osaki, Shinagawa-ku, Tokyo
Tel. No.: (491) 8141-5
Products: Propeller shaft

DIESEL KIKI KABUSHIKI KAISHA
6, 3-chome, Marunouchi, Chiyoda-ku, Tokyo
Tel. No.: (271) 0884-6
Products: Fuel injection equipment, Multi lubrication equipment, Air conditioner

DOWA KINZOKU KOGYO K.K.
895, Shimura-Maeno-cho, Itabashi-ku, Tokyo
Tel. No.: (961) 5391-3
Products: Various metal, Bushing (Bimetal, Trimetal) Kelmet metal

EBINA DENKI SEISAKUSHO CO., LTD.
486, 3-chome, Nishi-Osaki, Shinagawa-ku, Tokyo
Tel. No.: (491) 1236, 6323
Products: Switch for automobile

EIKO ELECTRICAL INDUSTRY CO., LTD.
3, 5-chome, Shiba Shinbashi, Minato-ku, Tokyo
Tel. No.: (431) 1840, 5051, 2326, 6046, 7016
Products: Heater plug, Resistant coil, Battery switch, Heater signal for diesel cars

FUJI ASBESTOS INDUSTRY CO., LTD.
22, 2-chome, Azusawa-cho, Itabashi-ku, Tokyo
Tel. No.: (901) 4406, 3596
Products: Brake lining, Clutch facing

FUJI HORN SEISAKUSHO CO., LTD.
114, 1-chome, Setagaya, Setagaya-ku, Tokyo
Tel. No.: (421) 3686
Products: Electric horn, Stop switch

FUJI SEIKO CO., LTD.
365, 1-chome, Higashi-Nakanobu, Shinagawa-ku, Tokyo
Tel. No.: (781) 1345, 4632, 3378
Products: Thermostat

FUJI VALVE CO., LTD.
775, 3-chome, Kojiya-cho, Ota-ku, Tokyo
Tel. No.: (741) 0711-5
Products: Engine valve

FUKOKU SPRING MANUFACTURING CO., LTD.
36, Tsutsumine, Kawasaki City, Kanagawa Pref.
Tel. No.: Kawasaki (3) 2405, 2407
Products: Automobile leaf spring, Torsion bar spring

FUKUSAN DENKI KOGYO CO., LTD.
2758, 1-chome, Kojiya-cho, Ota-ku, Tokyo
Tel. No.: (731) 2356
Products: Switch

FUTABA DENKI SEISAKUSHO CO., LTD.
4, 1-chome, Fukagawa-Kiyosumi-cho, Koto-ku, Tokyo
Tel. No.: (641) 1312
Products: Charging relay switch, Electric system

GASKET KOGYO CO., LTD.
28, 5-chome, Azabu-Miyamura-cho, Minato-ku, Tokyo
Tel. No.: (481) 1830-4
Products: Gasket, Packing

GOKO SEISAKUSHO CO., LTD.
50, 6-chome, Shiba-Shinbashi, Minato-ku, Tokyo
Tel. No.: (431) 8261-5
Products: Car heater, Automotive equipment

HACHIEI INDUSTRIAL CO., LTD.
34, Shiba-kotohiracho, Minato-ku, Tokyo
Tel. No.: (501) 3341-3
Products: Universal joint, Repair kit

HAKKOSHA KOGYO CO., LTD.
2, 2-chome, Higashi-Jyujo, Kita-ku, Tokyo
Tel. No.: (911) 7171-5
Products: Head lamp, Tail light

HAMANO KIKAKU KOGYO CO., LTD.
1793, Umeta-cho, Adachi-ku, Tokyo
Tel. No.: (888) 3171-5
Products: Oil seal

HASHIMOTO TEKKO K.K.
807, 3-chome, Takadaminami-cho, Toshima-ku, Tokyo
Tel. No.: (982) 7196-8
Products: Windshield, Sash door, etc.

HATA SEIHAN TEKKOSHO GOSHI-KAISHA
61, Taishido, Setagaya-ku, Tokyo
Tel. No.: (421) 1288
Products: Muffler

HAYASHI SPRING SEISAKUSHO CO., LTD.
918, Shimura-Maeno-cho, Itabashi-ku, Tokyo
Tel. No.: (961) 3887, 5671
Products: Speedometer cable, Brake cable, Choke throttle control wire, Wiper motor cable

K.K. HIGUCHI DENKYU SEISAKUSHO
605, Karagasaki-machi, Meguro-ku, Tokyo
Tel. No.: (712) 1503, 4366
Products: Auto lamp bulb

HINODE AUTO MANUFACTURING CO., LTD.
285, Taishido, Setagaya-ku, Tokyo
Tel. No.: (421) 1806
Products: Bolt, Nut, Pin

HIROSE DENKI KOGYO CO., LTD.
554, 4-chome, Kita-Shinagawa, Shinagawa-ku, Tokyo
Tel. No.: (441) 6137-9
Products: Head lamp, Tail lamp, Side lamp

HITACHI, LTD.
4, 2-chome, Otemachi, Chiyoda-ku, Tokyo
Tel. No.: (211) 1411
Products: Electric equipment and Carburettor for automobile

HITACHI METALS INDUSTRY CO., LTD.
12, 2-chome, Marunouchi, Chiyoda-ku, Tokyo
Tel. No.: (281) 4131, 4141
Products: Gear, etc.

HORIKIRI SPRING SEISAKUSHO CO., LTD.
951, Horikiri-cho, Katsushika-ku, Tokyo
Tel. No.: (691) 5138
Products: Suspension spring

ICHIKAWA SEISAKUSHO CO., LTD.
246, Shimo-maruko, Ota-ku, Tokyo
Tel. No.: (731) 7171-9
Products: Head lamp, Tail lamp, Back mirror, Accessories

GOSHI-KAISHA ICHIKIN SEISAKUSHO
60, Shiba-Nishikubo-Tomoe-cho, Minato-ku, Tokyo
Tel. No.: (431) 1010-2
Products: Head lamp, Tail light

IKUYO CHEMICAL INDUSTRY CO., LTD.
870, 1-chome, Machiya, Arakawa-ku, Tokyo
Tel. No.: (891) 2221-5
Products: Rubber part

INOUE SLEEVE CO., LTD.
531, 4-chome, Kita-Shinagawa, Shinagawa-ku, Tokyo
Tel. No.: (441) 2156-7
Products: Cylinder sleeve, Valve guide

ISHIKAWA GASKET CO., LTD.
1, Shiba-Nishikubo-Akefune-cho, Minato-ku, Tokyo
Tel. No.: (501) 0371-5
Products: Gasket, Packing

GOSHI-KAISHA ISHIKAWA TEKKOSHO
5, 1-chome, Umayabashi, Sumida-ku, Tokyo
Tel. No.: (622) 0319
Products: Tie rod and assembly, Shackle pin

ISHIKAWA LAMP MFG. CO., LTD.
4, 2-chome, Kiyosumi-cho, Fukagawa, Koto-ku, Tokyo
Tel. No.: (641) 9181-5
Products: Automotive lamp, Accessories

ISHINO GASKET INDUSTRY CO., LTD.
10, Shiba-Nishikubo-Akefune-cho, Minato-ku, Tokyo
Tel. No.: (501) 1481-4
Products: Gasket, Packing, Micro filter

ISODA METAL KOGYO CO., LTD.
485, Yaguchi-cho, Ota-ku, Tokyo
Tel. No.: (731) 3463, 5772, 3647-8
Products: Crank-shaft bearing

IZUMI AUTOMOTIVE INDUSTRY CO., LTD.
339, 4-chome, Sakuragi-cho, Omiya, Saitama Pref.
Tel. No.: (Omiya) 326, 398
Products: Piston, Cylinder, Cylinder liner

IZUMI MOTOR CO., LTD.
718, 4-chome, Kita-Shinagawa, Shinagawa-ku, Tokyo
Tel. No.: (441) 1281-5
Products: Steering wheel, Plastic parts

JAPAN ELECTRIC CLOCK CO., LTD.
346, 2-chome, Nakameguro, Meguro-ku, Tokyo
Tel. No.: (712) 2156-9
Products: Auto motor clock

JAPAN MOTOR WHEEL CO., LTD.
23, 3-chome, Minami-rokugo, Ota-ku, Tokyo
Tel. No.: (731) 2171-5
Products: Wheel for automobiles

JIDOSHA BUHIN SEIZO CO., LTD.
400, Hommachi-Ichiba-cho, Tsurumi-ku, Yokohama
Tel. No.: (Tsurumi) 4081-3
Products: King pin

JIDOSHA DENKI KOGYO CO., LTD.
354, Katase, Fujisawa, Kanagawa Pref.
Tel. No.: (Fujisawa) 2754, 2502
Products: Starter switch

JIDOSHA KIKI KABUSHIKI KAISHA
81, 2-chome, Nagata-cho, Chiyoda-ku, Tokyo
Tel. No.: (58) 1206
Products: Power actuator for brakes and steering, Leveling valve for air-suspension of vehicles

JIDOSHA NEJI KOGYO K.K.
1416, Futo-cho, Kohoku-ku, Yokohama
Tel. No.: (Tsunashima) 202, 368, 465
Products: Auto bolt & nut

KANEGAFUCHI MACHINE MFG. CO., LTD.
7, Kanda-Kamakura, Chiyoda-ku, Tokyo
Tel. No.: (251) 0254, 0296
Products: Engine valve

KANTO SEIKI CO., LTD.
453, 1-chome, Inatsuke-machi, Kita-ku, Tokyo
Tel. No.: (901) 3145
Products: Auto meter

KASHIYAMA INDUSTRY CO., LTD.
34, Shiba-Tamura-cho, Minato-ku, Tokyo
Tel. No.: (431) 4089, 5489
Products: Bearing, Bushing

K.K. KATAYAMA KOGYOSHO
92, 7-chome, Araijuku, Ota-ku, Tokyo
Tel. No.: (761) 0568
Products: Door hinge, Products made by flush-butt welding, Brake rod & Stabilizer pillar

KATO HATSUJYO CO., LTD.
51, Iwaicho, Hodogaya-ku, Yokohama
Tel. No.: Chojyamachi (3) 5231-3
Products: All kinds of wire & leaf springs

KATO RASHI SEISAKUSHO CO., LTD.
2183, 4-chome, Higashi-Komatsugawa, Edogawa-ku, Tokyo
Tel. No.: (651) 0440, 6162, 6167
Products: Automotive bolt, Nut, Screw, Stud, Pin, Nipple

KAWASAKI KOGYO K.K.
4618, Mukaijima-cho, Shimada, Shizuoka Pref.
Tel. No.: (Shimada) 2178
Products: Tow-tenjack, Bumper jack, Grease-pump

KAYABA INDUSTRY CO., LTD.
1, 1-chome, Shibaura, Minato-ku, Tokyo
Tel. No.: (451) 5141, 8156
Products: Shock absorber, Jack

KEIHIN KIKI MFG. CO., LTD.
64, Chofu-Chidori-cho, Ota-ku, Tokyo
Tel. No.: (751) 6127-9
Products: Thermostat

KINUGAWA RUBBER INDUSTRIAL CO., LTD.
24, Honden-Kawabata-cho, Katsushika-ku, Tokyo
Tel. No.: (691) 0961-5
Products: Oil brake cup, etc.

KITAHARA SEISAKUSHO CO., LTD.
408, Daimachi, Hachiojo City, Tokyo
Tel. No.: (Hachioji) 2173, 3847
Products: Air horn, Magnetic valve, Safety valve, Triple airhorn, Low pressure indicator

KOBAYASHI DENKI SEISAKUSHO CO., LTD.
1021, 2-chome, Higashi-Togoshi, Shinagawa-ku, Tokyo
Tel. No.: (781) 3343, 4220, 4337
Products: Condenser

KOBAYASHI SEISAKUSHO CO., LTD.
33, 3-chome, Nishirokugo, Ota-ku, Tokyo
Tel. No.: (731) 1676
Products: Distributor assembly, Ignition parts

KOITO ELECTRIC MFG. CO., LTD.
28, Shiba-Takanawa-Minami-cho, Minato-ku, Tokyo
Tel. No.: (441) 7241
Products: Automobile electric apparatus, Aircraft electrical parts

KOKUSAN KIKI KABUSHIKI KAISHA
193, Kita-Kojimachi, Ota-ku, Tokyo
Tel. No., Cable Add.: (741) 1441-4
Products: Water pump, Fuel filter, Air cleaner, etc.

KONISHI SEISAKUSHO CO., LTD.
19, 1-chome, Akasaka-Demma-cho, Minato-ku, Tokyo
Tel. No.: (408) 2967, 3774-5
Products: Distributor cap, Contact arm & point

K.K. KUMOSHITA SEISAKUSHO
207, Yukigaya, Ota-ku, Tokyo
Tel. No.: (781) 2189
Products: Oil pump assembly

KYOSAN DENKI CO., LTD.
1, 1-chome, Nishi-Ginza, Chuo-ku, Tokyo
Tel. No.: (561) 3631, 3610
Products: Fuel pump, Vacuum controller, Gasoline strainer

LIFE ELECTRIC LAMP CO., LTD.
27, Toyowakecho, Shibuya-ku, Tokyo
Tel. No.: (401) 3868, 4251
Products: Auto lamp bulbs

MARUENU MANUFACTURING CO., LTD.
217, Nakazato-machi, Kita-ku, Tokyo
Tel. No.: (821) 3141, 7965
Products: Electric wiper, Car-heater, Auto-fan

MARUHACHI ELECTRIC CO., LTD.
25, 4-chome, Taihei-cho, Sumida-ku, Tokyo
Tel. No.: (622) 3273
Products: Electric horn

MARUI INDUSTRY CO., LTD.
7, Kanda-Sakae-cho, Chiyoda-ku, Tokyo
Tel. No.: (831) 2191-4
Products: Head lamp

MARUKO KEIHOKI CO., LTD.
1880, Kami Maruko, Maruko-machi, Chiisagata-gun, Nagano Pref.
Tel. No.: (Maruko) 146, 147
Products: Electric horn

MASADA SEISAKUSHO YUGEN KAISHA
10257, Fuchu, Tokyo
Tel. No.: (Musashi Fuchu) (0236) 3435-7
Products: Hydraulic jack

MATSUI WORKS
390, 1-chome, Nishi-Okubo, Shinjuku-ku, Tokyo
Tel. No.: (351) 2870, 7040
Products: Universal joint kit

MIKUNI SHOKO CO., LTD.
4, Kanda-Gokencho, Chiyoda-ku, Tokyo
Tel. No.: (831) 1256
Products: Carburetter, Pump, Filter, Heater, etc.

MITSUBA ELECTRIC MFG. CO., LTD.
9, Nijukki-cho, Shinjuku-ku, Tokyo
Tel. No.: (341) 7080, 7685
Products: Electric horn, Windshield, Wiper, Flasher and Relay

MITSUBISHI ELECTRIC MANUFACTURING CO., LTD.
2, 2-chome, Marunouchi, Chiyoda-ku, Tokyo
Tel. No.: (211) 1631, 2231
Products: Magnet dynamo, Regurator

MITSUBISHI STEEL CO., LTD.
8, 2-chome, Marunouchi, Chiyoda-ku, Tokyo
Tel. No.: (211) 3271, 3281
Products: Spring, Rolled steel bar, Cold finished steel bar, Rock drill steel bar, MK magnet

MITSUIKE KOGYO CO., LTD.
832, Shimo-Sueyoshi-machi, Tsurumi-ku, Yokohama
Tel. No.: (Yokohama) (5) 8931-4
Products: Muffler ass'y, Brake disk

MITSUYA SEIKO CO., LTD.
101, 2-chome, Fukuro-cho, Kita-ku, Tokyo
Tel. No.: (901) 2952, 2953
Products: King pin, Bush

MIYAKE SEISAKUSHO CO., LTD.
2481, Kita-Kojiya, Ota-ku, Tokyo
Tel. No.: (741) 1358, 1816
Products: Engine piston (Automobile, Motor-bicycle, Compressor, Tractor)

MIYAKO HYDRAULIC BRAKE MFG. CO., LTD.
8, 2-chome, Shiba-Minami-Sakuma-cho, Minato-ku, Tokyo
Tel. No.: (591) 2470
Products: Hydraulic brake, Cylinder parts, Repair kit, Lining, Hose, Switch and Fluid

MIYAMOTO ELECTRIC HORN CO., LTD.
628, 5-chome, Higashi-Komatsugawa, Edogawa-ku, Tokyo
Tel. No.: (651) 0215, 5787
Products: Electric horn, Horn relay

MIYOSHI ASBESTOS CO., LTD.
30, Shiba-Takanawa-Minami-cho, Minato-ku, Tokyo
Tel. No.: (441) 6093-4, 7151-2
Products: Asbestos-textiles, Asbestos brake-lining, Pipe-insulation, Asbestos-cement insulation

MIYOSHI SEISAKUSHO CO., LTD.
1029, Shimura-Maeno-cho, Itabashi-ku, Tokyo
Tel. No.: (961) 0010
Products: Voltage regulator

MIZUNO SHOKO CO., LTD.
33, Shiba-Kotohira-cho, Minato-ku, Tokyo
Tel. No.: (501) 9678-9
Products: Starter drive ass'y, Hose clamps

MORI KAGAKU KOGYO CO., LTD.
991, Shimura-Maeno-cho, Itabashi-ku, Tokyo
Tel. No.: (961) 0575, 1761
Products: Distributor cap & rotor

MURATA SPRING MFG. CO., LTD.
17, 1-chome, Okachimachi, Daito-ku, Tokyo
Tel. No.: (831) 1360, 1361, 7868, 1444-5
Products: Valve spring, Clutch spring, Thin plate spring

MUSASHI OIL SEAL MANUFACTURE CO., LTD.
3, Shiba-Tamura-cho, Minato-ku, Tokyo
Tel. No.: (431) 0905, 3917, 8550
Products: Oil seal

NAGATO METAL KOGYO CO., LTD.
414, Shimomaruko-cho, Ota-ku, Tokyo
Tel. No.: (731) 0176-9
Products: Kelmet shaft bearing, White shaft bearing, Crank shaft bearing

K.K. NAIGAI SEIKOSHO
2, 1-chome, Minato-cho, Chuo-ku, Tokyo
Tel. No.: (551) 1111-5, 9116
Products: Piston pin, King pin, Kit, Shackle pin

NAKAMURA JIDOSHA KOGYO K.K.
5, 2-chome, Tsukiji, Chuo-ku, Tokyo
Tel. No.: (541) 1061, 8567
Products: Radiater, Propeller shaft

NAKANO SPRING CO., LTD.
1, 4-chome, Nishi-Shibaura, Minato-ku, Tokyo
Tel. No.: (451) 3920, 3978
Products: Chassis spring

NAMAI INDUSTRIAL CO., LTD.
8, 3-chome, Shiba-Tamura-cho, Minato-ku, Tokyo
Tel. No.: (591) 5748, 7884, 1565, 1729, 4515
Products: Parts of automobile, bus, jeep, track, & scooter

NICHIBEI KOGYO CO., LTD.
491, 4-chome, Minami-Shinagawa, Shinagawa-ku, Tokyo
Tel. No.: (491) 0051, 0052
Products: Lamp

NIHON PLAST CO., LTD.
7, 3-chome, Shiba-Nakamonzen-cho, Minato-ku, Tokyo
Tel. No.: (431) 7746
Products: Plastics moldings (Steering wheel, Meter cover, Nylon parts, etc.)

NIKKO ELECTRIC INDUSTRY CO., LTD.
19, 1-chome, Higashi-Rokugo, Ota-ku, Tokyo
Tel. No.: (731) 6186-9
Products: Electrical equipment for diesel engine

NILES PART CO., LTD.
5, 4-chome, Kojiya-cho, Ota-ku, Tokyo
Tel. No.: (741) 0609, 1268, 1768
Products: Automotive switch

NIPPON ASBESTOS CO., LTD.
3, 6-chome, Ginza-Nishi, Chuo-ku, Tokyo
Tel. No.: (571) 5701-9
Products: Asbestos brake lining, Clutch facing

NIPPON AUTO RADIO CO., LTD.
3, Nakano-Ekimae, Nakano-ku, Tokyo
Tel. No.: (381) 7773
Products: Auto motor radio

NIPPON DUST KEEPER CO., LTD.
5, 1-chome, Ginza, Chuo-ku, Tokyo
Tel. No.: (561) 9226-9
Products: Oil seal, Grease seal

NIPPON GEAR KOGYO CO., LTD
151, 4-chome, Higashi-Shinagawa, Shinagawa-ku, Tokyo
Tel. No.: (491) 8161-5
Products: Gear and Shaft

NIPPON HATSUJO KABUSHIKI KAISHA
1, Isogo-cho, Isogo-ku, Yokohama
Tel. No.: Yokohama (3) 5331-9
Products: Leaf spring, Coil spring, Wire spring

NIPPON KIKAKI SEISAKUSHO CO., LTD.
428, 5-chome, Kita-Shinagawa, Shinagawa-ku, Tokyo
Tel. No.: (441) 3094-7
Products: Carburettor flange

NIPPON OIL SEAL CO., LTD.
1222, 5-chome, Kojiya-cho, Ota-ku, Tokyo
Tel. No.: (741) 0775-9
Products: Oil seal, Unit seal

NIPPON PISTON RING CO., LTD.
6, 1-chome, Shiba-Tamura-cho, Minato-ku, Tokyo
Tel. No.: (541) 7411-9
Products: Pistonring, Piston, Cylinder sleeve & Liner

NIPPON RADIATOR CO., LTD.
40, 3-chome, Sakae-machi-dori, Nakano-ku, Tokyo
Tel. No.: (381) 7121-6
Products: Radiator

NIPPON ROKAKI K.K.
19, 3-chome, Tamagawa-Todoroki-cho, Setagaya-ku, Tokyo
Tel. No.: (701) 1161-5
Products: Air cleaner, Oil filter, Silencer, Oil cooler

NIPPON SHOCK ABSORBER CO., LTD.
622, Kitakase, Kawasaki City, Kanagawa Pref.
Tel. No.: Kawasaki (2) 7361
Products: Shock absorber

NIPPORI SPRING SEISAKUSHO CO., LTD.
16, 2-chome, Kanda-Kaji-cho, Chiyoda-ku, Tokyo
Tel. No.: (251) 1275, 5947
Products: Coil spring

NISHINA KOGYO COMPANY, LTD.
2, 7-chome, Shiba-Shinbashi, Minato-ku, Tokyo
Tel. No.: (431) 7700, 7770
Products: Cylinder, Piston pin, Valve guide

NISSIN AUTOMOBILE PARTS MFG. CO., LTD.
14-3, 4-chome, Haneda, Ota-ku, Tokyo
Tel. No.: (741) 0677, 1501
Products: Clutch plate, Clutch facing, Brake lining

NISSIN BOSEKI CO., LTD.
3, Nihonbashi-Yokoyama-cho, Chuo-ku, Tokyo
Tel. No.: (661) 1101-9
Products: Brake lining, Clutch facing

NITTAN VALVE MFG. CO., LTD.
6, 1-chome, Nishi-Hatchobori, Chuo-ku, Tokyo
Tel. No.: (551) 9301-5
Products: Engine valve

NITTO SEIMITSU KOGYO CO., LTD.
822, Yaguchi-cho, Ota-ku, Tokyo
Tel. No.: (731) 0225, 0978, 6687
Products: Piston pin, Crank pin, Needle roller, Needle bearing

OGU VALVE SEIZOSHO CO., LTD.
352, Yashiro, Yashiro-cho, Hanishina-gun, Nagano Pref.
Tel. No.: (Yashiro) 26
Products: Tire valve

OH-IZUMI MFG. CO., LTD.
410, Nukui-cho, Nerima-ku, Tokyo
Tel. No.: (991) 1101-5
Products: Thermostat, Varistor, Electrical contact point

OKAMOTO GLASS CO., LTD.
65, 6-chome, Oshima-machi, Koto-ku, Tokyo
Tel. No.: (681) 9126-8
Products: Glass

OKUBO HAGURUMA KOGYO K.K.
598, 3-chome, Tsurumaki-cho, Setagaya-ku, Tokyo
Tel. No.: (411) 0171-4
Products: Gears & Shaft, Speed-reducer, Gear motor, Transmission

ONISHI SEISAKUSHO CO., LTD.
536, 4-chome, Minami-Shinagawa, Shinagawa-ku, Tokyo
Tel. No.: (491) 4988, 6215
Products: Speedometer cable

ORIHASHI MFG. CO., LTD.
311, Kita-kojiya, Ota-ku, Tokyo
Tel. No.: (741) 0911, 1225
Products: Bushing, Thrust washer (bimetal, casting)

OSHIMA ELECTRIC WORKS
Fujikura, Hosen-mura, Nitta-gun, Gunma Pref.
Tel. No.: (Ota) 2363
Products: Lamp, Switch, Lock & Key, Wire

PRESS STEEL WORKS CO., LTD.
1, Shiohama-cho, Kawasaki City, Kanagawa Pref.
Tel. No.: Kawasaki (2) 2511-6
Products: Frame, Axle case, Fender, Wheel

RIKEN GOSEIJUSHI CO., LTD.
3, 6-chome, Ginza Chuo-ku, Tokyo
Tel. No.: (571) 1820, 3191-5
Products: Cam gear, Timing gear

RIKEN PISTON RING IND. CO., LTD.
4, 3-chome, Nihombashi Hongoku-cho, Chuo-ku, Tokyo
Tel. No.: (241) 1161-4
Products: Pistonring, Cylinder liner, Cylinder block, Piston fitting

SAITAMA KIKI MFG. CO., LTD.
650, Shimo-Ochiai, Yono, Saitama Pref.
Tel. No.: (Urawa) 7186-9
Products: Oil brake, Shock absorber, Oil pump, Water pump

SAKAGAMI SEISAKUSHO CO., LTD.
5, 4-chome, Kinshi-cho, Sumida-ku, Tokyo
Tel. No.: (631) 1175-9
Products: Gasket, Packing

SAKURAI WORKS CO., LTD.
389, Yoyogi-Sanya-cho, Shibuya-ku, Tokyo
Tel. No.: (371) 0653, 4311
Products: Autometer, Hydrometer, Inspection lamp, Wiper arm & Blade

SAN-EI GASKET KOGYO CO., LTD.
5639, 5-chome, Kami-Itabashi-cho, Itabashi-ku, Tokyo
Tel. No.: (961) 3065, 3534
Products: Gasket, Packing

SANKYO RADIATOR CO., LTD.
658, Owada-cho, Hachioji City, Tokyo
Tel. No.: (Hachioji) (2) 7171
Products: Radiator, Oil cooler, Car heater, Condenser

SANNO MFG. CO., LTD.
119, 2-chome, Omori-cho, Ota-ku, Tokyo
Tel. No.: (761) 9581, 9820
Products: Kelmet, Bearing metal

SANWA SEIKI MANUFACTURING CO., LTD.
80, Nakazato, Yono, Saitama Pref.
Tel. No.: (Urawa) 7191-5
Products: Air compressor, Air brake, Leveling valve, Vacuum pump

SAWAFUJI ELECTRIC CO., LTD.
398, Shimura-Nakadai, Itabashi-ku, Tokyo
Tel. No.: (933) 1181, 1579
Products: Magnet, Starter, Generator, Swing motor

SEIKO ISUZU JIDOSHA CO., LTD.
22, Ejiricha-machi, Shimizu, Shizuoka Pref.
Tel. No.: Shimizu (2) 0111
Products: Piston, Tappet

SHIN NIPPON DROP FORGING CO., LTD.
147, Tanabeshinden, Takenoshita-Kouchi, Kawasaki City, Kanagawa Pref.
Tel. No.: Kawasaki (3) 2631-5
Products: Axle shaft

SHIN TOYO CLOCK CO., LTD.
12, 1-chome, Okachimachi, Taito-ku, Tokyo
Tel. No.: (831) 9111-5
Products: Auto meter

SHINAGAWA ELECTRIC WIRE CO., LTD.
2503, Kotake-cho, Nerima-ku, Tokyo
Tel. No.: (991) 1172-5
Products: Automotive low-tension & high-tension wire, Wire harness assembly

SHINMITSUBISHI JUKOGYO CO., LTD.
10, 2-chome, Marunouchi, Chiyoda-ku, Tokyo
Tel. No.: (211) 3411, 3421, 3431
Products: Engine valve

SHIRATORI GASKET COMPANY
9, 2-chome, Shiba-Atago-cho, Minato-ku, Tokyo
Tel. No.: (431) 3625
Products: Gasket, Packing

SHIROKI KINZOKU KOGYO K.K.
50, 5-chome, Higashi-Shinagawa, Shinagawa-ku, Tokyo
Tel. No.: (491) 8221-4
Products: W/D Frame, Wind shield frame, Wind regulator, Special clip

SHOWA KOATSU KOGYO CO., LTD.
4, 1-chome, Ginza-Higashi, Chuo-ku, Tokyo
Tel. No.: (561) 6201
Products: Speedometer cable & Control wire

SHOWA SEIKI CO., LTD.
3451, 1-chome, Minami-machi, Nerima-ku, Tokyo
Tel. No.: (991) 3451
Products: Fuel pump assembly, Diaphragm

SMC METAL CO., LTD.
4, 3-chome, Demma-cho, Akasaka, Minato-ku, Tokyo
Tel. No.: (408) 2058, 2560
Products: Crankshaft, Connecting rod, Cam shaft bearing

STANLEY ELECTRIC CO., LTD.
605, 2-chome, Naka-Meguro, Meguro-ku, Tokyo
Tel. No.: (712) 1111-6
Products: Auto lamp bulb, Miniature lamp bulb, Sealed beam, Selenium rectifier, etc.

SUZUKI METAL PRODUCT CORPORATION
375, Shimura-Shimizu-cho, Itabashi-ku, Tokyo
Tel. No.: (961) 5271-4
Products: Automotive accessories

K. K. TAIYO SEISAKUSHO
51, Azabu Fujimi-cho, Minato-ku, Tokyo
Tel. No.: (451) 1621-2
Products: Steam cleaner

TAKEBE TEKKOSHO CO., LTD.
495, 4-chome, Kita-shinagawa, Shinagawa-ku, Tokyo
Tel. No.: (441) 0131-8
Products: Body parts, Heater & Cooler

TAKUBO KOGYO CO., LTD.
15, Mikawadai-machi, Azabu, Minato-ku, Tokyo
Tel. No.: (481) 5906
Products: Hydraulic oil jack, Garage-jack, Oil press

TANAKA INSTRUMENT CO., LTD.
998, Kamiochiai, Yono, Saitama Pref.
Tel. No.: (Omiya) 10, 100
Products: Electric wind shield wiper

TANIGUCHI ENG. WORKS CO., LTD.
3996, 8-chome, Omori, Ota-ku, Tokyo
Tel. No.: (761) 3204, 3690
Products: High pressure grease gun, Lubrication equipment, Reel hose

TEIKOKU PISTON RING CO., LTD.
7, 3-chome, Yaesu, Chuo-ku, Tokyo
Tel. No.: (271) 2826-9
Products: Pistonring set, Cylinder liner

TERAOKA SEISAKUSHO CO., LTD.
1120, 2-chome, Nishi-Sinagawa, Sinagawa-ku, Tokyo
Tel. No.: (491) 1141
Products: Diaphragm

T. J. S. PISTON INDUSTRIAL CO., LTD.
18, 3-chome, Nishirokugo, Ota-ku, Tokyo
Tel. No.: (731) 1936, 4837
Products: Piston

TOA DENSO CO., LTD.
4, Kaizuka, Kawasaki City, Kanagawa Pref.
Tel. No.: Kawasaki (3) 4653, 4865
Products: Car-heater, Converter, Invertor

TOHO SHACKLE CO., LTD.
9, 1-chome, Azabu-Iigura-cho, Minato-ku, Tokyo
Tel. No.: (481) 1446, 7788
Products: Suspension parts

TOKAI RIKA CO., LTD.
2, 1-chome, Nihombashi-Muromachi, Chuo-ku, Tokyo
Tel. No.: (241) 4615-8
Products: Switch, Lock & Key for automobile, aircraft and communication instrument

TOKUSYU KOSAKU CO., LTD.
5511, Morigasaki, Ota-ku, Tokyo
Tel. No.: (761) 0563, 8051
Products: Oil seal

TOKYO BUHIN KOGYO CO., LTD.
270, Oginaka-cho, Ota-ku, Tokyo
Tel. No.: (738) 0151-5
Products: Water pump, Oil pump, Brake equipment, Shock absorber

TOKYO DROP FORGING CO., LTD.
758, 1-chome, Higashi-Osaki, Shinagawa-ku, Tokyo
Tel. No.: (491) 5725-7
Products: Crank shaft, Front axle

TOKYO GASKET CO., LTD.
389, Oginaka-cho, Ota-ku, Tokyo
Tel. No.: (738) 2527
Products: Gasket, Packing

TOKYO KIKI ENGINEERING CO., LTD.
2, 1-chome, Nakajima, Kawasaki City, Kanagawa Pref.
Tel. No.: Kawasaki (2) 3591-7
Products: Shock absorber, Oil brake, Air brake

TOKYO PRESS KOGYO CO., LTD.
35, 6-chome, Oshima-cho, Koto-ku, Tokyo
Tel. No.: (681) 8166-9
Products: Frame bumper

TOKYO RADIATOR MANUFACTURING CO., LTD.
21, 3-chome, Fujisaki-cho, Kawasaki City, Kanagawa Pref.
Tel. No.: Kawasaki (2) 3501-5
Products: Radiator

TOKYO ROKA KOGYOSHO YUGENKAISHA
370, 2-chome, Koenji, Suginami-ku, Tokyo
Tel. No.: (229) 2604, (311) 4064, 3165
Products: Various metal bushing (Bimetal, Trimetal), Kelmet metal

TOKYO SEISAKUSHO CO., LTD.
713, 1-chome, Omiya-mae, Suginami-ku, Tokyo
Tel. No.: (398) 0821-2
Products: King pin, Piston pin, Kelmet

TOKYO SHIBAURA ELECTRIC CO., LTD.
2, 5-chome, Ginza-Nishi, Chuo-ku, Tokyo
Tel. No.: (571) 5711, 8131
Products: Auto lamps, Sealed beam

TOKYO TOKI CO., LTD.
240, Ichinotsubo-Nakamura-dori, Kawasaki City, Kanagawa Pref.
Tel. No.: Kanagawa (047) 3121-5, 4133, 4311
Products: Oil filter, Air cleaner

TONICHI SEISAKUSHO CO., LTD.
516, 4-chome, Kitashinagawa, Shinagawa-ku, Tokyo
Tel. No.: (491) 1141-5
Products: Torque wrench

TOTO SANGYOSHA CO., LTD.
2, Shiba-Kamiya-cho, Minato-ku, Tokyo
Tel. No.: (431) 3575, 4403
Products: Automobile piston

THE TOYO RADIATOR CO., LTD.
7, 1-chome, Ginza, Chuo-ku, Tokyo
Tel. No.: (561) 8636-8
Products: Radiator, Oil cooler

TOYO SEIKI CO., LTD.
2, Shiba-Mita-Toyooka-cho, Minato-ku, Tokyo
Tel. No.: (451) 4086, 7429
Products: Switch, Electric system

THE TSUBAKIMOTO CHAIN MFG. CO., LTD.
2, 3-chome, Kyobashi, Chuo-ku, Tokyo
Tel. No.: (281) 6051-5
Products: Timing chain

TSUCHIYA MANUFACTURING CO., LTD.
537, 2-chome, Takadaminami-cho, Toshima-ku, Tokyo
Tel. No.: (982) 6161-4
Products: Air cleaner, Oil filter, Fuel filter, Oil cooler

TSUJITANI SEISAKUSHO CO., LTD.
158, 6-chome, Ogu-machi, Arakawa-ku, Tokyo
Tel. No.: (891) 9506
Products: Tire pumps

TSURUOKA SPRING SEISAKUSHO
1, 5-chome, Hirakawabashi, Sumida-ku, Tokyo
Tel. No.: (622) 5633, 9633
Products: Coil spring, speedometer cable

USUI KOKUSAI SANGYO K. K.
131, Nagasawa, Shimizu-mura, Sunto-gun, Shizuoka Pref.
Tel. No.: (Mishima) 0497, 0008 (Numazu) 4950
Products: Exhaust pipe, Bush rod, Brake pipe, Coil push

WAKO KOGYO CO., LTD.
183, 2-chome, Nakamachi, Kawaguchi City, Saitama Pref.
Tel. No.: Kawaguchi (082) 3245, 4487
Products: Hydraulic jack

YAMADA LUBRICATOR MANUFACTURING CO.,LTD.
1-2, 3-chome, Irifune-cho, Chuo-ku, Tokyo
Tel. No.: (551) 1141-5
Products: Grease pump, Grease nipple

YAMAGUCHI ELECTRIC INDUSTRIES CO., LTD.
260, Ikejiri-cho, Setagaya-ku, Tokyo
Tel. No.: (421) 5771-2
Products: Automobile electric part, Switch

YAMAGUCHI MFG. CO., LTD.
24, Shiba-Toranomon, Minato-ku, Tokyo
Tel. No.: (591) 3053, 8775, 8735
Products: Wheel cap, Head lamp door, Door handle, Auto radio antenna

YAMAGUCHI SEISAKUSHO CO., LTD.
24, 1-chome, Amanuma, Suginami-ku, Tokyo
Tel. No.: (391) 3538
Products: Electric horn

YAMAMOTO RADIATOR CO., LTD.
1475, 3-chome, Machiya, Arakawa-ku, Tokyo
Tel. No.: (891) 4141-3
Products: Radiator & Oil-cooler for internal combustion engine

YAMAMOTO SPRINGS & RAIL SWITCHES MFG. CO., LTD.
5, 4-chome, Yaesu, Chuo-ku, Tokyo
Tel. No.: (281) 3411, 3412
Products: Various kinds of spring for car and mobile, Rail switch for national railway

YASUI SANGYO CO., LTD.
2, 3-chome, Minami-Rokugo, Ota-ku, Tokyo
Tel. No.: (731) 4374
Products: Hydraulic garage jack, Steam cleaner, Hydraulic press

YAZAKI ELECTRIC WIRE MFG. CO., LTD.
2, 5-chome, Shiba-Tamura-cho, Minato-ku, Tokyo
Tel. No.: (431) 7171-9
Products: All kinds of electric wire

YAZAKI METER CO., LTD.
2, 5-chome, Shiba-Tamura-cho, Minato-ku, Tokyo
Tel. No.: (431) 7171-7
Products: All kinds of auto meter

YUSHIN SEIKI INDUSTRY CO., LTD.
24, 4-chome, Shiba-Shinbashi, Minato-ku, Tokyo
Tel. No.: (431) 1065, 3115, 8311
Products: Switch

CENTRAL AREA

AICHI KOGYO CO., LTD.
50, Nakayama, Kariya, Aichi Pref.
Tel. No.: (Kariya) 501
Products: Water pump, Wheel cylinder, Oil pump, Gear

AISAN KOGYO CO., LTD.
100, Hara Kyowa, Obu-cho, Chita-gun, Aichi Pref.
Tel. No.: (Obu) 27, 414, 419
Products: Carburetter, Fuel pump, Oil pump, Oil brake, Water pump

ASAHI WORKS, LTD.
1, 1-chome, Hozen, Kuma, Kariya, Aichi Pref.
Tel. No.: (Kariya) 384
Products: Wiper motor

BANNO KOGYO CO., LTD.
1, 4-chome, Matsugae, Naka-ku, Nagoya
Tel. No.: Nagoya (24) 4558, 3370, 6614-6
Products: Electric wiper

T.K. CARBURETTER CO., LTD.
118, Yamanote-Mizubo, Toyota City, Aichi Pref.
Tel. No.: (Toyota) 630, 1006
Products: Carburetter

CHUKYO DROP FORGING CO., LTD.
Hatsutsubo, Sarugiri-machi, Kita-ku, Nagoya
Tel. No.: Nagoya (4) 3398, 3689, 3690
Products: Spring seat, Rear shaft, Front suspension, Engine lever, Kick lever, Rear suspension

CHUO SPRING CO., LTD.
68, Kamishioda, Narumi, Aichi-gun, Aichi Pref.
Tel. No.: (Narumi) 134, 226
Products: Laminated spring, Helical spring, Steel wire spring, Thin flat spring, Washer-look steel spring

CHUYO SPRING CO., LTD.
11, 7-chome, Rokuban, Atsuta-ku, Nagoya
Tel. No.: Nagoya (66) 0862, 3527
Products: Clutch disc, Wire spring, Flat spring

DAIDO METAL CO., LTD.
Tokyo Office: 15, Akasaka, Tameike, Minato-ku, Tokyo
Tel. No.: (481) 6716, 7621
Products: Bearing metal

IMAI KOSAKUSHO
27, Mukoda Gokiso-cho, Naka-ku, Nagoya
Tel. No.: Mizuho (88) 2950, 3423, 4105
Products: Drum, Hub, Bracket, Hanger, Shackle

IMASEN ELECTRIC IND. CO., LTD.
5, 2-chome, Sakuramachi, Naka-ku, Nagoya
Tel. No.: Nagoya (9) 1801, 1802, 1918
Products: Electric vibrate horn, Knight horn

KAWABE KIKAI KOSAKUSHO CO., LTD.
622, Hon-machi, Kameyama, Mie Pref.
Tel. No.: (Kameyama) 113, 163
Products: Tie rod end assembly

KINJO WHEEL FACTORY, LTD.
20, 8, Nagata-Hon-machi, Kanazawa, Ishikawa Pref.
Tel. No.: Kanazawa (3) 5411, (2) 5611
Products: Disc wheel

KOJIMA PRESS CO., LTD.
30, 3-chome, Shimoichiba, Toyota City, Aichi Pref.
Tel. No.: (Koromo) 253
Products: Air cleaner case

KOROMO IRON WORKS CO., LTD.
Jinchu, Toyota City, Aichi Pref.
Tel. No.: (Toyota) 248, 460
Products: Brake shoe complete, Hand brake lever, Fan blade, etc.

MARUHATI INDUSTRY CO., LTD.
8, 3-chome, Buhei-cho, Nakaku, Nagoya
Tel. No.: Nagoya (24) 2646, 3156, 3273
Products: Air cleaner case, Brake shoe, Master cylinder, Oil tunk, Brake drum, Strap

MEIDO IRON WORKS CO., LTD.
1, 1-chome, Tomifune, Nakagawa-ku, Nagoya
Tel. No.: Nagoya (32) 3778, 3893
Products: Bolts, Nuts & Motor parts, Motor screw

NAGOYA RUBBER CO., LTD.
9, 1-chome, Yabushita, Nishi-ku, Nagoya
Tel. No.: Nagoya (53) 6521-5
Products: Plastic steering wheel, Piston cup, Brake hose, Coating pipe

NAGOYA SCREW MANUFACTURING CO., LTD.
5, 1-chome, Taiko-dori, Nakamura-ku, Nagoya
Tel. No.: Nagoya (54) 8441
Products: Bolt, Hub bolt, Bushing

NATIONAL JIDOSHA KOGYO K.K.
1, 2-chome, Hioki-dori, Nakamura-ku, Nagoya
Tel. No.: Nagoya (54) 5787
Products: Valve guide, Tappet, Locket shaft, King pin

NIPPON DENSO CO., LTD.
1, Kariya-Mitamayama, Kariya, Aichi Pref.
Tel. No.: (Kariya) 364-9
Products: Electric horn, Radiator, Distributor, Cap, Starter pinion, Contact arm & Points changing relay switch, Generator, Starter, Distributors, Rotor, Ignition coil

THE NIPPON TOKUSYU TOGYO KAISHA, LTD.
17, 1-chome, Horita-dori, Mizuho-ku, Nagoya
Tel. No.: Nagoya (88) 1521
Products: NGK spark plug

NISHIOKA MALLEABLE IRON INDUSTRY CO., LTD.
88, Takaoka-cho, Hekikai-gun, Aichi Pref.
Tel. No.: (Aichi Takaoka) 130, 46
Products: Spring bracket, Spring shackle, Hub, Drum, Cylinder sleeve

OHASHI IRON WORKS, LTD.
37, 2-chome, Otobashi-dori, Nakagawa-ku, Nagoya
Tel. No.: Nagoya (32) 2719, 2854
Products: Oil level gage, Rod complete, Axle ring complete

PACIFIC INDUSTRIAL CO., LTD.
1703, Miwa-cho, Ogaki City, Gifu Pref.
Tel. No.: (Ogaki) 3166-9
Products: Standard tire valve, Valve cores and valve accessory

SEIKE JIDOSHA KOGYO CO., LTD.
61, 1-chome, Honen, Chigusa-ku, Nagoya
Tel. No.: Nagoya (73) 2894
Products: Cylinder sleeve, Hub, Drum, Bracket

SHIN-DAINIPPON SPRING WORKS CO., LTD.
18, Shin-Nakane, Kariya, Aichi Pref.
Tel. No.: (Kariya) 1434, 1435
Products: Seat cushion spring, Window

SHINKAWA INDUSTRY CO., LTD.
31, Rokkenyashiki, Hekinan, Aichi Pref.
Tel. No.: (Hekinan) 1600-3
Products: Clutch disc, Clutch cover, Fly wheel, Rear axle shaft, Steering center shaft, Shock absober, Bumper jack, Door lock

TAKEUCHI INDUSTRIAL CO., LTD.
1, 1-chome, Kiyokawa, Nakagawa-ku, Nagoya
Tel. No.: Nagoya (32) 2341, 2342
Products: Mechanical auto jack

TAIHO KOGYO CO., LTD.
234, Midori, Yamanote, Koromo-shi, Aichi Pref.
Tel. No.: (Koromo) 225, 610
Products: Bush

TOGO MANUFACTURING CO., LTD.
4384, Haruki, Togo-mura, Aichi-gun, Aichi Pref.
Tel. No.: (Miyoshi) 11, 101
Products: Spring

K. K. TSUDA TEKKOSHO
2, 1-chome, Shigehara-Tetcho, Kariya, Aichi Pref.
Tel. No.: (Kariya) 901
Products: Hub bolt, Hub nut, U bolt

YUSOKI KOGYO K. K.
102, Kamihama, Handa, Aichi Pref.
Tel. No.: (Handa) 495
Products: Manufacture and repair of automobile body and parts (disk wheel)

WESTERN AREA

ASAHI DENGYO K.K.
68, 3-chome, Tamade-Hondori, Nishinari-ku, Osaka
Tel. No.: Osaka (66) 8821-2
Products: Switches for auto

ASAHI DENKI SEISAKUSHO K.K.
174, Hosyutsu, Jyoto-ku, Osaka
Tel. No.: Osaka (97) 2135-6
Products: White bearing

ASAHI HATSUJO KOGYO CO., LTD.
42, 3-chome, Honda, Nishi-ku, Osaka
Tel. No.: Osaka (53) 1660, (54) 1417
Products: Chassis spring

ASAHI METAL INDUSTRIAL CO., LTD.
68, 2-chome, Nakatsu Hamadori, Oyodo-ku, Osaka
Tel. No.: Osaka (37) 6655-8
Products: Tire valve

AWAJI PACKING MANUFACTURING CO., LTD.
618, 2-chome, Awai-honmachi, Higashi-Yodogawa-ku, Osaka
Tel. No.: Osaka (37) 0877
Products: Cylinder head, Gasket, etc.

BUNKA JIDOSHA BUHIN KOGYO CO., LTD.
276, Higashi-Oji, Kishiwada City, Osaka Pref.
Tel. No.: (Kishiwada-Yamanao) 106
Products: All kinds of bushing and pin for automobiles

CABLE KOGYO CO., LTD.
27, 1-chome, Takaido-Nishi, Fuse, Osaka
Tel. No.: Osaka (72) 1073, 5604
Products: Speedometer cable, Flexible tube assembly

THE CENTRAL AUTOMOBILE INDUSTRY CO., LTD.
25, 4-chome, Nakanoshima, Kita-ku, Osaka
Tel. No.: Osaka (44) 5677, 5991
Products: Rear axle shaft, Tie rod end, U.J. kit, Sterling parts

CHIKUMA SEISAKUSHO
13, Saiin-Minami-Takada-cho, Ukyo-ku, Kyoto
Tel. No.: Mibu (84) 4335-7
Products: Oil pump, Water pump

DAIDO KINZOKU KOGYO CO., LTD.
60, 3-chome, Otomo, Ikuno-ku, Osaka
Tel. No.: Osaka (73) 8131-3
Products: Hab bolt & nut, Spring pin, Bracket, etc.

DAIKIN SEISAKUSHO CO., LTD.
18, 1-chome, Nakagawa, Ikuno-ku, Osaka
Tel. No.: Osaka (73) 5331-5
Products: Clutch disc assembly, Clutch-pressure plate assembly, etc.

DAITO PRESS KOGYO CO., LTD.
6, 1-chome, Oimazato-Honmachi, Higashinari-ku, Osaka
Tel. No.: Osaka (98) 3221
Products: Back mirror, Grease pump

FUJI ELECTRIC CO., LTD.
37, 3-chome, Nakagawa, Ikuno-ku, Osaka
Tel. No.: Osaka (73) 1558-9
Products: Regulator, relays, Starter switch, Condenser, etc.

FUJI KOGYO CO., LTD.
78, 1-chome, Kumano, Toyonaka, Osaka
Tel. No.: Osaka (53) 1457, 5414, 7288
Products: Third arm joint, Vendex gear, Tie rod end, Rear shaft

FURUKAWA SEIBYO CO., LTD.
420, 4-chome, Kujo-Makadori, Nishi-ku, Osaka
Tel. No.: Osaka (53) 1714
Products: U-bolt, Spring center bolt

HANSHIN TRANSFORMER MFG. CO., LTD.
17, 2-chome, Miyako-dori, Nada-ku, Kobe
Tel. No.: Kobe (8) 4097, 1117
Products: Ignition coil

HIGUCHI MACHINERY INDUSTRIAL CO., LTD.
343, Unobe, Ibaraki City, Osaka Pref.
Tel. No.: (Ibaraki) 2421
Products: Piston pin, King pin

HIKARI SEIKO CO., LTD.
20, Yamashina-Higashino-Koyabu, Higashiyama-ku, Kyoto
Tel. No.: (Yamashina) 201
Products: Adjustable reamer, Adjustable pilot reamer

HIRAI KOGYO CO., LTD.
2, 3-chome, Nagasu-Nakadori, Amagasaki City, Hyogo Pref.
Tel. No.: Amagasaki (48) 5958, 9848
Products: Piston pin, King pin

IKUNO MECHANICAL INDUSTRY CO., LTD.
28, 3-chome, Nakagawa, Ikuno-ku, Osaka
Tel. No.: Osaka (73) 1166
Products: King pin, Shackle pin

JAPAN ENGINE VALVE MFG. CO., LTD.
77, 2-chome, Nakagawa, Ikuno-ku, Osaka
Tel. No.: Osaka (73) 0292, 0884, 6554
Products: Engine valve, Valve rocker arm shaft, Valve tappet, Valve guide, Piston pin, King pin

KAMIBISHI DENKI SEIZO CO., LTD.
11, Kita-Imazaike-cho, Ikeda-City, Osaka Pref.
Tel. No.: Ikeda (076) 8733
Products: Switches for auto

KANAI SHARIN KOGYO CO., LTD.
27, Komoe, Toyonaka, Osaka
Tel. No.: Osaka (39) 2021-3
Products: Disc wheel, Devided wheel

KANSAI VALVE GUIDE SEISAKUSHO, LTD.
194, 2-chome, Otomo, Ikuno-ku, Osaka
Tel. No.: Osaka (73) 4741
Products: Engine valve guide

KEYSTER PRECISION WORKS, LTD.
19, Umeta, Kita-ku, Osaka
Tel. No.: Osaka (34) 4380, 7897, 7898
Products: Carburetter parts and Fuel pump parts

KOKUSAKU KOGYO CO., LTD.
8, 1-chome, Fukae-Higashi, Higashinari-ku, Osaka
Tel. No.: Osaka (97) 7744-6
Products: Universal joint, Tie rod end, etc.

KOYO DENKI CO., LTD.
20, 3-chome, Nakagawa, Ikuno-ku, Oaska
Tel. No.: Osaka (73) 4593
Products: Electric system

KUSHIRO ASBESTOS INDUSTRIAL CO., LTD.
135, Yasunaka, Yao City, Osaka Pref.
Tel. No.: Yao (029) 2603, 2092
Products: Brake lining, Clutch facing

KYOTO MACHINERY CO., LTD.
50, Funado, Kissho-in, Minami-ku, Kyoto
Tel. No.: Kyoto-shimo (5) 9071-6
Products: Hand tool (Open end wrench, Offset box, Wrench, etc.)

KYOTO MACHINERY TOOL CO., LTD.
15, Nakaai, Nishinokyo, Nakakyo-ku, Kyoto
Tel. No.: Kyoto (84) 1026, 2031, 9812
Products: Automotive wrench

MAEDA METAL INDUSTRIES, LTD.
34, 2-chome, Fukae-Higashi, Higashinari-ku, Osaka
Tel. No.: Osaka (97) 1351-3
Products: Socket wrench, Valve seat cutter, Expansion reamer

MURAI KOGYOSHO CO., LTD.
11, Nakano-cho, Daihoji, Minami-ku, Osaka
Tel. No.: Osaka (27) 4946-7
Products: Hub, Drum, Rear shaft, Oil ring gear

MURO METAL INDUSTRY MFG. CO., LTD.
1368, Oaza-Fujisaka, Hirakata City, Osaka Pref.
Tel. No.: Hirakata (0204) 8108
Products: Motor parts (Oil seal, Shim, Band & Parts, etc.)

NAIGAI SEIKI SEISAKUSHO
51, 4-chome, Naniwa-Hachijo-dori, Amagasaki City, Hyogo Pref.
Tel. No.: (48) 8396
Products: King pin, Piston pin

NAKAJIMA SEISAKUSHO, LTD.
23, 2-chome, Nakagawa-cho, Ikuno-ku, Osaka
Tel. No.: Osaka (73) 3255-6
Products: Hub bolt, Spring shackle pin

NEW TAKARAZUKA INDUSTRIAL CO., LTD.
25, Kita-Daimotsu, Amagasaki, Hyogo Pref.
Tel. No.: Osaka (48) 8801-2
Products: Water pump, Shackle pin, Bracket, Brake parts, etc.

NIKKO METAL INDUSTRY CO., LTD.
1457, Owada, Nishiyodogawa-ku, Osaka
Tel. No.: Osaka (47) 3231-3
Products: Electric horn for automobiles

NIPPO AUTOMOBILES INDUSTRY CO., LTD.
124, 1-chome, Kashiwazato, Nishiyodogawa-ku, Osaka
Tel. No.: Osaka (47) 2355-9
Products: Direction indicator, Vacuum horn, Back mirror

THE NIPPON AIR BRAKE CO., LTD.
2058, 3-chome, Wakinohama, Fukiai-ku, Kobe
Tel. No.: Fukiai (2) 1515
Products: Automotive air brake, Oil brake, Door control

NIPPON ELECTRIC MACHINERY MFG. CO., LTD.
77, 2-chome, Ikuno-Tajima, Ikuno-ku, Osaka
Tel. No.: Osaka (73) 2654, 2655
Products: Generator, Distributor, Voltage regulator, Starter switch, Point arm, Cap, Rotor, Switch, etc.

NIPPON KIZAI KOGYO CO., LTD.
19, 1-chome, Kusunoki, Sakai City, Osaka Pref.
Tel. No.: (Sakai) 881, 882
Products: Rear axle shaft & other auto parts

NIPPON PILLAR MANUFACTURING CO., LTD.
27, 3-chome, Nonakaminami-dori, Higashiyodogawa-ku, Osaka
Tel. No.: Osaka (37) 1974, 1975
Products: Gasket, Gland packing, Mechanical seal

NIPPON WICO CO., LTD.
72, 1-chome, Otomo, Ikuno-ku, Osaka
Tel. No.: Osaka (73) 2630, 2639
Products: Connecting rod

OSAKA CLUTCH INDUSTRY CO., LTD.
60, 1-chome, Ajiro-kita, Fuse, Osaka
Tel. No.: Osaka (72) 2412, 5018
Products: Clutch disk for automotive spare parts

K. K. OSAKA FLEXIBLE KOGYOSHO
205, 5-chome, Kitano, Oimazato, Higashinari-ku, Osaka
Tel. No.: Osaka (98) 0817-8
Products: Speedometer cable

OSAKA GASKET KOGYO K.K.
32, 2-chome, Tsukamoto, Higashi-Yodogawa-ku, Osaka
Tel. No.: Osaka (37) 2696, 5585
Products: Manifold-gasket, Packing, Cylinder head gasket

OSAKA MOTOR WHEEL CO., LTD.
27, 1-chome, Nishigamono, Joto-ku, Osaka
Tel. No.: (45) 4037-9
Products: Motor wheel, Rear axle-casing

OSAKA NAGAYANAGI CORK INDUSTRY CO., LTD.
37, 1-chome, Nishigamono, Jyoto-ku, Osaka
Tel. No.: Osaka (97) 4652-5
Products: Cork gasket, Cork sheet

SAKURA KOGYO KABUSHIKI KAISHA
50, Itsukaichi, Ibaraki, Osaka
Tel. No.: Osaka-Ibaraki (0262) 2581-3
Products: Piston & Piston pin

K. K. SANKEI SEISAKUSHO
52, Minami Tamatsukuri, Tennoji-ku, Osaka
Tel. No.: Osaka (75) 3297, 3814
Products: Switch

SANKO SENZAI KOGYO CO., LTD.
14, Nishiura-cho, Umezu, Ukyo-ku, Kyoto
Tel. No.: Kyoto (86) 1141-5
Products: Piano wire, Steel wire, Oil tempered wire, Tire bead wire, Engine valve spring, Seat spring & all other wire spring

SANYO JIDOSHA BUHIN SEIZO K. K.
22, 5-chome, Fukae-Nishi, Higashinari-ku, Osaka
Tel. No.: Osaka (97) 3443
Products: Hub bolt, Shakle, Shackle pin, U-bolt

SANYO KOGYO CO., LTD.
22, 4-chome, Nishi-Nakashima, Higashi-Yodogawa-ku, Osaka
Tel. No.: Osaka (37) 4697
Products: Driving mirror, Switch, Hand wiper

SHIGEHARA TEKKOSHO
305, Hosyutsu, Jyoto-ku, Osaka
Tel. No.: Osaka (33) 5965
Products: Vendex gear

SHIKISHIMA SEIKO CO., LTD.
101, Oaza-Shoya, Mishima, Mishima-gun, Osaka Pref.
Tel. No.: Fukita (38) 0535, 0793
Products: Light alloy piston

SUN SEAL METAL WORKS, LTD.
439, 2-chome, Kita-Oimazato, Higashinari-ku, Osaka
Tel. No.: Osaka (97) 2773-4
Products: Sun oil seal

TOKUSHU HEN-ATSUKI CO., LTD.
49, 1-chome, Tsukamoto, Higashiyodogawa-ku, Osaka
Tel. No.: Osaka (37) 4478-9
Products: Ignition coil

TOYO DENSOHIN CO., LTD.
37, 4-chome, Tagawa-dori, Higashiyodogawa-ku, Osaka
Tel. No.: Osaka (37) 3159
Products: Ignition coil

TOYOSHIMA SPRING MANUFACTURING CO., LTD.
111, 3-chome, Kamifukushima-kita, Fukushima-ku, Osaka
Tel. No.: Osaka (45) 4184, 4928
Products: Auto leaf springs

TOX METAL CO., LTD.
59, 6-chome, Kamisuetsugu, Higashisumiyoshi-ku, Osaka
Tel. No.: Osaka (79) 0788, 4888
Products: Bearing metal, Vacuum control

TSUMATANI SEISAKUSHO
67, 2-chome, Nakagawa, Ikuno-ku, Osaka
Tel. No.: Osaka (73) 3051-2
Products: Joint bearing, Oil line, Stud-bolt, Hexagon bolt

YAMATO SEIKOSHO K. K.
83, 3-chome, Kami-Fukushima, Fukushima-ku, Osaka
Tel. No.: Osaka (45) 3155
Products: King pin bush, Water pump bush, All kinds of bushing for automobiles

YONEDA SEISAKUSHO CO., LTD.
634, 3-chome, Shinkawa, Naniwa-ku, Osaka
Tel. No.: Osaka (64) 6331-2
Products: Tire valve, Valve inside, Air back valve

YUNO KOGYO CO., LTD.
148, 4-chome, Higashi-Tsumori, Nishinari-ku, Osaka
Tel. No.: Osaka (53) 0222, 0250, 0300, 0865, 2866
Products: Wheel

YUTANI SPRING MANUFACTURING CO., LTD.
130, Takatsugu, Sanda, Hyogo Pref.
Tel. No.: (Sanda) 168, 444
Products: Leaf spring for cars

INDEX

Arranged in Manufacturers' Alphabetical Order

Manufacturer	Kind of Vehicle	Model	Page
AICHI MACHINE INDUSTRY CO., LTD.	Truck	Cony 360	166
	Three-Wheeler	Cony AA29	211
		Giant AA24LHS	211
		Giant AA24T	211
DAIHATSU KOGYO K. K.	Truck	Daihatsu Vesta FPOL	166
		Daihatsu Vesta FPO	167
	Tank Lorry	Daihatsu Vacuum Car FPOE	176
	Dump Truck	Daihatsu Vesta FPOD	193
	Three-Wheeler	Daihatsu Midget DK-2 Standard	200
		Daihatsu Midget MPA Handy Wagon	201
		Daihatsu Midget DK-2 Station Wagon	201
		Daihatsu Midget DK-2 Light Van	201
		Daihatsu Midget DK-2 Canvas Van	202
		Daihatsu Midget MPA Panel Van	202
		Daihatsu Midget DK-2 Mail Van	202
		Daihatsu SKC-7	203
		Daihatsu PL-7	203
		Daihatsu PF8-TL	203
		Daihatsu PM10	204
		Daihatsu PO13-T	204
		Daihatsu Dump Truck PO8-D	204
		Daihatsu Fire Engine	205
		Daihatsu Pack Master	205
		Daihatsu Tractor & Trailer	205
FUJI HEAVY INDUSTRIES, LTD.	Passenger Car	Subaru 360	138
	Motor Scooter	Rabbit Minor S-201	215
		Rabbit Junior S-82S	215
		Rabbit Superflow S-601	215
FUJI KIKAI CO., LTD.	Motorcycle	Road King	225
FUJI MOTORS CORPORATION	Motorcycle	Gasuden BC-D	224
		Gasuden FB	236
		Gasuden GW-5	236
FUJI PRECISION MACHINERY CO., LTD.	Passenger Car	Prince Gloria BLSI	137
		Prince Skyline Deluxe ALSID	136
		Prince Skyline ALSIE (Export Model)	136
		Prince Skyline Standard ALSIS	137
	Bus	Prince Micro Bus AQVH-B	150
	Commercial Vehicle	Prince Skyway Light Van ALVG	156
		Prince Route Van AQVH	157
		Prince New Miler Light Van ARVF	156
		Prince Skyway Pick-Up ALPE	157
	Truck	Prince Clipper AQTI	163
		Prince New Miler ARTH	162
	Tank Lorry	Prince Clipper Vacuum Car	176
		Prince New Miler Vacuum Car	176
	Dump Truck	Prince Clipper	193
HEALTH MOTOR INDUSTRIAL CO., LTD.	Motorcycle	Emuro Deluxe ED-110	228
		Emuro Mighty FC-610	236
		Emuro EL-500	236
HINO MOTORS, LTD.	Passenger Car	Renault Hino PA	140
	Bus	Hino BD	143
		Hino BG	143
		Hino Bus Chassis BG	143
		Hino Commerce Mini Bus	150
	Commercial Vehicle	Hino Commerce Van	156
	Truck	Hino TH	172
		Hino TE	172

Manufacturer	Kind of Vehicle	Model	Page
	Dump Truck	Hino TA	187
		Hino ZG	187
		Hino ZH	186
HIRANO SEISAKUSHO, LTD.	Motor Scooter	Hirano Popet	217
		Hirano Pop Manlee FN125	217
		Hirano Pop Manlee FN175	217
HONDA MOTOR CO., LTD.	Motorcycle	Honda Super Cub C-100	220
		Honda Benly C-92	222
		Honda Dream CS-71	230
HOPE JIDOSHA CO., LTD.	Three-Wheeler	Hope Star	209
ISUZU MOTOR CO., LTD.	Passenger Car	Hillman Minx de Luxe	140
	Bus	Isuzu BA540	146
		Isuzu BC150	146
		Isuzu BX550	147
		Isuzu BB550 Bus Chassis	147
		Isuzu BX540 Bus Chassis	147
		Isuzu Elf Micro Bus TL221	150
	Truck	Isuzu Elf TL251	160
		Isuzu TX550	171
		Isuzu TX640-W	171
		Isuzu TW540	171
	Tank Lorry	Isuzu TD150	174
	Fire Engine	Isuzu Fire Fighting TX440	179
	Dump Truck	Isuzu TD140	190
		Isuzu TS540	190
ITAGAKI CO., LTD.	Motorcycle	Million Sunlight	221
		Queen Sunlight Junior	225
		Royal Sunlight	225
		Queen Sunlight	225
ITO MOTOR CO., LTD.	Motorcycle	IMC YB-II	228
		IMC U	237
		IMC R	237
KATAKURA CYCLE CO., LTD.	Motorcycle	Katakura Auto K-60	228
		Katakura Auto 202	233
KAWASAKI MEIHATSU INDUSTRY CO., LTD.	Motorcycle	Meihatsu Ace	226
		Meihatsu Super	226
		Meihatsu Crown	237
MARUSHO MOTORCYCLE INDUSTRIAL CO., LTD.	Motorcycle	Lilac CS28	223
		Lilac LS18	235
		Lilac LS38	235
MEGURO MANUFACTURING CO., LTD.	Motorcycle	Meguro Cadet CA	222
		Meguro Junior S5	230
		Meguro YA	230
		Meguro Stamina Z7	230
MINSEI DIESEL ENGINEERING CO., LTD.	Bus	Minsei B80	144
		Minsei "Condor" RF91	144
		Minsei "Condor" 6RFL-101A	145
		Minsei RX102	144
	Truck	Minsei T80	170
	Tank Lorry	Minsei T80	175
	Fire Engine	Minsei Discharging Tower Vehicle T80-S	179
	Dump Truck	Minsei T80-S	186
MITAKA FUJI INDUSTRIAL CO., LTD.	Truck	Paddle PD33	167
	Three-Wheeler	Musashi MF21	212
MITSUBISHI HEAVY INDUSTRIES, REORGANIZED CO., LTD.	Passenger Car	Mitsubishi 500	139
	Three-Wheeler	Mitsubishi Pet Leo Standard LT10	208
		Mitsubishi Pet Leo Light Van LT11	208
		Mitsubishi Pet Leo Canvas Van LT10	208
		Mitsubishi TM15-F	209
		Mitsubishi TM18-BH	209
	Truck	Mitsubishi "Jupiter" T10-DA·T11-GA	161
		Mitsubishi "Jupiter" T11-GBH	161
		Mitsubishi "Jupiter" T22-DBH	161
	Fire Engine	Mitsubishi "Jeep" CJ3B-J10	177
	Jeep Type	Mitsubishi "Jeep" CJ3B-J3	180
		Mitsubishi "Jeep" CJ3B-J10	180
	Dump Truck	Mitsubishi "Jupiter" T22D-D	192
	Motor Scooter	Silver Pigeon C-300	214

Manufacturer	Kind of Vehicle	Model	Page
		Siver Pigeon C-200	214
		Silver Pigeon C-110	214
MITSUBISHI NIPPON HEAVY-INDUSTRIES, LTD.	Bus	Mitsubishi Fuso B520	148
		Mitsubishi Fuso R710	148
	Truck	Mitsubishi Fuso T33	169
	Dump Truck & Construction Equipment	Mitsubishi Fuso T320D	189
		Mitsubishi Fuso W11D	189
		Mitsubishi Fuso T52	188
		Mitsubishi Fuso Concrete Mixer T320	194
		Mitsubishi Fuso Truck Tractor W21	195
		Mitsubishi Fuso Truck Tractor T350	194
		Mitsubishi Fuso Truck Crane T360	198
		Mitsubishi Fuso Truck Crane W25A	198
		Mitsubishi Motor Scraper WTS	195
		Mitsubishi Motor Grader LGII	197
		Mitsubishi Tractor Shovel BS30	196
		Mitsubishi Bulldozer BE10	197
		Mitsubishi Bulldozer BF	196
MITSUI PRECISION MACHINERY & ENGINEERING CO., LTD.	Three-Wheeler	Humbee EF11	210
		Humbee Light Van EF11	210
		Humbee Surry EF11	210
MIYATA WORKS, LTD.	Motorcycle	Miyapet II	220
		Asahi Deluxe II LA	223
NISSAN MOTOR CO., LTD.	Passenger Car	Datsun Bluebird P310-U	134
		Datsun Sports Car S211	134
		Austin A50 de Luxe	140
	Bus	Nissan UG690	149
		Nissan Junior Micro Bus KC42	150
	Commercial Vehicle	Datsun 4-Door Station Wagon WP211	152
		Datsun 2-Door Station Wagon VG221	153
		Datsun Ranch Sedan UP221	152
		Datsun Pick-Up PG222-U	153
	Truck	Nissan Junior Caball C43	160
		Nissan Junior B42	160
		Nissan G680	170
		Nissan UG680	170
	Tank Lorry	Nissan TG680	175
	Fire Engine	Nissan F680	178
		Nissan Junior FRB42	178
	Jeep Type	Nissan Patrol Station Wagon W4W65	183
		Nissan Patrol 4W66	183
		Nissan Carrier 4W73	183
	Dump Truck	Nissan DUG680	185
		Nissan DG680	185
OKAMURA MFG. CO., LTD.	Passenger Car	Mikasa Touring	139
	Commercial Vehicles	Mikasa Mark II	152
		Mikasa Mark I	153
RIKUO MOTORCYCLE CO., LTD.	Motorcycle	Rikuo FB	232
		Rikuo AC	232
		Rikuo RT	232
ROCKET CO., LTD.	Motorcycle	Queen Rocket 125F	228
		Queen Rocket 200R	233
SHIN MEIWA INDUSTRY CO., LTD.	Motorcycle	Pointer Junior PF-III	227
		Pointer Senior PSB-II	227
		Pointer Comet PCB-II	235
		Pointer Ace PAT-II	235
SHOWA WORKS, LTD.	Motorcycle	Light Cruiser SL-III	227
		Marien 125	227
		Cruiser SC-II	234
		Hosk 350 FA	234
		Hosk 500 Twin DB	234
		Hosk 500 Single GA	234
SUZUKI MOTOR CO., LTD.	Commercial Vehicle	Suzulight TL	151
	Motorcycle	Suzuki Sel Pet	221
		Colleda Seltwin SB	222
		Colleda ST-6A	222
		Colleda 250 TM-2	229

Manufacturer	Kind of Vehicle	Model	Page
		Colleda Twin Ace TA	229
TOKYO HATSUDOKI CO., LTD.	Motorcycle	Tohatsu New Birdy GB	224
		Tohatsu Arrow LA	224
		Tohatsu Arrow LB	224
		Tohatsu Hurry TA	232
TOKYU KUROGANE MOTOR CO., LTD.	Commercial Vehicle	Kurogane Light Van NCV	157
	Truck	Kurogane Nova KN-1500	164
		Kurogane NB	165
		Kurogane Baby Canvas Wagon KB-360	165
		Kurogane Baby Carrier KB-360	164
		Kurogane Baby Commercial KB-360	165
	Dump Truck	Kurogane NBD	192
	Three-Wheeler	Kurogane KW8	212
		Kurogane KY10	212
TOSHO MOTORS CO., LTD.	Motor Scooter	Pandora TS-1	216
	Motorcycle	Echo SE	221
TOYO KOGYO CO., LTD.	Truck	Mazda D1100 (DTA81)	166
		Mazda D1500 (DUA12S)	167
	Three-Wheeler	Mazda K360 (KTBA43)	206
		Mazda T600 (TEA45)	206
		Mazda MBR81	206
		Mazda T1100 (TTA81)	207
		Mazda HBR12S	207
		Mazda T1500 (TUA12S)	207
TOYOMOTORS CO., LTD.	Motorcycle	Toyomotor FHA	229
		Toyomotor FJA	237
TOYOTA MOTOR CO., LTD.	Passenger Car	Toyopet Crown Custom RS22L	132
		Toyopet Crown Deluxe RS21	133
		Toyopet Crown RS20	132
		Toyopet Corona PT10	133
	Bus	Toyota DR10 (DR15)	149
		Toyota DB85	149
	Commercial Vehicle	Toyopet Crown Custom Wagon RS27LG	154
		Toyopet Masterline Light Van RS26V	155
		Toyopet Coronaline PT16V	155
		Toyopet Route Van RK85V	155
		Toyo-Ace Light Van PK20V	155
		Toyopet Masterline Pick-Up RS26	154
		Toyopet Masterline Utility RS26-P	154
	Truck	Toyopet Stout RK30	162
		Toyopet Stout RK35-B	162
		Toyopet Dyna RK85	163
		Toyo-Ace PK20	163
		Toyota FA80 (95-H)	173
		Toyota DA80(95)	172
		Toyota Cargo Truck FW10	173
		Toyota Cargo Truck DW10	173
	Tank Lorry	Toyota FA80	175
	Fire Engine	Toyota FA74	179
		Toyota FC74	178
		Toyota FJ24	177
	Jeep Type	Toyota Land Cruiser Wagon FJ28	182
		Toyota Land Cruiser Hardtop FJ25-D	182
		Toyota Land Cruiser Canvastop FJ2	182
		Toyota Weapon Carrier FQ10	182
	Dump Truck	Toyota DH90	188
TSUBASA INDUSTRY CO., LTD.	Motorcycle	Tsubasa Fighter	223
		Tsubasa Falcon	233
YAMAGUCHI BICYCLE MFG. CO., LTD.	Motorcycle	Yamaguchi Auto-Pet BP-50	220
		Yamaguchi Auto-Pet	221
		Yamaguchi Supertwin 125	226
		Yamaguchi Sel Super 350	226
		Yamaguchi Deluxe 800S	233
YAMAHA MOTORCYCLE CO., LTD.	Motor Scooter	Yamaha Scooter	216
	Motorcycle	Yamaha 125	223
		Yamaha 250	231
		Yamaha 250S (Standard)	231
		Yamaha 250S (Racer)	231
		Yamaha 250S (Scrambler)	231

LATEST CAR SUPPLEMENT

TO

GUIDE TO THE MOTOR INDUSTRY OF JAPAN
1960 EDITION

So many new-model cars have been introduced since the closing time of this publication that we insert here this supplement with photos and brief specifications of these latest models which were introduced from November, 1959 to May, 1960. As to the latest trucks, buses, motorcycles and motor scooters, detailed information will be given on another occasion.

MAZDA R360 COUPE KRBB

Overall Length: 2,980 mm Overall Width: 1,290 mm Overall Height: 1,290 mm Wheelbase: 1,760 mm Vehicle Weight: 380 kg No. of Seats: 4 Engine: Forced air cooling, 4 cycle 2 cyl 356 cc 16 PS 5,300 rpm 90 km/h. Clutch: Single dry plate. No. of Speeds: forward 4 reverse 1 Tire: front 4.80–10, 2 P rear 4.80–10, 2 P

TOYO KOGYO PRODUCT

MAZDA R360 COUPE KRBC

Overall Length: 2,980 mm Overall Width: 1,290 mm Overall Height: 1,290 mm Wheelbase: 1,760 mm Vehicle Weight: 380 kg No. of Seats: 4 Engine: Forced air cooling, 4 cycle 2 cyl 356 cc 16 PS 5,300 rpm 85 km/h Clutch: Single dry plate. Transmission: Torque converter. Tire: front 4.80–10, 2 P rear 4.80–10, 2 P

TOYO KOGYO PRODUCT

Latest Car Supplement

SUBARU 360 COMMERCIAL
Overall Length: 2,995 mm　　Overall Width: 1,300 mm
Overall Height: 1,360 mm　Wheelbase: 1,800 mm　Vehicle
Weight: 400 kg　No. of Seats: 2　Engine: Forced air cooling, 2 cycle 2 cyl 356 cc 16 HP 4,500 rpm 83 km/h
Clutch: Single dry plate.　Transmission: Constant mesh, selective sliding gear.　No. of Speeds: forward 3 reverse 1　Gear Ratio: 1st 3.106, 2nd 1.590, 3rd 1.000 reverse 3.624　Tire: front 4.50—10, 2P　rear: 4.50—10, 2p
FUJI HEAVY PRODUCT

SUBARU 360 CONVERTIBLE
Overall Length: 2,995 mm　　Overall Width: 1,300 mm
Overall Height: 1,360 mm　Wheelbase: 1,800 mm　Vehicle
Weight: 385 kg　No. of Seats: 4　Engine: Forced air cooling, 2 cycle 2 cyl 356 cc 16 HP 4,500 rpm 83 km/h
Clutch: Single dry plate.　Transmission: Constant mesh, selective sliding gear.　No. of Speeds: forward 3 reverse 1　Gear Ratio: 3—1.000 2—1.590 1—3.106 R—3.624　Tire: front 4.50—10, 2P rear 4.50—10, 2P
FUJI HEAVY PRODUCT

SUBARU 360 SEDAN
Overall Length: 2,995 mm　　Overall Width: 1,300 mm
Overall Height: 1,360 mm　Wheelbase: 1,800 mm　Vehicle
Weight: 385 kg　No. of Seats: 4　Engine: Forced air cooling, 2 cycle 2 cyl 356 cc 16 HP 4,500 rpm 83 km/h
Clutch: Single dry plate.　Transmission: Constant mesh, selective sliding gear.　No. of Speeds: forward 3 reverse 1　Gear Ratio: 3—1.000 2—1.590 1—3.106 R—3.624　Tire: front 4.50—10, 2P　rear: 4.50—10, 2P
FUJI HEAVY PRODUCT

MITSUBISHI 500
Overall Length: 3,140 mm　　Overall Width: 1,390 mm
Overall Height: 1,380 mm　Wheelbase: 2,065 mm　Vehicle
Weight: 490 kg　No. of Seats: 4　Engine: Forced air cooling, 4 cycle 2 cyl 493 cc 20 HP 90 km/h.　Clutch: Single dry plate.　Transmission: Synchromesh in second and top speeds.　No. of Speeds: forward 3 reverse 1　Gear Ratio: 1st 3.417, 2nd 1.789, 3rd 1.120, reverse 3.417　Tire: front 5.20—12, 2PR　rear 5.20—12, 2PR.
MITSUBISHI 500 in the photo on p. 139 is the one which was displayed at the Tokyo Motor Show in November, 1959. At that time its front grille had been demounted because of being offered for the public design-contest. Later its design was decided and the car is now on sale since April, 1960.
MITSUBISHI REORGANIZED PRODUCT

Latest Car Supplement

TOYOPET CORONA PT20

Overall Length: 3,990 mm Overall Width: 1,490 mm Overall Height: 1,440 mm Wheelbase: 2,400 mm No. of Seats: 5 Engine: Overhead valve, in line, 4 cycle 4 cyl 997 cc 45 PS 5,000 rpm 110 km/h. Clutch: Single dry plate. Transmission: Synchromesh in 2nd & top gears. No. of Speeds: forwards 3 reverse 1 Gear Ratio: 1st 3.647, 2nd 1.807, 3rd 1.000, reverse 4.863 Tire: 5.60—13, 4 P
TOYOTA MOTOR PRODUCT

TOYOPET TIARA RT20

Overall Length: 3,990 mm Overall Width: 1,490 mm Overall Height: 1,440 mm Wheelbase: 2,400 mm Vehicle Weight: 980 kg No. of Seats: 4 Engine: Pushrod overhead valve in detachable head, 4 cycle 4 cyl 1,453 cc 65 HP 4,500 rpm 130 km/h Clutch: Single dry plate with rubber torsion dampers. Transmission: Synchromesh in 2nd & top gears, remote control, all gears of helical type for quietness and long life. No. of Speeds: forward 3 reverse 1 Gear Ratio: 1st 3.059, 2nd 1.645, 3rd direct, reverse 4.079 Tire: 5.60—13, 4 P
TOYOTA MOTOR PRODUCT

NISSAN CEDRIC

Overall Length: 4,410 mm Overall Width: 1,680 mm Overall Height: 1,520 mm Wheelbase: 2,530 mm Vehicle Weight: 1,170 kg No. of Seats: 6 Engine: Gasoline, water-cooled, overhead valve, 4 cycle 4 cyl 1,488 cc 71 PS 5,000 rpm 130 km/h Clutch: Single dry plate with rubber torsion dampers. Transmission: Synchromesh in 2nd, 3rd & top gears, remote control. No. of Speeds: forward 4 reverse 1. Gear Ratio: 1st 3.945, 2nd 2.402, 3rd 1.490, top 1.000 reverse 5.159 Tires: 6.40—14, 4 P
NISSAN MOTOR PRODUCT

NISSAN CEDRIC DELUXE

Overall Length: 4,410 mm Overall Width: 1,680 mm Overall Height: 1,520 mm Wheelbase: 2,530 mm Vehicle Weight: 1,195 kg No. of Seats: 6 Engine: Gasoline, water-cooled, overhead valve, 4 cycle 4 cyl 1,488 cc 71 PS 5,000 rpm 130 km/h Clutch: Single dry plate with rubber torsion dampers. Transmission: Synchromesh in 2nd, 3rd & top gears, remote control. No. of Speeds: forward 4 reverse 1 Gear Ratio: 1st 3.945, 2nd 2.402, 3rd 1.490, top 1.000 reverse 5.159 Tire: 6.40—14, 4 P.
NISSAN MOTOR PRODUCT

Latest Car Supplement

PRINCE SKYLINE STANDARD

Overall Length: 4,390 mm   Overall Width: 1,675 mm   Overall Height: 1,535 mm   Wheelbase: 2,535 mm   Vehicle Weight: 1,315 kg   No. of Seats: 6   Engine: Gasoline, overhead valve, water-cooled, 4 cycle 4 cyl 1,484 cc 70 HP 4,800 rpm 130 km/h   Clutch: Hydraulically actuated dry single plate type.   Transmission: Synchromesh in 2nd, 3rd & top, remote control.   No. of Speeds: forward 4 reverse 1   Gear Ratio: 4.625   Tire: front 6.40 14, 6 P (tubeless) rear 6.40 14, 6 P (tubeless)
FUJI PRECISION PRODUCT

PRINCE SKYLINE
EXPORT MODEL
1,484 cc & (1,862 cc)

Overall Length: 4,380 mm   Overall Width: 1,675 mm   Overall Height: 1,535 mm   Wheelbase: 2,535 mm   Vehicle Weight: 1,315 (1,325) kg   No. of Seats: 6   Engine: Gasoline, overhead valve, water-cooled, 4 cycle 4 cyl 1,484 (1862) cc 73 (83) HP 4,800 (4,800) rpm 130 (135) km/h   Clutch: Hydraulically actuated dry single plate type.   Transmission: Synchromesh in 2nd, 3rd & top, remote control.   No. of Speeds: forward 4 reverse 1   Gear Ratio: low 4.18, 2nd 2.87, 3rd 1.59 top 1.00 reverse: 5.50 (low 4.18, 2nd 2.64, 3rd 1.59 top 1.00 reverse 5.50)   Tire: front 6.40 14, 4 P (tubeless) rear 6.40 14, 4 P (tubeless)
FUJI PRECISION PRODUCT

PRINCE SKYLINE DELUXE

Overall Length: 4,380 mm   Overall Width: 1,675 mm   Overall Height: 1,535 mm   Wheelbase: 2,535 mm   Vehicle Weight: 1,340 kg   No. of Seats: 6   Engine: Gasoline, overhead valve, water-cooled, 4 cycle 4 cyl 1,484 cc 70 HP 4,800 rpm 130 km/h   Clutch: Hydraulically actuated dry single plate type.   Transmission: Synchromesh in 2nd, 3rd & top, remote control.   No. of Speeds: forward 4 reverse 1   Gear Ratio: 4.625   Tire: front 7.00-14, 4 P (tubeless) rear 7.00 14, 4 P (tubeless)
FUJI PRECISION PRODUCT

PRINCE GLORIA

Overall Length: 4,380 mm   Overall Width: 1,675 mm   Overall Height: 1,535 mm   Wheelbase: 2,535 mm   Vehicle Weight: 1,360 kg   No. of Seats: 6   Engine: Gasoline, overhead valve, water-cooled, 4 cycle 4 cyl 1,862 cc 80 HP 4,800 rpm 135 km/h   Clutch: Hydraulically actuated dry single plate type.   Transmission: Synchromesh in 2nd, 3rd & top, remote control.   No. of Speeds: forward 4 reverse 1   Gear Ratio: 4.625   Tire: front 7.00-14, 4 P (tubeless) rear 7.00 14, 4 P (tubeless)
FUJI PRECISION PRODUCT

IN JAPAN WITH FLOYD CLYMER

Clymer found Toyopet test track fast and steeply banked.

Toyopet's 4-cylinder engine is neatly mounted in rugged chassis.

Testing the Toyopet Crown Sedan, Clymer stops for a chat with two English-speaking motorcyclists in Japan's colorful countryside.

Part of rough obstacle course on Toyopet's test grounds.

Small truck with girl driver transports Toyopet engines from one part of factory to another.

Export official at Yamaha factory checks Clymer out on a 2-stroke twin Yamaha. Yamaha also builds pianos, guitars, harmonicas and other musical instruments.

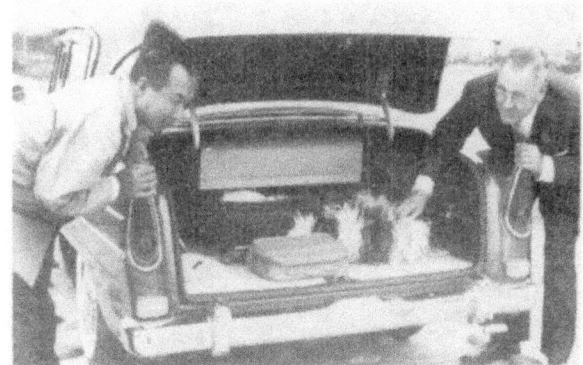
This is not a skunk in the rear end of Toyopet but a duster which driver used often to keep car spick and span.

In rural Japan Clymer met this interesting grandmother with child on back.

IN JAPAN WITH FLOYD CLYMER

Clymer on Suzika's Colleda in front of Shinto Shrine on factory grounds where employees may worship.

The Suzilite small vehicle.

Tester turns Colleda bike over to Clymer.

And Clymer proceeds to give it a workout, both forward and backward, on test track.

Clymer gives the Suzilight car a working-over on rough ground.

Suzika cycles ready for shipment.

Colleda test rider jump-testing at test course.

Suzilight station wagon has amazing room for small vehicle.

IN JAPAN WITH FLOYD CLYMER

Another Japanese bike is the Yamaguchi, shown here in front of P.X. at Zama.

A motorcycle officer gives citation to a truck violator on country road. Note the officer fingerprints violator on the spot, using folding inkpad.

Clymer inspects first Datsun (1923) in the lobby of Nisson Company office.

Typical Japanese school children seem more interested in camera than in the Toyopet, near Nagoya.

Testing Datsun near Hammamatsu, with Fiat, Rambler and Metropolitan dealer sign in the background.

Foreman guides Clymer and Datsun export officials through busy factory.

Busy factory of Honda Motorcycle Company, one of three factories.

Japanese girl inspectors appear happy as Datsun officials and Clymer look at their work.

IN JAPAN WITH FLOYD CLYMER

Clymer makes notes on the Datsun "Ladybird" Sports Car, accompanied by officials. "Jeep-type" Datsun is in background.

Toyopet Crown and factory officials with car on the test track obstacle course.

Toyopet Export Dep't. officials near factory.

Workmen on engine assembly line of Datsun Bluebird.

Clymer and export official with long line of Toyopets at factory grounds.

Toyopet sponsors a track near Nagoya where new drivers can practice for tough driver's license tests.

Inside Nissan Motor Co. (Datsun) plant at Tokyo.

License Inspector with three students, receiving instruction on driver technique at Nagoya track. Only 15% of applicants pass tough driver's license test on first try. They must also describe functions of car units such as pistons, valves, differential, carburetor, etc.

ARE YOU:
INTERESTED IN EUROPEAN, IMPORT & EXOTIC AUTOMOBILES?

DO YOU:
DO YOUR OWN MAINTENANCE?

If you answered yes to either of these questions, then you should check out our automobile books and manuals. We have included a sample listing of some of our featured marques. However, for complete details and the most up-to-date information, please visit our website.

— www.VelocePress.com —

The fastest growing specialist USA publisher of niche market automotive books and manuals.

All VelocePress titles are available through your local independent bookseller, Amazon.com or direct from VelocePress. Wholesale customers may also purchase direct or from the Ingram Book Group.

AUTOBOOKS WORKSHOP MANUALS

ALFA ROMEO GIULIA 1300, 1600, 1750, 2000 1962-1978 WSM
AUSTIN HEALEY SPRITE, MG MIDGET 1958-1980 WSM
BMW 1600 1966-1973 WSM
BMW 2000 & 2002 1966-1976 WSM
BMW 2500, 2800, 3.0 & 3.3 1968-1977 WSM
BMW 316, 320, 320i 1975-1977 WSM
BMW 518, 520, 520i 1973-1981 WSM
FIAT 1100, 1100D, 1100R & 1200 1957-1969 WSM
FIAT 124 1966-1974 WSM
FIAT 124 SPORT 1966-1975 WSM
FIAT 125 & 125 SPECIAL 1967-1973 WSM
FIAT 126, 126L, 126 DV, 126/650 & 126/650 DV 1972-1982 WSM
FIAT 127 SALOON, SPECIAL & SPORT, 900, 1050 1971-1981 WSM
FIAT 128 1969-1982 WSM
FIAT 1300, 1500 1961-1967 WSM
FIAT 131 MIRAFIORI 1975-1982 WSM
FIAT 132 1972-1982 WSM
FIAT 500 1957-1973 WSM
FIAT 600, 600D & MULTIPLA 1955-1969 WSM
FIAT 850 1964-1972 WSM
JAGUAR E-TYPE 1961-1972 WSM
JAGUAR MK 1, 2 1955-1969 WSM
JAGUAR S TYPE, 420 1963-1968 WSM
JAGUAR XK 120, 140, 150 MK 7, 8, 9 1948-1961 WSM
LAND ROVER 1, 2 1948-1961 WSM
MERCEDES-BENZ 190 1959-1968 WSM
MERCEDES-BENZ 220/8 WSM
MERCEDES-BENZ 220B 1959-1965 WSM
MERCEDES-BENZ 230 1963-1968 WSM
MERCEDES-BENZ 250 1968-1972 WSM
MERCEDES-BENZ 280 1968-1972 WSM
MG MIDGET TA-TF 1936-1955 WSM
MINI 1959-1980 WSM
MORRIS MINOR 1952-1971 WSM
PEUGEOT 404 1960-1975 WSM
PORSCHE 911 1964-1973 WSM
PORSCHE 911 1970-1977 WSM
RENAULT 16 1965-1979 WSM
RENAULT 8, 10, 1100 1962-1971 WSM
ROVER 3500, 3500S 1968-1976 WSM
SUNBEAM RAPIER, ALPINE 1955-1965 WSM
TRIUMPH SPITFIRE, GT6, VITESSE 1962-1968 WSM
TRIUMPH TR2, TR3, TR3A 1952-1962 WSM
TRIUMPH TR4, TR4A 1961-1967 WSM
VOLKSWAGEN BEETLE 1968-1977 WSM

BROOKLANDS BOOKS & ROAD TEST PORTFOLIOS (RTP)

AC CARS 1904-2009
ALFA ROMEO 1920-1933 ROAD TEST PORTFOLIO
ALFA ROMEO 1934-1940 ROAD TEST PORTFOLIO
BRABHAM RALT HONDA THE RON TAURANAC STORY
BUGATTI TYPE 10 TO TYPE 40 ROAD TEST PORTFOLIO
BUGATTI TYPE 10 TO TYPE 251 ROAD TEST PORTFOLIO
BUGATTI TYPE 41 TO TYPE 55 ROAD TEST PORTFOLIO
BUGATTI TYPE 57 TO TYPE 251 ROAD TEST PORTFOLIO
DELAHAYE ROAD TEST PORTFOLIO
FERRARI ROAD CARS 1946-1956 ROAD TEST PORTFOLIO
FIAT 500 1936-1972 ROAD TEST PORTFOLIO
FIAT DINO ROAD TEST PORTFOLIO
HISPANO SUIZA ROAD TEST PORTFOLIO
HONDA ST1100/ST1300 PAN EUROPEAN 1990-2002 RTP
JAGUAR MK1 & MK2 ROAD TEST PORTFOLIO
LOTUS CORTINA ROAD TEST PORTFOLIO
MV AGUSTA F4 750 & 1000 1997-2007 ROAD TEST PORTFOLIO
TATRA CARS ROAD TEST PORTFOLIO

VELOCEPRESS AUTOMOBILE BOOKS & MANUALS

ABARTH BUYERS GUIDE
AUSTIN-HEALEY 6-CYLINDER WSM
BMW 600 LIMOUSINE FACTORY WSM
BMW 600 LIMOUSINE OWNERS HAND BOOK & SERVICE MANUAL
BMW ISETTA FACTORY WSM
BOOK OF THE CARRERA PANAMERICANA - MEXICAN ROAD RACE
COMPLETE CATALOG OF JAPANESE MOTOR VEHICLES
DIALED IN - THE JAN OPPERMAN STORY
FERRARI 250/GT SERVICE AND MAINTENANCE
FERRARI 308 SERIES BUYER'S AND OWNER'S GUIDE
FERRARI BERLINETTA LUSSO
FERRARI BROCHURES AND SALES LITERATURE 1946-1967
FERRARI BROCHURES AND SALES LITERATURE 1968-1989
FERRARI GUIDE TO PERFORMANCE
FERRARI OPP, MAINTENANCE & SERVICE H/BOOKS 1948-1963
FERRARI OWNER'S HANDBOOK
FERRARI SERIAL NUMBERS PART I - ODD NUMBERS TO 21399
FERRARI SERIAL NUMBERS PART II - EVEN NUMBERS TO 1050
FERRARI SPYDER CALIFORNIA
FERRARI TUNING TIPS & MAINTENANCE TECHNIQUES
HOW TO BUILD A FIBERGLASS CAR
HOW TO BUILD A RACING CAR
IF HEMINGWAY HAD WRITTEN A RACING NOVEL
JAGUAR E-TYPE 3.8 & 4.2 WSM
LE MANS 24 (THE BOOK THAT THE FILM WAS BASED ON)
MASERATI BROCHURES AND SALES LITERATURE
MASERATI OWNER'S HANDBOOK
METROPOLITAN FACTORY WSM
MGA & MGB OWNERS HANDBOOK & WSM
OBERT'S FIAT GUIDE
PERFORMANCE TUNING THE SUNBEAM TIGER
PORSCHE 356 1948-1965 WSM
PORSCHE 912 WSM
SOUPING THE VOLKSWAGEN
TRIUMPH TR2, TR3, TR4 1953-1965 WSM
VEDA ORR'S NEW REVISED HOT ROD PICTORIAL
VOLKSWAGEN TRANSPORTER, TRUCKS, STATION WAGONS WSM
VOLVO 1944-1968 ALL MODELS WSM

VELOCEPRESS MOTORCYCLE BOOKS & MANUALS

AJS SINGLES 1955-65 350cc & 500cc (BOOK OF)
ARIEL 1939-1960 4 STROKE SINGLES (BOOK OF)
ARIEL LEADER & ARROW 1958-1964 (BOOK OF)
ARIEL MOTORCYCLES 1933-1951 WSM
ARIEL PREWAR MODELS 1932-1939 (BOOK OF)
BMW M/CYCLES R26 R27 (1956-1967) FACTORY WSM
BMW M/CYCLES R50 R50S R60 R69S (1955-1969) FACTORY WSM
BSA BANTAM (BOOK OF)
BSA ALL FOUR-STROKE SINGLES & V-TWINS 1936-1952 (BOOK OF)
BSA OHV & SV SINGLES - 250cc 1954-1970 (BOOK OF)
BSA OHV & SV SINGLES 1945-54 250-600cc (BOOK OF)
BSA OHV SINGLES 350 & 500cc 1955-1967 (BOOK OF)
BSA PRE-WAR MODELS TO 1939 (BOOK OF)
BSA TWINS 1948-1962 (BOOK OF)
BSA TWINS 1962-1969 (SECOND BOOK OF)
DOUGLAS PRE-WAR ALL MODELS 1929-1939 (BOOK OF)
DOUGLAS POST-WAR ALL MODELS 1948-1957 FACTORY WSM
DUCATI 160cc, 250cc & 350cc OHC MODELS FACTORY WSM
HONDA 50 ALL MODELS UP TO 1970 INC MONKEY & TRAIL (BOOK OF)
HONDA 90 ALL MODELS UP TO 1966 (BOOK OF)
HONDA MOTORCYCLES 125-150 TWINS C/CS/CB/CA WSM
HONDA MOTORCYCLES 250-305 TWINS C/CS/CB WSM
HONDA MOTORCYCLES C100 SUPER CUB WSM
HONDA MOTORCYCLES C110 SPORT CUB 1962-1969 WSM
HONDA TWINS & SINGLES 50cc TO 305cc 1960-1966 (BOOK OF)
LAMBRETTA ALL 125 & 150cc MODELS 1947-1957 (BOOK OF)
LAMBRETTA LI & TV MODELS 1957-1970 (SECOND BOOK OF)
MATCHLESS 350 & 500cc SINGLES 1945-1956 (BOOK OF)
MATCHLESS 350 & 500cc SINGLES 1955-1966 (BOOK OF)
NORTON 1938-1956 (BOOK OF)
NORTON DOMINATOR TWINS 1955-1965 (BOOK OF)
NORTON MOTORCYCLES 1957-1970 FACTORY WSM
NORTON PREWAR MODELS 1932-1939 (BOOK OF)
ROYAL ENFIELD 736cc INTERCEPTOR FACTORY WSM
ROYAL ENFIELD 250cc & 350cc SINGLES 1958-1966 (SECOND BOOK OF)
SUZUKI 50cc & 80cc UP TO 1966 (BOOK OF)
SUZUKI T10 1963-1967 FACTORY WSM
SUZUKI T20 & T200 1965-1969 FACTORY WSM
TRIUMPH PRE-WAR MOTORCYCLE 1935-1939 (BOOK OF)
TRIUMPH MOTORCYCLES 1937-1951 WSM
TRIUMPH MOTORCYCLES 1945-1955 FACTORY WSM
TRIUMPH TWINS 1956-1969 (BOOK OF)
VELOCETTE ALL SINGLES & TWINS 1925-1970 (BOOK OF)
VESPA 1951-1961 (BOOK OF)
VINCENT MOTORCYCLES 1935-1955 WSM

www.VelocePress.com

Please check our website:

www.VelocePress.com

for a complete
up-to-date list of
available titles